Automatic Item Generation

D0084360

Automatic item generation (AIG) represents a relatively new and unique research area where specific cognitive and psychometric theories are applied to test construction practices for the purpose of producing test items using technology. The purpose of this book is to bring researchers and practitioners up-to-date on the growing body of research on AIG by organizing in one volume what is currently known about this research area. Part I begins with an overview of the concepts and topics necessary for understanding AIG by focusing on both its history and current applications. Part II presents two theoretical frameworks and practical applications of these frameworks in the production of item generation. Part III summarizes the psychological and substantive characteristics of generated items. Part IV concludes with a discussion of the statistical models that can be used to estimate the item characteristics of generated items, features one future application of AIG, describes the current technologies used for AIG, and also highlights the unresolved issues that must be addressed as AIG continues to mature as a research area.

Comprehensive—The book provides a comprehensive analysis of both the theoretical concepts that define automatic item generation and the practical considerations required to implement these concepts.

Varied Applications—Readers are provided with novel applications in diverse content areas (e.g., science and reading comprehension) that range across all educational levels—elementary through university.

Mark J. Gierl is Professor of Educational Psychology and Director of the Centre for Research in Applied Measurement and Evaluation in the Department of Educational Psychology, Faculty of Education, at the University of Alberta. He holds the Canada Research Chair in Educational Measurement.

Thomas M. Haladyna is Professor Emeritus, Arizona State University. He is the author of numerous books in the field of educational assessment and test item development, including the much praised *Handbook of Test Development.*

Automatic Item Generation

Theory and Practice

Edited by
Mark J. Gierl and Thomas M. Haladyna

Routledge
Taylor & Francis Group

NEW YORK AND LONDON

P-M
Au 823
2013

First published 2013
by Routledge
711 Third Avenue, New York, NY 10017

Simultaneously published in the UK
by Routledge
2 Park Square, Milton Park, Abingdon, Oxon OX14 4RN

Routledge is an imprint of the Taylor & Francis Group, an informa business

Library of Congress Cataloging in Publication Data

Automatic item generation: theory and practice / edited by
Mark J. Gierl, Thomas M. Haladyna.
    p. cm.
    Includes bibliographical references and index.
    1. Educational tests and measurements. 2. Educational psychology.
    I. Gierl, Mark J. II. Haladyna, Thomas M.
    LB3051.A89 2012
    371.26—dc23
    2012006911

ISBN: 978–0–415–89750–1(hbk)
ISBN: 978–0–415–89751–8(pbk)
ISBN: 978–0–203–80391–2 (ebk)

Typeset in Minion
by Swales & Willis Ltd, Exeter, Devon

Printed and bound in the United States of America
by Edwards Brothers, Inc.

Contents

Figures and Tables

Figures

Tables

Acknowledgments

We would like to thank the chapter authors for contributing their expertise and insights on automatic item generation for this project: Hollis Lai, Isaac Bejar, Richard Luecht, Kristen Huff, Cecilia Alves, James Pellegrino, Pamela Kaliski, Jacqueline Leighton, Joanna Gorin, Susan Embretson, Edith Aurora Graf, James Fife, Sandip Sinharay, Matthew Johnson, Meisam Yazdchi, Todd Mortimer, and Eleni Stroulia. You are all a pleasure to work with—and we sincerely appreciate your commitment to this project. We would also like to thank Lane Akers and Julie Ganz at Taylor and Francis for their help and expert guidance in preparing this book.

I
Initial Considerations for Automatic Item Generation

1

Automatic Item Generation

An Introduction

Mark J. Gierl and Thomas M. Haladyna

A major motivation for this book is to improve the assessment of student learning, regardless of whether the context is K-12 education, higher education, professional education, or training. The *Standards for Educational and Psychological Testing* (AERA, APA, & NMCE, 1999) described assessment in this way:

> Any systematic method of obtaining information from tests and other sources, used to draw inferences about characteristics of people, objects, or programs. (p. 112)

A test or exam is one of the most important sources of information for the assessment of student learning. Our book is devoted to improving assessment of student learning through the design, development, and validation of test items of superior quality that are used for tests that improve assessment.

Although automatic item generation (AIG) has a relatively short history, it holds much promise for many exciting, innovative, and valuable technologies for item development and validation. The chapters in this book provide a coordinated and comprehensive account of the current state of this emerging science. Two concepts of value to readers in this volume are the content and cognitive demand of achievement constructs. Every test item has a content designation and an intended cognitive demand. The content of an achievement construct is generally considered as existing in one of two types of domains. The first type of domain consists of using knowledge, skills, and strategies in complex ways. A review of national, state, and school district content standards for reading, writing, speaking, and listening, and mathematical and scientific problem solving provides good examples of this first type of domain. The second type of domain focuses on a single cognitive ability. Abilities are complex mental structures that grow slowly (Lohman, 1993; Messick, 1984; Sternberg, 1998). For credential testing in the professions, the domain consists of tasks performed in that profession (Raymond & Neustel, 2006). A domain, therefore, represents one of these cognitive abilities. Kane (2006a, 2006b) refers to these tasks as existing in a target domain. Test items are intended to model the tasks found in the target domain. The reference to knowledge, skills, and ability refers to either of these two types of constructs as they exist in current, modern measurement theory and practice.

Cognitive demand refers to the mental complexity in performing a task. The task might be a test item where the learner selects among choices or the learner creates a response to an item, question, or command. One critic referred to the classification of cognitive demand as a conceptual "swamp," due to the perfusion of terms used to describe various types of higher-level thinking (Lewis & Smith, 1993). More recently, Haladyna and Rodriguez (in press) listed 25 different terms signifying higher-level thinking. For our purpose no taxonomy of higher-level thinking has been validated or widely accepted on scientific grounds, and none is advocated. However, several contributors of this book describe useful methods for uncovering ways to measure complex, cognitive behaviors via AIG.

Our introductory chapter has two main sections. The first section presents a context for change in educational measurement that features AIG. The second section provides a brief summary of the chapters in this book, as well as highlighting their interrelationships.

A Context for Automatic Item Generation

The Greek philosopher Heraclitus (c. 535 BC–475BC) provided some foresight into the state of 21st century educational measurement when he claimed that *the only constant was change*. The evolution of educational measurement—where interdisciplinary forces are stemming from the fusion of the cognitive sciences, statistical theories of test scores, professional education and certification, educational psychology, operations research, educational technology, and computing science—is occurring rapidly. These interdisciplinary forces are also creating exciting new opportunities for both theoretical and practical changes. Although many different examples could be cited, the state of change is most clearly apparent in the areas of computer-based testing, test design, and cognitive diagnostic assessment. These three examples are noteworthy as they relate to the topics described in this book, because changes in computerized testing, test design, and diagnostic testing will directly affect the principles and practices that guide the design and development of test items.

Example #1: Computer-Based Testing

Computer-based testing, our first example, is dramatically changing educational measurement research and practice because our current test administration procedures are merging with the growing popularity of digital media, along with the explosion in internet use to create the foundation for new types of tests and testing resources. As a historical development, this transition from paper- to computer-based testing has been occurring for some time. Considerable groundwork for this transition can be traced to the early research, development, and implementation efforts focused on computerizing and adaptively administering the *Armed Services Vocational Aptitude Battery*, beginning in the 1960s (see Sands, Waters, & McBride, 1997). A computer-adaptive test is a paperless test administered with a computer, using a testing model that implements a process of selecting and administering items, scoring the examinee's responses, and updating the examinee's ability estimate after each item is administered. This process of selecting new items based on the examinee's responses to the previously administered items is continued until a stopping rule is satisfied where there is considerable confidence in the accuracy of the score. The pioneers and early proponents of computer-adaptive testing were motivated by the potential benefits of this testing approach, which included shortened tests without a loss of measurement precision, enhanced score reliability particularly for low- and high-ability examinees, improved test security, testing on-demand, and immediate test scoring and reporting. The introduction and rapid expansion of the internet has enable many recent innovations in computerized testing. Examples include computer-adaptive multistage testing (Luecht, 1998; Luecht & Nungester, 1998; see also Luecht, this volume), linear on-the-fly testing (Folk & Smith, 2002), testlet-based computer adaptive testing (Wainer & Kiely, 1987; Wainer & Lewis, 1990), and computerized mastery testing (Lewis & Sheehan, 1990). Now, many educational tests which were once given in a paper format are now administered by computer via the internet. Many popular and well-known tests can be cited as examples, including the *Graduate Management Admission Test*, the *Graduate Record Examination*, the *Test of English as a Foreign Language*, the *Medical Council of Canada Qualifying Exam* Part I, and the American Institute of Certified Public Accountants *Uniform CPA Examination*. Education Week's 2009 *Technology Counts* also reported that almost half the U.S. states now administer some form of internet-based computerized educational test.

Internet-based computerized tests offer many advantages to students and educators, as compared to more traditional paper-based tests. For instance, computers enable the development of innovative item types and alternative item formats (Sireci & Zenisky, 2006; Zenisky & Sireci, 2002); items on computer-based tests can be scored immediately, thereby providing examinees with instant feedback (Drasgow & Mattern, 2006); computers permit continuous testing and testing on-demand (van der Linden & Glas, 2010). But possibly the most important advantage of computer-based testing is that it allows testing agencies to measure more complex performances by integrating test items and digital media to substantially improve the measurement of complex thinking (Bartram, 2006; Zenisky & Sireci, 2002).

The advent of computer-based, internet testing has also raised new challenges, particularly in the area of item development. Large numbers of items are needed to develop the item banks necessary for computerized testing because items are continuously administered and, therefore, exposed. As a result, these item banks need frequent replenishing in order to minimize item exposure and maintain test security. Unfortunately, traditional item development content requires experts to use test specifications, and item-writing guides to author each item. This process is very expensive. Rudner (2010) estimated that the cost of developing one operational item using the current approach in a high-stakes testing program can range from $1,500 to $2,000 per item. It is not hard to see that, at this price, the cost for developing a large item bank becomes prohibitive. Breithaupt, Ariel, and Hare (2010) recently claimed that a high-stakes 40-item computer adaptive test with two administrations per year would require, at minimum, a bank containing 2,000 items. Combined with Rudner's per item estimate, this requirement would translate into a cost ranging from $3,000,000 to $4,000,000 for the item bank alone. Part of this cost stems from the need to hire subject-matter experts to develop test items. When large numbers of items are required, more subject-matter experts are needed. Another part of this cost is rooted in the quality-control outcomes. Because the cognitive item structure is seldom validated and the determinants of item difficulty are poorly understood, all new test items must be field tested prior to operational use so that their psychometric properties can be documented. Of the items that are field tested, many do not perform as intended and, therefore, must be either revised or discarded. This outcome further contributes to the cost of item development. Haladyna (1994) stated, for example, that as many as 40% of expertly created items fail to perform as intended during field testing, leading to large numbers of items being either revised or discarded. In short, agencies that adopt computer-based testing are faced with the daunting task of creating thousands of new and expensive items for their testing programs. To help address this important task, the principles and practices that guide AIG are presented in this book as an alternative method for producing operational test items.

Example #2: Test Design

Although the procedures and practices for test design and development of items for traditional paper-and-pencil testing are well established (see Downing & Haladyna, 2006; Haladyna, 2004; Schmeiser & Welch, 2006), advances in computer technology are fostering new approaches for test design (Drasgow, Luecht, & Bennett, 2006; Leighton & Gierl, 2007a; Mislevy, 2006). Prominent new test design approaches that differ from more traditional approaches are emerging, including the cognitive design system (Embretson, 1998), evidence-centered design (Mislevy, Steinberg, & Almond, 2003; Mislevy & Riconscente, 2006), and assessment engineering (Luecht, 2006, 2007, 2011). Although the new approaches to test design differ in important ways from one another, these approaches are united by a view that the *science of educational assessment* will prevail to guide test design, development, administration, scoring, and reporting practices. We highlight the key features in one of these approaches, assessment engineering (AE) (Luecht, Chapter 5, this volume). AE is an innovative approach to measurement practice where engineering-based principles and technology-enhanced processes are used to direct the design and development of tests as well as the analysis, scoring, and reporting of test results. This design approach begins by defining the construct of interest using specific, empirically derived construct maps and cognitively based evidence models. These maps and models outline the knowledge and skills that examinees need to master in order to perform tasks or solve problems in the domain of interest. Next, task models are created to produce replicable assessment resources. A task model specifies a class of tasks by outlining the shared knowledge and skills required to solve any type of task in that class. Templates are then created to produce test items with predictable difficulty that measure the content for a specific task model. Finally, a statistical model is used for examinee response data collected from the template-generated test items in order to produce scores that are validly interpretable and reliable.

The science of assessment is central to AE. Item development is guided by the initial specification of the construct map as well as the articulation of the task models. A construct map is a cognitively based model of test performance that specifies the knowledge, skills, and abilities required to solve tasks and perform competently in the content area of interest. These cognitive competencies, in turn, serve as the basis for task model development. The task model provides a more concrete representation of the knowledge and skills specified in the construct map. It serves as the test specifications for defining classes of tasks to be performed, by outlining the knowledge, skills, and abilities required to solve any type of task within a specific class. Task models also identify content and auxiliary features within the class that will affect the cognitive complexity and, hence, difficulty of task performance. To ensure that items within a class measure the same content and produce the same item difficulty, a template is used. A template outlines the structure, content, and constraints required to produce items that measure the specific content defined in the task model. Each template, therefore, is a specific representation of a task model, meaning that the item measures the content outlined in the task model and performs at predictable level of difficulty. Because task models and templates are aligned according to content, cognitive complexity, and statistical properties, multiple templates can be created for a single task model, thereby providing the basis for item generation. AIG works by first specifying the knowledge, skills, and abilities in the construct map, operationalizing these cognitive performances in the task model, and then designing templates to produce items that measure these performances. Hence, AIG is governed by manipulating the number of templates per item model. When large numbers of items are needed, multiple templates are created for each task model.

This brief summary focusing on the item development process helps to highlight how AE differs from more traditional test designs. With AE, construct maps and task models guide the specification of knowledge, skills, and abilities that will be measured by the items. These maps and models also identify the content areas and auxiliary features that affect item difficulty. By using construct maps and task models, the developer has much more control over the specific skills measured by the items as well as their psychometric characteristics. The item development and generation process is governed by templating. As a result, the unit of analysis for item generation is the template. When more items are required, more templates are developed. Because the templates are aligned to the task models, the items generated from the templates allow both cognitive inferences and predictable psychometric characteristics. Conversely, with a more traditional test design, test specifications and judgments from content experts guide much of the process used to create test items. Currently, most large-scale educational testing programs are developed from test specifications (Leighton & Gierl, 2007b). A set of test specifications is generated by content experts as a two-way matrix outlining the content areas and cognitive demand measured by the items on the test (Schmeiser & Welch, 2006). Because content experts have extensive knowledge and experience with the examinees, curriculum, and learning environment, they develop test items for each cell in the test specifications by anticipating the cognitive processes that examinees will use to answer items correctly in different content areas. Item development, with a traditional approach, is a manual process where each item is treated by the content expert as a single and, largely, isolated unit that is individually created, reviewed, and formatted. Hence, the unit of analysis for item generation is the individual test item. When more items are required, more content experts are needed. Because the items are individually authored by different content experts using general content-by-skill test specifications, the psychometric characteristics of the items are often unpredictable because the cognitive item structure is not carefully documented and the content and auxiliary features that could affect item difficulty are not monitored during development.

This comparison between AE and traditional test design helps to highlight some of the potential strengths of using new approaches in test design to generate items. But even with the use of AE, pressing questions for item development remain unanswered. For example, how do we ensure that the cognitive demand outlined in the construct maps and operationalized in the task models are measured by the generated test items? How can construct maps and task models be used to identify the content areas and item features that affect the statistical properties of the items? What is the development process used to create task models, templates, and test items? How do we ensure that the content and psychometric properties of the generated items are similar within one task model class but different between other related but distinct task model classes? In short, agencies that adopt new test designs are faced with the daunting tasks of implementing procedures, processes, and steps for item development that have a limited empirical foundation and little or no precedent in an operational testing program. In this book, we describe solutions that can be used to address some of these daunting tasks by describing item development guidelines, strategies, and practical examples that help to illustrate how new test design principles can inform item-writing practices to promote AIG.

Example #3: Cognitive Diagnostic Assessment

Our third example comes from the growing empirical body of research in cognitive diagnostic assessment (CDA). A CDA is a test designed to measure the specific knowledge and skills required to solve items in a particular content area for the purpose of providing examinees with feedback on their cognitive problem-solving strengths and weaknesses One way to produce this diagnostic summary is with a cognitive information-processing approach where the psychology of test performance is modelled to yield scores that measure examinees' problem-solving ability. Because test performance is both unobservable and complex, a model is required to link the examinees' problem-solving ability with our interpretations of test performance. The development and use of a cognitive model of task performance provides one approach for identifying and measuring knowledge and skills so they can be connected with test performance and score interpretations (Leighton & Gierl, 2007b). A cognitive model in educational measurement refers to a simplified description of human problem solving on standardized tasks at some convenient grain size or level of detail in order to facilitate explanation and prediction of students' performance, including their strengths and weaknesses. Cognitive models provide an interpretative framework that can guide item development so that test performance can be connected to specific inferences about examinees' cognitive problem-solving ability.

Cognitive models for CDA have at least four defining characteristics (Gierl, Alves, Roberts, & Gotzmann, 2009). First, the model contains content specified at a fine grain size because it magnifies the construct that underlies test performance. Second, the knowledge and skills must be measurable, meaning that knowledge and skills in the model must be specified in a way that will permit a test developer to create an item to measure some specific knowledge or skill. Third, the knowledge and skills must be instructionally relevant and meaningful to a broad group of educational stakeholders, including the students, parents, and teachers. Fourth, a cognitive model will often reflect a hierarchy of ordered tasks within a domain because cognitive processes share dependencies and function within a network of interrelated knowledge and skills and the complex application of knowledge and skills that represent an ability. Tests based on cognitive models can be developed so that test items directly measure specific types of content and cognitive complexity, thereby allowing examinees' test item performance to be linked to their strengths and weaknesses. Once the cognitive models contain these four defining characteristics, they can then be used to guide item development so that these test items measure specific content with a specific cognitive demand.

Gierl, Alves, et al. (2009) described the development of cognitive models on the *Preliminary SAT/National Merit Scholarship Qualifying Test* (*PSAT*). The *PSAT* is a standardized test created by the College Board that allows students to practice for the SAT Reasoning Test as well as enter the National Merit Scholarship Corporation programs. The *PSAT* measures critical reading, mathematics problem solving, and writing. The purpose of the project was to investigate diagnostic scoring and reporting procedures so that examinees would receive more specific information about their problem-solving strengths and weaknesses in mathematics. Cognitive models were created in four content areas in mathematics. Three content specialists, who were experienced college mathematics professors and College Board test developers, created cognitive models in each content area. The content specialists drew on their knowledge and experiences in teaching mathematics and in writing *PSAT* test items and their review of the document, *College Board Standards for College Success: Mathematics and Statistics* (2006), which outlines the knowledge and skills that students should master for college success. Thirty-nine cognitive models containing 134 ordered diagnostic tasks seen as measurable and instructionally relevant were identified across the four *PSAT* content areas in mathematics. In other words, to measure *PSAT* mathematics skills for cognitive diagnosis, 134 items would be required if the diagnostic test contained *one item per skill*. To increase reliability for each subscore, at least three items per subscore would be needed (see Gierl, Cui, & Zhou, 2009) meaning that the diagnostic test would require 402 items. CDAs require test items that measure specific competencies outlined in a cognitive model in order to pinpoint the knowledge and skills that examinees use to respond to items. This precision serves as an important strength in CDA because it allows the test developer to provide more targeted feedback to the examinee about their achievement as well as helping the instructor to identify the specific areas where remediation is required. However, to provide this type of fine-grained, instructionally focused feedback, large numbers of meticulously created items must be developed. Hence, CDA requires large numbers of items that measure content with great cognitive demand. As our example illustrates, at minimum, 134 items are needed to measure *PSAT* mathematics, with a better estimate being 402 items. This scenario, again, presents an overwhelming item development challenge, particularly in a traditional test development context where single items with unspecified cognitive features are manually created at a very high cost. In this book, we describe how important new developments in the study of the psychology that underlies test performance may contribute to our AIG theories and methods.

Overview of the Book

AIG may be used to address the item development challenges posed by rapid changes occurring in areas such as computer-based testing, test design, and cognitive diagnostic assessment (Drasgow et al., 2006; Embretson & Yang, 2007; Irvine & Kyllonen, 2002). AIG represents a relatively new but quickly evolving research area where cognitive and psychometric theories are welded to develop a computerized technology for AIG.

AIG requires two steps. First, test development specialists develop item models or item templates that highlight the features or elements in the task that can be manipulated. Second, the elements in the item model are then manipulated to generate new items with the aid of computer-based algorithms. If the elements that affect item difficulty can also be identified and controlled in step 1, then the generated items in step 2 do not require separate calibration because statistical models can be used to estimate their psychometric characteristics without the need for item pre-testing. With this two-step process, hundreds or even thousands of new and, potentially, statistically calibrated items can be created from a single item model. Not surprisingly, AIG is seen by many testing practitioners as a "dream come true", given the high costs and laborious processes required for traditional item development. Part of our intention in writing this book is to begin to accumulate, organize, and document the theories and practices required to make this dream a reality.

We contend that the field is closer to achieving the dream of AIG than many people realize. Since the publication of the last book on this topic—*Item Generation for Test Development*, edited by Sidney Irvine and Patrick Kyllonen, in 2002—significant progress has been made in both the theory and practice of AIG. The purpose of this book is to bring researchers and practitioners up-to-date on the growing body of research on AIG by presenting what is currently known about this topic. Our volume is organized around the theoretical foundation and practical applications of AIG. By focusing on theory and practice, we will present a comprehensive analysis of the concepts that define AIG as well as the practical considerations required to implement these concepts in order to produce large numbers of useful test items. Part I (Initial Considerations for Automatic Item Generation) begins with an overview of the concepts and topics necessary to understand the basic principles in AIG. Part II (Connecting Theory and Practice in Automatic Item Generation) illustrates how two new frameworks for test design can be used to generate actual test items. Part III (Psychological Foundations for Automatic Item Generation) describes how research in the psychology of test performance can contribute to AIG. Part IV (Technical Developments in Automatic Item Generation) concludes with a discussion of how methodological developments in statistics and computing science are promoting item generation.

Part I—Initial Considerations for AIG

Our book begins with the current chapter, which is intended to introduce the reader to the topic of AIG by briefly highlighting some of the factors that have created a pressing need for alternative approaches to item development, by defining and describing the role of item models in the generative process, and by summarizing the purpose of the subsequent chapters. Next, we provide a historical context. The history of AIG is spread across books, chapters, published manuscripts, and conference papers. To consolidate this literature, Tom Haladyna describes the history, precedents, and motivation guiding research and practice in AIG in chapter 2. Chapter 3, by Mark Gierl and Hollis Lai, offers a detailed description of the methods and practices used to create item models. They illustrate how both the weak and strong theory approach to AIG, as advocated by Drasgow et al. (2006), can be used for item model development. Isaac Bejar, in chapter 4, argues that AIG can increase the validity of our interpretation of test scores by providing evidence to support our assumption about construct representation as well as by promoting construct preservation across test administrations. In short, he provides a description of how AIG can enhance our validity arguments and thereby contribute to the larger discussion about the valid meaning and interpretation of test scores.

Part II—Connecting Theory and Practice in AIG

Two important test design frameworks have emerged in the last decade to dramatically change how educational and psychological testing specialists view the design and development of educational and psychological testing. Neither framework was well developed when *Item Generation for*

Test Development (Irvine & Kyllonen, 2002) was first published. But both frameworks are now influencing how tests are designed and items are developed. These frameworks are featured in our book. The first test design framework that is changing how educational and psychological testing specialists view the design of tests and the development of items is assessment engineering. Richard Luecht, the developer of assessment engineering (AE), describes his approach in chapter 5. He begins with an outline of the AE test design principles and then connects these principles to item generative methods. Building on the description of AE presented in chapter 5, Hollis Lai and Mark Gierl then demonstrate, in chapter 6, how these principles can be used in a practical testing context to generate test items for exams in mathematics and reading comprehension. The second test design framework, described in chapter 7, is called evidence-centered design (ECD). Kristen Huff, Cecilia Alves, James Pellegrino, and Pamela Kaliski describe how ECD can be used to promote AIG by describing this design approach, as well as illustrating how the ECD principles can be used in a practical testing context to generate items for the Biology content area on the *College Board's Advanced Placement* exam. Taken together, the chapters in this section provide the reader with a comprehensive and detailed account of how new test design principles can be combined with AIG practices to produce thousands of items.

Part III—Psychological Foundations for AIG

Three different, complementary perspectives on the psychology of test performance are presented in Part III. In chapter 8, Jacqueline Leighton begins by describing how research in the learning sciences can contribute to AIG by helping to identify the item features that affect the psychometric properties of the generated items. An important discussion on the development and use of a cognitive model is also presented. In chapter 9, Joanna Gorin and Susan Embretson focus, specifically, on how research and methodological advances in cognitive psychology contribute to the development of item models and the generation of items in both the ability and achievement domains. Much of their discussion is framed using the metaphor of AIG as experimental design. In chapter 10, Edith Aurora Graf and James Fife provide a fitting conclusion to this section by focusing on the cognitive factors that affect the psychometric characteristics for generated quantitative reasoning items in the domain of mathematics. They focus on the link between outcomes from studies using difficulty modeling and AIG.

Part IV—Technical Developments in AIG

Important methodological developments in statistics and computing science, as they relate to AIG, are presented in the final section of our book. Sandip Sinharay and Matthew Johnson describe, in chapter 11, the statistical methods currently used to estimate the psychometric characteristics of the generated items. The authors provide a comprehensive, readable summary of the statistical models that are currently available. Next, in chapter 12, Richard Luecht provides a detailed description and illustration of how AIG can be integrated into computerized adaptive testing (CAT) using principles and practices in AE. He provides an excellent overview of CAT as well as those concepts in AIG that are directly applicable to CAT. In chapter 13, Todd Mortimer, Eleni Stroulia, and Meisam Yazdchi, provide a unique software development perspective by describing how a desktop computer program for item generation called IGOR (**Item GeneratOR**), initially developed by Gierl, Zhou, and Alves (2008), was migrated into a web-based application. They also emphasize why creating and using web-based systems are important for the future of AIG research. Thomas Haladyna and Mark Gierl then conclude this volume, in chapter 14, by summarize the main points from all preceding chapters and synthesize the theoretical and practical implications of the work described in this book. They also describe some directions and challenges for future AIG research.

Summary

Computer-based testing is proliferating. Tests are now routinely administered over the internet, where students respond to test items containing text, images, tables, diagrams, sound, and video. However, the growth of computer-based testing is only one example of change in educational measurement. Developments in test design, such as assessment engineering, and testing procedures, including cognitive diagnostic assessment, have focused attention on the need for larger numbers of new and alternative items and item types. AIG is the process of using item models to generate test items with the aid of computer technology. AIG can be used to initially develop item banks and then replenish the banks needed for computer-based testing and cognitive diagnostic assessment. The purpose of this book is to highlight for researchers and practitioners what is currently known about the growing body of research on AIG. Our intention is to create a book that will appeal to researchers and practitioners alike because our focus is on both the theoretical foundation and practical applications of AIG. This book was prepared with the goal of providing the most complete and up-to-date description on AIG. It is also intended to provide the reader with the knowledge required to understand the logic underlying AIG, as well as a sample of practical applications that provide the know-how to actually begin the process of generating test items.

References

AERA, APA, & NMCE (American Educational Research Association, American Psychological Association, National Council on Measurement in Education). (1999). *Standards for Educational and Psychological Testing.* Washington, DC: American Educational Research Association.

Bartram, D. (2006). Testing on the internet: Issues, challenges, and opportunities in the field of occupational assessment. In D. Bartram & R. Hambleton (Eds.), *Computer-based testing and the internet* (pp. 13–37). Hoboken, NJ: Wiley.

Breithaupt, K., Ariel, A., & Hare, D. (2010). Assembling an inventory of multistage adaptive testing systems. In W. van der Linden & C. Glas (Eds.), *Elements of adaptive testing* (pp. 247–266). New York, NY: Springer.

The College Board. (2006). *College Board Standards for College Success: Mathematics & Statistics.* New York, NY: The College Board.

Downing, S. M., & Haladyna, T. M. (Eds.) (2006). *Handbook of test development.* Mahwah, NJ: Lawrence Erlbaum Associates.

Dragsow, F., Luecht, R. M., & Bennett, R. (2006). Technology and testing. In R. L. Brennan (Ed.), *Educational measurement* (4th ed., pp. 471–516). Washington, DC: American Council on Education.

Dragsow, F., & Mattern, K. (2006). New tests and new items: Opportunities and issues. In D. Bartram & R. Hambleton (Eds.), *Computer-based testing and the internet* (pp. 59–76). Hoboken, NJ: Wiley.

Embretson, S. (1998). A cognitive design system approach to generating valid tests: Application to abstract reasoning. *Psychological Methods, 3,* 300–396.

Embretson, S. E., & Yang, X. (2007). Automatic item generation and cognitive psychology. In C. R. Rao & S. Sinharay (Eds.), *Handbook of Statistics: Psychometrics, Volume 26* (pp. 747–768). North Holland, UK: Elsevier.

Folk, W. G., & Smith, R. L. (2002). Models for delivery of CBTs. In C. Mills, M. Potenza, J. Fremer, & W. Ward (Eds.), *Computer-based testing: Building the foundation for future assessments* (pp. 41–66). Mahwah, NJ: Erlbaum.

Gierl, M. J., Alves, C., Roberts, M., & Gotzmann, A. (2009, April). *Using judgments from content specialists to develop cognitive models for diagnostic assessments.* In J. Gorin (Chair), How to Build a Cognitive Model for Educational Assessments. Paper presented in symposium conducted at the annual meeting of the National Council on Measurement in Education, San Diego, CA.

Gierl, M. J., Cui, Y., & Zhou, J. (2009). Reliability of attribute-based scoring in cognitive diagnostic assessment. *Journal of Educational Measurement, 46,*293–313.

Gierl, M. J., Zhou, J., & Alves, C. (2008). Developing a taxonomy of item model types to promote assessment engineering. *Journal of Technology, Learning, and Assessment, 7*(2). Retrieved from http://www.jtla.org.

Haladyna, T. (1994). *Developing and validation multiple-choice test items.* Hillsdale, NJ: Lawrence Erlbaum Associates.

Haladyna, T. M. (2004). Developing and validating multiple-choice test items (3rd ed.). Mahwah, NJ: Lawrence Erlbaum Associates.

Haladyna, T. M., & Rodriguez, M. C. (in press). *Developing and validating test items.* New York, NY: Routledge.

Irvine, S. H., & Kyllonen, P. C. (Eds.) (2002). *Item generation for test development.* Hillsdale, NJ: Erlbaum.

Kane, M. T. (2006a). Content-related validity evidence. In S. M. Downing & T. M. Haladyna (Eds.), *Handbook of test development* (pp. 131–154). Mahwah, NJ: Lawrence Erlbaum Associates.

Kane, M. T. (2006b). Validation. In R. L. Brennan (Ed.), *Educational measurement* (4th ed., pp. 17–64). Phoenix, AZ: Greenwood.

Leighton, J. P., & Gierl, M. J. (2007a). *Cognitive diagnostic assessment for education: Theory and applications.* Cambridge, UK: Cambridge University Press.

Leighton, J. P., & Gierl, M. J. (2007b). Defining and evaluating models of cognition used in educational measurement to make inferences about examinees' thinking processes. *Educational Measurement: Issues and Practice, 26,* 3–16.

Lewis, A. & Smith, D. (1993). Defining higher-order thinking. *Theory into Practice, 32*(3), 131–137.

Lewis, C., & Sheehan, K. (1990). Using Bayesian decision theory to design a computer mastery test. *Applied Psychological Measurement, 14,* 367–386.

Lohman, D. F. (1993). Teaching and testing to develop fluid abilities. *Educational Researcher, 22,* 12–23.

Luecht, R. M. (1998). Computer assisted test assembly using optimization heuristics. *Applied Psychological Measurement, 22,* 224–236.

Luecht, R. M. (2006, September). *Assessment engineering: An emerging discipline.* Paper presented in the Centre for Research in Applied Measurement and Evaluation, University of Alberta, Edmonton, AB, Canada.

Luecht, R. M. (2007, April). *Assessment engineering in language testing: From data models and templates to psychometrics.* Invited paper presented at the annual meeting of the National Council on Measurement in Education, Chicago, IL.

Luecht, R. M. (2011, February). *Assessment design and development, version 2.0: From art to engineering.* Invited paper presented at the annual meeting of the Association of Test Publishers, Phoenix, AZ.

Luecht, R. M., & Nungester, R. J. (1998). Some practical examples of computer-adaptive sequential testing. *Journal of Educational Measurement, 35,* 229–249.

Messick, S. (1984). The psychology of educational measurement. *Journal of Educational Measurement, 21,* 215–237.

Mislevy, R. J. (2006). Cognitive psychology and educational assessment. In R. L. Brennan (Ed.), *Educational Measurement* (4th ed., pp. 257–305). Phoenix, AZ: Greenwood.

Mislevy, R. J., & Riconscente, M. M. (2006). Evidence-centered assessment design. In S. M. Downing & T. Haladyna (Eds.), *Handbook of test development* (pp. 61–90). Mahwah, NJ: Lawrence Erlbaum Associates.

Mislevy, R. J., Steinberg, L. S., & Almond, R. G. (2003). On the structure of educational assessments. *Measurement: Interdisciplinary Research and Perspectives, 1,* 3–67.

Raymond, M. R., & Neustel, S. (2006). Determining the content of credentialing examinations. In S. M. Downing & T. Haladyna (Eds.), *Handbook of test development* (pp. 181–223). Mahwah, NJ: Lawrence Erlbaum Associates.

Rudner, L. (2010). Implementing the *Graduate Management Admission Test* computerized adaptive test. In W. van der Linden & C. Glas (Eds.), *Elements of adaptive testing* (p. 151–165), New York, NY: Springer.

Sands, W. A., Waters, B. K., & McBride, J. R. (1997). *Computerized adaptive testing: From inquiry to operation.* Washington, DC: American Psychological Association.

Schmeiser, C. B., & Welch, C. J. (2006). Test development. In R. L. Brennan (Ed.), *Educational measurement* (4th ed., pp. 307–353). Westport, CT: National Council on Measurement in Education and American Council on Education.

Sireci, S. G., & Zenisky, A. L. (2006). Innovative item formats in computer-based testing: In pursuit of improved construct representation. In S. M. Downing & T. M. Haladyna (Eds.), *Handbook of test development* (pp. 329–348). Mahwah, NJ: Lawrence Erlbaum Associates.

Sternberg, R. J. (1998). Abilities are forms of developing expertise. *Educational Researcher, 27,* 11–20.

van der Linden, W., & Glas, C. A. W. (2010). *Elements of adaptive testing.* New York: Springer.

Wainer, H., & Kiely, G. L. (1987). Item clusters and computerized adaptive testing: A case for testlets. *Journal of Educational Measurement, 24,* 185–201.

Wainer, H., & Lewis, C. (1990). Toward a psychometrics for testlets. *Journal of Educational Measurement, 27,* 1–14.

Zenisky, A. L., & Sireci, S. G. (2002). Technological innovations in large-scale assessment. *Applied Measurement in Education, 15,* 337–362.

2

Automatic Item Generation
A Historical Perspective

Thomas M. Haladyna

Introduction

The validity of a test score interpretation depends on many factors. One of the most important is the quality of items that comprise the test. That is why item development and validation is so expensive.

Ironically, the science of item development and validation has lagged far behind statistical theories of test scores and its attendant technologies (for example, item response theory, differential item function, and equating). This perception was voiced long ago by Cronbach (1970) and echoed by Roid and Haladyna (1980; 1982) and Nitko (1985). Although the scientific basis for item development and validation is increasing, there is much more work to do (Haladyna & Rodriguez, in press). Most guidance on item writing comes from the aggregated wisdom and experience of testing specialists. This guidance was summarized as a set of item-writing guidelines (see Haladyna & Downing, 1989a; 1989b; Haladyna, Downing, & Rodriguez, 2002). That is why early pioneers in item development like Ebel (1951) and Wesman (1971) considered item writing to be part science and part art. There has always been a subjective nature to item writing. Bormuth (1970) railed against subjectivity. His theory for developing items from prose passages appeared in his acclaimed book *On a Theory of Achievement Test Items*. From long ago to today, item development continues to be the most expensive and most time-consuming aspect of test development. Fortunately, we have many reached milestones that have contributed to a growing science of AIG. This chapter presents a brief history of these milestones and their influence on current AIG. The chapter begins with the presentation of this history in Part 1 and concludes with a discussion of four perspectives that are the result of this history and that will affect AIG's future.

Part 1: The History of AIG

This part of the chapter presents major milestones in AIG, dating from the middle of the last century to the present. What is interesting about this history is its diversity, lack of cohesion among the contributors, and disconnectedness from current theory and research. In other words, there have been no unification or unifying themes in AIG. We have theories of item development that involve AIG and we have non-theoretical, prescriptive methods that are practical and provide help to item developers until such time as AIG can take over the burden of facilitating item development in operational testing programs. Although AIG is not yet a unified science of item development, this volume gives evidence that the field is healthy and growing.

This history can be summarized by acknowledging the following milestones in AIG:

1. Prose-based AIG (Bormuth, 1970);
2. Facet theory (Guttman, 1953; 1959);
3. Item forms (Hively, 1974);
4. Concept formation (Markle & Tiemann, 1970); and
5. The 1998 ETS Invitational Seminar, which resulted in the publication of *Item Generation for Test Development* (Irvine & Kyllonen, 2002).

Current AIG can be traced to concepts and principles that these pioneers in AIG introduced and refined.

AIG From Prose

As most learning involves reading, it seems reasonable to generate test items from prose that represent the intent of what is to be learned. That was exactly what Bormuth proposed (Bormuth, 1970). The motivation for Bormuth's theory of item generation from prose was that conventional item writing is subjective and inefficient. Criterion-referenced testing was the impetus for creating tests that faithfully matched instructional objectives. Now such matching is a routine feature for local, state, and national achievement tests (see Webb, 2006). With testing professional competence, it is widely advocated and practiced to conduct a survey of the profession in order to identify the tasks performed, which are then the basis for a test of this professional ability (see Raymond & Neustel, 2006).

Bormuth's theory began with some assumptions. Item writing should not be subjective. Two item writers using the same content and item specifications should produce similar, high-quality items. Roid and Haladyna (1978), using very strict item-writing guidelines and very specific content specifications, produced parallel sets of items that differed significantly in difficulty. Even under these conditions, item writing was too subjective. From Bormuth's perspective, the process of item writing should be automated and item-writer subjectivity eliminated. From personal experience, the survival rate of newly written items developed traditionally after many rigorous reviews can be as low as 50% to 60%.

Bormuth's theory itself came from earlier research on cloze testing for reading comprehension. Early experiments involved syntactic transformations of prose referred to as wh-transformations. If a prose passage read: *The boy rode the horse.* the wh-transformation became: *Who rode the horse?* The wh- referred to who, what, when, and where. What followed was a theory that lacked detail and efficiency. In subsequent years, a team of researchers refined Bormuth's theory and simplified his algorithms for prose transformation (Finn, 1975; Roid & Haladyna, 1978). Subsequent research showed that the simplified algorithms worked, that teachers could be trained to use the algorithms, and the statistical properties of the items were good.

However, some setbacks and limitations were noted along the way. The prose had to be well written. Also, key sentences had to be chosen: not any sentence was subject to transformation. The cognitive demand of these items seemed to be recall. As comprehension has been universally deemed more important, the theory's technology lacked the capacity to paraphrase the chosen prose sentences. Specific discussion of procedures and the simplified algorithm can be found in Roid and Haladyna (1982). This theory appears to be abandoned. There are no current reports of how this original work was adapted or improved. Nonetheless, current AIG has no replacement theory for AIG for prose passages. As reading continues to be a principal basis for learning, having an AIG theory for prose would be a major advance in this young science.

Facet Design

Test theorists and instructional developers of the 1960s and 1970s were interested in a theory where the whole of achievement is contained in a domain, which contains all possible tasks. Referred to as *domain-referenced testing*, it contrasted with criterion-referenced testing, which depended on a set of instructional objectives developed by curriculum experts. Domain-referenced testing is very consistent with Kane's recent orientation to the target domain and the universe of generalization (Kane, 2006a). One way to explicate a construct is to identify all possible tasks that one can perform. These tasks comprise a domain. All of instruction is based on this domain, and tests of achievement are samples from this domain. Interestingly, credentialing testing seems to be moving in that direction. Professional competence consists of a domain of tasks, and a test of this competence samples from this domain.

The term *facet design* was used by Guttman (1959), but with acknowledgment that facet design is an idea that originated in personality testing (Roid & Haladyna, 1980, p. 128). In short, the theory resonated with the classic Cronbach and Meehl (1955) conceptualization of construct validity—that a construct/ability could be defined operationally. Facet design has this objective.

The device used in facet design is the *mapping sentence*. By developing many mapping sentences, the content of any domain is ordered and limited only to the mapping sentences. Guttman's schema was organized via a taxonomy of cognitive behavior that had two dimensions, with three categories in each dimension. Thus, facet design proposed a system for defining the universe of content in the form of these mapping sentences and then empirically validating its success. Facet theory included operationally defining content and validating it via its statistical structure. Mislevy's evidence-based learning comes closest to resembling this approach, because it has a logical structure and an empirical basis for testing its validity (Mislevy & Haertel, 2007; Mislevy & Riconscente, 2006).

The mapping sentence is the means by which test items are developed. Each mapping sentence has fixed and variable parts. Each of the variable aspects in the mapping sentence is called a *facet*. An example of a very elementary set of mapping sentences appears in Figure 2.1. Every dental student must know the name and number of the 32 teeth in the adult dentition. The basis is the Universal Coding System. The entire domain consists of 64 items. Adding the juvenile dentition of 20 teeth, the domain increases to 104 test items.

We have many benefits for the facet design. Distractors are algorithmically formed. There is no item-writer subjectivity, but the mapping sentences are constructed subjectively by the subject-matter experts (SMEs). Contiguity exists among the facets that provide diagnostic information if performance is poor. A rich opportunity is provided for formative and summative testing experiences from the same set of item-generating methods. Also, parallel test forms are easily generated. Computerization of these methods is possible.

> A first-year dental student is given the name of a tooth in the adult dentition (32 teeth) and must state the number of that tooth using the Universal Coding System.
>
> A first-year dental student is given the number of a tooth in the adult dentition (32 teeth) and must state the name of the tooth.

Figure 2.1 Example of a mapping sentence

Although the claims for these benefits are true, facet design has its limitations as well. The mapping sentence from one item developer is not necessarily the same mapping sentence from another item developer. Considerable effort must be given to developing mapping sentences. Also, the degree of mapping should be comprehensive and not sample from the domain. Finally, we have no research to report on the success of facet design, as presented by Guttman.

Item Forms

Current-day AIG has its greatest applicability with constructs that are scientific, technical, or quantitative. The simplest example is addition of two integers that range from 1 to 999. Here we have many test items that can be generated very rapidly.

Although Hively and his colleagues have done most to advance the idea of an item form, it was Osburn (1968) who first proposed it. The concept is a lesson to be learned in current education. Rather than teach to a test containing items that count in a summative test, teaching is aimed at a repertoire of test items that may appear in a test. Thus, a test score is an estimate of domain performance. Teaching the specific items on a summative test established bias.

What is an item form? As Osburn (1968) explained, it generates items that have a fixed syntactic structure. It has several variable elements, much like Guttman's facets. It defines a class of sentences by limiting the range of the replacement sets. Think of a sentence with blanks that are replaced by numbers or concepts to form the item.

The item form might be the following:

Existing item: Find the median for the following sale items at your local grocer.

Super Cola{ B }3 12-packs $8

Cool Cola{ B }2 12-packs for $5

Double Cola{ B }4 12-packs for $9

Which is the best value?

Simple Item Form: Given the advertised price for buying a 12-pack of diet soda from your local grocer, calculate the price per can.

Your local grocery store offers Double Cola:{ 3 }12-packs for{ 8 }dollars.

Replacement Sets: Replacement sets are A and B. A can vary from one to five. B can vary from $2.00 to $15.00 in integers.

Your local grocery store offers Double Cola:{ A }12-packs for{ B }dollars.

This simple example is quantitative and has a limited number of variations. Most item forms have to be carefully constructed so that the variations do not create ridiculous problems.

For instance, without a conditional relationship between A and B in the above example, a problem might ask the student to calculate a unit price for a single 12-pack advertised for $15.

An added condition might limit the variations to unit prices that fall between $1.00 and $2.00 per six-pack. In modern AIG terms, this is a *constraint*.

At the time that item forms were being studied, the use of computers to create item forms was of keen interest (Millman & Westman, 1989). The contribution of computer technology to AIG is featured in this book in chapter 13.

Item forms have many obvious advantages. First, items of a quantitative nature can be generated rapidly without using item writers. Domains of items are created. Quantitative story problems can be produced abundantly in such areas as statistics, chemistry, accountancy, financial analysis, banking, and pharmacy. The random generation of such items can be used to create formative and summative tests. Also, existing items can be used as a basis for an item form.

Some disadvantages also should be reported. First, any achievement domain will have to have many item forms in order to have a complete mapping of the domain. Also, there is much work in developing item forms.

Research on *item forms* seems to have ended in the mid 1980s. Ironically, current methods for AIG appear to employ aspects of item form technology that was so popular in the 1970s and 1980s.

Generating Test Items That Measure Concept Learning

The Bloom taxonomy and other approaches to defining types of learning have long agreed that recall is the most basic type of learning, and comprehension/understanding is the next higher level. After that, most taxonomic systems involve the use of knowledge and skills in complex ways. Some of these ways have names, but, as Haladyna and Rodriguez (in press) show, the literature is flooded with terms for different kinds of higher-level thinking. There is no standard set of terms.

Merrill (1994) promoted the idea that all knowledge can be defined as existing in four categories: facts, concepts, principles, and procedures. This simple, effective taxonomy provides a useful way to organize knowledge. The learning of concepts is a major aspect of K-12 education and in all professional/training schools and academies. Toward that end, many researchers in the 1960s through the 1980s worked on and developed a technology for item generation that measured concepts. Markle and Tiemann (1970) are credited with advancing this work, but many others influenced it. Richard Anderson (1972) advocated testing concepts by paraphrasing definitions of a concept. Simple verbatim recall is not sufficient. This idea of paraphrasing to write test items was expanded to include examples.

The most generic examples are:

Which of the following best defines {concept}?

Which of the following is an example of {concept}?

A full exposition of their work can be found in these references (Roid & Haladyna, 1982, chapter 9; Markle & Tiemann, 1970). They provided four major points for understanding how to analyze concepts and produce test items rapidly.

Defining a Concept

A dictionary definition might look like this: An idea created by mentally combining relevant characteristics. To help us, we define a concept, give examples and non examples, and list relevant characteristics of that concept. Concepts exist in all fields of learning, from literature (homonym), German language (dipthong), physics (free vector), and dentistry (endodontics).

All concepts have critical attributes, a set of examples and non examples, and variable attributes that may not seem relevant but produce variety of that concept. By combining critical attributes with variable attributes, we produce a variety of examples.

Contrasting concepts are identities, which are singular. A car is a concept, but a Lamborghini Aventador is an identity. We can generate lists of concepts to be learned and avoid learning identities, unless it is important to memorize identities.

Attributes of Concepts

All concepts have attributes. However, we have two types: critical and variable. For instance, a chair is a one-person seat with a back support and a sitting position, which are critical attributes. Chairs have variable attributes, which include constructional material, arms, rocker, or size. Variable attributes are irrelevant. As noted previously, in modern AIG terminology, variable attributes are constraints.

Testing for Generalization and Discrimination

Generalization is the ability to see a new version of a concept, one that has not been presented before. Identification is based on an understanding of critical attributes. A child sees a wolf hound and identifies it as a dog but rejects a coyote as a dog. Discrimination is the ability to classify an object as a member of a concept class despite attributes that are similar to other concepts. The general context for generalization and discrimination is discerning examples and non examples.

Listing and Sampling Examples and Non Examples

The crux of item generation for testing concept mastery is generating examples and non examples. Can this be done automatically? The technology for generating these examples seems to be based on the SMEs.

This work on concept testing has been extended to coordinating concepts and principles. A deeper reading of concept learning as proposed by Markle and Tiemann (1970) and reviewed by Roid and Haladyna (1982) reveals a systematic way of generating many items that measure discrimination. Prescriptive methods for generating test items have long since employed these ideas to measure cognitive learning outcomes.

Concept learning and concept testing is one of the easiest for which items can be generated. The thrust of testing for learning now comes from cognitive psychology, but the origins of concept learning appear to emanate from the work of psychologists of the 1960s and 1970s. The testing industry has not yet mined the wealth of material that was produced then and now for concept testing.

Educational Testing Service Seminar on Item Generation

Following the appearance of the Roid and Haladyna (1982) book on item generation, the next major milestone was the publication of *Item Generation for Test Development* (Irvine and Kyllonen, 2002). This book was the byproduct of a seminar held at the Educational Testing Service that included 25 contributors from a variety of disciplines. The publication includes a variety of perspectives for item generation that included work done in the United Kingdom (UK) and recent work in the United States. There is no adequate way to summarize this work, due to its diversity. Some of the chapters deal with aptitude testing, which is different from achievement testing. Other chapters deal with cognitive and measurement theories that provide a basis for the construct being measured. A few chapters report projects where item generation is operational.

Irvine (2002) argued that three measurement paradigms exist for AIG, which are referred to as R-models, L-models, and D-models. The R-models deal with what we know as conventional testing programs that measure achievement. The L-models deal with time-based measurement such as timed testing. D-model are used for prediction purposes. Computers are more central in AIG with variations in display modes, information types, and response modes. Irving reported progress in the UK on item generation, dating from the mid 1980s to the time of this book's publication. One of the objectives was the study and control of item difficulty. For the most part, this work centered on psychological testing of mental abilities such as represented in the Guilford structure-of-the intellect model.

Generative Testing

The term *generative testing* is attributed to Isaac Bejar (2002) and his continuing research on item generation. He advocated a thorough analysis of the construct to be measured, as it should be.

Model-based generative testing is concerned with a domain of tasks that has been identified as consistent with construct definition. The target domain suggested by Kane (2006a; 2006b) seems to be the focus in generative testing. Another type of generative testing is characterized at the grammatical level, which dates back to Bormuth's prose-based theory for item generation.

The heart of generative testing is isomorphs, which are generated items with similar psychometric properties. Thus, difficulty and discrimination can be controlled. The devices used to produce isomorphs are item models, a term first introduced by LaDuca, Staples, Templeton, and Holzman (1986). Not all item models are designed to standardize item difficulty and discrimination. In some settings, it is important to vary difficulty in order to accommodate efficient measurement at different levels in the continuum. The term *task model* was also introduced to designate constructed response item objectively scored (CROS).

Several important principles are featured in the research by Bejar. First, construct analysis is essential to having an effective AIG. Item and task models are important to explicate the target domain. These item and task modes can be designed to be content equivalent, which is why the term *isomorph* is used. Other item and task models can be designed to vary in some way and are referred to as *variants*. The process of building item and task models in isomorph and variant forms is iterative, with the opportunity for empirical verification of item responses. Thus, data collection and analysis are vital aspects of generative testing.

The central claim for this approach to item generation is that the characteristics of test items (difficulty and discrimination) are under control, due to the design of the item models. Thus, the need for field-testing of items may be avoided if research shows the validity of the item generation methods.

In summary, the argument for generative testing is that all the important work is done on the front end with construct analysis and building an adequate supply of item and task models that fully explicate the construct being measured. Once this is done, the expense of item generation and testing is lowered considerably. Because of the complexity of some of these item and task models, the analysis of item responses and item response patterns requires more sophisticated methods of analysis that likely include item response theory. The result is that AIG has a bright future when a technology is created for construct analysis and developing these item and task models in isomorph and variant forms.

Many papers provide a rich source of information on generative testing (Bejar, 1993; 1996; 2002; 2009; Bejar & Yocom, 1991; Bejar, Lawless, Morley, Wagner, Bennett, & Revuelta, 2003).

Prescriptive Item Generation Methods

Given the gaps in theory and research on item generation and the slow and uneven development of AIG dating back to the early 1960s, we have had periodic introductions of prescriptive methods for item generation. These methods have no strong link to any theory but may resemble or capitalize on implied technologies from these past attempts at item generation. Two prescriptive item generation methods are the item shells and the mapping sentence. The mapping sentence was illustrated in Figure 2.1. Each method has proven useful for item development. Each method is serviceable and easy to implement.

Item shells are hollow items based on empirical study of items in an item bank that are performing quite well. The syntactical structure of the stem is retained, but content is removed. What remains is a stem that provides a basis for generating similar items. The item shell has some of the elements of the modern item model but is less constrained and offers the item writer more freedom in choosing content to complete the stem and more freedom to create options.

The technique was created in response to the need to train item writers who were preparing to write items for the North American Pharmacist Licensure Examination (NABPLEX), which measures a candidate's knowledge of the practice of pharmacy (Haladyna & Shindoll, 1989). These item writers were chosen on the basis of the subject-matter expertise in pharmacy but often lacked experience in writing test items. Many of these item writers experienced *writer's block*.

Haladyna and Rodriguez (in press) provide many examples of generic item shells, but the most effective item shells come directly from an extant item bank. SMEs review items in the bank, pull the best items out, and transform them into item shells by stripping out the content. One might think of the content as variants in AIG item models, but the main difference is the emphasis on modeling existing items with no reference to options.

Table 2.1 provides a partial list of published articles on item shells, with the subject-matter or professional competence tested. As the table implies, the item shell technique has had success in diverse fields.

Future of Practical, Prescriptive Item Generation Methods

Until such time as AIG is a refined science with a well-developed technology, these prescriptive remedies for item generation seem to work well with item developers who have subject-matter expertise but lack item-writing ability and experience. Item shells and mapping sentences are viable item-development methods until such time that AIG methods achieve the goal of generating many items that have a predictable, controllable difficulty and discrimination, and, at the same time, map the desired content at an appropriate cognitive demand.

Part 2: Four Perspectives Arising From This History

Four perspectives influenced past efforts to develop AIG and each will influence future efforts as well. The first is how we define the content of any test. The second is the cognitive demand of each test item. Test developers and their sponsors want test items that are cognitively complex and engaging to test takers. The third is the role of validity in item development. Will AIG improve the validity of test score interpretations? The fourth involves item formats.

The Content of Tests and Test Items

The most fundamental step in developing any test is to define the construct. Cronbach and Meehl (1955) referred to this as *construct formulation*. It benefits test developers to know exactly what they are measuring. The content of any cognitive test and its test items seem to originate from one of two sources.

Traditional behavioral learning theory is associated with the criterion-referenced movement that started in the 1960s. Tests were thought to be representative samples from a domain of instructional objectives. Hence the term *domain-referenced testing* was often preferred over *criterion-referenced testing*. In K-12 achievement testing in most states today, this tradition is still followed. Items are

Table 2.1 Studies involving item shells

Study	Subject
Solano-Flores (2001)	Science
Morrison & Free (2001)	Nursing
Sheaet al. (1992)	Medicine
Enright & Morley, & Sheehan (2002)	Graduate Record Examination–Quantitative
Haladyna (1991)	Statistics, art history
Simon (1989)	Reading comprehension
Draaijer, Hartog, & Wageningen (2007)	Higher education
Liu & Haertel (2011)	Science

developed from learner outcome statements. The organization and structure of content is developed by curriculum experts, but the basis continues to be instructional objectives. This approach to testing is a residue of behavioral learning theory that emphasized acquiring knowledge and skills and, to a small extent, the application of knowledge and skills in complex ways.

The second source of content is based on cognitive learning theory, which Snow and Lohman (1989) once characterized as a loose confederation of theorists and researchers working on the same problems. One constant in cognitive learning theory is that what we are developing and testing are cognitive abilities (Lohman, 1993; Messick, 1984; Sternberg, 1998). Each cognitive ability is a slow-growing mental structure that includes knowledge and skills and the capacity to use knowledge and skills in complex ways to perform tasks that are relevant to that construct. In public education, these cognitive abilities are reading, writing, speaking, and listening (the language arts), and mathematical and scientific problem solving, and critical thinking that is used in many subject matters, including social studies. In the testing for professional competency, these abilities include accountancy, architecture, dentistry, medicine, nursing, and teaching, among many others. To measure a professional competency requires SMEs to identify a domain of tasks that are representative of this ability. A test is a representative sample of that domain, and a test score is an estimate of this ability. In fact, a practice analysis is a survey of a profession whereby the most important and frequently performed tasks are identified, and these results are used to define the content of future credentialing tests.

Given these two competing traditions for defining and measuring constructs, we have some dissonance in how AIG grows in the future. AIG seems to accommodate both approaches to defining content. However, behavioral learning theory is waning in importance, and cognitive learning theory appears to be increasingly important (Mislevy, 2006). That said, the focus of AIG should be on defining cognitive abilities and creating items that reflect with high fidelity those tasks that best represent this ability. If AIG focuses on technologies that foster behavioral learning theories, this technology will surely be abandoned because cognitive learning theory is emerging as the dominant learning theory. As AIG continues to develop, the role of cognitive psychology is becoming stronger, and developers of AIG technology seem to be united in thinking that construct definition must be done, and cognitive learning theory may be the mechanism for construct definition.

The Cognitive Demand of Items

Since the publication of the cognitive taxonomy by Bloom and his colleagues (Bloom et al., 1956), interest has been keen on writing test items that reflect different types of cognitive demand. The unfortunate and heavy reliance on memory-type items in the past underscored a need to create test items that are more cognitively engaging.

Unfortunately, there is no existing cognitive taxonomy that works. The Bloom cognitive taxonomy is enormously popular, but a hard look at the research underlying it reveals that item and test performance does not conform to these taxonomic categories (Haladyna & Rodriguez, in press). Most achievement-testing programs appear to be comfortable with the idea of sampling knowledge and skills, but the cognitive taxonomy is seldom used. A simpler system for categorizing the cognitive demand of test items seems to be knowledge, skills, and the ability to apply knowledge and skills for performing complex tasks.

The overriding and unsolvable dilemma with respect to cognitive demand is that it is dependent on the developmental level of the test takers. Novices tend to use more complex cognitive strategies to respond to test items and experts tend to work from memory. Thus, no item has a definitive cognitive demand. The cognitive demand for any item depends on who is responding to the test item. Until such time as we have a unified approach to defining cognitive demand, AIG will struggle with the dilemma of developing items with a known cognitive demand. However, the cognitive demand will certainly be more extensive than recall.

Validity

As stated previously, AIG will be successful to the extent that it improves validity or, at least, makes item development more efficient and maintains validity. Any past or future technology for AIG needs to work in a framework of current validity theory if it wants to be successful. Validity is that important.

Validity is an evolving concept. According to Cronbach and Meehl (1955), the most fundamental approach to creating any cognitive test involves three steps: (1) construct formulation (definition), (2) construct explication, and (3) construct validation. We define what we want to measure and describe our purpose for testing. The term *explication* refers to developing a test. Validation is the investigative process by which we garner evidence supporting each test score interpretation and use.

Validity is said to be a property of a test score interpretation. Kane (2006a, 2006b) has provided many useful insights into a way of thinking about validating test score interpretations. Any cognitive ability consists of a domain of tasks to be performed. The *target domain* is said to be the actual tasks performed that exemplify the domain. The *universe of generalization* is the operational set of tasks that we use for tests. For our purposes, it is an item bank. Item validation seeks evidence that each task/item does what it is supposed to do. As any test is a representative sample from that domain, each item should be proven to measure desired content with a predictable cognitive demand for beginning and advanced learners.

The same standards that we apply for the validity of test score interpretations should be applied to the validity of each item response interpretation. As the item is the basic building block of each test, we might think of validation as servicing both tests and test items. As the item is a basic building block of the test, it generates a scorable response that should be validly interpreted. Thus a parallelism exists for items and item scores and tests and test scores regarding validity. AIG needs to attend to the demands of the modern view of validity, which appears to be in the context of cognitive learning theory and the idea that cognitive abilities are the targets for testing. AIG must produce items that are cognitively engaging and complex if the technology will contribute to more validly measuring these constructs. At the heart of validity is the need to define the construct in the context of a cognitive theory (Embretson, 2002).

Anatomy of Test Items

Standardization is a goal in testing. We like all aspects of test development to be uniform, orderly, principled, predictable, and understandable. As noted previously, the quest for a precise test score that is validly interpretable is contingent on effectively performing test items. One area of standardization is item format. Toward that end, Bennett and Ward's (1993) edited book dealt with item formats and each format's capabilities for content and cognitive demand. Textbooks on classroom testing treat this subject extensively as well, dating from long ago to the present. A variety of item formats exist and are popularly used in these textbooks (Haladyna, 1992a; 1992b, 2004, Haladyna & Rodriguez, in press; Haladyna, Downing, & Rodriguez, 2002). From a body of theory and research, a reasonable conclusion is that each item format has the capability of measuring different types of content and cognitive demand. However, in some circumstances some formats seem to have greater fidelity to the construct. For instance, if the construct is writing ability, then a test format needs to elicit writing. In other circumstances, we can weigh benefits and losses of using or not using certain formats.

Item formats can be clearly separated into three distinct categories: Selected-response (SR), constructed-response that is objective scored (CROS), and constructed-response that is subjectively scored (CRSS). Table 2.2 summarizes the characteristic of these three item formats. More extensive

Table 2.2 Basic anatomy of item formats

Type	Stimulus	Response	Scoring	Random error	Systematic error
Selected response (SR)	Question/partial sentence	Choose from a list	Objective	Usually very low with longer tests	No
Constructed response objectively scored (CROS)	Command/question	Create	Objective	Usually very low with longer tests	No
Constructed response subjectively scored (CRSS)	Command/question	Create	Subjective	Usually high because tests have few items	Yes, comes from subjective scoring

treatment of item formats can be found in Haladyna and Rodriguez (in press). They show the extensive variety that exists within each category and the variety of content and cognitive demand possible with each format.

As noted in Table 2.2, the SR response is objectively scored. Because of that, random error associated with the reliability coefficient is very small if the test is long enough. Systematic error arising from scoring is absent. The CROS format is very much like the SR format but the answer is supplied by the examinee. As with the SR format, random error can be very small if the test is long enough. The CRSS format is preferred for measuring complex tasks that comprise an ability. For instance, to measure writing, students must write. SR does not have sufficient fidelity for the measurement of writing ability.

Three issues with item format affect AIG. Each is serious enough to warrant attention. First, previous and current AIG theories and attendant technologies are wedded to four- and five-option SR item formats. Theory, research, and practicality argue for two or three options (Haladyna & Downing, 1993; Haladyna, 2004, Haladyna & Rodriguez, in press; Rodriguez, 2004). Simply stated, most options in four- and five-option items do not perform as they should. Adding fourth and fifth options to items that are better suited to three options makes it very challenging. Distractors are supposed to represent logical errors in order to have diagnostic value. AIG has a serious challenge to create fourth and fifth options that have this diagnostic value.

Second, AIG focuses on the conventional SR format. A variety of other SR formats exist that are very useful in testing programs. For instance, the testlet is increasingly popular, due to the fact that it simulates complex performance testing that is usually obtained with the CRSS format. Other formats such as true/false, multiple true/false, and extended matching should be included in future AIG technology.

Third, CROS and CRSS formats are not yet part of the technology in AIG. Yet, in test development, the need for items in all formats is urgent. As performance testing is increasing in scope, due to its naturally higher fidelity to constructs that imply performance of tasks, more work is needed in AIG for CROS and CRSS formats.

Summary

This chapter has chronicled the short history of AIG that started in the late 1960s and continues today. The early work of theorists like Bormuth, Guttman, Hively and Tiemann, and Markle provides a foundation for future work on AIG. Theoretical development and an emerging technology have grown very slowly. The future is clearly linked to cognitive learning theory and partnerships of cognitive psychologists and measurement specialists. Item models seem to be at the heart of the future of AIG, but, as Embretson (2002) advocates, a structure of construct definition set in a cognitive learning theory seems very desirable, with empirical verification at the item level. The road ahead for AIG seems daunting but achievable.

References

Anderson, R. C. (1972). How to construct achievement tests to assess comprehension. *Review of Educational Research, 42*, 145–170.

Bejar, I. I. (1993). A generative approach to psychological and educational measurement. In N. Frederiksen (Ed.), *Test theory for a new generation of tests* (pp. 323–357). Hillsdale, NJ: Lawrence Erlbaum Associates.

Bejar, I. I. (1996). *Generative response modeling: Leveraging the computer as a test delivery medium* (ETS RR-96–13). Princeton, NJ: ETS.

Bejar, I. I. (2002). Generative testing: From conception to implementation. In S. H. Irvine & P. C. Kyllonen (Eds.), *Item generation for test development* (pp. 199–218). Mahwah, NJ: Lawrence Erlbaum Associates.

Bejar, I. I. (2009). Model-based item generation: A review of recent research. In S. E. Embretson (Ed.), *Measuring psychological constructs: Advances in model-based approaches*. Washington, DC: American Psychological Association Books.

Bejar, I. I., Lawless, R. R., Morley, M. E., Wagner, M. E., Bennett, R. E., & Revuelta, J. (2003). A feasibility study of on-the-fly item generation in adaptive testing. *Journal of Learning, Technology and Assessment 2*(3), 2–29.

Bejar, I. I., & Yocom, P. (1991). A generative approach to the modeling of isomorphic hidden figure items. *Applied Psychological Measurement, 15*(2), 129–137.

Bennett, R. E., & Ward, W. C. (Eds.) (1993). *Construction versus choice in cognitive measurement: Issues in constructed response, performance testing, and portfolio assessment*. Hillsdale, NJ: Lawrence Erlbaum Associates.

Bloom, B. S., Engelhart, M. D., Furst, E. J., Hill, W. H., & Kratwohl, D. R. (1956). *Taxonomy of educational objectives*. New York: Longmans Green.

Bormuth, J. R. (1970). *On a theory of achievement test items*. Chicago: University of Chicago Press.

Cronbach, L. J. (1970). [Review of *On the theory of achievement test items*]. *Psychometrika, 35*, 509–511.

Cronbach, L. J., & Meehl, P. E. (1955). Construct validity in psychological tests. *Psychological Bulletin, 52*, 281–302.

Draaijer, S., & Hartog, R. J. M. (2007). Design patterns for digital item types in higher education. *E-Journal of Instructional Science and Technology, 10*(1), 1–32.

Ebel, R. L. (1951). Writing the test item. In E. F. Lindquist (Ed.), *Educational measurement* (1st ed., pp. 185–249). Washington, DC: American Council on Education.

Embretson, S. E. (2002). Generating abstract reasoning items with cognitive theory. In S. H. Irvine, & P. C. Kyllonen (Eds.), *Item generation for test development* (pp. 219–250). Mahwah, NJ: Lawrence Erlbaum Associates.

Enright, M. K., Morley, M., & Sheehan, K. M. (2002). Items by design: The impact of systematic feature variation of item statistical characteristics. *Applied Measurement in Education, 15*(1), 49–74.

Finn, P. J. (1975). A question writing algorithm. *Journal of Reading Behavior, 4*, 341–367.

Guttman, L. (1953). Image theory for the structure of quantitative variates. *Psychometrika, 18*(4), 277–296.

Guttman, L. (1959). Introduction to facet design and analysis. *Acta Psychologica, 15*, 130–138.

Haladyna, T. M. (1991). Generic questioning strategies for linking teaching and testing. *Educational Technology: Research and Development, 39*, 73–81.

Haladyna, T. M. (1992a). Context dependent item sets. *Educational Measurement: Issues and Practices, 11*, 21–25.

Haladyna, T. M. (1992b). The effectiveness of several multiple-choice formats. *Applied Measurement in Education, 5*, 73–88.

Haladyna, T. M. (2004). *Developing and validating multiple-choice test items* (3rd ed.). Mahwah, NJ: Lawrence Erlbaum Associates).

Haladyna, T. M., & Downing, S. M. (1989a). A taxonomy of multiple-choice item-writing rules. *Applied Measurement in Education, 1*, 37–50.

Haladyna, T. M., & Downing, S. M. (1989b). The validity of a taxonomy of multiple-choice item-writing rules. *Applied Measurement in Education, 1*, 51–78.

Haladyna, T. M. & Downing, S. M. (1993). How many options is enough for a multiple-choice test item. *Educational and Psychological Measurement, 53*(4), 999–1010.

Haladyna, T. M., Downing, S. M., & Rodriguez, M. C. (2002). A review of multiple-choice item-writing guidelines for classroom assessment. *Applied Measurement in Education, 15*(3), 309–334.

Haladyna, T. M., & Rodriguez, M. C. (in press). *Developing and validating test items*. New York, NY: Routledge.

Haladyna, T. M., & Shindoll, R. R. (1989). Item shells: A method for writing effective multiple-choice test items. *Evaluation and the Health Professions, 12*, 97–104.

Hively, W. (1974). Introduction to domain-referenced testing. *Educational Technology, 14*(6), 5–10.

Irvine, S. H. (2002). The foundations of item generation for mass testing. In S. H. Irvine & P. C. Kyllonen (Eds.), *Item generation for test development* (pp. 3–34). Mahwah, NJ: Lawrence Erlbaum Associates.

Irvine, S. H., & Kyllonen, P. C. (Eds.) (2002). *Item generation for test development*. Mahwah, NJ: Lawrence Erlbaum Associates.

Kane, M. T. (2006a). Content-related validity evidence. In S. M. Downing & T. M. Haladyna (Eds.), *Handbook of test development*, pp. 131–154. Mahwah, NJ: Lawrence Erlbaum Associates.

Kane, M. T. (2006b). Validation. In R. L. Brennan (Ed.), *Educational measurement* (4th ed.) pp. 17–64. Westport, CT: American Council on Education/Praeger.

LaDuca, A., Staples, W. I., Templeton, B., & Holzman, G. B. (1986). Item modelling procedure for constructing content–equivalent multiple-choice questions. *Medical Education, 20*, 53–56.

Liu & Haertel, G. (2011) Large-scale assessment technical report. Report Series Published by SRI International.

Lohman, D. F. (1993). Teaching and testing to develop fluid abilities. *Educational Researcher, 22*, 12–23.

Markle, S. M., & Tiemann, P. W. (1970). *Really understanding concepts*. Champaign, IL: Stipes.

Merrill, M. D. (1994). *Instructional design theory*. Englewood Cliffs, NJ: Educational Technology Publications.

Messick, S. (1984). The psychology of educational measurement. *Journal of Educational Measurement, 21*, 215–237.

Millman, J., & Westman, R. S. (1989). Computer-assisted writing of achievement test items: Toward a future technology. *Journal of Educational Measurement, 26*, 177–190.

Mislevy, R. (2006). Cognitive psychology and educational assessment. In R. L. Brennan (Ed.), *Educational measurement* (4th ed., pp 257–305). Westport, CT: American Council on Education/Praeger.

Mislevy, R., & Haertel, G. (2007). Implications of evidence-centered design for educational testing. *Educational Measurement: Issues and Practice, 25*(4), 6–20.

Mislevy, R.J., & Riconscente, M. M. (2006). Evidence-centered assessment design. In S. M. Downing & T. Haladyna (Eds.), *Handbook of test development* (pp. 61–90). Mahwah, NJ: Erlbaum.

Nitko, A. J. (1985). [Review of Roid and Haladyna's *A technology for test item writing*]. *Journal of Educational Measurement, 21*, 201–204.

Osburn, H. G. (1968). Item sampling for achievement testing. *Educational and Psychological Measurement, 28*, 95–104.

Raymond, M., & Neustel, S. (2006). Determining the content of credentialing examinations. In S. M. Downing and T. M. Haladyna (Eds.), *Handbook of Test Development* (pp. 181–223). Mahwah, NJ: Lawrence Erlbaum Associates.

Rodriguez, M. R. (2004). Three options are optimal for multiple-choice items: A meta-analysis of 80 years of research. *Educational Measurement: Issues and Practice, 24*(2) 3–13.

Roid, G. H., & Haladyna, T. M. (1978). The use of domains and item forms in the formative evaluation of instructional materials. *Educational and Psychological Measurement, 38*, 19–28.

Roid, G. H., & Haladyna, T. M. (1980). Toward a technology of test item writing. *Review of Education Research, 50*, 293–314.

Roid, G. H. & Haladyna, T. M. (1982). *A technology for test-item writing*. New York: Academic Press.

Shea, J. A., Poniatowski, P. A., Day, S. C., Langdon, L. O., LaDuca, A., & Norcini, J. J. (1992). An adaptation of item modeling for developing test-item banks. *Teaching and Learning in Medicine, 4*, 19–24.

Simon M. G. (1989). *Use of item shells to construct higher level test-items in reading comprehension*. Paper presented at the annual meeting of the American Educational Research Association, San Francisco.

Snow, R. E., & Lohman, D. F. (1989). Implications of cognitive psychology for educational measurement. In R. L. Linn (Ed.), *Educational measurement* (3rd ed., pp. 263–332). New York: American Council on Education and Macmillan.

Solano-Flores, G. (2001). On the development and evaluation of a shell for generating science performance assessments. *International Journal of Science Education, 21*(3), 293–315.

Sternberg, R. J. (1998). Abilities are forms of developing expertise. *Educational Researcher, 27*(3), 11–20.

Webb, N. (2006). Identifying content for student achievement tests. In S. M. Downing & T. M. Haladyna (Eds.), *Handbook of test development*, pp. 155–180. Mahwah, NJ: Lawrence Erlbaum Associates.

Wesman, A. G. (1971). Writing the test item. In R. L. Thorndike (Ed.) *Educational measurement* (2nd ed., pp. 99–111). Washington, DC: American Council on Education.

3

Using Weak and Strong Theory to Create Item Models for Automatic Item Generation

Some Practical Guidelines with Examples

Mark J. Gierl and Hollis Lai

Automatic item generation (AIG), in its most ambitious form, is the process of using item models to generate statistically calibrated items, with the aid of computer technology. The role of the content specialist is critical for the task of designing and developing meaningful item models. The role of computer technology is critical for the task of systematically combining large numbers of elements in each model to produce items. The role of statistical theory is critical for the task of linking item features to the psychometric characteristics of the generated items. By combining content expertise, computer technology, and statistical theory, content specialists can create item models that yield large numbers of statistically calibrated test items. The purpose of this volume, in fact, is to describe how recent advances in educational measurement theory and practice are contributing to each of these three critical AIG roles. The purpose of this chapter is to focus, more specifically, on the first role, which is the design and development of item models.

An item model (Bejar, 1996, 2002; Bejar, Lawless, Morley, Wagner, Bennett, & Revuelta, 2003; LaDuca, Staples, Templeton, & Holzman, 1986) has been described using different terms, including a schema (Singley & Bennett, 2002), blueprint (Embretson, 2002), template (Mislevy & Riconscente, 2006), form (Hively, Patterson, & Page, 1968), frame (Minsky, 1974), and shell (Haladyna & Shindoll, 1989). Even in this volume, the phrases item model and item template are often used synonymously to describe the variables in an assessment task that can be used for generation, which include the stem, the options, and the auxiliary information. The stem is the part of an item model which contains context, content, item, and/or the question the examinee is required to answer. The options include the alternative answers, with one correct option and one or more incorrect options or distracters. For multiple-choice item models, both stem and options are required. For open-ended or constructed-response item models, only the stem is created. Auxiliary information includes any additional content, in either the stem or the option, required to generate an item, including text, images, tables, diagrams, sound, and/or video.

The stem and options can be further divided into elements. Elements are often denoted either as strings, which are non-numeric values, or as integers, which are numeric values. By systematically manipulating the elements, large numbers of items can be generated from a single item model. If the generated items, sometimes called instances of the item model, are intended to measure content with comparable psychometric characteristics (e.g., similar difficulty levels), then the generated items are called isomorphs (Bejar, 2002). When the goal of item generation is to create isomorphic instances, only the incidental elements are manipulated. Incidental elements serve as surface features of the item model that may cause the generated instances to appear different from one another, but these surface features are not expected to alter an item's psychometric characteristics, such as the difficulty level. If the instances are intended to measure content with different psychometric characteristics, then the generated items are called variants. When the goal of item generation is to create variant instances, the incidental elements can be manipulated, but, more importantly, the radical elements must also be manipulated in the item model. Radical elements are the deep features of the item model that are expected to alter an item's psychometric characteristics (Irvine, 2002).

Content specialists have the critical role of designing and developing the item models and, after the items are generated, of reviewing the instances or samples of the instances. The principles, standards, and practices that guide traditional item development (cf. Case & Swanson, 2002; Downing & Haladyna, 2006; Schmeiser & Welch, 2006) still provide the foundational concepts necessary for developing item models. Some item model examples are available in the literature (e.g., Bejar et al., 2003; Case & Swanson, 2002; Gierl, Zhou, & Alves, 2008), which can guide practice. However, there are currently no published studies describing either the principles or practices required to develop item models. Hence, the purpose of this chapter is to describe and illustrate how item models can be created using a "weak" and "strong" theory approach to AIG (Drasgow, Luecht, & Bennett, 2006).

Item Model Development Using Weak Theory

Drasgow et al. (2006) advised content specialists to engage in the challenging task of item model development using a combination of design guidelines and principles discerned from experience, theory, and research. They proposed two approaches. The first is item model development from weak theory. With this approach, design guidelines are used to create item models that generate isomorphic instances. As a starting point, they suggest identifying a parent item. The parents can be found by reviewing items from previous test administrations, by drawing on an inventory of existing test items, or by creating the parent item directly. Regardless of the starting-point used, the parent item highlights the underlying structure of the model, thereby providing a point of reference for creating alternative items (the parent item can also be thought of as a rendering model; see Luecht, chapter 5 this volume). When the goal of using weak theory is to generate statistically calibrated items, then the content specialist's task is to manipulate those elements in the parent item that yield generated items with similar psychometric characteristics (i.e., item difficulty). Alternatively, when the goal of using weak theory is to generate items that are not statistically calibrated (in this case, the generated items will still need to be field tested), then the content specialist's task is to manipulate those elements that yield large numbers of instances of the parent item through the generative process. This second goal is seldom the purpose of weak-theory AIG, although it can be used to generate items needed to initially develop banks or to replenish the banks as items are retired.

One important drawback of using weak theory for item model development, particularly when the goal is to generate statistically calibrated items, is that relatively few elements can be manipulated in the model because their effect on the psychometric characteristics of the generated items is poorly anticipated. That is, content specialists who initially identify the elements in the item model must draw on any source of available information, which, typically, is their professional experience and expectations, to anticipate how these manipulations will alter the psychometric characteristics of the items. Unfortunately, these predictions are often inaccurate. Moreover, by restricting the element manipulations to a small number, the generated items may have the undesirable quality of appearing too similar to one another. In our experience, isomorphic items generated from weak theory are referred to pejoratively by many content- and test-development specialists as "clones". Clones are often perceived to be generated items that are easy to produce, unlike more traditional items; clones are believed to be easy to detect by coaching and test preparation companies, and therefore of limited use in operational testing programs; and clones are often seen as a simplistic product from an overly simple item-development process, compared to a more sophisticated traditional test item, which is a complex product from a more sophisticated item-development process. In short, content specialists are rarely impressed with item clones produced from weak theory, particularly when the underlying item model is thought to be discernible through the generated instances.

To begin to address the problem of generating discernible clones, Gierl et al. (2008) described a taxonomy of item model types. The purpose of this taxonomy was to provide content specialists with design guidelines for creating item models, and also to help the specialists to create models that yield more diverse generated items. Gierl et al.'s (2008) strategy in promoting item generation diversity was to systematically combine and manipulate those elements in the stem and options typically used for item-model development. Recall, the stem is the section of the model used to formulate context, content, and/or questions. The elements in the stem can function in four different ways. Independent indicates that the element(s) in the stem are unrelated to one another. Hence, a change in one stem element will not affect the other stem elements. Dependent indicates that all element(s) in the stem are related to one other. Mixed include both independent and dependent elements in the stem, where at least one pair of stem elements is related. Fixed represents a constant stem format with no variation or change.

The options contain the response alternatives for a multiple-choice item model. The elements in the options can function in three different ways. Randomly selected options refer to the manner in which the distracters are selected from their corresponding content pools. The distracters in this case are selected randomly. Constrained options mean that the keyed option and the distracters are generated according to specific constraints, such as formulas or calculation. Fixed options occur when both the keyed option and distracters are fixed and therefore do not change across the generated items in the model.

A matrix of item model types can then be produced by crossing the four stem and three option element variables. Gierl et al. (2008) claimed that the taxonomy is useful because it provides the guiding principles necessary for designing diverse item models by outlining their structure, function, similarities, and differences. It can be used to ensure that content specialists do not design item models where the same elements are manipulated or where the same item model structure is used, thereby yielding more diversity in the generative process. Finally, the taxonomy can be used to train content specialists on how to design and develop item models. Ten functional combinations were created from the 12 possible stem-by-options element combinations (the two combinations that were excluded where a fixed stem and constrained options, which produces an infeasible item model type, and a fixed stem and fixed options, which produces a traditional multiple-choice item). Gierl et al. (2008) also produced two examples for each of the 10 cells in the taxonomy, thereby creating 20 examples in total, to illustrate each unique combination. Their examples were drawn from diverse content areas in the achievement domain, including science, social studies, language arts, and mathematics.

To illustrate the logic and some of the concepts related to item-model development using weak theory, two examples are presented here. Each example was developed by two content specialists who were experienced classroom teachers and who also had extensive knowledge, skills, and practice in developing items for large-scale educational achievement tests. The item model in Figure 3.1 measures the concept of adaptation in Grade 9 science. It is represented as a dependent stem with randomly selected options and no auxiliary information. The stem contains three strings (S1, S2, and S3). These strings draw on content from three separate pools. These content pools could be seen as the universe of all permissible content in this model. For example, S1 is the animal-type content pool, meaning that all animals with adaptive strategies could be placed in this pool. In our example, the pool includes four animals with adaptive strategies: white-tailed jackrabbit, white-tailed ptarmigan, long-tailed weasel, and artic fox. Because other animals also have adaptive strategies, they could also be included in this pool to expand the generative capacity of this model. The decision about which animals to include in the pool serves as the statistical difficulty "driver" in this example, meaning that different animals could elicit different item difficulty estimates. Using weak-theory AIG, the goal is most often to select those animals that would yield items with a similar level of difficulty. S2 includes content on animal habitat. In our example, three habitats are presented: prairie, mountains, and tundra. Other habitats expected to yield generated items with a similar difficulty level could be included. S3 includes content on the animal's adaptive characteristics. Two characteristics are described in this model, fur and feathers. S1, S2, and S3 are dependent stem elements in this example, as the choice of animal affects the animal's habitat and adaptive characteristics. Also, it is assumed that some of the animals in S1 could live in more than one habitat in S2. The options are randomly selected from a fixed list of incorrect options: ecosystem, niche, species, community, and population. It is assumed that the incorrect options yield comparable and consistent examinee response processes and, hence, difficulty estimates across the generated items. IGOR (which stands for item generator) is a Java desktop software application developed by Gierl et al. (2008) to systematically combine the elements in a model to generate test items (see also Mortimer, Stroulia, & Yazdchi, this volume). IGOR was used with this item model to generated 480 instances. A sample of four from the 480 generated items is presented in Table 3.1.

Parent item :

> A white-tailed jackrabbit living on the prairie is a consumer, and has fur that changes color with the seasons.
>
> The above description is an example of an organism's _____.
>
> A. species
>
> B. niche
>
> C. ecosystem
>
> D. adaptation

Item model:

Stem	A S1 living on the S2 is a consumer, and has S3 that changes color with the seasons. The above description is an example of an organism's _____.
Elements	S1 Range: "white-tailed jackrabbit", "white-tailed ptarmigan", "long-tailed weasel", "arctic fox" S2 Range: "prairie", "mountains", "tundra" S3 Range: "fur", "feathers"
Options	Key: adaptation Distractors: ecosystem, niche, species, community, or population
Auxiliary information	None
Key	D

Figure 3.1 Science item model measuring the concept of adaptation

Table 3.1 A sample of four generated items produced from the grade 9 science item model in Figure 3.1

2. A white-tailed jackrabbit lives on the prairie and is a consumer, and has fur that changes color with the seasons. The above description is an example of an organism's _____.

   a. community
   b. adaptation
   c. ecosystem
   d. niche

169. A white-tailed ptarmigan lives on the tundra and is a consumer, and has feathers that change color with the seasons. The above description is an example of an organism's _____.

   a. adaptation
   b. population
   c. community
   d. niche

303. A long-tailed weasel lives on the prairie and is a consumer, and has fur that changes color with the seasons. The above description is an example of an organism's _____.

   a. adaptation
   b. ecosystem
   c. population
   d. niche

373. An arctic fox lives on the mountain and is a consumer, and has fur that changes color with the seasons. The above description is an example of an organism's _____.

   a. ecosystem
   b. niche
   c. population
   d. adaptation

The item model in Figure 3.2 measures the concept of rounding in Grade 3 mathematics. It is represented as a mixed stem with constrained options and auxiliary information. The stem contains two strings (S1, S2), two integers (I1, I2), and no auxiliary information. S1 could be described as the content pool that includes all containers for small objects. In our example, four containers are included in this model. To expand the generative capacity of this model, additional containers could be added. S2 is the content pool with small objects. In our example, six small objects are specified. The vocabulary used to describe the containers and the objects in the containers would be chosen to ensure that the generated items have a comparable difficulty level. The integers specify the number of containers (I1) and the number of small objects in the containers (I2). I1 includes three values, from 3 to 5 in increments of 1. I2 includes 10 values, from 101 to 299 in increments of 19. The magnitude of the integers would be selected so that the difficulty estimates of the generated items are similar to one another. The string elements are independent, whereas the integer elements are dependent, hence the stem is mixed. The options are selected from specific string and integer combinations and, hence, constrained in this example. When IGOR was used with this item model, 576 instances were generated. A sample of four from the 576 generated items is presented in Table 3.2.

Item Model Development Using Strong Theory

Another way to create item models is using the strong-theory approach. Drasgow et al. (2006) describe strong theory as the process where a cognitive model is used to specify and then manipulate those elements that affect the difficulty level of the generated items using a theoretical account of test performance. Cognitive theory helps to highlight both the examinees' knowledge and skills required to solve the item as well as the content features in the item that affect difficulty. Drasgow et

Parent Item:

> A teacher has 3 boxes that each contains 176 drinking straws. After combining the straws in all 3 boxes, the TOTAL number of straws is closest to
> A. 170 straws
> B. 180 straws
> C. 540 straws
> D. 600 straws

Item model:

Stem	A teacher has I1 S1 that each contains I2 S2. After combining the S2 in all I1 S1, the TOTAL number of S2 is closest to
Elements	I1 Value Range: 3 – 5 by 1 I2 Value Range: 101 – 299 by 19 S1 Range: "boxes", "trays", "bowls", "bags" S2 Range: "straws", "cubes", "blocks", "marbles", "chocolate", "rings"
Options	A. ROUND (I2) to nearest 10s * (I1-1) S2 B. ROUND (I2) to nearest 100s * (I1+0.5) S2 C. ROUND (I2) to nearest 10s *I1 S2 D. ROUND (I2) to nearest 10s * (I1+1) S2
Auxiliary Information	None
Key	C

Figure 3.2 Math item model measuring estimation and rounding

al. (2006) claim that, by modeling the interaction between the examinee and the content, it is possible to predict and therefore control the psychometric characteristics of the generated items. This approach, when successful, has the added benefit of yielding a strong inferential link between the examinees' test-item performance in a specific content area and the interpretation of the examinees' test score because the model features that elicit the item characteristics are predictive of test performance (Bejar, 1993; see also Bejar, this volume).

To date, the use of strong theory for AIG has focused on the psychology of specific response processes, such as spatial reasoning (Bejar, 1990) and abstract reasoning (Embretson, 2002), where articulate cognitive models of task performance exist (see also the chapters in Part III of this volume). Unfortunately, few comparable cognitive theories exist to guide our item-development practices (Leighton & Gierl, 2011) or to account for test performance in broad content areas typical of those found on most educational achievement tests (Ferrara & DeMauro, 2006; Schmeiser & Welch, 2006).

Table 3.2 A sample of four generated items produced from the grade 3 mathematics item model in Figure 3.2

5. A teacher has 3 boxes that each contain 177 straws.
    After combining the straws from all 3 boxes, the TOTAL number of straws is closest to

    a. 360 straws
    b. 540 straws
    c. 700 straws
    d. 720 straws

114. A teacher has 4 boxes that each contain 234 cubes.
      After combining the cubes from all 4 boxes, the TOTAL number of cubes is closest to

    a. 690 cubes
    b. 900 cubes
    c. 920 cubes
    d. 1150 cubes

225. A teacher has 3 trays that each contain 253 blocks.
      After combining the blocks from all 3 trays, the TOTAL number of blocks is closest to

    a. 500 blocks
    b. 750 blocks
    c. 1000 blocks
    d. 1050 blocks

305. A teacher has 4 boxes that each contain 215 marbles.
      After combining the marbles from all 4 boxes, the TOTAL number of marbles is closest to

    a. 660 marbles
    b. 880 marbles
    c. 900 marbles
    d. 1100 marbles

In an attempt to illustrate the use of a strong-theory approach to item-model development for AIG in a broad content area, we drawn on an example from medical-licensure testing in the content area of surgery. Admittedly, our example is incomplete, as it does not possess all of the characteristics of strong theory as we described it. For instance, our example is not based on cognitive theory. However, it does help to demonstrate how a design principle for generating items can yield both a cognitive model for describing task performance in surgery and an integration process that uses this model to produce new items.

Figures 3.1 and 3.2 highlight the item model structure commonly associated with weak-theory AIG. For strong-theory AIG, we propose a different representation. Figure 3.3 contains a cognitive model structure for AIG using the content for a medical-licensure testing example in surgery. This structure outlines the knowledge and skills required in medical problem solving to make diagnostic inferences. It is presented in three panels. The top panel identifies the problem and its associated scenarios. The middle panel specifies the relevant sources of information. The bottom panel highlights the salient features, which include both the elements and constraints, within the relevant sources of information specified in the middle panel.

To generate items using a strong-theory approach, we begin by identifying the problem area and the associated scenarios for this area. As shown in Figure 3.3, we are generating items that allow us to measure an examinee's ability to diagnose complications with gallstones. Five different scenarios are associated with this problem in our example: cholangitis, acute cholangitis, biliary cholic, pancreatitis, and gall bladder perforation.

Next, we specify the relevant sources of information for this problem. The relevant information sources were identified by two content specialists who were both experienced item writers and practicing physicians. The sources were patient presentation, physical examination results, and laboratory results. Additional sources of information could be identified to expand the generative capacity

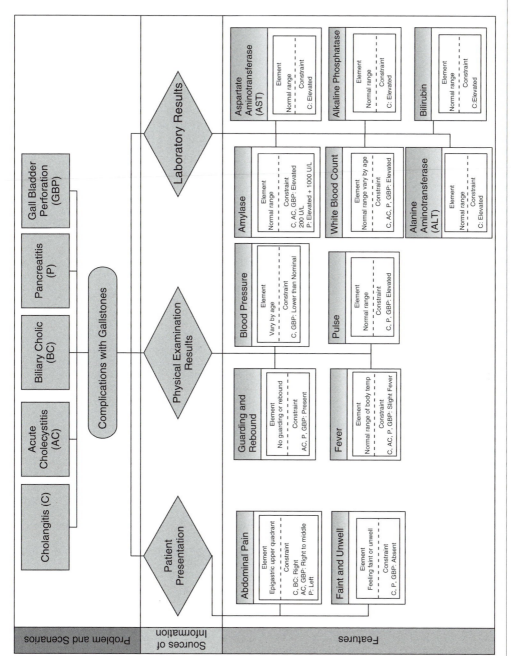

Figure 3.3 Cognitive model specifying the knowledge and problem-solving skills required to diagnose complications with gallstones

of this model. For example, a fourth information source that was identified, but not manipulated for this model, is the patient's physical characteristics (e.g., a 60-year-old woman). Different sources of information, framed by different educational and testing problems, could also be specified (e.g., focusing the evaluation in this example solely on the permissible range of different laboratory test results for diagnosing cholangitis).

Finally, we highlight the salient features within the relevant information. These features can be viewed as the universe of all permissible features relevant to the problem. In our example, the two content specialists claimed that Patient Presentation had two features: abdominal pain and feeling faint and unwell. Again, other types of presentation features could be included to expand the generative capacity of the model. Each feature, in turn, contains two nested components. The first nested component for a feature is the element. Elements contain content specific to each feature that can be manipulated for item generation. For the abdominal pain feature of the Patient Presentation information source in our example, epigastric upper quadrant is the element. This element has three values: right, right to middle, and left. The second nested component for a feature is the constraint. Each element is constrained by the scenarios specific to this problem. For instance, cholangitis and biliary cholic are associated with right epigastric upper quadrant pain (i.e., C, BC: Right, at the bottom left side in Figure 3.3), acute cholecystitis and gall gladder perforation are associated with right-to-middle epigastric upper quadrant pain, and pancreatitis is associated with left epigastric upper quadrant pain. For the faint and unwell feature of the Patient Presentation information source in our example, feeling faint or unwell is the element. This element has two values: present or absent. Each element is again constrained by the scenarios specific to this problem. Acute cholangitis and biliary cholic are associated with feeling faint and unwell, whereas cholangitis, pancreatitis, and gall gladder perforation are not. The remaining features, elements, and constraints for diagnosing complications with gallstones across the five scenarios for each information source are presented in Figure 3.3.

The content presented in the cognitive model structure in Figure 3.3 can be viewed in two ways. First, it serves as a pragmatic rendering model necessary for item generation with a software program like IGOR. The purpose of the rendering model is to link the problem (diagnosing complications with gallstones) and the associated scenarios (cholangitis, acute cholangitis, biliary cholic, pancreatitis, and gall bladder perforation) in the top panel to the features (abdominal pain, feeling faint and unwell, guarding and rebound, fever, blood pressure, pulse, amylase, white blood cells, aspartate amniotransferase, alanine aminotransferase, alkaline phosphatase, amylase level, bilirubin) in the bottom panel through the information sources (patient presentation, physical examination outcomes, laboratory test results) in the middle panel. This prescriptive link is used for item generation, as the features can be inserted in their appropriate information sources, as outlined in Figure 3.4, subject to the elements and their constraints. For the medical-licensure testing example in surgery, IGOR generated 240 items using the cognitive model structure in Figure 3.3. A sample of four from the 240 generated items is presented in Table 3.3.

Second, Figure 3.3 serves as an explicit cognitive model where the problem-solving knowledge and skills required to diagnose complications with gallstone are identified and, if desired, evaluated. Norman, Eva, Brooks, and Hamstra (2006), for instance, describe "problem representation" as an

---

A 60-year-old woman has been booked for a laparoscopic cholecystectomy for symptomatic gallstones. Prior to surgery, she <**Patient Presentation**>. She has had rigors. <**Physical Examination Results**>. <**Laboratory Results**>. Which of the following is the most likely diagnosis?

Figure 3.4 Item model used to measure examinees' ability to diagnose complications with gallstones

Table 3.3 A sample of four generated items produced from the surgery item model in Figure 3.3

23. A 60-year-old woman is scheduled for a cholecystectomy. Prior to her surgery, she presents to the Emergency Department with epigastric pain in the left upper quadrant. She also has a fever and has been faint and unwell. Upon physical examination revealed guarding and rebound, elevated temperature and pulse. Lab work revealed extremely high amylase and elevated WBC count.
Which one of the following is the most likely diagnosis?

    a. Pancreatitis
    b. Peritonitis
    c. Perforated gall bladder
    d. Bilia cholic

112. A 60-year-old woman has recently undergone surgery for treating symptomatic gallstones. After her surgery, she presents to the Emergency Department with epigastric pain in the right to middle upper quadrant. She also has a fever and has been feeling faint and unwell. Upon physical examination revealed guarding and rebound, drop in blood pressure and a rise in temperature and pulse. Lab work revealed slightly elevated amylase and elevated WBC count.
Which one of the following is the most likely diagnosis?

    a. Perforated gall bladder
    b. Peritonitis
    c. Duodenal ulcer
    d. Pancreatitis

189. A 60-year-old woman has been booked for a cholecystectomy. Prior to her surgery, she presents to the Emergency Department with epigastric pain in the right upper quadrant that is sharp in intensity, but comes and goes. She also has a fever and has been fainting and unwell. Upon physical examination revealed a higher than normal pulse, low blood pressure and a fever. Lab work revealed elevation in WBC, amylase, AST, ALT, ALP, and bilirubin.
Which one of the following is the most likely diagnosis?

    a. Cholangitis
    b. Peritonitis
    c. Perforated gall bladder
    d. Pancreatitis

203. A 60-year-old woman has been booked for surgery for treating symptomatic gallstones. Prior to her surgery, she presents to the Emergency Department with epigastric pain in the right to middle upper quadrant. She also has a fever. Upon physical examination revealed guarding and rebound and a fever. Lab work revealed blood pressure 72 over 52, white blood count to be 2.3×10^{10}/L, with AST in expected ranges, ALT normal, alkaline phosphatase normal and amylase in a normal range.
Which one of the following is the most likely diagnosis?

    a. Perforated gall bladder
    b. Peritonitis
    c. Cholecystitis
    d. Pancreatitis

important way to organize and study the content and processes required in expert medical reasoning. The cognitive model in Figure 3.3 can serve as a problem representation, as described by Norman et al. (2006), because it highlights the problem, the scenarios, the sources of information, and the cognitive features used to study the reasoning and thinking processes of medical examinees. The same cognitive model is used to identify and organize the information necessary for generating items. One important outcome of using a cognitive model structure for AIG, like the example presented in Figure 3.3, is that the quality of the model can also be evaluated. Bordage and Lemieux (1991), for example, created a list of qualifiers to evaluate diagnostic problem representations (see also Bordage, Connell, Chang, Gecht, & Sinacore, 1997; Nendaz & Bordage, 2002). They first coded the features, signs, and symptoms in the problem. Then, they organized the coded information for a particular problem representation to evaluate and characterize the level of expertise. The organization of the representation can vary. For instance, they described one level as "reduced", meaning that the representation has few features, with no linkages among the features. A higher level of organization was described as "elaborated", meaning that the representation had extensive features with clear linkages. Bordage et al. (1997) also demonstrated that an increase in level of organization in the representation was associated with diagnostic accuracy.

Unlike the weak-theory approach, where the determinants of item difficulty for the manipulated elements in the model must be discerned through the guidelines, judgments, and experiences of the content specialists, a strong-theory approach provides a cognitive model and some associated design principles for predicting the psychometric characteristics of the generated items. In our strong-theory example, the cognitive model structure in Figure 3.3 was created by two content experts. This representation guides the detailed rendering process needed for item generation, where different configurations of the information in the representations can be used to generate items. But the quality of the representations can also be evaluated. In our example, the features and information sources, along with their organization as specified by the elements and the constraints, form the cognitive model representation for diagnosing complications with gallstones across five different scenarios. The coding scheme developed by Bordage and his colleagues to predict diagnostic accuracy could also be applied to the cognitive model specified in our example to predict the difficulty (i.e., diagnostic accuracy) of the generated items. Item models with different representation qualities should yield generated items with different difficulty levels. In our example, strong theory is used, first, to produce a representation of the examinees' knowledge and skills and, second, to link the organization of these cognitive skills to the problem, information sources, and item features for the purpose of generating test items. Although we have not yet estimated the difficulty levels for the generated items, our description is intended to help illustrate how a strong-theory approach can be used to specify and manipulate content that could affect the difficulty of the generated items.

Comparing Weak- and Strong-Theory Approaches to AIG

The purpose of this chapter was to focus on the process of item-model development by describing and illustrating how content specialists can create the models necessary for item generation. The process of using statistical methods and models to, in turn, calibrate the items generated from the item models is described in Sinharay and Johnson (this volume). With weak theory, a combination of outcomes from research, theory, and experience provide the guidelines necessary for identifying and manipulating those elements in the model that yield generated items that are expected to have comparable levels of difficulty. The weak-theory approach to developing item models is well suited to broad content domains where few theoretical descriptions exist on the knowledge and skills required to solve test items (Drasgow et al., 2006). The main drawback of using weak theory is that item difficulty for the generated items is unpredictable and, therefore, relatively few elements in the model can be manipulated. And, with only a small number of element manipulations, the generated items may be overtly similar to one another. Gierl al. el. (2008) described a taxonomy of item-model types that yields more diverse model structures. We presented two examples of how weak-theory AIG could be used to create item models that, in turn, could generate items in Grade 9 Science and Grade 3 Mathematics.

If we cast the weak-theory approach (see Figures 3.1 and 3.2) into the cognitive model structure (see Figure 3.3), then some of the limitations of weak theory become apparent. The Grade 9 science adaptation example, presented initially in Figure 3.1, is recast as a cognitive model structure in Figure 3.5. Because little explicit information is available to guide item-model development with weak theory, content specialists must rely on loose guidelines and personal judgments to identify and manipulate those elements in the model that yield generated items expected to yield comparable levels of difficulty. The consequence of having little information for model development using weak theory is quickly apparent. For the adaptation example, there is only one general problem, the concept of adaptation, and no associated scenarios in the top panel. There are no explicit sources of information in the middle panel for this example. As judged by the structure of the parent item, the features

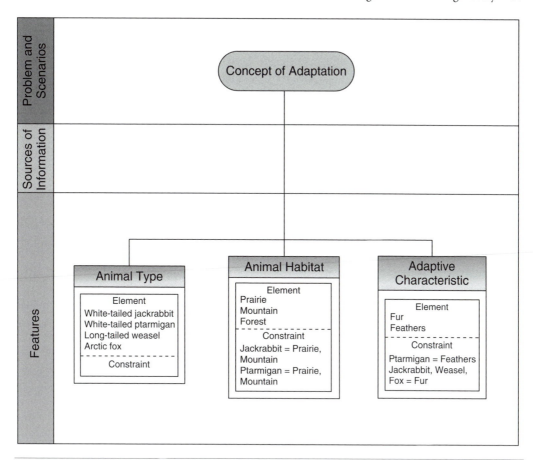

Figure 3.5 Adaptation example in Figure 3.1 cast as a cognitive model structure

provide the content for the bottom panel. As a rendering model, the Figure 3.5 example links the problem in the top panel to the features in the bottom panel. However, there are no specific sources of information in the middle panel. Hence, item generation is governed by inserting the features into the problem, as outlined in the parent item. The Figure 3.5 example can be used to identify content for item generation, but it fails to identify the knowledge and skills required to make inferences about what examinees' might understand or how they might solve the generated adaptation items.

With strong theory, a cognitive model of item difficulty serves as the principled basis for identifying and manipulating those elements that yield generated items with predictable psychometric characteristics. The methods used to structure and manipulate the elements are complex, relative to the weak-theory approach. We showed how a cognitive model structure could be created to link the test purpose to the elements required for item generation in the content area of surgery (see Figure 3.3). In our example, the cognitive model was created by first specifying the purpose, along with its applicable scenarios. Next, the sources of information needed to diagnose complications with gallstones across the five scenarios were identified. Finally, the features for each information source were articulated. Each feature, in turn, contains elements and constraints. The elements and constraints outline the content specific to each diagnostic scenario required for item generation. The benefit of using strong theory is that item difficulty for the generated items is expected to be more predictable and, as a result, the generated items may be calibrated without the need for extensive field or pilot testing because the factors that govern the item difficulty level can be specified and, therefore, explicitly modeled and controlled. Unfortunately, few cognitive theories currently exist to guide our item-development practices, thereby limiting the practical applications of strong theory. To begin to overcome this problem, we presented an example of a strong-theory approach as it applies to medical-licensure testing in surgery. Our example was incomplete because it was not based on a cognitive theory of item difficulty in surgery. However, it was guided by design principles, it did yield a cognitive model for describing task performance in surgery, and it provided a method to link the organization of the knowledge and skills in the cognitive model to the elements and constraints needed for item generation. The cognitive model in our example could also be used to study the features that affect the item-difficulty estimates.

Conclusions

Research on item models is warranted and now sorely needed. Item models provide the foundation required for operational AIG. Hence, the theory and practices that underlie item model development must be studied. Currently, there is little focused research on item model development. While we recommend that researchers and practitioners use the principles, standards, and practices that guide traditional item development as a starting-point for creating item models, this recommendation is inherently limited because models are not items. Hence, much more research is required on how to design, develop, and evaluate the methods, processes, and procedures used to create items models using both weak and strong theory. As a starting-point, we recommend working closely with content specialists in diverse content areas to begin to better understand how to design and develop item models, but also to carefully document the methods and procedures used to create these models. Research must also be conducted to evaluate the properties of these models by focusing on their generative capacity (i.e., the number of items that can be generated from a single item model), as well as their generative veracity (i.e., the usefulness of the generated items, particularly from the viewpoint of content specialists). These quantitative (i.e., generative capacity) and qualitative (i.e., generative veracity) characteristics are both essential to study and document as we begin to assess the strengths, the weaknesses, and, ultimately, the applicability of AIG in operational testing situations.

Acknowledgement

The authors would like to thank the Medical Council of Canada for their support with this research. However, the authors are solely responsible for the methods, procedures, and interpretations expressed in this study. Our views do not necessarily reflect those of the Medical Council of Canada.

References

Bejar, I. I. (1990). A generative analysis of a three-dimensional spatial task. *Applied Psychological Measurement, 14*, 237–245.

Bejar, I. I. (1993). A generative approach to psychological and educational measurement. In N. Frederikson, R. J. Mislevy, & I. I. Bejar (Eds.), *Test theory for a new generation of tests* (pp. 323–359). Mahwah, NJ: Erlbaum.

Bejar, I. I. (1996). *Generative response modeling: Leveraging the computer as a test delivery medium* (ETS Research Report 96-13). Princeton, NJ: Educational Testing Service.

Bejar, I. I. (2002). Generative testing: From conception to implementation. In S. H. Irvine & P. C. Kyllonen (Eds.), *Item generation for test development* (pp.199–217). Hillsdale, NJ: Erlbaum.

Bejar, I. I., Lawless, R., Morley, M. E., Wagner, M. E., Bennett, & R. E., Revuelta, J. (2003). A feasibility study of on-the-fly item generation in adaptive testing. *Journal of Technology, Learning, and Assessment, 2*(3). Available from http://www.jtla.org.

Bordage, G., Connell, K. J., Chang, R. W., Gecht, M. R., Sinacore, J. M. (1997). Assessing the semantic content of clinical case presentations: Studies of reliability and concurrent validity. *Academic Medicine, 72*,S37–S39.

Bordage, G., & Lemieux, M. (1991). Semantic structures and diagnostic thinking of experts and novices. *Academic Medicine, 66*,S70–S72.

Case, S. M., & Swanson, D. B (2002). *Constructing written test questions for the basic and clinical sciences* (3rd ed.). Philadelphia, PA: National Board of Medical Examiners.

Downing, S. M., & Haladyna, T. M. (2006). *Handbook of test development.* Mahwah, NJ: Erlbaum.

Drasgow, F., Luecht, R. M., & Bennett, R. (2006). Technology and testing. In R. L. Brennan (Ed.), *Educational measurement* (4th ed., pp. 471–516). Washington, DC: American Council on Education.

Embretson, S. E. (2002). Generating abstract reasoning items with cognitive theory. In S. H. Irvine & P. C. Kyllonen (Eds.), *Item generation for test development* (pp. 219–250). Mahwah, NJ: Erlbaum.

Ferrara, S. & DeMauro, G. E. (2006). Standardized assessment of individual achievement in K-12. In R. L. Brennan (Ed.), *Educational measurement* (4th ed., pp. 579–621). Westport, CT: National Council on Measurement in Education and American Council on Education.

Gierl, M. J., Zhou, J., & Alves, C. (2008). Developing a taxonomy of item model types to promote assessment engineering. *Journal of Technology, Learning, and Assessment, 7*(2). Retrieved from http://www.jtla.org.

Haladyna, T., & Shindoll, R. (1989). Items shells: A method for writing effective multiple-choice test items. *Evaluation and the Health Professions, 12,* 97–106.

Hively, W., Patterson, H. L., & Page, S. H. (1968). A "universe-defined" system of arithmetic achievement tests. *Journal of Educational Measurement, 5,* 275–290.

Irvine, S. H. (2002). The foundations of item generation in mass testing. In S. H. Irvine & P. C. Kyllonen (Eds.), *Item generation for test development* (pp. 3–34). Mahwah, NJ: Lawrence Erlbaum Associates.

LaDuca, A., Staples, W. I., Templeton, B., & Holzman, G. B. (1986). Item modeling procedures for constructing content-equivalent multiple-choice questions. *Medical Education, 20,* 53–56.

Leighton, J. P., & Gierl, M. J. (2011). *The learning sciences in educational assessment: The role of cognitive models.* Cambridge, UK: Cambridge University Press.

Minsky, M. (1974). A framework for representing knowledge. *MIT-AI Laboratory Memo 306.*

Mislevy, R. J., & Riconscente, M. M. (2006). Evidence-centered assessment design. In S. M. Downing & T. Haladyna (Eds.), *Handbook of test development* (pp. 61–90). Mahwah, NJ: Erlbaum.

Nendaz, M. R., & Bordage, G. (2002). Promoting diagnostic problem representation. *Medical Education, 36,* 760–766.

Norman, G., Eva, K., Brooks, L., & Hamstra, S. (2006). Expertise in medicine and surgery. In K. A. Ericsson, N. Charness, P. J. Feltovich, & R. R. Hoffman (Eds.), *The Cambridge handbook of expertise and expert performance* (pp. 339–353). Cambridge, UK: Cambridge University Press

Schmeiser, C. B., & Welch, C. J. (2006). Test development. In R. L. Brennan (Ed.), *Educational measurement* (4th ed., pp. 307–353). Westport, CT: National Council on Measurement in Education and American Council on Education.

Singley, M. K., & Bennett, R. E. (2002). Item generation and beyond: Applications of schema theory to mathematics assessment. In S. H. Irvine & P. C. Kyllonen (Eds.), *Item generation for test development* (pp. 361–384). Mahwah, NJ: Erlbaum.

4
Item Generation
Implications for a Validity Argument

Isaac I. Bejar

One sense of "item generation" that immediately comes to mind is the capability of producing a large number of operational items by algorithmic or automated means, ready to be administered, or at least pretested. The perceived advantage in that case is efficiency, especially if the items contain graphic elements that are rendered in an automated fashion in the generation process. Such graphic elements are common in mathematics and are typically handled manually by specialized staff, which adds greatly to the cost of producing such items.

The efficiencies made possible by item generation are not insignificant, and are relevant to the arguments presented below concerning construct preservation. However, item generation as defined here *entails an accounting of the variability in item difficulty, not just the efficient production of the items.* Such an accounting of the psychometric attributes of items can be used in supporting the assumption of construct representation of test scores, which is one of the assumptions that needs to be critically evaluated in appraising an interpretive validity argument (Kane, 2006, p. 46). Similarly, the ability to create test content in this fashion is relevant in order to avert some threats to validity, thereby preserving validity.

Figure 4.1 presents a vision of item generation in a K-12 context inspired, on the one hand, by research on how students learn (Pellegrino, Chudowsky, & Glaser, 2001), and, on the other hand, by evidence-centered assessment design (Mislevy, Steinberg, & Almond, 2003), whereby the assessment starts with a detailed analysis of the construct and research surrounding the construct, and the purpose of the assessment. The construct and purpose of the assessment inform all design decisions. Figure 4.1 suggests that research on student learning, together with content standards, such as the Common Core State Standards (CCSS) under Race to the Top (Department of Education, 2010, April 9), are input to the assessment design process.

Other important sources of information are the practical and theoretical bases for item writing as well as relevant policy specifications regarding the levels of excellence targeted by the assessment. Under Race to the Top, those categorizations correspond to educational mileposts that indicate whether students are on track to completing their secondary education successfully. For example, the Partnership for Assessment of Readiness for College and Careers (PARCC) (2010, June 23, p. 63) consortium has indicated that the Partnership will set four performance level classifications that signal student performance against the CCSS and benchmarks for college and career readiness.

To classify students accurately into each of those levels, and to obtain accurate aggregate estimates, the design of the test will need to take those classifications into account, rather than define the levels *after* the assessment has been completed (see Cizek & Bunch, 2007, p. 222). This means specifying more precisely the difficulty of the items that will be optimal for discriminating among students at different policy-relevant levels of proficiency (Bejar, 2010). That is, those policy-relevant levels of proficiency, although typically obtained by standard-setting methods *after* the test has been developed, should, instead, be seen as specifications for the test (Bejar, Braun, & Tannenbaum; Huff & Plake, 2010). Those specifications include the psychometric attributes of the items once the design of the test has been sufficiently settled and the items can be scaled by a suitable Item Response Theory (IRT) model.

As suggested by Figure 4.1, with theoretical, content, and policy-relevant considerations in hand, obtained as a preamble to test content production, the next step is to produce item and task models. Item and task models are, respectively, the specifications for producing multiple-choice items (e.g., Bejar, et al., 2003) and constructed-response items (e.g, Mislevy, Steinberg, & Almond, 2002). When the item and task models are sufficiently detailed, item-generation methods can be used to expedite and make more efficient the process of producing test content aligned with the decisions to be made based on the scores. A model-based approach to producing items has practical as well as theoretical advantages, as compared to what has been historically an item-centric approach of producing test content. (See also Hendrickson, Huff, & Luecht, 2010 for a discussion of the process in the context of the redesign of the Advanced Placement examination, as well as Huff, Alves, Pellegrino, & Kaliski, this volume). Item and task models, as I am using the term, formalize the specifications for test content into templates, a set of variables and constraints on those variables, such that it becomes possible to produce instances of such models, that is, actual items that have predetermined psychometric attributes.[1]

The development of item and task models requires empirical work, not unlike pre-testing, until it is possible to produce instances that behave psychometrically according to expectations. Not incidentally, much can be learned from that process. For example, when the difficulty of instances of item or task model departs from expectation, regardless of whether it is due to limitations in our theoretical or practical knowledge, an opportunity is created to refine theoretical and practical item-writing knowledge (Graf, Peterson, Steffen, & Lawless, 2005).

With item and task models available, the production of items is a matter of *instantiating* the models to produce actual items to be delivered. Figure 4.1 makes a distinction between several test-delivery scenarios. Specifically, the item and task models can be used to instantiate actual items to be administered at a subsequent time, or they can be instantiated during the administration of a test. Figure 4.1 distinguishes three cases. In one case, the models are used to generate the items offline. A second possibility is to instantiate items on the fly, *during* the testing process, as illustrated by Bejar et al. (2003). The third possibility is that, in addition to generating multiple-choice items on the fly, constructed-response items that can be scored objectively are generated on the fly, together with the required scoring key, as previously discussed by Mislevy, Winters, Bejar, Bennett, & Haertel (2010) and Bejar and Graf (2010), and further illustrated by Fife (2011, April) and Graf and Fife (this volume). An example for mathematics items is provided later in the chapter.

Item and task models can be designed to produce isomorphic instances, that is, items having the same psychometric attributes. Item and task models also can be conceived to produce variants that systematically vary psychometric attributes, such as difficulty. The latter requires a far more detailed understanding of the response process (Bejar, 2009). In either case, the generated items have associated *expected* psychometric attributes that are homogeneous, in the first case, and vary predictably in their psychometric parameters, in the second case. While specific instances may not have been pretested, a successfully calibrated item or task model can produce items that are precalibrated, and, thus, require little or no pretesting prior to operational use.

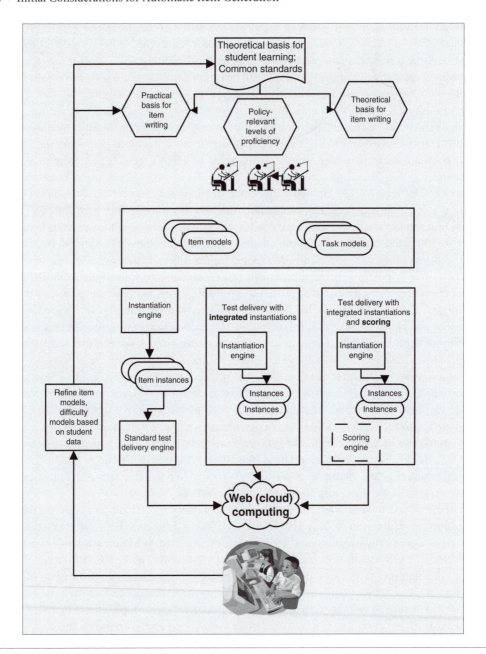

Figure 4.1 Conception of item generation including automated scoring of constructed responses and a feedback loop

The psychometric modeling of item and task models can take the form of a hierarchical item response model (e.g., Embretson & Yang, 2007; Glas, Linden, & Geerlings, 2010; Johnson, Sinharay, & Bradlow, 2007; Sinharay, Johnson, & Williamson, 2003). Embretson (2011) provides a review of such models. Essentially, such hierarchical item-response models describe the mean and variance of the instances' item parameters. As implied by Figure 4.1, once the test is administered, the expectations about the behavior of item-model instances can be evaluated to verify that they are homogeneous or vary predictably in difficulty. When that is not the case, typically the item and task models need to be revised (Graf, et al., 2005) rather than discarded. Given this conception of item generation, what are the implications for validity? To answer that question, I first discuss the concept of *construct representation* (Embretson, 1983) and introduce a new term, *construct preservation.*

Construct Representation

One implication of item generation for validity is enhancing construct representation. The formulation of construct validity by Cronbach and Meehl (1955) emphasized the relationship among scores, and did not dwell on the principles for constructing a test. Loevinger (1957) noted the point at the time, but it was not until much later, after the so-called cognitive revolution, that construct validity was expanded to include not just the relationship among scores but also the theoretical basis for the content of the test, i.e., construct representation (Embretson, 1983). That is, the relationships among scores, compelling as they might be in suggesting the meaning of scores, still leave open the possibility that those relationships could be due to sources other than the construct we postulate, until we know more about what is behind the scores, so to speak. Bringing information to the validation table about the construction of the test greatly enhances what we can say about the scores by augmenting the information about the relationship among scores with a deeper understanding of the psychological *processes* behind the scores. This is distinct from the idea of content validity that was popular for part of the 20th century, but lost momentum. A recent attempt was made to revive content validity (Lissitz & Samuelsen, 2007). However, this attempt was not well received, in part because the concept is unnecessary in light of the idea of construct representation (Mislevy, 2007), a point that had been previously made (Messick, 1989).

The revival of cognitive psychology led to a rapprochement between cognitive psychology and psychometrics (Carroll, 1974; Pellegrino, Baxter, & Glaser, 1999; Whitely, 1976), including expansions of item-response models that could accommodate hypotheses about the response process. The first such expansion was extending the Rasch model to decompose the difficulty parameter, the Linear Logistic Test Model (Fischer, 1973). Subsequently, construct representation served to formalize the integration of cognitive theory and psychometric modeling: "In construct representation studies, item properties, such as item difficulty and response time, are mathematically modeled from the stimulus features that represent cognitive processes" (Embretson, 2004). Importantly, such modeling makes it feasible to impute the item parameter estimates of instances of items and task models that have not been explicitly administered yet. That is, the model is calibrated by a suitable psychometric model based on a few instances and the resulting calibration is assumed to apply to other instances.[2] Item generation as conceived here takes advantage of that possibility.

In short, item generation and construct representation go hand in hand, as will be illustrated below, following the discussion on construct preservation.

Construct Preservation

A second implication of item generation for validity that I'd like to discuss is "construct preservation." The term is useful because in today's testing environment multiple threats to score validity are present, especially under computer-based testing, where testing can take place in multiple localities over a period of days. When tests were given at a few well-controlled administrations it could be assumed that occasion and location did not introduce significant threats to validity, except perhaps in the case of irregularities.

A long-standing threat is the possibility that some test takers have obtained pre-knowledge about the content of the test. This was amply demonstrated with the introduction of adaptive testing. It quickly became apparent that it was important to control the exposure of items in order to maintain the validity of scores (Sympson & Hetter, 1985) and minimize the overlap of items across students (Davey & Nering, 2002).

The assessments that will be produced as part of Race to the Top (Department of Education, 2010) may experience similar threats. The plan is for a common assessment to be used by a large number of states. It is unlikely that all states can test on the same date, and yet the content of the test must remain confidential in order to be fair to all and to ensure that the comparisons among jurisdictions are valid. If the same form were to be used, then knowledge about its content could be disseminated to jurisdictions that tested later in the cycle, unless comparable forms were used in different jurisdictions. (For an in-depth discussion of the many implications of comparability under Race to the Top, see Marion and Perie, 2011). Item generation can facilitate the creation of multiple comparable forms and help to preserve the construct being measured.

In short, through item generation it is possible to strengthen construct representation. Similarly, I argued that item generation can help to preserve validity in high-stakes environments by, for example, enabling the creation of multiple comparable forms more efficiently.

Implications for Validity and Some Examples

To examine in more detail the implications of item generation for validity, we adopt the perspective advocated by Kane (2006), namely, of viewing validation as argumentation. The approach does not represent a new "type" of validity but, rather, an approach to organizing the evidence to support score interpretation by means of a Toulmin (1958) argument. That is, validation is making (and maintaining) a case for score interpretation by stating the assumptions being made to justify the score interpretation, an interpretive validity argument, and, importantly, providing evidence to support those assumptions in order to arrive at a validity argument. Counter-arguments to the suggested score interpretation can be raised, of course, and need to be addressed and rebutted in order to uphold the desired score interpretation.

Figure 4.2 illustrates an interpretive validity argument. Observed performance (datum) on a test is linked to an interpretation or inference (claim) by means of a set of warrants or assumptions. That linkage is potentially attenuated, to the extent that caveats are needed if counter-arguments are not adequately rebutted, in which case qualifiers to the score interpretation are needed in the formulation of the validity argument.

To see the implications of item generation for validity, I have associated specific warrants to construct representation and construct preservation. Specifically, the scoring and theory-based interpretation warrants proposed by Kane (2006) are strongly relevant in connection with the assumption of construct representation. For construct preservation, the warrant concerned with score comparability, generalization, together with security of test content and the maintenance of scoring standards are strongly linked to construct preservation.[3] In short, item generation has implications for the assumptions in an interpretive validity argument. In addition, the approach to item generation discussed above involves a recurrent evaluation, a reappraisal of construct representation, by examining the items produced from item and task models. I elaborate further below.

Construct Representation

According to Figure 4.2, construct representation is supported by evidence for theory-based score interpretation and the appropriateness of the scoring process. I discuss them in that order.

Kane (2006) distinguishes between interpretive arguments for traits and theoretical constructs. The latter is appropriate in the present context, given the view of item generation as driven by research

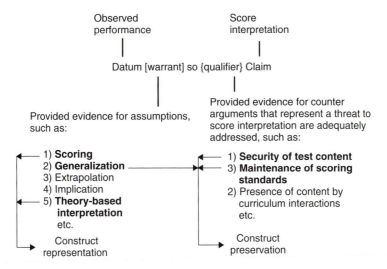

Figure 4.2 Interpretive validity argument

on student learning. That is, we view a test as what Kane calls "indicators of theoretical constructs" (p. 43). Kane adds: "A theory provides guidance on how to develop indicators for its constructs" (p. 44). When a test is developed based on theory, "we assume that the theory provides a sound explanation for the relevant phenomena and that indicators provide appropriate estimates of the constructs in the theory" (p. 44). The warrant for such an assumption is the theory (p. 44).

Merely referring to a theory is not sufficient to establish construct representation. We can choose a theory and claim that we have developed a test based on that theory, and further assert that the scores from such a test have specific theoretical attributes as a result. However, it is also necessary to demonstrate that the theoretically expected results are actually observed. Kane (p. 44) notes:

> Any prediction about observable attributes that can be made from the theory provides a potential empirical check on the theory. These empirical checks include predictions about performance or behavior in various contexts or by various groups, correlational evidence, and the results of experimental studies. To the extent that the predictions are verified, the plausibility of the theory is enhanced, and therefore, the plausibility of the theory-based interpretation is enhanced.

Item generation as conceived here entails predictions about observable psychometric attributes *of items*. The attributes of items, in the form of parameter estimates from a suitable psychometric model, are, to the extent that they are well-predicted, corroborating evidence in favor of the theory on which item construction is based. Of course, that evidence also enhances "the plausibility of the theory-based interpretation." That is, there is a symbiotic relationship between theory and test development based on item generation, as implied by the box on the left of Figure 4.1, and as has been noted previously by Bejar (1993, p. 351), when items in a test have been generated according to theory "the administration of a test becomes a psychological experiment, which in turn may lead to the improvement of both theories and tests."

For example, certain features of an item could be hypothesized to contribute to its difficulty according to a relevant theory for that domain. As part of the item-generation process, those features can be manipulated systematically following the theory, or held constant with the expectation that difficulty will be well predicted or held constant, respectively. These two cases have been described as item generation based on strong and weak theory, respectively, a distinction introduced by Drasgow, Luecht, & Bennett (2006). In either case, a natural symbiosis develops between the implementation of a test and the relevant theories used in designing the test.

Construct Representation: An Example

What is the evidence that items can be generated in such a way that they have well-predicted psychometric parameter estimates? Reviews of the literature are available covering several domains (Bejar, 1993; Bejar, 2009). However, in what follows I illustrate the symbiosis between testing and theory alluded to in Figure 4.1.

An item type used formerly in the Graduate Record Examination (GRE), the analytical reasoning (AR) item sets, was subjected to an extensive series of studies at the University of Plymouth (Newstead, Bradon, Handley, Dennis, & Evans, 2006; Newstead, Bradon, Evans, & Dennis, 2002). The structure of the item sets is the same. A *scenario* is always an array consisting of at most seven elements (which can be radio segments, floors on a building, tracks on a CD, etc.) and the order in which they are to appear. The *stimulus* section introduces restrictions or additional information, in this case as to adjacency restrictions between elements of the array. Finally, the *stem* for an item is presented by stating, in this case, a specific adjacency condition and asking the order in which different segments might be played, given the preceding restrictions. Several items are generated from a given scenario, and stems are classified into (a) possible orders, (b) necessity, (c) possibility, and (d) impossibility items. Figure 4.3 shows a sample item.

The University of Plymouth's approach took advantage of its extensive background in the psychology of reasoning (Evans, 1989; Newstead, Pollard, Evans, & Allen, 1992), and the fact that, in addition to developing a model of difficulty, the goal was to generate items as well. One hypothesized source of difficulty was content or encoding effects, which means that the text needs to be processed in order to get to the logical structure, and necessarily would need to be part of any accounting of difficulty, regardless of the theoretical stance. The second hypothesized source of difficulty was complexity of rules, which would be theoretically aligned with rule-based approaches to reasoning (Braine, 1978; Rips & Conrad, 1983). The third source of difficulty was hypothesized to be a representational difficulty factor. The representational emphasis seemed natural, given that think-aloud protocols examined early in the project (Newstead et al., 2002) looked like mental models. Moreover, the explicit goal of generating items, not just understanding difficulty, also encouraged an approach that was highly representational.

The project was successful in that Newstead et al. (2002) were able to generate items algorithmically and predict the difficulty of those items. Equally relevant is the symbiotic relationship between testing and psychological theory, which in this case serves to evaluate two competing accounts of reasoning. Referring to the competing models of reasoning, Newstead et al. concluded that "mental model theorists will take comfort from the finding that semantic informativeness of a rule correlated negatively with difficulty … and from a finding that model variability score figured in our difficulty models" (Newstead, et al., 2006, p. 88). That is, the fact that difficulty could be predicted from an a priori analysis consistent with mental model theory was seen as supportive of mental model theory. However, they concluded that the GRE items were so rich that it was unlikely that a single theoretical accounting of difficulty was feasible.

The symbiosis between theory and test development was further illustrated by Rijmen and De Boeck (2001), who examined the difficulty of syllogistic reasoning items. They contrasted the two theoretical perspectives to deductive reasoning that played a role in the analysis of analytic reasoning: rule theories (e.g., Braine, 1978; Rips & Conrad, 1983) and mental model theory (Johnson-Laird, 1983). Rijmen and De Boeck (2001) pointed out that while different rules appear to require different

---

Scenario

An office building has exactly six floors, numbered 1 through 6 from bottom to top. Each of exactly six companies, F, G, I, J,K, and M, must be assigned an entire floor for office space. The floors must be assigned according to the following conditions:

Stimulus

F must be on a lower floor than G. I must be either on the floor immediately above M's floor or on the floor immediately below M's floor. J can be neither on the floor immediately above M's floor nor on the floor immediately below M's floor. K must be on floor 4.

Stem

If G is on floor 5, which of the following must be true?

Options

(A) F is on floor 1

(B) F is on floor 3

(C) I is on floor 1

(D) J is on floor 6

(E) M is on floor 2

Figure 4.3 Sample necessity item (see also Dennis, Handley, Bradon, Evans, & Newstead, 2002; Newstead, et al., 2002)

degrees of effort, and therefore contribute differentially to difficulty, rule theory itself does not provide the means for estimating a priori an item's difficulty. From a validity perspective this is not ideal because it still leaves unanswered the question as to why different rules are more difficult (Revuelta & Ponsoda, 1999, p. 247). By contrast, as noted by Rijmen and De Boeck (2001), mental model theory is more amenable to a priori predictions, due to how the reasoning process is framed, namely requiring that premises and situations be represented. That representation makes it possible to enumerate possible mental models. The assumed mental enumeration of mental models on the part of the test takers could serve as the basis for theoretical predictions of difficulty a priori, as demonstrated by Newstead et al (2006).

Many other examples illustrating the symbiotic relationship between item generation and construction representation are available (Bejar, 2009). Work on non-cognitive skills, which may be increasingly important in the context of 21st-century skills, such as personality tests (Mumford, Costanza, Connelly, & Johnson, 1996), situational judgment tests (Lievens & Sackett, 2007), or science tests (Solano-Flores, Jovanovic, & Bachman, 1999), call for a somewhat different set of considerations for item generation, but the basic principles discussed earlier seem to be equally applicable.

Construct Representation: An Example Involving Constructed Responses

A second example illustrating the implication of item generation for construct representation is concerned with the scoring in constructed-response item formats. The scoring assumption in an interpretive validity argument refers to the assumption that the scoring process is effective in recasting observed performance into predefined categories or score levels (Kane, 2006, p. 34). In the case of multiple-choice items those categories are typically "right" and "wrong" and the process is, by now, sufficiently well understood that it is not viewed as a source of validity threats, except under unusual circumstances, such as the malfunctioning of the equipment that is used in the scoring of answer sheets.[4] By contrast, the scoring of constructed responses does raise the possibility of inaccuracies purely from the scoring process, especially when scored by human raters (Bejar, Williamson, & Mislevy, 2006), and also in the case of automated scoring (Bejar, 2011).

Given the potential erosion of construct representation during the scoring of constructed responses, an important implication of item generation for validity is enabling the incorporation of constructed response formats into a test economically and without delaying score reporting. This means expanding item generation to include automated scoring of constructed responses. Such an expansion is important to the extent that the construct calls for such responses. Although the use of constructed responses has become common in educational surveys, such as the National Assessment of Educational Progress (NAEP), it remains less so in state testing at the moment. In fact, states that experimented with incorporating constructed responses (for example, Vermont, Nebraska, Maryland), have reverted to more conventional forms of assessment, for pragmatic reasons. Nevertheless, increased use of constructed response formats is likely for Race to the Top assessments. For example, the PARCC application (Partnership for Assessment of Readiness for College and Careers, 2010, June 23) noted that:

> both end-of-year and through-course, will include challenging *performance tasks and innovative, computer-enhanced items* that elicit complex demonstrations of learning and measure the full range of knowledge and skills necessary to succeed in college and 21st century careers. The inclusion of performance tasks will ensure that the assessments measure skills that are difficult to measure in on-demand assessments, and they will help model effective classroom instruction.

The possibility of economically incorporating constructed responses into a test by means of item generation, together with automated scoring of those responses, could make it possible to incorporate constructed response items more readily.

Figure 4.4 describes the item-generation process of constructed response items at a conceptual level. The process requires a set of variables and constraints that are sufficient to create instances, i.e., items, from an item model or a task model that are part of a shell or template. Among those variables are the theoretically driven variables that control difficulty, but also other aspects, such as the language in which the item is rendered, which is a variable under item generation (Higgins, Futagi,

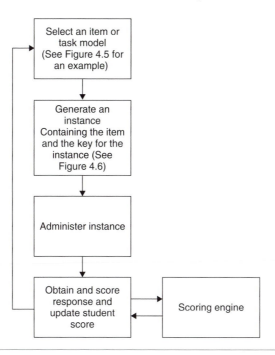

Figure 4.4 Item and scoring key generation

& Deane, 2005). In addition, as suggested by Figure 4.4, in the case of items requiring constructed responses, the scoring key must also be generated along with the items.

Figure 4.5 shows a simple mathematics task model based on a released NAEP Grade 8 item. Figure 4.6 shows two instances generated by the model. The key corresponding to the task model is given by

$$N_3 = \frac{(Total - N_1 J_1 - N_2 J_2)}{J_3}$$

Thus, any instance, generated by the model in Figure 4.5 is scorable by substituting the values of *Total*, N_1, J_1, N_2, J_2, and J_3 for that instance to obtain N_3. In this example, the scoring is fairly objective and the benefit of item generation to validity resides in making it feasible to incorporate constructed response formats economically and to score on the fly. An obvious advantage of on-the-fly automated scoring is that constructed response formats can be included as part of an adaptive test (Bejar & Graf, 2010).

In short, item generation, as conceived here, entails a feedback loop between theory and test development. Theory guides the conception of test content in sufficient detail that predictions about how items will behave are possible. When the test is administered, those predictions can be tested and amendments made to the theory, the test, or both, thereby constantly refreshing the evidence for construct representation. Similarly, by facilitating the creation and scoring of constructed response formats, item generation also has implications for construct representation when the construct calls for such formats.

Construct Preservation

Whereas construct representation is concerned with building-in the basis for score interpretation, construct preservation is concerned with maintaining and preserving the score interpretation. Figure

Description of model	Model template	Variables and constraints
A person has some number of objects to be distributed among three sets of friends. Friends within a given set receive the same number of objects. The number of friends in each set is unique, as are the number of objects to be distributed to each friend in each set.	*Name* had *Total Adjective Objects.* [He, She] gave the *Objects* to [his, her] friends. *N1* of [his, her] friends received *J1 Object(s)* each. *N2* of [his, her] friends received *J2 Object(s)* each. The rest received *J3 Objects* each. How many of [his, her] friends received exactly *J3Objects* from *Name*? Explain how you found your answer.	Name is a string variable which may assume a first name as a value. Objects is a string variable which may assume one of a list of objects as a value. Adjective is a string variable linked to Objects which may assume a value that corresponds to the Object value. N1 is an integer s.t. $2 \leq N1 \leq 8$ N2 is an integer s.t. $2 \leq N2 \leq 8$ N3 is an integer s.t. $2 \leq N3 \leq 8$ J1 is an integer s.t. $1 \leq J1 \leq 5$ J2 is an integer s.t. $1 \leq J2 \leq 5$ J3 is an integer s.t. $2 \leq J3 \leq 5$ Total = N1*J1 + N2*J2 + N3*J3 N1, N2, and N3 are unique J1, J2, and J3 are unique

Note. This example illustrates how to develop an item model using a released NAEP mathematics item as a source item. For the purposes of illustration, the model has been simplified. A technical specification requires additional variables and constraints. For example, in its current form, this model includes trivial variations that are identical except that the third and fourth sentences in the stem are reversed. Additional variables and constraints are also needed to ensure subject/verb agreement and the correct use of pronouns.

Figure 4.5 Sample task model (Authored by Aurora Graf)

4.2 suggests that two types of evidence would be important for that purpose: maintaining the security of the test content and maintaining scoring standards.

Specifically, score generalization could suffer when the same test is administered at different times in multiple jurisdictions,[5] since there is the potential for introducing an "occasion effect" that would reduce the generalizability of scores (e.g., Cronbach, Linn, Brennan, & Haertel, 1995). A potential solution to this problem is to have available multiple forms that are psychometrically equivalent but have no actual items in common. It is not easy to implement such a solution following the conventional practice of constructing forms and equating them retrospectively. An alternative is to rely on *form models* as proposed by Bejar and Graf (2010).

A form model is essentially a blueprint populated by item and task models. Instantiating the form model produces a test ready to be administered that is, in principle, comparable to any other form

---

1. Cynthia had 51 rare stamps. She gave the stamps to her friends. Three of her friends received 5 stamps each. Six of her friends received 2 stamps each. The rest received 3 stamps each. How many of her friends received exactly 3 stamps from Cynthia?

   Explain how you found your answer.

   Key: 8

---

2. Bruce had 43 commemorative coins. He gave the coins to his friends. Six of his friends received 5 coins each. Four of his friends received 1 coin each. The rest received 3 coins each. How many of his friends received exactly 3 coins from Bruce?

   Explain how you found your answer.

   Key: 3

Figure 4.6 Sample instances produced by task model in Figure 4.5. Clearly, in this case, the instances have a strong family resemblance. This can be avoided by having additional item models that introduce additional surface variability in the items produced

and yet sufficiently different that the possibility of pre-knowledge is reduced. Whether comparable forms are, in fact, produced by a form model needs to be evaluated, of course. However, to the extent that sufficiently comparable forms are generated to use as is, or to the extent that retrospective equating is more successful as a result of a more deliberate effort to produce comparable forms, item generation is an instrument for construct preservation.

At least two illustrations of construct preservation involving task modeling are available. The licensing test for architects (Kenney, 1997) was designed with construct preservation in mind. The test was designed in a such a way that different versions of the same design problem could be generated from a template (Bejar, 2002). Each candidate received a different set of instances from the set of task models comprising the different design problems a beginning architect is expected to have mastered. The design was adopted because it was anticipated that test takers would reveal the content of the test they took upon completing the examination.[6] Importantly, the automated scoring of responses to the multiple versions of a prompt or design problem was successfully implemented.

Another example is provided by the GR® revised General Test (rGRE). The assessment of writing in high-stakes contexts is vulnerable to threats to validity that erode the meaning of scores, such as lengthening their response in a construct-irrelevant manner, or wordiness (Powers, 2005). In the case of the GRE writing test, students have been known to engage in formulaic language that potentially could earn them a higher score. To minimize that possibility, multiple versions of prompts are created that require the student to address somewhat different points, depending on the version they are assigned. Research suggests that the different versions of a prompt function equivalently (Bridgeman, Trapani, & Bivens-Tatum, 2009).

Conclusions

Perhaps, the main appeal of item generation is, reasonably, the increases in efficiency that it affords. In this paper, an argument is presented that an additional advantage of item generation is its potential in enhancing a validity argument through better support for the assumption of construct representation, and by promoting construct preservation.

Specifically, I have argued that item generation can enhance construct representation directly by detailing the specifications for items and task models that take into account content specifications, and by relying on theoretical knowledge about student learning. Those detailed specifications, in turn, translate into expectation about the psychometric attributes of the items generated from item and task models. Upon administration of the test, those expectations can be evaluated. To the extent that the expectations are verified, evidence for construct representation is enhanced. When expectations are not fulfilled adequately, there is an incentive to revisit theoretical knowledge and revise items and task models, a feedback loop that is bound to enhance construct representation and theoretical knowledge. Construct representation is also potentially enhanced by the use of constructed response formats and automated scoring. The approach to item generation presented here makes it possible to incorporate, more readily, tasks that require constructed responses. Finally, the increase in efficiency that is possible with item generation makes it possible to prevent threats to validity, due, for example, to test security.

Acknowledgments

I want to express my appreciation to Michael Kane and David Williamson, who read an early version of this paper and provided me with useful suggestions. I also want to acknowledge the contributions of Paul De Boeck and Mary Pommerich, who offered valuable comments as discussants in the National Council of Measurement in Education (New Orleans, 2011), where this paper was first presented. Finally, I want to thank Jay Breyer and Jim Carlson for commenting on the more recent version of the chapter. Needless to say, any remaining errors are mine alone.

Notes

1 Although the process can be implemented manually, clearly it is more efficient to do so by means of software designed for the purpose. For mathematics, several software platforms are available for authoring item models (Gierl, Zhou, & Alves, 2008; Singley & Bennett, 2002). More general platforms are also available (Conejo, et al., 2004) that can deliver tests based on item models.

2 In a sense, this is no different than assuming that the calibration of a single item holds in future administrations where the same item appears. That is, we typically assume that position and context effects are negligible (T. Davey, personal communication, December 8, 2011). Under item generation, we further assume that the variability among the instances that remains after successfully developing and calibrating an item or task model is also negligible, an assumption that needs to be verified and monitored.

3 The generalization assumption has much broader implications not discussed here (see Kane, 2006, p. 35). Moreover, evidence for other assumptions that are less directly related to item generation is not explicitly discussed. For example, the credential of subject-matter experts involved in the design of the test is clearly relevant.

4 Perhaps the best illustration is the relatively recent scoring mishap in connection with the scoring of SAT answers sheets (Booz, May 26, 2006). Scoring of multiple-choice tests through scanning of answer sheets is a form of "automated scoring" based on the scanning. According to the report, a contributing factor to the scoring inaccuracies was the presence of high humidity where the answer sheets had been stored, which apparently affected the accuracy of the scanning process.

5 Of course, the administration of the same test when conditions are not controlled for, a possibility that has been explored in connection with Race to the Top (Marion & Perie, 2011, April), can create incomparable test scores even when the same test has been used.
6 Based on information on the website of the organization that administers the examination, the same process continues to this day. In this case, item generation is not automated. Instead, test developers create instances manually guided by a template.

References

Bejar, I. I. (1993). A generative approach to psychological and educational measurement. In N. Frederiksen, R. J. Mislevy & I. I. Bejar (Eds.), *Test theory for a new generation of tests* (pp. 323–359). Hillsdale, NJ: Erlbaum.

Bejar, I. I. (2002). Generative testing: From conception to implementation. In S. H. Irvine & P. C. Kyllonen (Eds.), *Item generation for test development* (pp. 199–218). Mahwah, New Jersey: Earlbaum.

Bejar, I. I. (2009). Recent developments and prospects in item generation. In S. E. Embretson (Ed.), *Measuring psychological constructs: Advances in model-based approaches* (pp. 201–226). Washington, DC: American Psychological Association Books.

Bejar, I. I. (2010). Application of evidence-centered assessment design to the advanced placement redesign: A graphic restatement. *Applied Measurement in Education, 23*, 378–391.

Bejar, I. I. (2011). A validity-based approach to quality control and assurance of automated scoring. *Assessment in Education, 18*(3), 319–341.

Bejar, I. I., Braun, H., & Tannenbaum, R. (2007). A prospective, predictive and progressive approach to standard setting. In R. W. Lissitz (Ed.), *Assessing and modeling cognitive development in school: Intellectual growth and standard setting* (pp. 31–63). Maple Grove: MN: JAM Press.

Bejar, I. I., & Graf, E. A. (2010). Updating the duplex design for test-based accountability in the twenty-first century. *Measurement: Interdisciplinary Research & Perspective, 8*(2), 110–129.

Bejar, I. I., Lawless, R. R., Morley, M. E., Wagner, M. E., Bennett, R. E., & Revuelta, J. (2003). A feasibility study of on-the-fly item generation in adaptive testing. *Journal of Technology, Learning, and Assessment, 2*(3). Available from http://www.jtla.org.

Bejar, I. I., Williamson, D. M., & Mislevy, R. J. (2006). Human scoring. In D. M. Williamson, R. J. Mislevy & I. I. Bejar (Eds.), *Automated scoring of complex tasks in computer-based testing* (pp. 49–82). Mahwah, NJ: Lawrence Erlbaum.

Booz, Allen & Hamilton, Inc. (May 26, 2006). SAT process review: Answer sheet processing. Available from http://www.collegeboard.com/prod_downloads/satscoreprocessing/SAT_Process_Review_Final_Report.ppt.

Braine, M. D. S. (1978). On the relation between the natural logic of reasoning and standard logic. *Psychological Review, 85*, 1–21.

Bridgeman, B., Trapani, C., & Bivens-Tatum, J. (2009). *Comparability of essay question variants*. Princeton, NJ: ETS.

Carroll, J. B. (1974). *Psychometric tests as cognitive tasks: A new "structure of intellect." Technical Report No. 4* (No. RB-74–16). Princeton, NJ: Educational Testing Service.

Cizek, G. J., & Bunch, M. B. (2007). *Standard setting: A guide to establishing and evaluating performance standards on tests*. Thousand Oaks, CA: Sage Publications.

Conejo, R., Guzmán, E., Millán, E., Trella, M., Pérez-De-La-Cruz, J. L., & Ríos, A. (2004). SIETTE: A web-based tool for adaptive testing. *International Journal of Artificial Intelligence in Education, 14*, 29–61.

Cronbach, L. J., Linn, R. L., Brennan, R. L., & Haertel, E. (1995). Generalizability analysis for educational assessments. *Educational and Psychological Measurement, 57*(3), 373–399.

Cronbach, L. J., & Meehl, P. E. (1955). Construct validity in psychological tests. *Psychological Bulletin, 52*, 281–302.

Davey, T., & Nering, M. (2002). Controlling item exposure and maintaining item security. In C. N. Mills, M. T. Potenza, J. J. Fremer & W. C. Ward (Eds.), *Computer-based testing: Building the foundation for future assessments*. Mahwah, NJ: Lawrence Erlbaum.

Dennis, I., Handley, S., Bradon, P., Evans, J., & Newstead, S. E. (2002). Approaches to modeling item-generative tests. In S. H. Irvine & P. C. Kyllonen (Eds.), *Item generation for test development* (pp. 53–71). Mahwah, NJ: Lawrence Erlbaum Associates.

Department of Education (2010, April 9). Overview information; Race to the Top Fund Assessment Program; Notice inviting applications for new awards for fiscal year (FY) 2010. *Federal Register, 75*(68), 18171–18185.

Dragsow, F., Luecht, R., & Bennett, R. E. (2006). Technology and testing. In R. L. Brennan (Ed.), *Educational measurement* (4th ed., pp. 471–515). Westport, CT: Praeger Publishers.

Embretson, S. E. (1983). Construct validity: Construct representation versus nomothetic span. *Psychological Bulletin, 93*, 179–197.

Embretson, S. E. (2004). The second century of ability testing: Some predictions and speculations. *Measurement: Interdisciplinary Research and Perspectives, 2*(1), 1–32.

Embretson, S. E. (2011, April). *Item generation and psychometrics: Overview of appropriate models*. Paper presented at the National Council of Measurement in Education, New Orleans.

Embretson, S. E., & Yang, Y. (2007). Automatic item generation and cognitive psychology. In C. R. Rao & S. Sinharay (Eds.), *Handbook of statistics: Psychometrics (Vol. 26)* (pp. 747–768). New York: Elsevier.

Evans, J. S. B. T. (1989). *Bias in human reasoning: Causes and consequences*. Hillsdale, NJ: Erlbaum.

Fife, J. (2011, April). *Integrating item generation and automated scoring*. Paper presented at the National Council of Measurement in Education, New Orleans.

Fischer, G. H. (1973). The linear logistic model as an instrument of educational research. *Acta Psychologica, 37*, 359–374.

Gierl, M. J., Zhou, J., & Alves, C. (2008). Developing a taxonomy of item model types to promote assessment engineering. *Journal of Technology, Learning, and Assessment, 7*(2), Retrieved from http://www.jtla.org.

Glas, C. A. W., Linden, W. J. v. d., & Geerlings, H. (2010). Estimation of the parameters in an item-cloning model for adaptive testing. In W. J. v. d. Linden & C. A. W. Glas (Eds.), *Elements of adaptive testing* (pp. 289–314). New York, NY: Springer.

Graf, E. A., Peterson, S., Steffen, M., & Lawless, R. (2005). *Psychometric and cognitive analysis as a basis for the revision of quantitative item models* (No. RR-05-25). Princeton, NJ: Educational Testing Service.

Hendrickson, A., Huff, K., & Luecht, R. (2010). Claims, evidence, and achievement-level descriptors as a foundation for item design and test specifications. *Applied Measurement in Education, 23*(4), 358–377.

Higgins, D., Futagi, Y., & Deane, P. (2005). *Multilingual generalization of the Model Creator software for math item generation* (Research Report No. RR-05-02). Princeton, NJ: Educational Testing Service.

Huff, K., & Plake, B. S. (2010). Innovations in setting performance standards for K-12 test-based accountability. *Measurement: Interdisciplinary Research & Perspective, 8*(2), 130–144.

Johnson-Laird, P. (1983). *Mental models.* Cambridge, MA: Harvard University Press.

Johnson, M. S., Sinharay, S., & Bradlow, E. T. (2007). Hierarchical item response models. In C. R. Rao & S. Sinharay (Eds.), *Handbook of statistics: Psychometrics (Vol. 26)* (pp. 587–606). New York, NY: Elsevier.

Kane, M. T. (2006). Validation. In R. L. Brennan (Ed.), *Educational measurement* (4th ed., pp. 17–64). Westport, CT: Praeger Publishers.

Kenney, J. F. (1997). New testing methodologies for the Architect Registration Examination. *CLEAR Exam Review, 8*(2), 23–28.

Lievens, F., & Sackett, P. R. (2007). Situational judgment tests in high stakes settings: Issues and strategies with generating alternate forms. *Journal of Applied Psychology, 92*(4), 1043–1055.

Lissitz, R., & Samuelsen, K. (2007). A suggested change in terminology and emphasis regarding validity and education. *Educational Researcher, 36*(8), 437–448.

Loevinger, J. (1957). Objective tests as instruments of psychological theory. *Psychological Reports, 3*, 653–694.

Marion, S., & Perie, M. (2011, April). *Some thoughts about comparability issues with "common" and uncommon assessments.* Paper presented at the National Council of Measurement in Education, New Orleans.

Messick, S. (1989). Validity. In R. L. Linn (Ed.), *Educational measurement* (3rd ed., pp. 13–103). New York, NY: American Council on Education.

Mislevy, R. J. (2007). Validity by design. *Educational Researcher, 36*(8), 463–469.

Mislevy, R. J., Steinberg, L. S., & Almond, R. G. (2002). On the roles of task model variables in assessment design. In S. H. Irvine & P. C. Kyllonen (Eds.), *Item generation for test development* (pp. 97–128). Mahwah, NJ: Lawrence Erlbaum Associates

Mislevy, R. J., Steinberg, L. S., & Almond, R. G. (2003). On the structure of educational assessments. *Measurement: Interdisciplinary Research and Perspectives, 1*(1), 3–62.

Mislevy, R. J., Winters, F. I., Bejar, I. I., Bennett, R. E., & Haertel, G. D. (2010). Technology supports for assessment design. In G. McGaw, E. Baker & P. Peterson (Eds.), *International Encyclopedia of Education* (3rd ed., Vol. 8, pp. 56–65). Oxford: Elsevier.

Mumford, M. D., Costanza, D. P., Connelly, M. S., & Johnson, J. F. (1996). Item generation procedures and background data scales: Implications for construct and criterion-related validity. *Personnel Psychology, 49*(2), 361–398.

Newstead, S. E., Bradon, P., S., H., Evans, J., & Dennis, I. (2002). Using the psychology of reasoning to predict the difficulty of analytical reasoning problems. In S. H. Irvine & P. C. Kyllonen (Eds.), *Item generation for test development* (pp. 35–51). Mahwah, NJ: Lawrence Erlbaum Associates.

Newstead, S. E., Bradon, P., Handley, S. J., Dennis, I., & Evans, J. S. B. T. (2006). Predicting the difficulty of complex logical reasoning problems. *Thinking & Reasoning, 12*(1), 62–90.

Newstead, S. E., Pollard, P., Evans, J. S. B. T., & Allen, J. L. (1992). The source of belief bias effects in syllogistic reasoning. *Cognition, 45*(3), 257–284.

Partnership for Assessment of Readiness for College and Careers (2010, June 23). *The Partnership for Assessment of Readiness for College and Careers (PARCC) application for the Race to the Top Comprehensive Assessment Systems competition.* Retrieved from http://www.fldoe.org/parcc/pdf/apprtcasc.pdf.

Pellegrino, J. W., Baxter, G. P., & Glaser, R. (1999). Addressing the "Two Disciplines" problem: Linking theories of cognition and learning with assessment and instructional practice. *Review of Research in Education, 24*, 307–353.

Pellegrino, J. W., Chudowsky, N., & Glaser, R. (2001). *Knowing what students know: The science and design of educational assessment.* Washington, DC: National Academy Press.

Powers, D. (2005). *"Wordiness": A selective review of its influence, and suggestions for investigating its relevance in tests requiring extended written responses* (RM-04-08). Princeton, NJ: Educational Testing Service.

Revuelta, J., & Ponsoda, V. (1999). Generación automática de ítems. In J. Olea, V. Ponsoda & G. Prieto (Eds.), *Test informatizados: Fundamentos y aplicaciones* (pp. 227–250). Madrid, Spain: Piramide.

Rijmen, F., & De Boeck, P. (2001). Propositional reasoning: The differential contribution of "rules" to the difficulty of complex reasoning problems. *Memory & Cognition, 29*(1), 165–175.

Rips, L. J., & Conrad, F. G. (1983). Individual differences in deduction. *Cognition and Brain Theory, 6*, 259–289.

Singley, M. K., & Bennett, R. E. (2002). Item generation and beyond: Applications of schema theory to mathematics assessment. In S. Irvine & P. Kyllonen (Eds.), *Item generation for test development* (pp. 361–384). Mahwah, NJ: Lawrence Erlbaum Associates, Inc.

Sinharay, S., Johnson, M. S., & Williamson, D. M. (2003). Calibrating item families and summarizing the results using family expected response functions. *Journal of Educational Behavioral Statistics, 28*(4), 295–313.

Solano-Flores, G., Jovanovic, R. J., & Bachman, M. (1999). On the development and evaluation of a shell for generating science performance assessments. *International Journal of Science Education, 29*(3), 293–315.

Sympson, J. B., & Hetter, R. D. (1985). *Controlling item exposure rates in computerized adaptive testing.* Paper presented at the Proceedings of the 27th Annual Meeting of the Military Testing Association, San Diego, CA.

Toulmin, S. E. (1958). *The uses of argument.* New York, NY: Cambridge University Press.

Whitely, S. E. (1976). Solving verbal analogies: Some cognitive components of intelligence test items. *Journal of Educational Psychology, 68*, 234–242.

II
Connecting Theory and Practice in Automatic Item Generation

5
An Introduction to Assessment Engineering for Automatic Item Generation

Richard M. Luecht

Introduction

Assessment engineering (AE) is a new way to approach the entire process of designing and developing tests, items and score scales (Luecht, 2006a, 2006b, 2007a, 2008, 2009, 2010, 2011). It is not a specific technology, nor is it a psychometric model. Rather, AE is a comprehensive framework for re-conceptualizing and then designing and implementing in a principled way an end-to-end system for efficiently and consistently building an enormous number of items and tests supporting one or more validly score scales.

AE shares many features and some terminology with other approaches to principled assessment design, including evidence-centered design (ECD; Mislevy, 2006; Mislevy, Steinberg, and Almond, 2003; Mislevy & Riconscente, 2006) and automatic item generation (AIG; Irvine and Kyllonen, 2002; Bejar & Yocom, 1991; Bejar, Lawless, Morley, Wagner, Bennett, & Revuelta, 2003; Embretson & Yang, 2006; Drasgow, Luecht & Bennett, 2006). For example, AE makes reference to *evidence models* and *claims* like ECD, and uses *item templates* in a manner that is consistent with AIG implementations of item models, families or shells. The AE framework relies on strong manufacturing-engineering design principles that facilitate efficient implementation and quality-control aspects of the entire assessment system with several operational goals: (1) to design and consistently measure the same intended construct(s) over time and conditions of measurement—for formative or summative purposes; (2) to fully or partially automate tedious, costly or time-consuming, human-dominant procedures; (3) to provide low-cost, scalable and efficient methods of producing large numbers of items that may not have to be individually pretested, calibrated and then discarded after operational use (or re-purposed); and (4) to relax some of the pressure on data-hungry psychometric calibration and scaling models to do the "heavy-lifting" in establishing and maintaining one or more score scales that measure the intended construct(s).

The need for principled assessment design is essential if we ever hope to implement useful formative and cognitive diagnostic assessments (see also chapter 1). Formative and cognitive diagnostic tests need to provide scores on multiple, instructionally sensitive scales that are capable of measuring targeted learning. The current discussion in many educational circles seems to support this requirement, arguing that formative and diagnostic assessments in the classroom should positively affect learning and teaching (e.g., Shepard 2000; Pellegrino, Baxter, & Glaser, 1999; Pellegrino,

Chudowsky & Glaser, 2001; Stiggins, 1997; Wilson & Sloane, 2000). There is also a need for tests that provide more informative score information and actionable, instructionally relevant insights about students' knowledge and skill strengths and weaknesses that can be integrated on a regular basis as part of the ongoing learning process. Summative tests—including tests that tangentially report domain-based subscores or strand scores—are typically not useful for diagnosing learning strengths or weakness, or helping teachers to make tangible instructional decisions (Leighton & Gierl, 2007; Gierl & Leighton, 2010; Luecht, Gierl, Tan & Huff, 2006). Educators need a different type of test capable of producing formatively useful *profiles* of student performance on a regular basis—ideally on demand. *That means designing tests to be multidimensional, not unidimensional.* This is the fundamental challenge that AE attempts to address: providing teachers and educators with trustworthy and useful multidimensional tests and associated scores to support formative assessments. Of course, AE can also benefit most other measurement applications, too. However, the greatest potential for AE may be realized for formative and diagnostic assessment—an area where traditional test development and psychometric practices have been recommended (e.g., Stiggins, 1997) but have demonstrated little tangible success. Luecht (2011) referred to the need for "*assessment design and development version 2.0*" to meet these types of challenges. AE is about changing the nature of the assessment data through intentional design.

An Overview of Assessment Engineering (AE)

AE employs manufacturing-engineering and strong quality-control principles and processes to direct the design, development and assembly as well as the analysis, scoring and reporting of examinations and assessment results. There are four core processes typically employed in AE: (1) construct mapping and evidence modeling; (2) building task models and task model maps; (3) designing templates and item writing; and (4) calibrating the assessment tasks and quality control. This chapter describes each of these processes and relates them to AIG.

Designing Construct Maps and Evidence Models

Successful and useful construct map design is an *iterative* process that articulates the ordered, proficiency-related claims that we wish to make at different levels of one or more construct-based scales.[1] Wilson (2005) calls this process *construct mapping*.

A construct map is an ordered (continuous or discrete) description of knowledge and skill-performance claims along an intended score scale. Developing a construct map involves carefully and thoughtfully laying out an ordered set of proficiency claims. The claims articulate what we would like to say about the knowledge and skill exhibited by an examinee scoring at any point along the implied score scale. Creating a construct map links the ultimate goal of devising a scale with meaningful, performance-based interpretations to every subsequent step in the assessment design and development process (Bejar, Braun, & Tannenbaum, 2007). The desired statistical properties of the scale, such as the location and amount of score precision needed, may not be fully understood at the earliest, conceptual phase of designing the construct map. But, from the very beginning of the design process, we should at least be able to visualize and/or concretely articulate how the knowledge and skills-proficiency claims are to be ordered and understand the basic cognitive complexity of tasks that would be required to support those claims. It is also important to recognize that the construct-mapping design process is iterative; any of the proficiency claims along the construct map can be modified, eliminated, re-aligned or augmented as needed to provide a thorough and well-articulated description of what it means to exhibit low, moderately low, moderate, moderately high or high proficiency on each construct.

The construct map can also be augmented with evidence models that describe the expected performance, including exemplars of work products or other concrete performance-based evidence that subject-matter experts would expect to see as justification that a particular student has exhibited the cognitive skills and knowledge implicitly or explicitly required by each proficiency claim (Mislevy et al., 2003; Mislevy & Riconscente, 2006). Figure 5.1 provides a conceptual construct map. The proficiency claims are described along the left side of the map and are aligned with the evidence models at the right. In practice, each construct map and associated evidence models would be far more detailed, but this example illustrates the general concept.

What is important from an AE perspective is to keep the goal up front—the intended scale(s) and valid interpretations of that/those scale(s). The proficiency claims along each construct should be incremental and consistent in detailing how proficiency is expected to change along the scale. Higher-order claims should explicitly build on proficiency claims at a lower level of the construct. In this manner, prerequisite knowledge and skills can be easily incorporated into the construct specification. If multiple constructs are included in the assessment specification, then it is essential to also specify how those constructs are expected to interact (i.e., establish expected covariance patterns among the constructs). Luecht, Gierl, Tan, and Huff (2006) provide some specific guidance in that regard.

The implication of construct mapping for AIG is clear. Creating templates and items without a clear sense of the construct(s) is potentially wasteful in terms of the cost and investment in resources to develop and validate those templates that, ultimately, may not provide very useful information. Visualizing the interpretation of a scale from the outset helps to keep the eventual test development on track and headed in the proper direction.

Task Modeling and Task Model Maps

A *task model* is a cognitively oriented specification for a class or family of items that integrates declarative knowledge components, relationships among those components, and cognitive skills, as well as relevant content, contexts and auxiliary features that affect the cognitive complexity of the task. The phrase *declarative knowledge* refers to more-or-less static representations of knowledge in memory. A system of declarative knowledge evolves from having many declarative knowledge components and

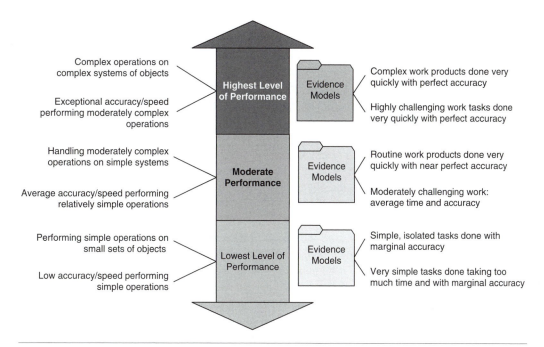

Figure 5.1 A generic construct map and associated evidence models

properties of those components related to one another in possibly complex ways. Dealing with a system of declarative knowledge should logically be more cognitively challenging than mentally working with an isolated fact or unitary declarative knowledge component. Cognitive skills—sometimes called *procedural knowledge*—are applied to the declarative knowledge components and relations, along with or in combination. A task model therefore specifies the declarative knowledge components, relevant properties of those components, relationships among the components, and cognitive skills required to successfully complete a family of similar task challenges.

Ideally, each task model specification *locates* that task relative to other task models, where more complex tasks are located higher on the scale and requiring greater proficiency to solve or otherwise appropriately respond to the item. This notion of locating a content-based task model on a scale may seem a bit foreign to test developers who are more accustomed to working with test specifications and to psychometricians who are used to "p-values" or calibrating the items to estimate their statistical difficulty. Here, we are talking about locating each task model by creating a detailed design specification that relates its cognitive complexity to the proficiency claims and associated evidence models, and that also helps to maintain the statistical difficulty and other psychometric characteristics (e.g., item discrimination, asymptotic noise, or patterns of residual covariance) for an entire family of items associated with it.

The phrase "task modeling" has been used in a number of ways (e.g., Mislevy et al., 2003; Mislevy, 2006; Mislevy & Riconscente, 2006; Luecht, 2006a, 2006b, 2007a, 2008, 2009; Luecht, Burke,& Devore, 2009; Luecht, Dallas,& Steed, 2010). Under the AE connotation, task models define a somewhat unique combination of cognitive skills applied to declarative knowledge objects required to support proficiency claims *within a specific region of the construct-based measurement scale*. Simply put, task models have a relative ordering in terms of complexity and difficulty with respect to other task models. Each task model forms the basis for creating multiple assessment task templates and eventually populating an item pool with large numbers of items that operate in a predictable manner—the item family. That is, each task model can be represented by multiple templates, and each template can generate multiple items. This provides enormous efficiencies to treat the task model as a family of templates and each template as a family of items. The relationships between task models, templates and items also lend themselves nicely to a hierarchical item response theory (IRT) calibration system and related, powerful quality-control mechanisms (e.g., Glas & van der Linden, 2003; Geerlings van der Linden, & Glas, 2010; Geerlings, Glas, & van der Linden, 2011; Glas, van der Linden, & Geerlings, 2010; Shu, Burke, & Luecht, 2010; see also Sinharay & Johnson, this volume).

Task modeling provides an alternative way to replace more traditional test specifications with a system of fairly elaborate cognitive specifications that detail every assessment task in a way that also takes into account depth of knowledge, required cognitive skills, and subject-specific content and contexts to describe a family of items that present similar challenges to the examinee and that statistically behave in an equivalent manner. The relative locations of the AE task models are later empirically validated—as are the associated templates and items discussed later in this chapter—using an appropriate, hierarchical psychometric calibration model. Ultimately, new items developed for well-behaved task-model families may not need to be pilot tested or otherwise exposed for very long. This creates the potential for tens, hundreds or even thousands of items to be produced for each task model—potentially realizing the goal of providing teachers with an enormous supply of items that measure progress immediately or when they need that information for formative instructional planning.

So what exactly is an AE task model? A task model can be represented graphically or using a task-model grammar (TMG) (Luecht, 2006a, 2006b, 2007, 2008; Luecht, Burke,& Devore, 2009; Luecht et al., 2010). The TMG statements replace the usual content coding familiar to test developers with a formal description of: (a) the combinations of defined declarative knowledge and skills needed to solve the task; (b) the information density and complexity of the task components (e.g., one simple component vs. a system of components with complex relations); (c) auxiliary information or tools that facilitate or complicate the task; and (d) other relevant attributes associated with each component and/or set of relations that might affect item difficulty (i.e., specific values and properties of the knowledge objects, relations or cognitive skills). For example, a very simple task model with one cognitive skill and only one knowledge object might be generically represented as $f(x1)$. A slightly more complex task model involving the same skill would be $f(x1, x2)$, where x1 and x2 denote two distinct knowledge objects to be manipulated. Finally, $f(g[x1, x2], x3)$ could represent an even more complex (difficult) set of tasks where x1, x2 and x3 are knowledge-objects, $f()$ is [again] the required skill, and $g[\cdot]$ represents a set of relations between x1 and x2). We would therefore hypothesize a difficulty ordering of these task models as: $f(x1) < f(x1, x2) < f(g[x1, x2], x3)$.

It is essential to *always* keep in mind that each task model has an intended location on the proficiency scale. Operationally, that location is maintained via the template and quality controls that apply to the family of items produced from each task model. The location provides an interpretation of the expected response to the intended level of challenge offered by the task model. The analogy of a hurdling competition in track and field can help to illustrate this notion of intentionally altering a challenge. Asking a person to walk around a track with no hurdles is certainly easier than asking the same person to run around the track with no hurdles. Running and jumping low hurdles is easier than running and jumping higher hurdles, or running a longer distance and still having to jump the low hurdles. Adding many [high] hurdles closer together is more difficult than spacing fewer [high] hurdles further apart. In the same way, we increment complexity by explicitly changing the challenge(s) via the task model specification.

A general form of a TMG statement for AE task models is:

$$action_2 \left[action_1 \left(is.related \left(object_1, object_2 \right), object_3 | context, aux.\ tools \right) \right] \tag{5.1}$$

This type of predicate calculus expression has been successfully used in cognitive text processing research to denote semantic complexity (Kintsch, 1988). The "actions" can differ in *ordered* complexity (e.g., *identify* is a lower complexity action than *analyze*) or functionally nested such as $action_1$ $(action_2((... action_m)))$ to denote complexity. "Objects" can likewise differ in complexity by assigning more or less relevant properties to them. Those properties are defined external to the predicate clause. "Objects" can also differ in number, where including more objects implies greater cognitive load and, correspondingly, greater complexity. "Objects" can also be made more complex by incorporating "relations" that vary in type (unidirectional, bidirectional, hierarchical) and can take on additional properties that might affect the complexity of the "relations". Finally, the "context" and "auxiliary tools" are included in the predicate clause and both have properties and controls that can alter the complexity of the task in predictable ways. An important advantage of this predicate calculus representation of task complexity is that it also lends itself nicely to modern, object-oriented database designs. The importance of connecting the complexity representation of cognitive skills and knowledge to specific, manipulable, data-based features should be apparent from the perspective of our goal to locate each task model (and its associated family of templates and items) on a particular proficiency scale.

The cognitive skills can be conveniently specified using *action verbs*. It is important to keep in mind that each action verb also needs to maintain its [ordinal] location relative to other action verbs. Therefore, it is important to construct a *list* of plausible action verbs, define each verb, and select those verbs that are as unambiguously meaningful as possible. For example, *understands* is not a very useful action verb, since it implies a rather obtuse set of cognitive operations that result in some equally poorly defined mental representation of a concept. We might instead prefer the use of more outcome-focused action verbs such as *analyze* and *compute*, provided that we explicitly define the types of skills associated with each verb. The definitions are essential for every verb, in order to ensure that each verb always represents the same primitive or constellation of skills across tasks associated with a particular construct.

Luecht et al. (2010) developed a series of task models for a multidimensional, high-school algebra and reading comprehension test by organizing the action verbs into *low, medium, high* categories of apparent cognitive skills. They defined action verbs in one of two ways: (1) as primitives and (2) as skill constructions. Primitives are verbs that have no need for an explicit reduced form. That is, inclusive verbs, by definition, have a fixed interpretation of location on the construct (e.g., identify or recognize are lower-level skills/actions than evaluate). Once defined, a primitive verb always maintains its relative ordering with respect to other action verbs, at least as used in describing the task models associated with a particular construct.[2] Actions representing multiple skill constructions must combine lower-level primitive clauses to form higher-order clauses. For example, *calculate*[*identify.method*[*data*]] defines a multistep computational procedure leading to a particular result. To avoid an excessive number of action verbs, skill constructions can also be denoted by qualifiers such as *calculate.simple* or *calculate.complex*, where the meaning insofar as level of skills should be obvious to the developers and carefully documented. For complex skill constructions, it may be preferred to assign a single verb or identifier to combinations of primitives for ease in referencing (e.g., *analyze*[*data*]= *calculate*[*identify.method*[*data*]]).

The TMG statements also indicate the declarative knowledge components—that is, the static or generated knowledge to which the cognitive skills are applied when the examinee encounters the actual items constructed from each task model. For example, asking the examinees to identify a theme in a paragraph composed of simple sentences and relatively common vocabulary should be easier than applying the same theme-identification skills to a passage containing obtuse vocabulary, somewhat complex grammatical constructions, and other passage features that increase the information density of the passage. Declarative knowledge components can range from simple concepts to an entire system of knowledge components linked together by complex relations among the components.

There are [at least] three general classes of declarative knowledge components that are acted upon by the examinee using the procedural skills: (a) *knowledge objects* (e.g., static or generated data, graphs, text or other information); (b) acceptable *relations* among the knowledge objects; and (c) *auxiliary tools/information* that define, elaborate or otherwise qualify knowledge components of each task. In general, dealing with more knowledge objects, using more complex knowledge objects, introducing [more] complex relations and offering fewer auxiliary tools or resources (or potentially punitive resources) will add to the overall information density and challenge the examinee more by increasing cognitive processing loads in working memory. In turn, requiring the examinee to contend with more complex knowledge components will tend to make the family of items for that task model more difficult—at least if procedural knowledge is held constant.

It is important to keep in mind that the location of each task model along the scale applies to an entire family of items that require the same constellation of skills operating on similarly complex declarative knowledge objects. Therefore, the entire family of items has the same intended relative difficulty, which is manipulated or controlled across task models by modifying the required procedural skills, or by manipulating the complexity of the declarative knowledge components, or both. A simple two-dimensional graphic helps to illustrate the potential interactions between procedural skills and declarative knowledge components insofar as charting a *trajectory* for the task model designs to adopt (see Figure 5.2). One can hold the procedural skill relatively constant and increase or decrease the relative location of each task model by incrementally making the declarative knowledge components more or less complex. Or, one might hold the complexity of the declarative knowledge components relatively constant and alter the task-model locations by requiring more or less complex procedural skills. Or, one might systematically change the task-model complexity by simultaneously changing both the procedural skills and declarative knowledge components. The

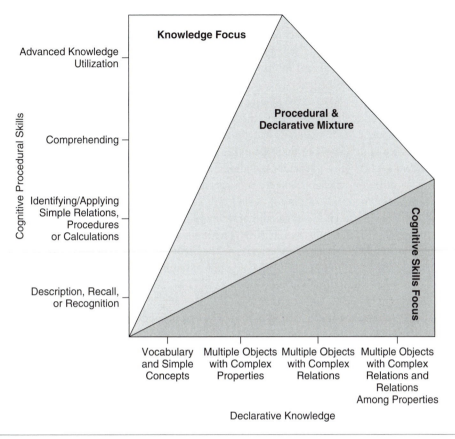

Figure 5.2 A declarative knowledge and procedural skill space with possible trajectories to guide construct specification

proper trajectory depends largely on the proficiency claims from the construct map. Again—everything in AE is done *by design*.

Since each task model has a location on the intended proficiency scale, it is relatively straightforward to conceptualize a concentration of task models at different points of the scale—ideally at key decision points tied to important proficiency claims along the construct map. This density simultaneously represents a specification for the amount of measurement precision needed at various points of the scale, similar to an IRT test information target. The full distribution of task models is called a *task model map* (TMM). A particular TMM represents the intended density distribution of task models as another design decision and naturally implies the need for more precision or information in service of either key decisions in some corresponding region of the construct map, or richer interpretations of performance in particular regions of the scale.

Because a task model incorporates relevant procedural skill requirements of the task, content representation and declarative knowledge load, and location along a scale, it is an *integrated* specification for a family of items that presents the same type of task challenges to every examinee under the same conditions, and where every item generated from the task model has approximately the same relative difficulty. We use templates, a data model and constraints on the template components, and empirical quality control mechanisms to ensure that the difficulties of all items in the family do not vary too much. If we wish to add performance-based interpretation to some region of the construct (scale), we would add one or more task models at those locations. It all becomes a matter of principled design where item difficulty and content are incorporated into every task model.

The relationship between the concentrations of task models on the TMM—aligned to proficiency claims on the construct map and psychometric measurement information needs—and item density is isomorphic. There is exactly one task model for every test item. However, multiple templates can be created for each task model and multiple items can be generated from each template (Luecht et al., 2010; Luecht et al., 2009; Lai, Gierl, & Alves, 2010). This approach to item creation attaches a strong engineering perspective to the design of task models and templates that allows items to be manufactured in large numbers (within the family of templates for a particular task model), all with similar operating characteristics. Provided that the manufactured items maintain an acceptable degree of tolerance with respect to their locations (difficulty and minimum discrimination), both the templates associated with a particular task model and items associated with a particular template can be viewed as randomly exchangeable from the perspectives of both validity and statistical control (i.e., variation is assumed to be a random event that can be integrated out for scoring purposes). Once the templates are validated—through iterative design and pilot testing—and shown to maintain the intended level of difficulty and sensitivity within acceptable tolerances, an obvious benefit is that pilot testing of individual items can be relaxed—possibly eliminated altogether for well-designed templates and task models. In much the same way that a manufacturing organization retrieves schematics and builds new components as needed, the templates can be stored and used to generate new items as needed.

The relationship between the construct map, TMM and individual task-model families comprising templates and items is depicted in Figure 5.3.

This idea of locating task models on a task-model map accomplishes three important goals: (1) it provides the basis for subsequently calibrating the task model to the scale; (2) it allows us to evaluate the measurement precision associated with a particular task model; and (3) it provides strong, empirically based quality control mechanisms to ensure that items created to represent a common task model perform similarly in a psychometric sense. In practice, each task model is represented by multiple, exchangeable templates. In turn, each template can be used to generate many items.

The task models serve two other purposes. First, the task models clearly link the proficiency claims on the construct map to the types of knowledge and skills instantiated by particular tasks on the eventual test forms. This would seem to provide a far stronger validity argument as to what the test score scale represents than is possible using traditional validity studies based on test specifications and content-coding taxonomies. With AE, we are basically saying that, as a student or other

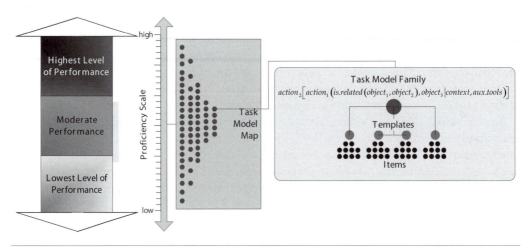

Figure 5.3 Linking templates and items to the task model map and construct map

examinee moves along the scale, the task models detail in a fairly elaborate way the unique *interaction* of levels and types of skills and knowledge that need to be demonstrated. Arguably, a construct map and associated task-model map represent what the valid operational definitions of performance along a particular scale fundamentally should be (e.g., Messick, 1994). Second, task models help to overcome the criticisms that item models usually only manipulate certain surface features of the item, such as names, quantities or simple verbs/grammatical constructions in a multiple-choice stem or in the distractors (e.g., Case & Swanson, 1998; Haladyna, 2004; Bejar et al., 2003)—essentially creating item clones. Cloning potentially restricts generalization or inferences beyond the content and rendered form of a specific parent item (see also Gierl & Lai, this volume). In contrast, as described below, a single AE task model is typically associated with multiple templates, providing potentially much better generalization to the intended interaction or union of cognitive skills and knowledge structures.

For testing programs that only generate a small number of summative assessment test forms each year, there may seem to be few apparent benefits in investing in the development of a task-model map, task models and the necessary iterative design steps and field testing needed to empirically validate the task models and templates. I would argue that any improvement in the test- and item-specification process is worthwhile to avoid the constant struggle to find items. For multidimensional, formative assessments, AE becomes almost essential. That is, the incremental demand for items over time (e.g., over the course of a semester or academic year) will quickly tax even the largest item banks. It is certainly not efficient or cost-effective to continue to conceptualize item writing as an "art form" where each item is crafted by subject-matter experts, pilot tested and then used for a limited engagement as an operational [scored] item.[3] For the formative assessment movement to succeed we need very large item banks with stable item-parameter estimates to support on-demand testing and score reporting, where the banks are sensitive to different traits.[4] This cannot be easily achieved without a carefully engineered item- and test-manufacturing system that builds items as well as tests to exacting specifications.

Designing Templates and Writing Items

In most manufacturing-engineering settings, every component and every assembly of components and every system of assemblies is carefully specified by design parameters. The design parameters specify the critical features of a unit, measurements and acceptable tolerances that lend themselves to schematics or blueprints that can be used to actually build the components, assemblies and systems. It is not so different in test design—at least not from an AE perspective.

A task model is a carefully constructed specification for a task that requires a particular challenge to the examinee. The challenge should be more or less difficult than other challenges and provide acceptable evidence about the proficiency claims of interest along the construct map. If the task challenge is intentionally altered (i.e., made more or less complex), then we would expect it to change the difficulty of items associated with that task model. Our point is that changes in difficulty should not be random outcomes as a function of possibly creative imagination (largely misunderstood features or content that one item writer chooses to include in his/her item and that another item writer ignores). This characterizes the fundamental problem with most test specifications. They are specifications that fail to provide any guidance about the intended difficulty of an item within a particular content category. As a result, it is almost impossible to hold item writers accountable for their items, except to look at adherence to the rather vague content requirements handed to them and, possibly, to evaluate the test statistics of their items after experimental pilot testing.

Under AE, items are part of a family created from one or more templates and the templates are constructed to maintain the interpretation of the declarative knowledge and procedural skills specified by a particular task model. Since a task model has an implicit location (at least a location ordered relative to other task models), the job of the templates and the item writers using the templates is to maintain that location/ordering. This presents an important improvement on the notion of quality assurance and quality control for template design and modification and for item writing. *Quality assurance* (QA) refers to ongoing procedures that evaluate procedures or outputs to detect patterns of aberrations that may signal a need to make alterations. *Quality control* (QC) refers to more proactive mechanisms that are put into place during a particular manufacturing procedure or operation in order to enforce adherence to a quality criterion. In the sense of AE, the templates are part of the QC system and QA would involve an ongoing attempt to make sure that the items in a template family are behaving similarly in terms of their operating characteristics.

Empirically determined variation in item and template operating characteristics is a useful and powerful way of judging quality, whether from a control or an assurance perspective (Luecht, 2008, 2009; Masters, 2010; Shu et al., 2010). Ultimately, we do care about the difficulty and other statistical operating characteristics of each item. Excessive variation of items within the template family and variation in difficulty of the templates within a task model are all causes of concern (Masters, 2010; Shu et al., 2010). We also need to make sure that the item discriminations (sensitivity) of items in task-model families exceed some minimum threshold.

As noted throughout this chapter, a task model should be designed to have a distinct location on a proficiency scale—relative to its difficulty. The QA and QC goals are to maintain each task-model location. A certain amount of variation in the item operating characteristics is fully acceptable at the level of templates and again at the level of items. These minimum levels, in an engineering sense, are viewed as manufacturing *tolerances*. Acceptable tolerances can be empirically derived through simulation (Shu, et al., 2010) or analytical means using pilot test results. Once the tolerances are determined, we use the templates as the primary mechanisms for modifying item operating characteristics to minimize variation and maintain those tolerances at the levels of item families within templates (Masters, 2010) and templates within task models (see, for example, Lai et al., 2010, Lai & Gierl, this volume).

An AE task template is composed of three components: (1) a *rendering model*; (2) a *scoring evaluator*; and (3) a *data model*. These three components jointly specify the presentation format, manipulable content and scoring rules for each template. A rendering model is a structured statement of the problem that can be used to generate two or more items. A task model can have multiple templates and therefore multiple rendering models.

A particular rendering model employs a specific item type. For example, Figure 5.4 shows some sample rendering models for multiple-choice test items in a medical context generated by Case and Swanson (1998). Bejar and Yocom (1991), Irvine and Kyllonen (2002), Bejar et al. (2003) and Haladyna (2004) also provide examples of rendering models—referring to them as item shells or item models.

As the label implies, rendering refers primarily to the interface and look-and-feel of the item, including its basic display functionality and any interactive components provided to the examinee (e.g., navigation controls, auxiliary tools, etc.). Rendering models can be extremely simple or quite complex, depending on the nature of the task model. For example, computer-based performance simulations may have multiple tasks, contexts and tools to be manipulated as part of the template (Luecht et al., 2009). The rendering model is reusable across items, meaning that only the content of the item changes. The National Assessment of Educational Progress (NAEP) provides some examples of potential rendering models for multiple-choice and constructed-response items measuring an implied assessment task model related to developing an interpretation when reading for information (National Assessment Governing Board, 2005). The NAEP website defines the general task and assessment claims as follows.

To develop an interpretation, the reader must extend initial impressions to develop a more complete understanding of what was read. This process involves linking information across parts of a text as well as focusing on specific information. Questions that assess this aspect of reading include

A (*patient description*) has (*abnormal findings*). Which [*additional*] finding would suggest/suggests a diagnosis of (*disease*₁) rather than (*disease*₂)?

<insert 5 plausible findings here, one best answer>

A (*patient description*) has (*symptoms and signs*). These observations suggest that the disease is a result of the (*absence or presence*) of which of the following (*enzymes*)?

<insert 5 plausible enzymes here, one best answer>

A (*patient description*) has (*symptoms and signs*). These observations suggest that the disease is a result of the (*absence or presence*) of which of the following (*mechanisms*)?

<insert 5 plausible mechanisms here, one best answer>

A (*patient description*) follows a (*specific dietary regime*). Which of the following conditions is most likely to occur?

<insert 4 plausible conditions here, one best answer>

A (*patient description*) has (symptoms, signs, or specific disease) and is being treated with (*drug or drug class*). The drug acts by inhibiting which of the following (*functions*)?

<insert 5 plausible functions here, one best answer>

A (*patient description*) has (symptoms, signs, or specific disease) and is being treated with (*drug or drug class*). The drug acts by inhibiting which of the following (*functions, processes*)?

<insert 5 plausible functions here, one best answer>

Figure 5.4 Sample rendering templates (adapted from Case and Swanson, 1998)

drawing inferences about the relationship of two pieces of information and providing evidence to determine the reason for an action.

Any number of rendering model statements could be generated and reformulated into either a multiple-choice or constructed-response item format. For example:

- What <event> marked a change in the plot or situation?
- What caused <the character> to <text-based event related to character>?
- Which of the following <text-based causes> caused <this event>?
- Which of the following is a likely <implications> of this <idea>?
- What will be the result of <this step> in <the directions>?

A scoring evaluator (Luecht, 2005, 2007b) is a formalized—ideally software-based, automated—process or "agent" for extracting and evaluating the response data that ultimately is used in scoring. For example, a correct-answer key scoring evaluator associated with a multiple-choice item typically matches a single response with a stored answer and produces a binary score, correct/incorrect. Luecht (2001, 2005) discussed more complex scoring evaluators for complex items, types, and pattern matches. Partial-credit and polytomous scoring evaluators are also relatively easy to conceptualize, extending this approach to almost any item types. For example, multiple-key scoring evaluators can be developed as a chain of single-key evaluators or operate on specified combinations from vector-valued arguments for the response variables and answer keys. Furthermore, the scoring evaluator's arguments, processing algorithm and assigned point values can easily be represented as database structures to facilitate access for item analysis and scoring. If automation is not possible, then we can also consider human scorers, using rubrics, to be the scoring evaluators. More complicated scoring evaluators are generally needed whenever we are forced to relax constraints on the rendering models or otherwise limit our controls. Conversely, more engineered assessment task controls introduced into the template design will tend to reduce the complexity of the scoring evaluator.

An assessment task template must also include a data model. A data model is a formal structure or specification that allows all of the fixed and variable data components of the task to be represented in a database, manipulated, replicated and assembled in a principled way. The *data* in a datamodel should be able to be stored in database fields, in self-defining XML data structures or some other structured, assessable representation amenable to building actual items by applying the stored or generated information from the data model to the template-rendering model. In essence, if the data for the data model is generated by a computer algorithm or some other automated mechanism the result is *automatic item generation* (AIG). In that sense, the AE framework applies equally well to AIG or human-generated content for the data model.

The data model also contains rubric data (e.g., answer keys) and any variety of item statistics used for test assembly and scoring. Finally, references to external exhibits or information required by the rendering model and the scoring evaluator(s) must also be included as part of the data model. There are obviously numerous ways to represent data, ranging from flat-file data structures to relational schemes to object-oriented frameworks. A detailed discussion of data models is beyond the scope of this chapter. However, incorporating a data model for each template forces assessment designers to come up with concrete structures for representing each assessment task, allowing common task-rendering or scoring features to be reused.

The structure of the templates should promote reusability and scalability of various data structures, content and scoring components. It is relatively straightforward to devise even complex, relational or object-based data hierarchies to represent these reusable, scalable components of the templates. From a test-development perspective, the use of templates reduces the need for item writers to creatively redefine the construct by their choices of items meant to represent nebulous content taxonomies. However, the use of templates also has important psychometric benefits. That is, templates are also meant to provide explicit controls on the difficulty and dimensionality of the items generated from each template. Properties of the rendering models and scoring evaluators that directly or indirectly affect difficulty and other item operating characteristics must be incorporated into the data models (i.e., represented by particular data-based attributes of the task) and specifically manipulated to reduce four sources of variation: (i) variance due to item difficulty and discrimination relative to other items generated from the same template (e.g., item discrimination, estimated "guessing" proportions, and covariances among the estimates) ; (ii) variance due to template difficulty relative to other templates generated from the same task model; (iii) intentional and unintentional dependencies introduced via the scoring evaluators that could indirectly result in bias or other adverse consequences; and (iv) residual covariance associated with templates and items that might lead to psychometric scaling complications (e.g., multidimensionality, differential item functioning, etc.). It becomes an empirical issue to experimentally discover and eventually manipulate the template features that control these sources of variance.

Developing and empirically validating multiple templates for each task model is probably the most complicated, but absolutely necessary, step in AE. The templates turn a conceptual task model into real test items. In addition to designing an appropriate rendering model for each template, the data model needs to capture useful difficulty drivers and features of the task that contribute to item difficulty. These difficulty drivers can be categorical variables or quantitative indices. An iterative process of task design, prototyping, analysis and data coding is needed to identify and capture in a structured way the task difficulty drivers and other manipulable task features that empirically affect the performance of items associated with that template. It needs to be emphasized that *empirical verification of the difficulty drivers is essential.* It is not necessary to identify all of the plausible difficulty drivers—just the ones that work reasonably well to explain changes in item performance for items generated from a common template and for templates associated with the same task model (Masters, 2010; Geerlings et al., 2010).

If the templates are well designed using AE principles, it should be apparent that item writing and test assembly will become relatively uncomplicated procedures. That is, the task-model maps provide a joint specification of the measurement information needs and the content of the test. In turn, each task model is associated with multiple templates capable of generating large numbers of items. If every item writer is required to use the templates, then item writing becomes an item production or manufacturing enterprise rather than a series of unique craft projects. From a validity perspective, allowing item writers too much flexibility in creating items—with or without the benefit of a test specification —introduces the possibility that each item writer will effectively redesign the construct and inherently modify the structure of the score scale.

Under AE, item writing should be less complicated and certainly more predictable than item-writing assignments based on broad test specifications. A particular template associated with a particular task model can be assigned to each item writer. The item writer then engages in either or both of two responsibilities. One item-writing responsibility is to provide *plausible* values for assessment task features (i.e., aspects of the task challenge, context or resources allowed by the template) that effectively control for difficulty and/or eliminate sources of nuisance dimensionality. The second responsibility is to provide surface-level, incidental changes to the rendering form of the item so as to provide multiple instantiations of each item. Admittedly, this makes item writing far less creative and more of a production-line manufacturing task. However, that is exactly what is needed in order to ensure acceptably consistent and high-quality items.

Psychometric Calibrations and Quality Control

The use of task models and templates implies that AE involves a decidedly confirmatory perspective about assessment where the item difficulties and other statistical characteristics of the items are somewhat predictable outcomes based directly on intentional and principled design decisions. Strong QC procedures are therefore needed to confirm that the system is working as intended. If not, we iteratively change the design until it does work. The idea of using task models and templates provides a convenient way of applying design-based control over the salient difficulty and dimensionality "drivers" that will ensure replication of the assessment features for a prescribed population of test takers. Focusing on a task model as the central unit (or parent) of a class of templates, we can employ statistical QC procedures to gauge and subsequently manage the variation that occurs among templates that, theoretically, belong to the same task model. The rather common goal of minimizing [random and systematic error] variance provides a concrete QC mechanism for evaluating the utility of multiple templates associated with a particular task model. That is, if the variation is sufficiently small, the task model and templates are "usable". If not, the templates must be adapted until an appropriate minimum amount of variance can be consistently achieved within the target population. Similarly, we can view each template as the central unit in a class of items generated from that template, where minimizing variance becomes the goal.

Consider a simple demonstration of how the task model and template design features lend themselves to QC. Using IRT, it is common to estimate at least two parameters for each item: a discrimination parameter, denoted a, representing the statistical sensitivity of each item to the underlying score scale, and a difficulty parameter, denoted b, that locates the item on the underlying score scale. The score scale is represented by the Greek letter θ ("theta"). The associated IRT two-parameter model for dichotomous data—that is, for data where an item response to item i is $u_i = 1$ if correct or $u_i = 0$ if incorrect—uses a particular mathematical expression to represent the probability of a correct response, given θ, a_i and b_i, as

$$\Pr\left(u_i = 1 \middle| \theta; a_i, b_i\right) = \frac{\exp\left[a_i\left(\theta - b_i\right)\right]}{1 + \exp\left[a_i\left(\theta - b_i\right)\right]} \tag{5.2}$$

(Lord 1980; Hambleton & Swaminathan, 1985)

Although the examinees' scores (estimates of θ) are certainly of interest, we will limit this discussion to the a- and b-parameter estimates.

When a large number of examinees are administered a particular item, we usually obtain fairly accurate and stable estimates of a_i and b_i. The stability of the estimates can be estimated by computing a standard error or error variance of estimate (Lord, 1980; Hambleton & Swaminathan, 1985). Larger standard errors or error variances imply that the item parameter estimates are less stable. For AE, since our goal is QC, we can generalize the item parameter estimates to either templates or task models. That is, we can conceptualize a and b as representing the discrimination and difficulty of an item, a template or a task model.[5] When the estimation error variance is small enough at the task-model level, we can calibrate the task models and use those estimates for all templates and items. When the error variance is too large at the task-model level, we can allow the calibration to migrate to the template level. In the "worst case"—that is, when AE task models and templates fail to control to a reasonable degree the difficulty and discrimination of the items—we do what we do now insofar as uniquely calibrating each item.

Figure 5.5 presents a visual example of two hypothetical distributions of estimates of a and b associated with two task models (or two templates). Each distribution assumes that a large number of items were generated for each task model and administered to comparable samples of test takers from a common population. Each family of items was treated as a type of "super item" and calibrated using a two-parameter logistic item response theory model (see Equation 5.1). The item parameter estimates represented by the distribution plotted in Figure 5.5a are too varied, suggesting that the task model may be somewhat poorly specified and/or the templates are not doing a good job of controlling item features that affect the difficulty of each item in the family. Figure 5.5b presents a far better-behaved task model family. The variation is only slightly larger than we would expect from estimation (sampling) error.

In practice, empirical studies or model-based simulation can be employed to determine the acceptable tolerances (i.e., required minimum level of variation in the item parameter estimates). This approach lends itself nicely to a formal hierarchical Bayes framework for subsequently calibrating task models, templates or even individual items. For example, there have been several promising applications of hierarchical IRT modeling to response data from items generated using fixed design features (Glas & van der Linden, 2003; Geerlings, van der Linden, & Glas, 2010; Glas et al., 2010; Geerlings et al., 2011). Similarly, Shu et al. (2010) demonstrated that, at least for simulated multidimensional IRT-generated data, this type of hierarchical calibration framework is rather robust and that accurate scores can be obtained for task-model- or template-calibrated items where the difficulty and discrimination parameter estimates have moderate to low standard errors of estimate. Luecht (this volume) demonstrates a similar finding insofar as using AIG for computerized adaptive testing (CAT).

The important point is that IRT calibration takes on a new role under AE: to provide empirically based *quality-control evidence* that test developers can use to guide the redesign of the templates and ultimately reduce undesirable variation in the item operating characteristics for every item gener-

(a) A Lower-Quality Task Model

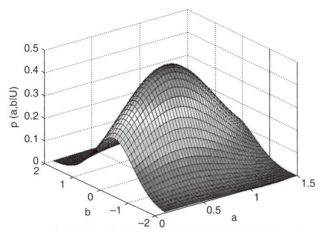

(b) A Higher-Quality Task Model

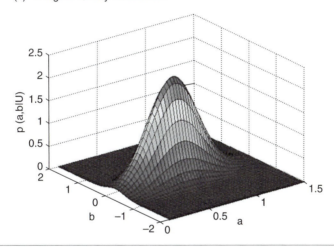

Figure 5.5 Hypothetical task models: (a) A lower-quality task model producing a smaller variance of operating characteristics; (b) A higher-quality task model producing a smaller variance of operating characteristics

ated from a particular task model. This iterative redesign and QC feedback process may seem to be time-consuming and expensive. But, it pays off by an order of magnitude in the end, since enough items can be generated from every well-behaved task model to all but eliminate security/item over-exposure risks and pretesting. Furthermore, it is possible to use the natural hierarchy between task models, templates and items to either collapse the data and/or employ hierarchical IRT calibration models that result in more stable estimates of the item statistics. In short, we have had the statistical machinery for some time to handle hierarchical calibrations (e.g., Glas & van der Linden, 2003). AE may provide the item and test-design framework to make use of that machinery.

Discussion

Modern psychometrics and traditional test-development practices may have taken testing as far as it can go. That is always the limitation of "version 1" of any product or service. It is time for "version 2.0," and AE represents one way to get there. Many states and testing organizations are discovering that as testing demands increase, the costs of item production can be enormous. The solution is to find a new design that allows organizations to manufacture as many items as needed for measuring as many traits as teachers need in order to provide remediation and improve their instructional practices.

Although automated test assembly (ATA) technology and related "modern" methods of test construction have made it possible to reconcile complex content requirements (constraints) with sometimes equally complex statistical objectives, the need for any reconciliation stems largely from a potential incompatibility between the content blueprint used to guide item writing, the statistical targets or objective functions, and the items actually generated by item writers. From an AE perspective, this potential incompatibility between demands (constraints and objectives) and supply (the items) represents a fundamental design flaw. If the items are not designed to meet the specifications, change the design.

Traditional test specifications are fundamentally flawed because they do not account for the statistical operating characteristics of the items. There are many examples in virtually every domain of items written to exactly the same content specifications that differ dramatically in difficulty and other operating characteristics. The use of AE task models, task-model maps, and templates attempts to correct the design flaw by advocating for an integrated test specification that makes substantive sense and that allows items to be written to a target location. Initially, the proposed locations are little more than hypotheses about the relative complexity (difficulty) of each task model. Using empirical data, those hypotheses can be refined until a complete description of each of the task challenges is evident, as one progresses from the lowest levels to the highest levels of the construct. Once a task-model location is fixed, the task templates and quality assurance/control mechanisms are used to maintain that location over time and contexts.

The utility of this AE approach should be obvious, especially when coupled with a solid psychometric calibration framework built on hierarchical estimation that capitalizes on the natural hierarchy between task models, templates and items. Suppose, for example, that we develop a task-model map for a 50-item test, with three templates (on average) for each task model, with strong quality controls to maintain difficulty of the family of items associated with each template. If each template is capable of generating a minimum of 100 items, we would have a 15,000-item pool comprising 300 items per task model. And not all of the items would need to be pilot tested. For a formative assessment, this size of an item bank would seem more than reasonable to support on-demand testing throughout a semester-long course. Geerlings et al. (2010, 2011), Glas et al. (2010), and Shu et al. (2010) have demonstrated through computer-generated data simulations that a hierarchical Bayes calibration system is fully feasible to support that size of any item bank, provided that investment is made, up front, to fully develop and validate the task models and templates.

It needs to be emphasized that designing useful task models, task-model maps and even templates are not arm-chair exercises carried out by subject matter experts, cognitive psychologists, or psychometricians. Rather, empirical data is used to iteratively and continually inform and improve the design process. The reward is a set of test specifications that integrate psychometric measurement needs with content in a meaningful way that provides tangible evidence about defined proficiency claims on a particular construct. When combined with other aspects of AE, these test specifications become part of a highly efficient assessment system.

There remains a lot of research to carry out before AE can realize its potential. However, the results and proof-of-concept work to date are promising and will, hopefully, help to pave the way for others to explore and improve on AE.

Notes

1 Affective or psychological constructs can likewise be treated as ordered attributes, behaviors or symptoms.
2 It is possible and even likely that action verbs will take on different meanings (and possibly, different relative sequencing) for different traits. That is fully acceptable, provided that the construct-specific context is retained as part of the definition of the verb.
3 To complicate matters further, most of our calibration/equating models are "data hungry," requiring somewhat substantial examinee sample sizes and sufficient connectivity in the data (i.e., at most, semi-sparse data sets) in order to accurately estimate item and person parameters. AE capitalizes on a natural hierarchy that exists between a task model, multiple templates associated with the task model, and multiple items associated with each template to estimate stable item parameters and to minimize misfit (variation of difficulty and discrimination) within templates and task models.
4 This perspective of multidimensionality being a prerequisite for diagnostic testing is arguably contrary to the attempts by some organizations to "re-purpose" large item banks containing previously used operational items calibrated to a unidimensional metric. The diagnostic utility of such items is questionable for purposes of reliably profiling strengths and weaknesses on instructionally sensitive metrics that can be legitimately remediated through teaching and instruction.
5 In practice, we have at least three options: (i) to collapse the data for templates or task models; (ii) to combine the item estimates to get template estimates or task-model estimates, weighed by their reciprocal error variances; or (iii) to fit a hierarchical IRT model to the data (Glas et al., 2010; Geerlings et al., 2010, 2011).

References

Bejar, I., Braun, H. I., & Tannenbaum, R. J. (2007), A prospective, predictive, and progressive approach to standard setting. In Lissitz, R. (Ed.) *Assessing and modeling cognitive development in school: Intellectual growth and standard setting.* Maple Grove, MN: JAM Press.
Bejar, I. I., Lawless, R. R., Morley, M. E., Wagner, M. E., Bennett, R. E., & Revuelta, J. (2003). A feasibility study of on-the-fly item generation in adaptive testing. *The Journal of Technology, Learning, and Assessment. 2(3)* (Available online: http://ejournals.bc.edu/ojs/index.php/jtla/article/view/1663/1505)
Bejar, I. I., & Yocom, P. (1991). A generative approach to the modeling of isomorphic hidden-figure items. *Applied Psychological Measurement,* 15(2). 129–137.
Case, S., & Swanson, D. (1998). *Constructing written test questions for the basic and clinical sciences, 3rd edition.* Philadelphia, PA: National Board of Medical Examiners.
Drasgow, F., Luecht, R. M., & Bennett, R. E. (2006). Technology and testing. In R. L. Brennan (Ed.). *Educational measurement, 4th Edition* (pp. 471–515). American Council on Education (ACE)/Praeger.
Embretson, S., & Yang, X. (2006). Automatic item generation and cognitive psychology. *Handbook of Statistics, 26,* 747–768.
Geerlings, H., Glas, C. A. W., & van der Linden, W. J. (2011). Modeling rule-based item generation. *Psychometrika, 76(2),* 337–359.
Geerlings, H., van der Linden, W. J., & Glas, C. A. W. (2010, April). *Optimal design of tests with Automated Item Generation.* Paper presented at the Annual Meeting of the National Council on Measurement in Education, Denver, CO.
Gierl, M. J., & Leighton, J. P. (2010, April). *Developing construct maps to promote formative diagnostic inferences using assessment engineering.* Paper presented at the Annual Meeting of the National Council on Measurement in Education, Denver, CO.
Glas, C.A.W., & van der Linden, W.J. (2003). Computerized adaptive testing with item cloning. *Applied Psychological Measurement, 27,* 247–261.
Glas, C.A.W., van der Linden, W.J., & Geerlings, H. (2010). Estimation of the parameters in an item-cloning model for adaptive testing. In W.J. van der Linden & C.A.W. Glas (Eds.), *Elements of adaptive testing* (pp. 289–314). New York: Springer.
Haladyna, T. M. (2004). *Developing and validating multiple-choice test items, 3rd edition.* Routledge.
Hambleton, R. K., & Swaminathan, H. (1985). *Item response theory: Principles and applications.* Boston: Kluwer.
Irvine, S. H., & Kyllonen, P. C. (2002). *Item generation for test development.* Psychology Press.
Lai, J., Gierl, M. J., & Alves, C. (2010, April). Using item templates and automated item generated principles for assessment engineering. In R. M. Luecht (Chair), *Application of assessment engineering to multidimensional diagnostic testing in an educational setting.* Paper presented in symposium conducted at the annual meeting of the National Council on Measurement in Education, Denver, CO.
Leighton, J. P., & Gierl, M. J. (2007). Defining and evaluating models of cognition used in educational measurement to make inferences about examinees' thinking processes. *Educational Measurement: Issues and Practice, 26,* 3–16.
Lord, F. M. (1980). *Applications of item response theory to practical testing problems.* Mahwah, NJ: Lawrence Erlbaum Associates.
Luecht, R. M. (2001, April). *Capturing, codifying and scoring complex data for innovative, computer-based items.* Paper presented at the Annual Meeting of the National Council on Measurement in Education, Seattle, WA.
Luecht, R. M. (2005). Item analysis. *Encyclopedia of Statistics in Behavioral Science.* London: Wiley.
Luecht, R. M. (2006a, May). *Engineering the test: From principled item design to automated test assembly.* Paper presented at the annual meeting of the Society for Industrial and Organizational Psychology, Dallas, TX.
Luecht, R. M. (2006b, September). *Assessment engineering: An emerging discipline.* Paper presented in the Centre for Research in Applied Measurement and Evaluation, University of Alberta, Edmonton, AB, Canada.
Luecht, R. M. (2007a, April). *Assessment engineering in language testing: From data models and templates to psychometrics.* Invited paper presented at the Annual Meeting of the National Council on Measurement in Education, Chicago, IL.

Luecht, R. M. (2007b). Using information from multiple choice distractors to enhance diagnostic score reporting. In J. Leighton & M. Gierl (Eds.), *Cognitive Diagnostic Assessment*. London: Cambridge University Press.

Luecht, R. M. (2008, October). *Assessment engineering in test design, development, assembly, and scoring*. Invited keynote presented at the Annual Meeting of East Coast Language Testing Organizations (ECOLT), Washington, DC.

Luecht, R. M. (2009, June). *Adaptive computer-based tasks under an assessment engineering paradigm*. Paper presented at the 2009 GMAC CAT Conference, Minneapolis, MN (in press, *Proceedings of the 2009 GMAC CAT Conference*).

Luecht, R. M. (2010, April). *Controlling difficulty and security for complex computerized performance exercises using assessment engineering*. Paper presented at the Annual Meeting of the National Council on Measurement in Education, Denver, CO.

Luecht, R. M. (2011, March). *Assessment design and development, version 2.0: From art to engineering*. Invited, closing keynote address at the Annual Meeting of the Association of Test Publishers, Phoenix, AZ.

Luecht, R. M., Burke, M., & Devore, R. (2009, April). *Task modeling of complex computer-based performance exercises*. Paper presented at the Annual Meeting of the National Council on Measurement in Education, San Diego, CA.

Luecht, R. M., Dallas, A., & Steed, T. (2010, April). *Developing assessment engineering task models: A new way to develop test specifications*. Paper presented at the Annual Meeting of the National Council on Measurement in Education, Denver, CO.

Luecht, R. M., Gierl, M. J., Tan, X., & Huff, K. (2006, April). *Scalability and the development of useful diagnostic scales*. Paper presented at the annual meeting of the National Council on Measurement in Education, San Francisco, CA.

Kintsch, W. (1988). The role of knowledge in discourse comprehension construction-integration model. *Psychological Review, 95*, 163–182.

Masters, J. S. (2010). *A comparison of traditional test blueprinting and item development to assessment engineering in a licensure context*. Unpublished doctoral dissertation. University of North Carolina at Greensboro.

Messick, S. (1994). The interplay of evidence and consequences in the validation of performance assessments. *Educational Researcher, 32*(2), 13–23.

Mislevy, R. J. (2006). Cognitive psychology and educational assessment. In R. L. Brennan (Ed.), *Educational measurement* (4th ed., pp. 257–306). Washington, DC: American Council on Education.

Mislevy, R. J., & Riconscente, M. M. (2006). Evidence-centered assessment design. In S.M. Downing & T. M. Haladyna (Eds.). *Handbook of test development* (pp. 61–90). Mahwah, NJ: Lawrence Erlbaum Associates.

Mislevy, R. J., Steinberg, L. S., & Almond, R. G. (2003). On the structure of educational assessments. *Measurement: Interdisciplinary Research and Perspectives, 1*, 3–66.

National Assessment Governing Board (2005). *The Nation's Report Card*. (http://nces.ed.gov/nationsreportcard).

Pellegrino, J. W., Baxter, G. P., & Glaser, R. (1999). Addressing the "two disciplines" problem: Linking theories of cognition and learning with assessment and instructional practice. In A. Iran-Nejad & P. D. Pearson (Eds.), *Review of research in education*. Washington, DC: American Educational Research Association.

Pellegrino, J., Chudowsky, N., & Glaser, R. (Eds.). (2001). *Knowing what students know: The science and design of educational assessment* (National Research Council's Committee on the Foundations of Assessment). Washington, DC: National Academy Press.

Shepard, L. A. (2000). The role of assessment in a learning culture. *Educational Researcher, 29*(7), 4–14.

Shu, Z., Burke, M., & Luecht, R. M. (2010, April). *Some quality control results of using a hierarchical Bayesian calibration system for assessment engineering task models, templates, and items*. Paper presented at the Annual Meeting of the National Council on Measurement in Education, Denver, CO.

Stiggins, R. J. (1997*). Student-centered classroom assessment*. Upper Saddle River, NJ: Prentice-Hall.

Wilson, M. (2005). *Constructing measures: An item response modeling approach*. Mahwah, NJ: Lawrence Erlbaum Associates.

Wilson, M., & Sloane, K. (2000). From principles to practice: An embedded assessment system. *Applied Measurement in Education, 13*(2), 181–208.

6

Generating Items Under the Assessment Engineering Framework

Hollis Lai and Mark J. Gierl

Introduction

Assessment Engineering (AE) is a comprehensive framework for managing test design, development, analysis, and reporting (see also Luecht, Chapter 5, this volume). AE can be used to develop formative and summative tests in an efficient manner that allow for detailed inferences to be made about multiple aspects of examinees' knowledge and skills. A systematic approach to developing test items is the centerpiece of AE, where each test item is developed to probe examinees' mastery on a specific set of skills and knowledge, and examinee response can then be used to guide instruction and student learning. This chapter demonstrates an item-generation process under the AE framework. Our demonstration is organized into four sections. First, we describe the similarities and differences between the traditional and AE process of item development. Second, we demonstrate how an item template, an intermediate representation of a test item, can be created from the process of AE. Third, we demonstrate how test items can be generated from item templates. Fourth, we discuss the implications of item development under the AE framework. By applying the AE framework to item generation, we hope to improve the current process of test development and ensure that test items are created in an efficient manner to promote reliable and valid inferences about examinees' knowledge and skills.

Overview of Item Development Practices

A common process of item development has been adopted as the de facto standard (Welch, 2006). In this process, test developers first define the purpose and content domains of the test. Then, item writers create items that are deemed representative of the content domains and should perform in a predictable manner (i.e., difficulty). This burden of balancing representativeness with predictable item performance became the "holy grail" of item writing. As items are written from the developer's interpretation of the required domain, very little theory is used to guide their interpretations (Osterlind, 1998; Schmeiser & Welch, 2006). As a result, item development is often considered to be an art (Hornke, 2002), where the skill of creating an optimal test item can be gained through experience. Past attempts to improve item-development processes have focused on increasing the specificity of the test construct (Welch, 2006) and enhancing the item-review process (Downing & Haladyna,

1997; Schmeiser & Welch, 2006). Although such attempts have increased item quality, the subjectivity of item writers' interpretations on test requirements have not been addressed. Moreover, the issue of subjectivity is further exacerbated when test requirements are ill defined.

In the past, tests were often designed under classical test theory where the most commonly used test designs did not require a large number of items or a balance in item representation across diverse content areas. The simplicity in such test design allows for a more stringent item-review process to be feasibly implemented for identifying poor items. But as more advanced models of scoring and testing became available, larger numbers of items are needed, and these items are scrutinized and evaluated more carefully. To highlight how complex assessment designs require many more test items, Breithaupt, Ariel, and Hare (2010) estimated that the number of items required for a 40-item adaptive test with two administrations per year is, at minimum, 2,000 items over a testing period of five years. This large item requirement is necessitated by item exposure, which invalidates an item for future use after administration to ensure that it is not used too frequently. The advancement of computer-based and adaptive testing methods has also contributed to the increase in demand for test items, implying that not only do item writers need to create items at an unprecedented rate, but items must also fit more specific categories and must adhere to higher psychometric standards. In short, item writers using the traditional approach are beginning to reach a point where they can no longer meet the demands of producing large numbers of high-quality test items.

Automatic Item Generation

AIG was developed specifically to address this increased demand for test items. By varying the attributes of an item in a systematic manner, AIG can be used to create multiple items, in an iterative fashion, under a common methodology (Kyllonen, 2002). Although AIG is theoretically promising, several practical hurdles remain. First, the current process of AIG requires knowing what aspects of an item affect difficulty. This predictive knowledge on difficulty is important for AIG, as it can be used to determine which element of an item should be varied. Second, creating items using AIG is only beneficial for algorithmic items with a minimum amount of supplementary information. In content-specific areas such as reading and writing, development of AIG items is limited, as multiple items using the same information cannot be administered. Third, as AIG clones multiple items for a common task, specific instructions are needed to guide item-template development. In the absence of such guidance, AIG would be prone to creating too many easy items, as these items are simpler to develop, as compared to more difficult items (Wainer, 2002). Hence, the quality of generated items can be improved by using a more systematic approach for creating item templates. In this chapter, we demonstrate how the AE approach of creating item templates in a systematic manner can be incorporated into the AIG process. By incorporating AE into AIG, our goal is to provide guidelines for systematically creating item templates, thereby improving the quality of generated items.

Assessment Engineering (AE)

AE is an innovative approach to test development where engineering principles are used to guide the development of an assessment (Luecht, 2007). AE is distinguishable from traditional test development by dividing each step of test development into its own systematic process. To guide the systematic development, knowledge and skills in a given content area are organized in the form of construct map or cognitive models. Moreover, skills in the cognitive model are anchored to an underlying scale of ability specific to the content area, commonly expressed as θ. By anchoring skills on a scale of ability, the cognitive model can be used to guide item development in AE. With these modifications, AE is capable of providing a more controlled process in creating tests and test items, which will lead to stronger inferences about student learning (Gierl, Zhou, & Alves, 2008).

The application of the AE framework for developing tests can be characterized by three distinct steps. First, AE defines an underlying scale of ability as the basis of mastering a content domain, where cognitive models are then used to define specific sets of knowledge and skills required to solve an assessment task. For this chapter, two specific areas in high school mathematics and reading are used as content domains. Knowledge and skills from each domain are structured into a cognitive model, where each piece of knowledge or skill relevant to domain mastery is defined on the scale of ability to guide item development. Second, task-level instructions are developed. Based on each scale of ability, a *task construct* is created to summarize the scale of ability into sets of sub-tasks, where different variations in levels of sub-task complexities create a different level of difficulty reflected on the scale of ability. *Task model*, a first-order logic representation of a unique set of sub-task complexities from the task construct, is a guide for developing items. Third, items and related information are generated. Using a task model, each unique combination of a sub-task required to create an item template is specified. An item template provides both the context and content to create multiple items under the same task model. In this chapter, we demonstrate the item-generation step of AE, where items are generated from templates that, in turn, are created from task models. Because item templates are a crucial component of AE, we provide a short description of what we mean by item template, we explain how these templates are defined, and we illustrate how templates can be used to generate items.

Item Templates

An item template can be generalized as a prototypical representation of multiple items for the purposes of item generation. In the context of AE, an item template is not only purposeful for AIG, but is also an explicit representation of a task model. The relationship of a task model to an item template can be described in the following way: a task model is an implicit set of instruction that provides the knowledge and skill requirements to be expressed on an item template, whereas an item template is an expression of those demands with the inclusion of item content. While each item template can only be an instance of one task model, multiple item templates can be created to represent the same task model. Figure 6.1 is an example of how a task model differs from an item template (also presented as item template 10 in Appendix A).

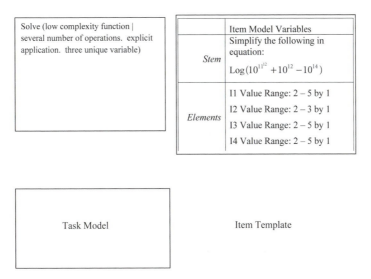

Figure 6.1 Example of a task model and an item template

An item template for generating selected-response items includes three components: stem, options, and auxiliary information. The item stem is where the question or task is posed to the examinee. The options, including the correct and incorrect responses, are selections that the examinee can choose as a response. Auxiliary information is additional multimedia presentation such as graphics, charts, and tables that are appended to facilitate the examinee's understanding on the item. Depending on the type of item, options and auxiliary information may not be presented, although every item would require a stem. To enable AIG, item templates also contain elements within each of the three components to elicit differences between items. To optimize different types of variation, elements of an item template can be conceptualized into two categories: a numerical variable, where elements are essentially a numerical value and can vary across items during generation in an algorithmic manner, or a text-based variable, where a precompiled set of possible texts are systematically substituted to create a unique item (Bejar, Lawless, Morley, Wagner, Bennett, & Revuelta, 2003). These two types of variations, expressed in the form of different elements, can produce unique items from a single template. Assuming that all elements are independent from one another, the maximum number of unique items that can be generated from an item template is the product of the ranges of all the elements specified,

$$n = \prod_e c_{ce}$$

where e is an element in the item template, and c is the range (i.e., number of choices) of that element. This expression demonstrates that the number of possible items that can be generated is theoretically promising. However, not all possible combinations of elements may be a fit for generating items.

The goal of generating task models in AE is to have a set of models that are representative across the entire scale of ability, as described in the cognitive model. The goal of AIG is to vary elements within the item template, in an iterative and systematic manner, to generate unique items that are comparable to one another psychometrically. This property, known as isomorphism, is a desired outcome for variations with an item template (Bejar, 2002). To ensure that all generated items have the same test characteristics, the range of elements can be manipulated and constraints can be placed on the elements during generation in order to discard unwanted items. However, determining how item templates can be constrained is often a complicated process. Currently, there are two prevalent approaches to constraining item templates: weak and strong theory (Gierl & Lai this volume).

In traditional item writing, few strategies exist for controlling item difficulty, but experienced item writers often have recommendations or guidelines to produce items with somewhat predictable psychometric characteristics. For example, test-wiseness, response length cueing, or eliminating two similar options are a few of many features that should be avoided when developing traditional items. This guideline approach is similar to the application of weak theory in AIG. Like traditional item writing, weak theory is an approach to control for isomorphism in generated items using guidelines based on prior experience. Namely, weak theory relies on the experience of test developers to heuristically guide what combination of elements would affect item difficulty. The main benefit of using weak theory to control for item difficulty in AIG is the simplicity of its implementation—item-writing guidelines are often available and can be generalizable to develop diverse types of item templates (Lai, Alves, Zhou, & Gierl, 2009). The drawback of using weak theory is the elusiveness of controlling difficulty itself. Heuristic approaches to constraining item difficulty have often failed because difficulty is neither easy to predict nor to control at the item syntax level (Dennis, Handley, Bradon, Evans, & Newstead, 2002; Gierl et al., 2008). As a result, items should be generated in a more deterministic manner, such that the reliance on guidelines and reviews to constrain item difficulty can be minimized. Instead, the estimation of item difficulty should be incorporated within the item-development process.

The strong-theory approach involves generating items from a known structure of knowledge where difficulty can be predicted (Irvine, 2002; Drasgow, Luecht, & Bennett, 2006). The use of cognitive modeling for item generation, where elements of items are controlled based on the features suggested in the cognitive theory, is one such example. Compared to weak-theory approaches, generating items from strong theory requires much more development effort. And while the application of strong theory can be a burdensome process, it does provide many benefits over other weak-theory approaches. For instance, item generation with strong theory allows for developers to control for item difficulty. With the use of a cognitive model, item difficulty can be controlled and manipulated at the cognitive-features level, where the addition or subtraction of skills included on a given item can be used to predict its difficulty, thereby allowing more complex inferences to be made about student responses. Also, by controlling difficulty beyond text similarities, strong theory allows more flexibility in the item-generation process. For example, when an item template generates two items that may use a different set of skills (and hence yield different difficulty levels), weak theory would suggest constraining the item template to eliminate one instance of the item. In contrast, AIG with strong theory would allow for the generation of both items, as long as there is a method to account for how the items vary in difficulty. Few studies have demonstrated this application, but, for the available applications, promising results were demonstrated only for some specific tasks (Embretson & Daniel, 2008). A strong-theory approach to item development is analogous to the conceptual process of AE. Therefore, by employing the AE framework to generate items from task models, we demonstrate an application of strong theory in item generation.

Creating Item Templates From Task Models

To create item templates under the AE framework, task models are needed. Each task model contains a unique set of cognitive instructions, dimensions of complexity, and required materials associated for testing. Luecht, Dallas, and Steed (2010) created 15 task models under the AE framework. In the current study, we continue the AE development process by creating one item template for each of the Luecht et al. (2010) task models to generate items. Our task models were developed using two cognitive models in the domains of Algebra and Functions (mathematics) and Determining the Meaning of Words and Sentences (reading comprehension). Both cognitive models were developed to evaluate student learning in Grade 9 (see Gierl & Leighton, 2010). While only one item template was created for each task model for the current study, it should be noted that it is possible to create multiple item templates for each task model, as numerous item templates can provide different context for the same set of instructions given by a task model.

With the task models available, creating item templates can be completed in a three-step process. First, given a task model, a relevant and appropriate context is needed to apply the features as described in the task model. Second, from the context of the item template, each feature of the task model is applied to the elements of the template until all constraints and instructions have been met. Third, the item template needs to be constrained so that non-cognitive, non-model related effects on difficulty are controlled. These effects include, but are not limited to, test-wiseness, content cueing, and appropriateness of options. In contrast to other demands of the task model, constraints placed at the item-template level are implemented algorithmically during the item-generation process. To demonstrate the development process, item templates 1 and 14 will be described in detail (the complete set of 15 item templates for mathematics and reading comprehension is presented in Appendix A).

Item Template 1: Mathematics

First, consider that the task model in Figure 6.2 is to be used to create item template 1(IT1) in the domain of Algebra and Functions.

Construct	Algebraic solutions to applied word problems
Task model specification	Apply (moderate distracting information | polynomial function.1 unknown. moderate complexity. few number of operations)

Figure 6.2 An example of a task model in algebraic solutions to applied word problems

This task model provides the instruction necessary to create item templates for a specific area within the domain of Algebraic Solutions to Applied Word Problems. Specifically, the task model outlines six requirements that an associated item template will have to meet: (1) items must be worded in an applicative manner, (2) the verbal load of the items must contain a moderate level of distracting information, (3) items must involve a polynomial function, (4) application of functions must contain one unknown variable, (5) the complexity of operations required in the items has to be at a moderate level for Grade 9 students, (6) only a few numbers of operations are needed to get the correct answer. Given this set of instructions, an item template for this task model can now be created.

The first step in creating an item template is to consider a context that both is applicable to the requirements of the task model and can be applied appropriately for generation. In the case of IT1, we chose to use the context "how far an airplane travels in a given time span during takeoff" (see Figure 6.3).

Development of IT1 did not include options or auxiliary information. With the context specified for the item template set, the second step is to iteratively implement the demands of the task model. Consider Figure 6.4 as a demonstration of how features from the task model can be iteratively incorporated into IT1. The changes made to the item template at each step are presented in bold.

As the item template incorporates more features required by the task model, the content of the item template grows and the subsequent items become more constrained (see Figure 6.4). Three points of clarification have to be made about this process. First, as different task models have different features and categories, each feature does not have to be modified in the order in which it was presented. Second, each feature from the task model should be integrated separately, as the iterative process would ensure that each feature of the task model has been represented. Third, the last feature of the task model, "few numbers of operations", was verified to be true in IT1 without modification to the item template.

After all features from the task model have been incorporated into the item template, the elements in the template will need to be checked throughout their ranges so as to ensure that item difficulty

	Item Template: Context
Stem	Suppose the distance traveled by an airplane at takeoff can be determined by the following equation in meters: [Equation] Distance airplane traveled after X seconds?

Figure 6.3 Context for item template 1 in mathematics

Features incorporated	Item Template 1
Context only	**Distance traveled by an airplane at takeoff can be determined by the following equation in meters:** [Equation] **Distance airplane traveled after X seconds?**
Verbs: *Apply*	Suppose the distance traveled by an airplane at takeoff can be determined by the following equation in meters: [Equation] How far would the airplane have traveled after X seconds?
Verbal load: *Moderate distraction*	**Suppose at takeoff, the distance traveled by a passenger jet on the runway can be determined by the following equation in meters:** [Equation] **Where S is the number of seconds the plane has traveled.** How far would the airplane have traveled after X seconds?
Complexity of function: *Polynomial*	Suppose at takeoff, the distance traveled by a passenger jet on the runway can be determined by the following equation in meters: **D = I1 S^2 + I2 S** Where S is the number of seconds the plane has traveled. How far would the airplane have traveled after X seconds?
Number of unknowns: *1*	Suppose at takeoff, the distance traveled by a passenger jet on the runway can be determined by the following equation in meters: D = I1 S^2 + I2 S Where S is the number of seconds the plane has traveled. How far would the airplane have traveled after **I3** seconds?
Complexity of operations: *Moderate*	Suppose at takeoff, the distance traveled by a passenger jet on the runway can be determined by the following equation in meters: D = I1 S^2 + I2 S Where S is the number of seconds the plane has traveled. How far would the airplane have traveled after I3 seconds? **Elements**: **I1 Value Range: 5 – 9 by 1** / **I2 Value Range: 2 – 9 by 1** / **I3 Value Range: 10 – 20 by 1**

Figure 6.4 An illustration of incorporating task model demands in item templates

has been controlled. In the case of IT1, two modifications were added to the item template to ensure that no elements are the same within the generated items (see Figure 6.5). The modifications are: (1) number of seconds should not end in multiples of 10 and (2) the value I1 should not be equal to the value of I2.

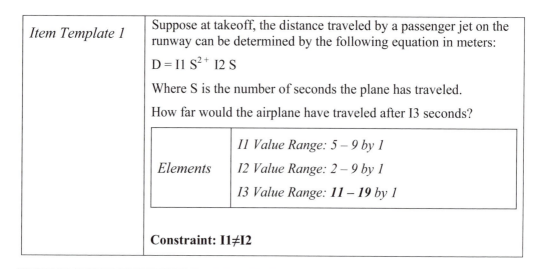

Item Template 1	Suppose at takeoff, the distance traveled by a passenger jet on the runway can be determined by the following equation in meters: $D = I1\ S^{2\,+}\ I2\ S$ Where S is the number of seconds the plane has traveled. How far would the airplane have traveled after I3 seconds?

	Elements	*I1 Value Range: 5 – 9 by 1* *I2 Value Range: 2 – 9 by 1* *I3 Value Range: **11 – 19** by 1*

Constraint: I1≠I2

Figure 6.5 Item template 1 with template-level constrains

Item Template 14: Reading Comprehension

There is a tendency for item templates to favor algorithmic-based domains such mathematics, therefore the process of developing an item template in a non-math related domain is also demonstrated to illustrate how the generation process in these two areas compare and contrast. The item template illustrated here (IT14) was created from a task model from the Determining the Meaning of Words and Sentences domain from Gierl and Leighton (2010). Consider the following task model:

Define (words | esoteric familiarity, independent cuing, high information)

In contrast to IT1, the task model for IT14 requires more demanding features. Furthermore, the dimensions of features used in this task model are less definitive, where most features have to consider the expected student reading level. The requirements for IT14 are listed in Table 6.1.

One of the challenges in developing item templates for reading comprehension is that the underlying algorithmic pattern for the template may not be apparent, or may not even exist. In the case of IT14, the features must be incorporated with the context of the items. Development of the context for IT14 was completed iteratively. A SAT word list was used to ensure that the verbs used in the item template met the reading level requirements of the task model. Also, as the item template calls for the use of multiple choices as response options, the context of the options of the items also had to be considered. The process of developing the context of the item is demonstrated in Figure 6.6.

With the context information established in the item template, the remaining features from the task model can now be incorporated. As options will also be used in this item template, features of

Table 6.1 List of cognitive features required for IT14

Dimensions	Level
Action Verbs	Define
Objects	Words
Context.Familiarity	Esoteric
Context.Cuing	High
Context.Information density	High

The Assessment Engineering Framework • 85

Features incorporated	Context of the Item Template
Context.Familiarity: Esoteric	Explain: S1 S1: ameliorate, congeal, elicit, myriad
Context.Cuing: High	Explain S1 **in the context of S6** S1: ameliorate, congeal, elicit, myriad **S6: He ameliorated the situation by apologizing.** **The cement congealed in the short amount of time.** **The child elicited anger when his candy was taken away.** **There was a myriad of plastic balls in the ball pit.**
Context.Information Density: High	Explain S1 in the context of S6 S1: ameliorate, congeal, elicit, myriad **S6: He tried to ameliorate the situation by talking to his friends about his problems.** **The cement has yet to congeal in the short amount of time.** **The child elicited a range of emotions from happiness to sadness.** **The myriad of shoes made it difficult to walk across the hallway.**

Figure 6.6 Determining the context of IT14

the task model must fit with the options. In an item template, the underlying relationship of the item with the answer can be used to control variability in the generated items. Figure 6.7 outlines the process of developing IT14.

After incorporating all the features from the task model into the item template, constraints are then appended in order to ensure the quality of the generated items. For example, since the key of IT14 varied depending on the sentence presented in the stem, the options would then also have to appear accordingly with the appropriate stem and answer key (see Figure 6.8).

Following the same development process, the remaining 13 item templates are presented in Appendix A. With item templates completed, items can now be generated using AIG.

Generating Items from Item Templates

Using an *Item GeneratOR* aptly named IGOR (see Gierl et al., 2008 for a description of IGOR; see also Yazdchi, Mortimer, & Stroulia, this volume), item templates are formatted into IGOR to

Features	Item Template 14
Context of Item Template	Explain S1 in the context of S6 S1: ameliorate, congeal, elicit, myriad S6: He tried to ameliorate the situation by talking to his friends about his problems. The cement has yet to congeal in the short amount of time. The child elicited a range of emotions from happiness to sadness. The myriad of shoes made it difficult to walk across the hallway. **Option 1 : Synonym of key** **Option 2: Antonym of key** **Option 3: Synonym of similar sounding (but unrelated) word**
Action verbs: Define	**Define** the following term S1 in the sentence S6 S1: ameliorate, congeal, elicit, myriad S6: He tried to ameliorate the situation by talking to his friends about his problems. The cement has yet to congeal in the short amount of time. The child elicited a range of emotions from happiness to sadness. The myriad of shoes made it difficult to walk across the hallway. **Option 1 : Synonym of key** **Option 2: Antonym of key** **Option 3: Synonym of similar sounding (but unrelated) word**
Objects: Words	Define the following term S1 in the sentence S6 S1: ameliorate, congeal, elicit, myriad **Key (S2): to make the situation better, to solidify, to draw out, numerous** **Option 1 (S3): to complicate, to soften, to interpret, few** **Option 2 (S4): to define , to mix together, to differ, different** **Option 3 (S5): to measure, to hide , to define, selection** S6: He tried to ameliorate the situation by talking to his friends about his problems. The cement has yet to congeal in the short amount of time. The child elicited a range of emotions from happiness to sadness. The myriad of shoes made it difficult to walk across the hallway.

Figure 6.7 An illustration of the development process for IT14

Constraints	Item Template 14
Options presented in the same order as key	Definethe following term S1 in the sentence S6 S1: ameliorate, congeal, elicit, myriad Key (S2): to make the situation better, to solidify, to draw out, numerous Option 1 (S3): to complicate, to soften, to interpret, few Option 2 (S4): to define , to mix together, to differ, different Option 3 (S5): to measure, to hide , to define, selection S6: He tried to ameliorate the situation by talking to his friends about his problems. The cement has yet to congeal in the short amount of time. The child elicited a range of emotions from happiness to sadness. The myriad of shoes made it difficult to walk across the hallway. **S1 = S2 = S3 = S4 =S5 = S6**

Figure 6.8 Constraining for the answer key of IT14

generate items. Specifically, IGOR creates items by iterating all combinations of elements in the item template, where each combination is a unique item. The numbers of items generated from each item template are presented in Table 6.2.

Based on the 15 item templates, a total of 10,301 items can be generated using IGOR. To demonstrate the product of these item templates without all the items, a selection of items

Table 6.2 The number of generated items from 15 item templates

Item template #	Element 1	Element 2	Element 3	Element 4	Element 5	Number of items
Mathematics						
1	5	8	9			355
2	2	3	3			18
3	8	6	4	4		762
4	20	9	33			5940
5	3	3	3			27
6	3	2	2			12
7	8					8
8	4	4	4	4	4	896
9	5	3	13	11		2132
10	4	2	4	4		128
Reading comprehension						
11	5					5
12	5					5
13	4					4
14	4					4
15	5					5
Total number of generated items						10301

from IT1 and IT14 are presented in Appendix B. The results from IGOR demonstrate that non-mathematic item templates generate significantly fewer items as compared to math item templates, at least in our examples. Although some item templates are capable of generating a large number of items, the median number of our generated items from each item template is 18.

Conclusions and Discussion

In this chapter, we demonstrated how items can be generated under the AE framework. Item generation is guided by task models, where cognitively based features are incorporated into the test items during the development process. To demonstrate the incorporation of these features across multiple items, 15 item templates were created in order to ensure that all features in the task model were reflected in the generated items. Finally, the use of AIG with 15 item templates generated a total of 10,301 items that measures a known set of features. As the process of generating items under AE is relatively new, many benefits have yet to be realized. As well, many challenges remain. Next, we discuss a few potential benefits, and some associated limitations, in applying the AE framework for item generation.

Using the AE framework to generate items is an attempt to improve the current item-development process. Specifically, the traditional test-development process can be enhanced by drawing on three principal steps from AE item generation outlined in this chapter. First, the use of task models to develop item templates allows items to be related more explicitly to the test construct. Second, task models are developed from a cognitive model, hence test scores can provide detailed information about students' thinking and problem-solving skills. For example, students' score results can be used to support inferences about knowledge and skill mastery more finely than the overall test score. This type of information can enhance score feedback for students and parents, and can also be used to guide instruction for teachers. Third, the use of item templates allows AIG to generate seemingly different items that probe the same set of cognitive features. Under the AE framework, the process of item generation differs from weak theory, where items generated under AE are designed to test a specific set of cognitive skills. The benefit of this generation process is that it can be used to populate large item banks in a systematic manner.

There are also some key limitations with generating items under the AE framework. First, generating items under the AE framework is problematic for language- and content-rich domains. This was evident in the development of our item templates, where five item templates from Determining the Meaning of Words and Sentences generated a total of only 23 items. Although AE was able to generate items specific to the set of features specified in the task model, it is likely that domains such as Determining the Meaning of Words and Sentences would require more item templates under the same task model, should a large amount of items be needed. Second, although the AE process is able to generate an abundance of meaningful items, the issue of field testing this abundance of items may be problematic. Results from the theoretical work in this area have shown promise. Studies have suggested that generated items could be calibrated using an item-family model rather than an item-specific model (Sinharay, Johnson, & Williamson, 2003; Glas & van der Linden, 2003), while calibrated item generation, where items are generated concurrently, based on a combination of the cognitive and item features, have also been suggested (Gierl & Lai, in press), but thus far no study has provided a practical solution to calibrating and field testing large banks of generated items. Third, the AE process of developing items is not well suited to some testing situations, due to the large amount of development work needed to support the AE processes. To generate items under AE, as we have done in this chapter, rigorous development effort was required, on the creation of the cognitive and task models. While this process of development is feasible for a large-scale testing, it may be too costly for testing programs that do not have up-start resources to develop cognitive models of learning. In other words, generating items under AE is a systematic process capable providing a large number of quality test items, but the price of implementation is still unknown.

In summary, we demonstrated how items can be generated under the AE framework. This systematic process of item development can be used to address the growing demand facing testing organizations that require more items. The use of a systematic process for guiding item template development ensured that detailed features are included in each generated item. Current test-development practices rely heavily on the test developer's experience. The use of a systematic process helps to overcome the current approach to item development, such that large numbers of test items can be generated effectively to populate item banks for satisfying the demands of varying cognitive complexity levels within a test construct.

References

Bejar, I. (2002). Generative testing: From conception to implementation. In S. H. Irvine & P. C. Kyllonen (Eds.), *Item generation for test development* (pp. 199–217). Hillsdale, NJ: Erlbaum.

Bejar, I., Lawless, R., Morley, M., Wagner, M., Bennett, R., & Revuelta, J. (2003). A feasibility study of on-the-fly item generation in adaptive testing. *Journal of Technology, Learning, and Assessment, 2*(3). Available from http://www.jtla.org.

Breithaupt, K., Ariel, A., & Hare, D. (2010). Assembling an inventory of multistage adaptive testing systems. In W. van der Linden & C. Glas (Eds.), *Elements of adaptive testing* (p. 247–266), New York, NY: Springer.

Dennis, I., Handley, S., Bradon, P., Evans, J., & Newstead, S., (2002) Approaches to modeling item-generative tests. In S. H. Irvine & P. C. Kyllonen (Eds.), *Item generation for test development*. Mahwah, NJ: Erlbaum.

Downing, S. M., & Haladyna, T. M. (1997). Test item development: Validity evidence from quality assurance procedures. *Applied Measurement in Education, 10,* 61–82.

Drasgow, F., Luecht, R. M., & Bennett, R. (2006). Technology and testing. In R. L. Brennan (Ed.), *Educational measurement* (4th ed., pp. 471–516). Washington, DC: American Council on Education.

Embretson, S., & Daniel, R. (2008). Understanding and quantifying cognitive complexity level in mathematical problem solving items. *Psychological Science Quarterly, 50,* 328–344.

Glas, C., & van der Linden, W. (2003). Computerized adaptive testing with item cloning. *Applied Psychological Measurement, 27,* 247–261.

Gierl, M. J., & Lai, H. (in press). The role of item models in automatic item generation. *International Journal of Testing.*

Gierl, M. J., & Leighton, J. (April, 2010). *Developing cognitive models and constructed maps to promote assessment engineering.* Paper presented at the annual meeting of the National Council on Measurement in Education, Denver, CO.

Gierl, M. J., Zhou, J., & Alves, C. (2008). Developing a taxonomy of item model types to promote assessment engineering. *Journal of Technology, Learning, and Assessment, 7*(2). Retrieved January 1, 2010 from http://www.jtla.org.

Hornke, L. (2002) Item-generation models for higher order cognitive functions. In S. H. Irvine & P. C. Kyllonen (Eds.), *Item generation for test development* (pp. 159–178). Mahwah NJ: Erlbaum.

Irvine, S. (2002). The foundations of item generation for mass testing. In S. H. Irvine & P. C. Kyllonen (Eds.), *Item generation for test development* (pp. 3–34). Mahwah, NJ: Erlbaum.

Lai, H., Alves, C., Zhou, J., & Gierl, M. (May, 2009). *Using automatic item generation to address current test development issues.* paper presented at the annual meeting of the Canadian Society for Studies in Education, Ottawa, ON.

Luecht, R. (April, 2007). *Assessment engineering in language testing: From data models and templates to psychometrics.* Invited paper presented at the annual meeting of the National Council on Measurement in Education, Chicago, IL.

Luecht, R., Dallas, A., & Steed, T. (April, 2010). *Developing assessment engineering task models: A new way to develop test specifications,* paper presented at the annual meeting of the National Council on Measurement in Education, Denver, CO.

Osterlind, S. (1998). *Constructing test items: Multiple-choice, constructed-response, performance, and other formats.* Boston, MA: Kluwer Academic Publishers.

Schmeiser, C., & Welch, C. (2006). Test development. In R. Brennan (Ed.), *Educational measurement* (4th ed.). Westport, CT: Praeger.

Sinharay, S., Johnson, M., & Williamson, D. (2003). Calibrating item families and summarizing the results using family expected response functions. *Journal of Educational and Behavioral Statistics, 28,* 295–313.

Wainer, H., (2002). On the automatic generation of test items: Some whens, whys, and hows. In S. H. Irvine & P. C. Kyllonen (Eds.), *Item generation for test development* (pp. 287–316). Mahwah, NJ: Erlbaum.

Welch, C. (2006) Item and prompt development in performance testing. In S. M. Downing & T. M. Haladyna (Eds.), *Handbook of test development* (pp. 303–327). Mahwah, NJ: Lawrence Erlbaum.

Appendix A

Appendix contains the set of 15 item templates created to demonstrate the process of item generation outlined in the paper.

Item Template 1

Construct	Algebraic Solutions to Applied Word Problems	
Task Model Specification	Apply (moderate distracting information|polynomial function.1 unknown. moderate complexity.few number of operations)	
	Dimensions	Level
	Verbs	Medium (Apply)
	Verbal Load	B
	Complexity of Function	A
	Number of Unknowns	A
	Complexity of Operations	B
	Number of Operations	B

	Item Template
Stem	Suppose at takeoff, the distance traveled by a passenger jet on the runway can be determined by the following equation in meters: $$D = I1\ S^2 + I2\ S$$ Where S is the number of seconds the plane has traveled. How far would the airplane have traveled after I3 seconds?
Elements	I1 Value Range: 5–9 by 1 *I2 Value Range: 2–9 by 1* *I3 Value Range: 11–19 by 1*
Auxiliary Information	None

Item Template 2

Construct	Algebraic Solutions to Applied Word Problems	
Task Model Specification	Solve (moderate distracting information| linear function.2 unknown. low complexity. few number of operations)	
	Dimensions	Level
	Verbs	Solve
	Verbal Load	B
	Complexity of Function	B
	Number of Unknowns	A
	Complexity of Operations	C
	Number of Operations	B

	Item Template
Stem	Julie takes a holiday every I1 years. Nicola takes a holiday every I2 years. Julie and Nicola both took a holiday in I3. The next year that they both take a holiday in the same year is
Elements	I1 Value Range: 2–4 by 2 I2 Value Range: 5–9 by 2 I3 Value Range: 2008–2010 by 1
Options	A. I3 + I1 B. I3 + I2 C. I3 + I1 + I2 D. I3 + lcm (I1, I2)
Auxiliary Information	None
Key	D

Item Template 3

Construct	**Algebraic Solutions to Applied Word Problems**
Task Model Specification	Solve (high distracting information| linear function.2 unknown. Moderate complexity. several number of operations)

Dimensions	Level
Verbs	Solve
Verbal Load	A
Complexity of Function	A
Number of Unknowns	A
Complexity of Operations	B
Number of Operations	C

	Item Template
Stem	Alan, Ben, and Cameron went on a trip for I1 days. They had each saved $I2 for the trip. The hotel where they stayed together was $I3 per night and they had spent $I4 for everything else. How much did each person have at the end of the trip?
Elements	I1 Value Range: 8–15 by 1 I2 Value Range: 500–1000 by 100 I3 Value Range: 80–140 by 20 I4 Value Range: 500–800 by 100
Options	a. $(I2 \times 3 - ((I3 \times I1) + I4))/3$

Item Template 4

Construct	**Algebraic Solutions to Applied Word Problems**
Task Model Specification	Recognize (moderate distracting information| linear function. 2 unknown. low complexity. few number of operations)

Dimensions	Level
Verbs	Recognize (low)
Verbal Load	B
Complexity of Function	A
Number of Unknowns	A
Complexity of Operations	C
Number of Operations	B

Item Model Variables

Stem	Carly earns $I1 an hour and her monthly expenses are $I2. Which of the following inequalities can be used to determine the number of hours, t, that Carly must work, in one month to save at least $I3?
Elements	I1 Value Range: 8–15 by 0.25 I2 Value Range: 500–1000 by 25 I3 Value Range: 100–300 by 25
Options	A. I1 t − I2 ≤ I3 B. I1 t + I2 ≤ I3 C. I1 t + I2 ≤ I3 D. I1 t − I2 ≤ I3
Auxiliary Information	None
Key	D

Item Template 5

Construct	**Algebraic Solutions to Applied Word Problems**
Task Model Specification	Recognize (no distracting information| linear function. 1 unknown. low complexity. simple number of operations)

Dimensions	Level
Verbs	Recognize
Verbal Load	C
Complexity of Function	B
Number of Unknowns	B
Complexity of Operations	C
Number of Operations	C

Item Template

Stem	Joe's Pizza sells I1 slices of vegetarian pizza for every I2 slices of pepperoni pizza sold. If I3 slices of vegetarian pizza slices are sold, then how many slices of pepperoni pizzas are sold?
Elements	I1 Value Range: 2–4 by 1 I2 Value Range: 5–7 by 1 I3 Value Range: 80–96 by 8
Options	A. I3 / I1 B. I3 / I1 +I2 C. (I1 + I2) *I3 D. (I3 * I2) / I1
Key	D

Item Template 6

Construct — **Algebraic Solution to Exponential Functions**

Task Model Specification — Recognize (low complexity function | few number of operations. Explicit application. two unique variable)

Dimensions	Level
Verbs	Recognize
Complexity of Function	C
Number of Operations	B
Clarity of Application	B
Number of Variables	B

Item Template

Stem	What kind of function can this equation be simplified into? $$\frac{5X^{I1}}{4X^{I2}} + \frac{3X^{I3}}{5X} + 56$$
Elements	I1 Value Range: 3–5 by 1 I2 Value Range: 1–2 by 1 I3 Value Range: 2–3 by 1
Options	A. Linear B. Quadratic C. Cubic D. Logarithmic

Item Model 7

Construct	**Algebraic Solution to Exponential Functions**
Task Model Specification	Recognize (low complexity function | few number of operations. Implicit application. one unique variable)

Dimensions	Level
Verbs	Recognize
Complexity of Function	C
Number of Operations	B
Clarity of Application	A
Number of Variables	C

Item Model Variables

Stem	Which of the following expressions represents (I1) (I1) (I1) (I1)?
Elements	I1 Value Range: –9 to –2 by 1
Options	A. $-(|I1|)^4$
	B. $(I1)^4$
	C. $-(|I1|^4)$
	D. $(I1^4)$
Key	B

Item Template 8

Construct	**Algebraic Solution to Exponential Functions**
Task Model Specification	Solve (moderate complexity function | few number of operations. explicit application. two unique variable)

Dimensions	Level
Verbs	Solve
Complexity of Function	B
Number of Operations	B
Clarity of Application	A
Number of Variables	B

Item Model Variables

Stem	Solve
	$11^{12^{13}} + 14^{15}$
Elements	I1 Value Range: 2–5 by 1
	I2 Value Range: 2–5 by 1
	I3 Value Range: 2–5 by 1
	I4 Value Range: 2–5 by 1
	I5 Value Range: 2–5 by 1

Item Template 9

Construct	**Algebraic Solutions to Applied Word Problems**
Task Model Specification	Solve (high distracting information| linear function. 1 unknown. low complexity. Several number of operations)

Dimensions	Level
Verbs	Solve
Verbal Load	A
Complexity of Function	B
Number of Unknowns	B
Complexity of Operations	C
Number of Operations	A

Item Model Variables

Stem	Gina works as a S1. She works I1 hours per week and makes $I2 per hour. She is paid weekly and I3% of her weekly wage is deducted for taxes. If Gina saves 1/4 of her paycheck every week, then how much money will she have saved at the end of 4 weeks?
Elements	S1 Range: "dishwasher", "cashier", "landscaper", "receptionist", "telemarketer" I1 Value Range: 25–40 by 0.5 I2 Value Range: 9–12 by 0.25 I3 Value Range: 15–25 by 1
Options	A. I3/100*I2*I1 B. (I3/100) * I2 * I1 C. (1-(I3/100))*I2*I1*4 D. (I3/100)*I2*I1*4
Key	C

Item Template 10

Construct	**Algebraic Solution to Exponential Functions**
Task Model Specification	Solve (low complexity function | several number of operations. explicit application. three unique variable)

Dimensions	Level
Verbs	Solve
Complexity of Function	C
Number of Operations	A
Clarity of Application	B
Number of Variables	A

	Item Model Variables
Stem	Simplify the following in equation:
	$Log(10^{11^{12}} + 10^{13} - 10^{14})$
Elements	I1 Value Range: 2–5 by 1
	I2 Value Range: 2–3 by 1
	I3 Value Range: 2–5 by 1
	I4 Value Range: 2–5 by 1

Item Template 11

Construct	*Determining the meaning of words and sentences*
Task Model Specification	Identify (words| very familiar, independent cuing, low information density)

Dimensions	Level
Action Verbs	Identify
Objects	Word
Relation	Explicit
Context.Familiarity	Very Familiar
Context.Cuing	Independent
Context.Information density	Low

	Item Template
Stem	Identify the word that is closely related to S1
Elements	S1: arcane, clamor, solicit, terse, hamper
	S2: obscure, shout, seek, concise, hinder
	S3: familiar, quiet, refuse, abstract, assist
	S4: old, calm, socialize, unclear, basket
	S5: abhor, placid, bilk, cower, hasten
Options	A. S2
	B. S3
	C. S4
	D. S5
Auxiliary Information	None

Item Template 12

Construct	*Determining the meaning of words and sentences*
Task Model Specification	Identify (simple phrases I context = somewhat familiar. moderate cuing. medium information density)

Dimensions	Level
Action Verbs	Identify
Objects	Simple Phrases
Relation	Explicit
Context.Familiarity	Somewhat Familiar
Context.Cuing	Moderate
Context.Information density	Medium

Item Template

Stem	Jack used the idiom "S1", what does he mean by that?
Elements	S1: Drop in the bucket, a silver lining, off the record, over the top, run out of steam S2: insignificant, optimistic, unofficially, extravagant, exhausted S3: important, pessimistic, officially, underwhelming, prepared S4: irrelevant, happy, to care about, important, arriving S5: savor, placid, scamp, equivocate, reinvigorated
Options	A. S2 B. S3 C. S4 D. S5
Auxiliary Information	None

Item Template 13

Construct	*Determining the meaning of words and sentences*
Task Model Specification	Identify (relations = implicit (complex phrases)I context = moderate familiarity. independent cuing. high information density)

Dimensions	Level
Action Verbs	Indentify
Objects	Complex Phrases
Relation	Implicit
Context.Familiarity	Moderate
Context.Cuing	Independent
Context.Information density	High

	Item Template
Stem	Identify the overall theme that best describes this sentence: S1
Elements	S1: Although he was too exhausted, he managed to struggle through and complete his task. Not only was he unable complete the task, he managed to destroy what he had completed previously. The team was able to finish the task ahead of time, thanks to their coach's encouragement. The team performed in such a strong manner that no other teams were able to defeat them. S2: perseverance, aggravation, motivation, invincible S3: difficulty, neglect, encouragement, fallible S4: hesitancy, frantic, enthusiasm, dependable S5: exhaustion, unlucky, talent, reliable
Options	A. S2 B. S3 C. S4 D. S5

Item Template 14

Construct	***Determining the meaning of words and sentences***
Task Model Specification	Define (words | esoteric familiarity, independent cuing, high information)

Dimensions	Level
Action Verbs	Define
Objects	Words
Relation	Explicit
Context.Familiarity	esoteric
Context.Cuing	High
Context.Information density	High

	Item Template
Stem	Define the following term S1 in the sentence S6
Elements	S1: ameliorate, congeal, elicit, myriad S2: to make the situation better, to solidify, to draw out, numerous S3: to complicate, to soften, to interpret, few S4: to define, to mix together, to differ, different S5: to measure, to hide, to define, selection S6: He tried to ameliorate the situation by doing more work. The material has yet to be congealed in the short amount of time. The child elicited a number of emotions, from happiness to anger to sadness. The myriad of shoes made it difficult to walk across the path.

Options	A. S2
	B. S3
	C. S4
	D. S5

Item Template 15

Construct	*Determining the meaning of words and sentences*
Task Model Specification	Define (words| context = very familiar. independent cuing)

Dimensions	Level
Action Verbs	Define
Objects	Words
Relation	Explicit
Context.Familiarity	Very Familiar
Context.Cuing	Independent
Context.Information density	Low

Item Template

Stem	Define this word: S1
Elements	S1: infallible, unambiguous, dismember, refine, unearth
	S2: perfect, clear, take apart, improve, find
	S3: wrong, unclear, put together, move back, hide
	S4: broken, confuse, reject, practice, guess
	S5: true, likable, invite, concise, to plant
Options	A. S2
	B. S3
	C. S4
	D. S5
Auxiliary Information	None

Appendix B

Appendix B contains a selection of generated items from IT1 and IT14.

Generated Items of Item Template 1

1. Suppose at takeoff, the distance traveled by a passenger jet on the runway can be determined by the following equation in meters:

   $D = 5S^2 + 2S$

   Where S is the number of seconds the plane has traveled.
   How far would the airplane have traveled after 11 seconds?

2. Suppose at takeoff, the distance traveled by a passenger jet on the runway can be determined by the following equation in meters:

   $D = 5S^2 + 8S$

   Where S is the number of seconds the plane has traveled.
   How far would the airplane have traveled after 14 seconds?

3. Suppose at takeoff, the distance traveled by a passenger jet on the runway can be determined by the following equation in meters:

   $D = 5S^2 + 8S$

   Where S is the number of seconds the plane has traveled.
   How far would the airplane have traveled after 17 seconds?

4. Suppose at takeoff, the distance traveled by a passenger jet on the runway can be determined by the following equation in meters:

   $D = 7S^2 + 5S$

5. Suppose at takeoff, the distance traveled by a passenger jet on the runway can be determined by the following equation in meters:

   $D = 7S^2 + 8S$

   Where S is the number of seconds the plane has traveled.
   How far would the airplane have traveled after 14 seconds?

6. Suppose at takeoff, the distance traveled by a passenger jet on the runway can be determined by the following equation in meters:

   $D = 7S^2 + 2S$

   Where S is the number of seconds the plane has traveled.
   How far would the airplane have traveled after 17 seconds?

7. Suppose at takeoff, the distance traveled by a passenger jet on the runway can be determined by the following equation in meters:

   $D = 9S^2 + 5S$

   Where S is the number of seconds the plane has traveled.
   How far would the airplane have traveled after 11 seconds?

8. Suppose at takeoff, the distance traveled by a passenger jet on the runway can be determined by the following equation in meters:

   $D = 9S^2 + 8S$

   Where S is the number of seconds the plane has traveled.
   How far would the airplane have traveled after 11 seconds?

9. Suppose at takeoff, the distance traveled by a passenger jet on the runway can be determined by the following equation in meters:

$D = 9S^2 + 2S$

Where S is the number of seconds the plane has traveled.

How far would the airplane have traveled after 14 seconds?

10. Suppose at takeoff, the distance traveled by a passenger jet on the runway can be determined by the following equation in meters:

$D = 9S^2 + 5S$

Where S is the number of seconds the plane has traveled.

How far would the airplane have traveled after 14 seconds?

Generated Items from Item Template 14

1. Define the following term ameliorate in the sentence:
   He tried to ameliorate the situation by talking to his friends about his problems.

   a. to make the situation better
   b. to define
   c. to complicate
   d. to measure

2. Define the following term congeal in the sentence:
   The cement has yet to congeal in the short amount of time.

   a. to mix together
   b. to solidify
   c. to hide
   d. to soften

3. Define the following term elicit in the sentence:
   The child elicited a range of emotions from happiness to sadness.

   a. to define
   b. to draw out
   c. to interpret
   d. to differ

4. Define the following term myriad in the sentence:
   The myriad of shoes made it difficult to walk across the hallway.

   a. different
   b. selection
   c. few
   d. numerous

7

Using Evidence-Centered Design Task Models in Automatic Item Generation

Kristen Huff, Cecilia B. Alves, James Pellegrino, and Pamela Kaliski

Introduction

The purpose of this chapter is to provide an illustration of how task models derived within an evidence-centered design framework can be used in automatic item generation (AIG). Particular focus is given to the role of *claims* and *evidence* in creating task models. The claims and evidence were developed as part of the project entitled *From Research to Practice: Redesigning Advanced Placement Science Courses to Advance Science Literacy and Support Learning with Understanding*, partly funded by NSF (Award #ESI-0525575).[1] The chapter begins with a brief overview of AIG and evidence-centered design (ECD). Next, a detailed example of a task model and an item template that was used as input into an AIG program is provided. The chapter concludes with suggestions for future directions in development of task models for use in AIG.

Test Development: Conventions and Innovations

Educators use a variety of tests for critical purposes: to measure students' strengths and weaknesses, to determine whether students are meeting educational objectives, to monitor progress over time, and to tailor programs and resources to student needs. Schools, districts, and states are held accountable based on student performance on end-of-year state-level summative tests. Teachers and principals must pass certification and licensing tests before they can be employed. Increasingly, educators are evaluated, in part, by how well their students perform on tests. Colleges and universities use student test scores for admissions and placement. Such high demands for educational testing come at a significant cost and with considerable effort. Thousands of test items must be developed to measure student performance in different subject areas, in different contexts, for different purposes. As a result, item development involves significant cost, time, and effort.

In conventional approaches to large-scale item and test construction, each item is individually developed by content specialists: the item is first written, then reviewed, revised, edited, and, finally, administered as a field test item, and then, if necessary, revised and field tested again—all before use in an operational context (Drasgow, Luecht, & Bennett, 2006; Schmeiser & Welch, 2006). As a result of this lengthy process, it becomes difficult to meet the ever-increasing demand for more test items, especially with the advancement of computer-based and adaptive testing methods where large numbers of items are required in order to implement continuous testing and where item exposure must be minimized to ensure test security (Drasgow, et al., 2006). Test items have the potential to be memorized and distributed to other examinees and, therefore, many items suffer an early retirement (i.e., removal from bank) and are no longer used (Fairon & Williamson, 2002). As a consequence, constant production of new items is required to replace old items that have been retired, thereby increasing the costs of tests. At the same time, developing replacement items often involves a time delay between writing and administering items, due to item review and pretesting procedures, which can interfere with a continuous testing process, while continuing to drive up the cost of testing (Fairon & Williamson, 2002).

The last few decades have seen an evolution in information technology that has influenced all aspects of life, including education. Advances in computer technology, artificial intelligence, and the internet are creating new possibilities and promises for educational testing. Together with the techonological changes, developments in cognitive science, statistics, the learning sciences, computer technology, and educational psychology are also creating profound changes in educational measurement (Gierl & Lai, 2011; Drasgow, et al., 2006; National Research Council, 2001, 2002). AIG is one of the promising examples of educational applications made possible by means of these advances. AIG is a computerized approach to item development that can supplement the conventional hands-on approach through the use of highly specified algorithms to automatically generate items. Although human intervention is present in early stages of the item-development process in AIG (e.g., creation of task models and item templates—see next section), the ultimate goal of AIG is to produce large numbers of high-quality items that require little human review prior to administration (Williamson, Johnson, Sinharay, & Bejar, 2002).

Overview of Important Concepts for Item Generation

AIG involves generating multiple-choice items[2] in an automated fashion using a predefined structure known as an *item template*[3] (Lai, Alves, & Gierl, 2009). Item templates must satisfy two requirements in order to be used successfully in AIG (Drasgow et al., 2006). First, item templates should be defined sufficiently for a computer to create instances of the template—that is, items—automatically according to a given algorithm. Second, determinants of item difficulty should be articulated well enough so that all of the items generated from the template have approximately the same statistical properties. In our research, *task models* (defined below) created within an ECD framework are used as a way to gather and organize the information that supports the fullfilment of these two requirements for item templates.

Evidence-Centered Design (ECD)

At its heart, assessment is a process of reasoning from imperfect evidence (Mislevy & Haertel, 2006; National Research Council, 2001). To ensure the validity of our inferences about student proficiency from test scores, we must have an evidentiary argument that explicates the relationships—both inferential and observed—among all the elements of the assessment (e.g., our inferences, the scores, our scoring and measurement models, the features of each item, test specifications and relation to domain, model of student cognition undergirding item design and measurement model, etc.). ECD is an approach for articulating critical components of the evidentiary argument throughout each step in the assessment design process. Building upon the work of Mislevy, Steinberg and Almond (2002), Huff, Steinberg, and Matts (2010) defined ECD as:

> a set of activities and artifacts that facilitate explicit thinking about (a) given the purpose of the assessment, what content and skills are both useful and interesting to *claim* about examinees;

(b) what is the reasonable and *observable* evidence in student work or performance required to support the claims; and (c) how *tasks* (items) can be developed within the constraints of the assessment to provide students with an optimal opportunity to provide the observable evidence that is consistent with their achieving the intended claim. (pp. 314–315).

Starting the assessment design process with an articulation of claims and the required evidence to support each claim, one is poised to design tasks (items) that are directly related to the inferences that will be eventually made from the final scores.

ECD is employed in the Advanced Placement (AP) redesign project for three reasons: to provide a foundation for alignment between what is taught in the course and measured on the examination; to help ensure the measurement of deep conceptual understanding through reasoning with discipline-specific content; and to help ensure construct equivalence across different forms of the exam (Huff et al., 2010). Detailed descriptions of the full ECD process used for AP are documented in other reports,[4] and summarizing here is beyond the scope of this chapter. However, central to understanding the use of ECD task models in AIG is the role of claims and evidence in developing task models.

Role of Claims and Evidence in creating Task Models

As mentioned above, one of the primary reasons why AP use ECD is to ensure that the tests measure deep conceptual understanding, that is the tests measure not only the science content knowledge that students need to master in order to be successful, but also the *science practices*, such as *construct an explanation, make a prediction*, or *use a model or representation*. As indicated by the *College Board Standards for College Success* in Science (*2009*), "Science practices must be taught and learned within the context of discipline-specific science content" (page 7). In their final report to NSF, the College Board (*2010*) state, "A practice is a way to coordinate knowledge and skills to accomplish a goal or task. It embodies scientific knowledge and, at the same time, enables it" (page 16). Due to the intricate relationship between science content and science practice, each claim represents an integration of science content and science practice. See Table 7.1 for an example.

The claim and evidence statements are rich with potential scenarios for learning and assessment. For example, in the claim in Table 7.1 what are the varieties of *behavioral responses* on which a student can collect data? Would it not follow that the types of behavioral responses would be dependent upon whether the student is dealing with cells, organisms, or populations? In turn, what are the varieties of cells for which a students can collect data? Varieties of organisms? Varieties of Populations? Additional

Table 7.1 Example of integration of science content and science practice in a claim (adapted from Bertenthal, Pellegrino and Huff, 2009)

Content	**Big Idea:** Living systems store, retrieve, transmit, and respond to information critical to life processes. **Enduring Understanding:** Transmission of non-heritable information results in changes within and between biological systems. **Supporting Understanding:** Organisms exchange information with each other in response to internal changes and external cues, which may change behavior.
Practice	The student can design a plan for collecting data to answer a particular scientific question.
Claim	The student can design a plan for collecting data to assess behavioral responses in cells, organisms, or populations to changes in external conditions.
Evidence to support claim	The work product consists of a narrative or protocol which includes the premise that cells, organisms, and populations detect changes in external conditions, respond to them, and exchange information to change behavior or responses. The work product consists of an experimental design which reflects acceptable scientific methodology and an organism (cell or population) of choice. Examples of experimental designs include, but are not limited to, concentrations of pheromones and numbers of mates attracted in insects; effect of light or darkness on flowering in plants; effect of temperature on reproductive cycles or behavior.

potential scenarios, such as type of experimental design or environmental changes, are found in the evidence statements. Capturing the potential scenarios that are appropriate and meaningful, given the purpose, use, and constraints of the assessment, is the first step in task model design. Further, task model design requires an expression of the scenario features as elements (or variables) and ranges (or values); these should be organized in a useful way, such as those elements and ranges related to what is provided to the student as stimulus versus what the student is expected to produce. The elements and ranges are an articulation of what is allowed to vary and what must be constrained in task design.

Allowable variations and constraints must serve two critical functions: to ensure the evidentiary focus of the task model and to target the task model at the appropriate level(s) of cognitive complexity. Maintaining evidentiary focus not only is a matter of excluding construct-irrelevant elements and ranges, but also is related to focusing on specific elements of evidence. For example, a task model could focus on select components of evidence, such as a cell's ability to detect changes in the environment, or an organism's response to changes in the environment. Ensuring that task models target the appropriate level of cognitive complexity is also a consideration that must remain front and center when determining elements and ranges. Sometimes, such as in the case of AP redesign, the claims and evidence themselves are targeted to specific proficiency levels (see Hendrickson, Huff, & Luecht, 2010; Plake, Huff, & Reshetar, 2010), which means that the elements and ranges associated with a specific task model will be of a more narrow range than when the claim and evidence on which the task model is built are meant to span the full range of proficiency to be measured on the test.

A useful concept in the creation of claims, evidence and task models is the *work product*. Although it may be counter-intuitive, it is a disadvantage to focus on the constraints of the test, specific tasks or item types when authoring claims, evidence, and task models. Rather, it is more useful to focus on the desired learning objective as the claim, the observable evidence that is required to support the claim, and the spectrum of work products that could potentially provide the evidence. The work product is not equivalent to the observable evidence but, rather, the vehicle by which it is transmitted; similarly, the task is not the evidence but, rather, a way to elicit the work product that will be evaluated in order to determine the degree to which it (the work product) contains the sought-after evidence. The most straightforward example is to consider a writing prompt, an essay, and a rubric. The writing prompt (i.e., the task administered to the student) shapes the work product (i.e. the essay, which is what is produced by the student), and the rubric allows for an evaluation of the essay against criteria to determine the value of the observed evidence (e.g., quality and characteristics of thesis statement, amount of and quality of evidence from text to support claims, appropriate use of academic vocabulary, etc.). The notion of a work product becomes especially critical in assessment-design contexts where multiple-choice items must be used. In task-model development where it is known a priori that the eventual items will need to be multiple-choice, one can overly constrain the task model to the detriment of the construct if the work product or observable evidence is conceptualized as a student interaction with a multiple-choice item. Instead, the work product must be visualized as the appropriate vessel for the observable evidence absent from the constraints of any given large-scale assessment. For example, if the claim is "student can summarize the key supporting details and ideas of a text" (adapted from *Common Core State Standards*, National Governors Association Center and Council of Chief State School Officers, 2010, p. 10), the design team should envision the observable features of a work product that is either a written or an oral summary, rather than a multiple-choice item. If the team does the latter, is the observable evidence for the claim, "Student bubbles in correct answer"? Such observable evidence would not get the design team very far along in the creation of viable task models. As such, a useful way to determine claims, evidence, and work products is to reference the domain of interest to which the results from the test will be generalized, not the constraints of the test.

Item Template as an Explicit Representation of a Task Model

Typically, one moves from the more general (claims and evidence) to the most specific (a particular item) by making a series of decisions that narrow the number of elements and ranges under consideration. Task models and item templates are organized collections of elements and ranges that are situated along this continuum (see Figure 7.1). Task models are at higher level of generality than an item template (Mislevy & Riconscente, 2006). The relationship of a task model to an item template is described by Lai et al. (2009) in the following way: "a task model is an implicit instruction set that provides the requirements for an item template, whereas an item template is an expression of those demands with the inclusion of item content" (p. 7). According to Zhou (2009), the defining difference between task models and templates is that the former provide the *theoretical* foundation for item development and the latter provide an *operational* foundation. Hendrickson et al. (2010) indicate that a task model becomes a template when the level of specificity is such that items can be produced. Although there are slightly different takes on exactly what distinguishes a task model from a template, it can be generally agreed upon that the level of specificity of a task model is subjective (see Hendrickson et al., 2010) but it is more general than an item template, and that a single task model can serve as the basis for one or more item templates (as will be demonstrated later in this chapter). Item templates, as noted earlier, have also been termed item models, schemas, item forms, and item shells. Similarly, the items produced from templates have been termed siblings, variants, instances, isomorphs, and clones. In AIG, item templates provide the necessary information for automatically generating items.

Templates are designed to generate items that elicit evidence for a targeted proficiency level and, therefore, have comparable psychometric properties. The comparable psychometric properties are dependent on the variables and constraints placed on the template (through articulation of the elements and ranges), and should be informed by a theory that articulates, for the given assessment purpose and use, the interplay among the three components of the assessment triangle (National Research Council 2001):

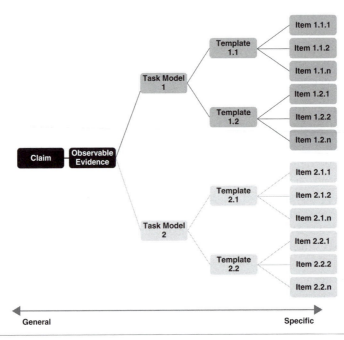

Figure 7.1 Continuum from claim to items (adapted from Hendrickson, Huff, & Luecht, 2010)

- *Student cognition*: How students' knowledge and skills develop as they progress along the proficiency continuum for the given domain,
- *Task complexity*: How different features, expressed as elements and ranges, of tasks impact the cognitive complexity, and
- *Interpretive framework*: How to interpret results of assessment.

The interpretive framework should include assumptions about opportunity to learn, which can affect item statistics and task design. For example, tasks that are designed to demand high levels of cognitive complexity based on a well-articulated theory of how students develop deep conceptual knowledge in a given domain could produce low observed difficulty statistics if the students have had the opportunity to learn and master that task. Similarly, tasks that demand very low cognitive complexity could produce very high observed difficulty statistics in instances where students have not had the opportunity to learn. As such, it is critical to consider cognitive complexity and difficulty statistics in appropriate context when evaluating the items that result from the template.

Illustration of AIG using ECD-based Task Models and Templates

The purpose of the present study was to illustrate how task models developed within an ECD framework can be used to automatically generate items. Subject-matter experts (SMEs) participated in the iterative processes of constructing task models and item templates, which included mining the claims and evidence statements for elements and ranges to be input into the task model and templates, and then reviewing item stems, keys, distractors, and template constraints. After these procedures were conducted, AIG was performed. These actions can be described in a three-step procedure: (1) creating task models, (2) creating item templates, and (3) item generation.

Step 1: Creating Task Models

After specifying claims and evidence, task models were created. Task models serve as a guide for creating item templates, which are the foundation for AIG. The task models are explicitly linked to the intended targets of measurement for the assessment—the claims—because claims and evidence are a primary source of task-model variables as demonstrated below.

A task model was developed for the following claim: The student can construct explanations for how DNA is transmitted to the next generation via the processes of mitosis, meiosis, and fertilization. This task model articulates the intended target of measurement, intended proficiency level of the construct, documentation of the evidence in student work required to support the claim, features that affect task complexity, and features that are irrelevant to the complexity of the task. Our task-model structure is based on an example provided by Luecht (2008). Figure 7.2 documents the key features of a task model for the claim.

The primary function of the task model is to guide the development of the subsequent templates and items, and ensure that the evidentiary focus is maintained and the desired and appropriate level of complexity is targeted. The first four lines of the task model represent the domain area of the task: Biology is the most general level of the construct; the primary context of the construct is cell division; and the claim that is the basis of this task model is included. The *evidence documentation* describes observable characteristics of student work that would warrant the claim about a student's ability to "construct explanations for how DNA is transmitted to the next generation via the processes of mitosis, meiosis and fertilization." In other words, if a student were to provide a *description of the purpose and products of mitosis and meiosis; a description of the behavior of the chromosomes during mitosis and meiosis; an explanation and a comparison and contrast of the processes of mitosis and meiosis; and could*

Construct Identifier:	Biology
Primary Context:	Cell division
Competency Claim	The student can construct explanations for how DNA is transmitted to the next generation via the processes of mitosis, meiosis, and fertilization.
Proficiency Level	Basic
	Evidence Documentation

	Evidence Documentation
1.	Description of the purpose of mitosis and meiosis
2.	Description of the products of mitosis and meiosis
3.	Description of the behaviour of the chromosomes during the phases of mitosis and meiosis
4.	Explanation of the processes of mitosis and meiosis
5.	Comparison and contrast of the processes of mitosis and meiosis
6.	Use and recognition of vocabulary specific to cell division

	Manipulable features of complexity
1.	Type of cell division (mitosis is simpler than meiosis)
2.	Number of steps in process (mitosis has fewer steps than meiosis)
3.	Type of statement/alternative (definition is less challenging than explanation)
4.	Use of vocabulary particular to cell division will increase complexity: ploidy, tetrads, synapsis, crossing over, sister chromatids, homologous chromosomes, segregation, equatorial plate, cytokinesis
5.	Phase of cell division in question; the events in some phases are more conceptually difficult than the events of other phases
6.	Making a comparison (more challenging) vs. selecting a true statement (less challenging)

	Features irrelevant to complexity
1.	Number of chromosomes in a cell
2.	Type of organism in which the processes occur

Figure 7.2 Task model for the AP biology cell division claim

use and recognize the vocabulary specific to cell division, then we would have all the evidence we need to support the claim described above. In large-scale assessment, however, we do not always have the opportunity to collect rich, performance-based tasks from students and must rely on multiple-choice items. So, rather than asking students to say, construct an explanation, multiple-choice items are designed from the observable evidence (demonstrated in the next section) and, as such, inferences about students' ability to construct an explanation are partially supported.

The next section of task model in Figure 7.2 identifies six manipulable features of task complexity identified by the SMEs. Although items with an evidentiary focus of, for example, *definition* are expected to be less challenging than items with an evidentiary focus of *explanation*, both are expected of students at the basic level of proficiency. Conversely, the features that are irrelevant to the task complexity, such as number of chromosomes in a cell, are also documented. The features that have an impact on and do not impact on task complexity are relevant to all templates derived from this task model, and should guide the identification of elements and ranges in the template.

Step 2: Creating Item Templates

An item template provides a method for generating a large number of items with similar contexts and statistical properties. Item templates are constructed by the application of the information contained in the task model to the three essential elements of the multiple-choice item: stem, options, and auxiliary information (such as a passage or diagram). For each template, the specification of which elements are fixed or allowed to vary is required. For example, the designers need to decide such things as: Will the same diagram be used for each item produced from the template, or will different diagrams be used as long as they meet specific criteria? In addition, for each template, the allowable variants (or ranges) must be specified. For example, if different diagrams are to be used, then what is the range of permissible diagrams? The number of elements that are fixed and the range of allowable variants determine where along the continuum of specificity the template is situated (see Figure 7.1). The more fixed elements and the fewer variants, the more likely that the items will be of similar psychometric characteristics, but the template may not be as generative as more flexible templates. The evidentiary focus of the template and the targeted task complexity should guide the determination of fixed and variable elements and the ranges. See Figure 7.3 for an example of one of several item templates generated from the task model in Figure 7.2.

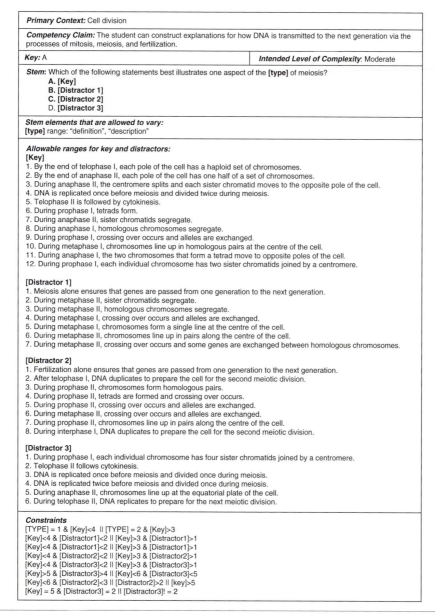

Primary Context: Cell division

Competency Claim: The student can construct explanations for how DNA is transmitted to the next generation via the processes of mitosis, meiosis, and fertilization.

| **Key:** A | **Intended Level of Complexity:** Moderate |

Stem: Which of the following statements best illustrates one aspect of the **[type]** of meiosis?
 A. **[Key]**
 B. **[Distractor 1]**
 C. **[Distractor 2]**
 D. **[Distractor 3]**

Stem elements that are allowed to vary:
[type] range: "definition", "description"

Allowable ranges for key and distractors:
[Key]
1. By the end of telophase I, each pole of the cell has a haploid set of chromosomes.
2. By the end of anaphase II, each pole of the cell has one half of a set of chromosomes.
3. During anaphase II, the centromere splits and each sister chromatid moves to the opposite pole of the cell.
4. DNA is replicated once before meiosis and divided twice during meiosis.
5. Telophase II is followed by cytokinesis.
6. During prophase I, tetrads form.
7. During anaphase II, sister chromatids segregate.
8. During anaphase I, homologous chromosomes segregate.
9. During prophase I, crossing over occurs and alleles are exchanged.
10. During metaphase I, chromosomes line up in homologous pairs at the centre of the cell.
11. During anaphase I, the two chromosomes that form a tetrad move to opposite poles of the cell.
12. During prophase I, each individual chromosome has two sister chromatids joined by a centromere.

[Distractor 1]
1. Meiosis alone ensures that genes are passed from one generation to the next generation.
2. During metaphase II, sister chromatids segregate.
3. During metaphase II, homologous chromosomes segregate.
4. During metaphase I, crossing over occurs and alleles are exchanged.
5. During metaphase I, chromosomes form a single line at the centre of the cell.
6. During metaphase II, chromosomes line up in pairs along the centre of the cell.
7. During metaphase II, crossing over occurs and some genes are exchanged between homologous chromosomes.

[Distractor 2]
1. Fertilization alone ensures that genes are passed from one generation to the next generation.
2. After telophase I, DNA duplicates to prepare the cell for the second meiotic division.
3. During prophase II, chromosomes form homologous pairs.
4. During prophase II, tetrads are formed and crossing over occurs.
5. During prophase II, crossing over occurs and alleles are exchanged.
6. During metaphase II, crossing over occurs and alleles are exchanged.
7. During prophase II, chromosomes line up in pairs along the centre of the cell.
8. During interphase I, DNA duplicates to prepare the cell for the second meiotic division.

[Distractor 3]
1. During prophase I, each individual chromosome has four sister chromatids joined by a centromere.
2. Telophase II follows cytokinesis.
3. DNA is replicated once before meiosis and divided once during meiosis.
4. DNA is replicated twice before meiosis and divided once during meiosis.
5. During anaphase II, chromosomes line up at the equatorial plate of the cell.
6. During telophase II, DNA replicates to prepare for the next meiotic division.

Constraints
[TYPE] = 1 & [Key]<4 || [TYPE] = 2 & [Key]>3
[Key]<4 & [Distractor1]<2 || [Key]>3 & [Distractor1]>1
[Key]<4 & [Distractor1]<2 || [Key]>3 & [Distractor1]>1
[Key]<4 & [Distractor2]<2 || [Key]>3 & [Distractor2]>1
[Key]<4 & [Distractor3]<2 || [Key]>3 & [Distractor3]>1
[Key]>5 & [Distractor3]>4 || [Key]<6 & [Distractor3]<5
[Key]<6 & [Distractor2]<3 || [Distractor2]>2 || [key]>5
[Key] = 5 & [Distractor3] = 2 || [Distractor3]! = 2

Figure 7.3 Item template for generating moderately challenging items on meiosis

In this template, the stem element *type* can be varied into two possible values: *definition* and *description*. Twelve keys and 21 distractors were identified. The distractors were identified by mining the information from the *big idea, enduring understanding,* and *supporting understanding* associated with the content in the claim (see Table 7.1 for an example of the richness of this information). Key options *1 to 3* concern meiosis' *definition*, and key options *4 to 12* are related to meiosis' *description*. All keys and distractors in this template correspond to the moderately challenging complexity level. The match among the keys and the distractors are delimited by constraints. For example, the first constraint *([TYPE]=1 & [Key]<4 || [TYPE]=2 & [Key]>3)* is an articulation of the relationship between the element *type* and the *key*. In other words, when *type* assumes the value *definition*, the *key* option should be one of the first three keys listed in Figure 7.3. Conversely, when *type* assumes the value of *description*, the key should assume one of the remaining nine values, starting with key number 4, in Figure 7.3. All the other constraints in this template are related to the match among keys and distractors. For instance, the last constraint of this template *([Key]=5& [Distractor3]=2||* *[Distractor3]!=2)*, specifies that the key option "Telophase II is followed by cytokinesis" has to be presented together with the distractor "Telophase II follows cytokinesis". This requirement was used to make the key and distractors parallel in form.

Step 3: Item Generation

An item generator called IGOR was used to produce items from this item template (see Gierl, Zhou, & Alves, 2008, for a description of the IGOR computer program; see also Yazdchi, Mortimer, & Stroulia, this volume). As discussed above, the number of generated items depends on several factors, including the number of elements in the stem, the range specified for the elements, the number of keys and distractors, and the number of constraints.

Three additional templates were created using similar elements and ranges as in the template above; the additional templates related to the intended cognitive complexity of the resulting items (i.e., more challenging meiosis items, less challenging mitosis items, and moderately challenging mitosis items). From these four templates, a total of 1,787 items were generated for our study (see Table 7.2).

IGOR creates items by combining all elements in the item template, subject to the specified constraints. A description of how to generate items using IGOR is presented in the item-generation process in the Appendix. One example of a generated item is presented in Figure 7.4.

Conclusions and Implications for Practice

The purpose of this chapter was to illustrate how ECD-based task models could be used to create item templates and automatically generate test items. Our study was also designed to bridge to two promising innovations in educational assessment: ECD and AIG. In particular, we demonstrated

Table 7.2 Number of generated items from the cell division template

	Keyed answers	Distractors	Number of items
Meiosis			
Template #1: Moderately challenging	12	24	1,473
Template #2: More challenging	6	13	78
Mitosis			
Template #3: Less challenging	9	9	40
Template #4: Moderately challenging	9	22	196
Total	**36**	**68**	**1,787**

Which of the following statements best illustrates one aspect of the mechanism of mitosis?

A. DNA is replicated once before mitosis and divided once during mitosis.
B. DNA is duplicated once before mitosis and divided twice during mitosis.
C. During telophase of mitosis, DNA replicates to prepare for the next mitotic division.
D. During anaphase of mitosis, homologous pairs of chromosomes move to opposite ends of the cell.

Figure 7.4 Example of one item generated with IGOR

that ECD-based task models can provide the required information at the level of specificity needed for item templates that are suitable for AIG. Recall that there are two requirements for AIG item templates: they should be specified at a level of detail sufficient for a computerized algorithm, such as IGOR, to produce items; and the determinants of task complexity should be articulated such that all of the items generated from the template have similar psychometric properties. It was outside the scope of this research project to administer the generated items to determine the degree to which their psychometric properties were similar. Nevertheless, we were pleased in being able to use the ECD-based task models to produce templates suitable for AIG (and produce lots of items!). Furthermore, we feel confident that the model of student cognition and learning in the biology domain, as embodied by the claims and evidence is a solid foundation for creating templates that can generate a great number of quality items.

Automatically generating items holds many potential benefits for assessment design and item development: (a) item development can occur more quickly because items are generated automatically; (b) challenges present in creating parallel test forms that yield comparable scores (i.e., measuring the same construct consistently and producing forms with similar psychometric properties) can be minimized because item templates can be used to generate large numbers of parallel items; (c) issues of test security become less of a concern because many test items are now available for creating tests; and (d) the costs involved in the item-development process can be significantly reduced. That said, the amount of time required to produce the claims, evidence, task model, and item templates was substantial and required very specialized content knowledge. Perhaps there are approaches to creating AIG templates that are more efficient than the one we used for our research; however, we are skeptical about the quality of templates that would be produced, absent an articulation of the fundamentals of ECD. That is, without answers to questions like *What claims do we want to make? What observable evidence is required to support those claims? What are the optimal situations (tasks) that we can construct to elicit this evidence from students?*, we doubt that the resulting templates would be useful for generating quality items. Articulating answers to these questions may be the best substitute available to us while we await theories that explain the relationship between student cognition in the domain of interest and task features that have an impact on cognitive complexity.

Future research and development efforts can build upon the work described in this chapter by exploring (a) how developing task models and templates may warrant the revision of claims and evidence, (b) the establishment of task model and template evaluation criteria that can be used throughout the design process to help improve quality; and (c) ways to make the process of task model and item template development more efficient without sacrificing quality. Huff et al. (2010) emphasize the iterative nature of the ECD process, and how the outputs of the design process improve through allowing for iteration. However, it was beyond the scope of this research to trace to what degree the SMEs' thinking about the claims and evidence evolved as they were developing the task models and item templates by considering sources of cognitive complexity and deciding whether elements should be fixed or allowed to vary, among other considerations and decisions. Plake et al. (2010) document how SMEs' thinking about claims and evidence evolved once they started to consider the relationships among claims, evidence, and proficiency levels, so it stands to reason that the SMEs would have a similar experience as a result of task model and template development.

The design of task models and templates is not a routine, step-by-step process with rigid guidelines. As such, we recommend that researchers and assessment designers explore the development of process steps and scaffolds, as well as evaluation criteria for use in task model and template design. For example, these criteria could be used to help designers identify to what degree the task model or template is at the appropriate level of specificity, the evidentiary foci are being maintained throughout the task model and template development, and the potential scalability of the task model or template. Such guidance would not only be useful in helping assessment designers with the process of task model and template development, but also has the potential of improving and guiding claim and evidence writing, such that the claims and evidence are written with applicability to task model and template development in mind.

Finally, as discussed above, the time and expertise required to construct the task models and item templates for this research project was substantial. More efficient approaches should be explored. For example, perhaps there are ways that claims and evidence could be written that would better suit them for use in task models, or, perhaps, technology (such as artificial intelligence or natural language processing) could be leveraged to do some of the "mining" described here.

As with most attempts at innovation, we must allow for practice to beget principle, as opposed to the more optimistic view that scientific principles always guide design. Fletcher indicated that "we built many bridges before we abstracted bridge-building techniques and principles" (2003, p. 30), which serves as an apt analogy here, as we have attempted to build a bridge between ECD-based task models and AIG, and we are also practicing in the absence of robust, scientific principles to guide our exploration. It is our hope that the work presented here is useful to other innovators interested in ECD, AIG or both.

Authors' Note

This project was completed with funds provided to the second author as part of the College Board Graduate Student Research Fellowship Program. The purpose of the program is to encourage and support developing young research scientists who wish to gain experience in conducting a program of research. We would like to thank the College Board for its support. However, the authors are solely responsible for the methods, procedures, and interpretations expressed in this study. Our views do not necessarily reflect those of the College Board.

Notes

1 This work was sponsored as a research project and no items produced by this project were or will be included on actual Advanced Placement (AP) examinations. This work was conducted simultaneously as the completion of the final NSF report, and as such the reader may encounter edited versions of the claims and evidence in the final NSF report. The AP Biology claims and evidence in both the final NSF report and this manuscript represent earlier versions of the materials used for current AP Biology course and assessment materials.

2 The research described in this chapter is concerned only with four-option multiple-choice items.

3 Generally speaking, in AIG literature, the term "item model" is used instead of "item template." To avoid confusion with the term "task model" (a critical component of ECD and the focus of this paper), we use the term "item template" throughout. The difference between task models and item templates is the focus of a later section of this chapter.

4 See NSF Final Report (College Board, 2010) and the 2010 fall/winter special issue of Applied Measurement in Education.

References

Bertenthal, M., Pellegrino, J., and Huff, K. (2009, May) *Leveraging research and practice: Building a large-scale, high stakes assessment that supports educational goals for teaching and learning.* Presentation at the annual conference of the American Educational Research Association, Denver, CO.

College Board (2009). *Science College Board standards for college success.* New York, NY: College Entrance Examination Board. Retrieved from http://professionals.collegeboard.com/ profdownload/Science_College_Board_Standards_for_College_Success_SCAS.pdf.

College Board (2010, May). *From research to practice: Redesigning AP science courses to advance science literacy and support learning with understanding.* Final report submitted to National Science Foundation, Award # ESI-0525575.

Drasgow, F., Luecht, R. M., & Bennett, R. E. (2006). Technology and testing. In R. L. Brennan (Ed.), *Educational measurement* (4th ed., pp. 471–515). Westport, CT: National Council on Measurement in Education and American Council on Education.

Fairon, C., & Williamson, D. (2002). Automatic item text generation in educational assessment. In *Proceedings of TALN 2002*, pp. 395–401.

Fletcher, J. (2003). Is it worth it? Some comments on research and technology in assessment and instruction. In *Technology and assessment: Thinking ahead: Proceedings of a workshop.* Washington, DC: Board on Testing and Assessment, Center for Education.

Gierl, M. J., & Lai, H. (2011). *The role of item models in automatic item generation.* CCSSO Symposium, Orlando, FL.

Gierl, M. J., Zhou, J., & Alves, C. B. (2008). Developing a taxonomy of item model types to promote assessment engineering. *The Journal of Technology, Learning, and Assessment, 7*(2), 1–51. Available from http://www.jtla.org.

Hendrickson, A., Huff, K. & Luecht, R. (2010). Claims, evidence, and achievement level descriptors as a foundation for item design and test specifications. *Applied Measurement in Education, 23,* 358–377.

Huff, K., Steinberg, L., & Matts, T. (2010). The promises and challenges of implementing evidence-centered design in large scale assessment. *Applied Measurement in Education, 23*(4), 310–324

Lai, H., Alves, C. B., & Gierl, M. J. (2009). *Using automatic item generation to address item demands for CAT.* Paper presented at the CAT Research and Applications Around the World, Minneapolis, MN.

Luecht, R. M. (2008). *Assessment engineering in test design, development, assembly, and scoring.* Presentation at East Coast Organization of Language Testers (ECOLT) Conference. Retrieved from:http://www.govtilr.org/Publications/ECOLT08-AEKeynote-RMLuecht-07Nov08%5B1%5D.pdf.

Mislevy, R.J., & Haertel, G. (2006). Implications for evidence-centered design for educational assessment. *Educational Measurement: Issues and Practice, 25,*6–20.

Mislevy, R. J., & Riconscente, M. M. (2006). Evidence-centered assessment design. In Downing, S. M., & Haladyna, T. M. (Eds.), *Handbook of test development* (pp. 61–90). Mahwah, NJ: Lawrence Erlbaum Associates.

Mislevy, R. J., Steinberg, L. S., & Almond, R. G.(2002). On the roles of task model variables in assessment design. In S. Irvine, & P. Kyllonen (Eds.), *Generating items for cognitive tests: Theory and practice.* (pp. 97–128). Hillsdale, NJ: Lawrence Erlbaum.

National Governors Association Center and Council of Chief State School Officers (2010). *Common Core State Standards for english language arts & literacy in history/social studies, science and technical subjects.* Washington, DC: Authors.

National Research Council (2001). *Knowing what students know: The science and design of educational assessment.* Committee on the Foundations of Assessment. J. W. Pellegrino, N. Chudowsky, and R. Glaser, Editors. Division of Behavioral and Social Sciences and Education. Washington, DC: National Academy Press.

National Research Council (2002). *Learning and understanding: Improving advanced study of mathematics and science in US high schools.* Committee on Programs for Advanced Study of Mathematics and Science in American High Schools. J. P. Gollub, M. W. Bertenthal, J. B. Labov, and P. C. Curtis, (Eds.) Center for Education, Washington, DC: National Academy Press.

Plake, B. S., Huff, K., & Reshetar, R. (2010). Evidence-centered assessment design as a foundation for achievement-level descriptor development and for standard setting. *Applied Measurement in Education, 23*:4, 342–357.

Schmeiser, C. B. & Welch, C. J. (2006). Test development. In R. L. Brennan (Ed.), *Educational measurement* (4th ed., pp. 307–353). Westport, CT: National Council on Measurement in Education and American Council on Education.

Williamson, D. M., Johnson, M. S., Sinharay, S., & Bejar, I. (2002). *Hierarchical IRT examination of isomorphic equivalence of complex constructed response tasks.* Paper presented at the American Educational Research Association, New Orleans, LA.

Zhou, J. (2009). *A review of assessment engineering principles with select applications to the certified public accountant examination.* Technical Report prepared for the American Institute of Certified Public Accountants. Retrieved from: http://www.cpa-exam.org/download/Zhou-A-Review-of-Assessment-Engineering.pdf.

Appendix

Generating Items from the .xmls files

A short description of the item-generation process is presented here. More detailed information can also be found in the 'Help' menu of the IGOR software.

Step 1. Double click the IGOR icon:

IGOR v1.03
Executable Jar File
2.01 MB

Step 2. Open the. xml file, for example, from "Report3\xml files\Natural Selection":

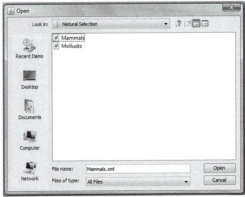

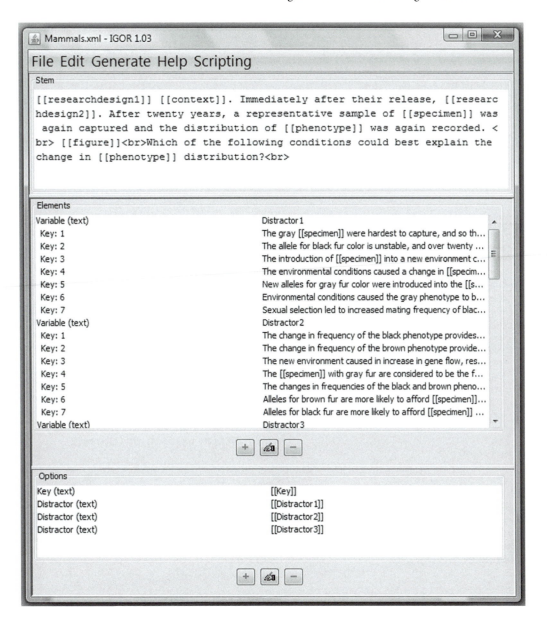

Mammals.xml - IGOR 1.03

File Edit Generate Help Scripting

Stem

[[researchdesign1]] [[context]]. Immediately after their release, [[researc
hdesign2]]. After twenty years, a representative sample of [[specimen]] was
again captured and the distribution of [[phenotype]] was again recorded. <
br> [[figure]]
Which of the following conditions could best explain the
change in [[phenotype]] distribution?

Elements

Variable (text)	Distractor 1
Key: 1	The gray [[specimen]] were hardest to capture, and so th...
Key: 2	The allele for black fur color is unstable, and over twenty ...
Key: 3	The introduction of [[specimen]] into a new environment c...
Key: 4	The environmental conditions caused a change in [[specim...
Key: 5	New alleles for gray fur color were introduced into the [[s...
Key: 6	Environmental conditions caused the gray phenotype to b...
Key: 7	Sexual selection led to increased mating frequency of blac...
Variable (text)	Distractor 2
Key: 1	The change in frequency of the black phenotype provides...
Key: 2	The change in frequency of the brown phenotype provide...
Key: 3	The new environment caused in increase in gene flow, res...
Key: 4	The [[specimen]] with gray fur are considered to be the f...
Key: 5	The changes in frequencies of the black and brown pheno...
Key: 6	Alleles for brown fur are more likely to afford [[specimen]]...
Key: 7	Alleles for black fur are more likely to afford [[specimen]] ...
Variable (text)	Distractor 3

+ 🖉 −

Options

Key (text)	[[Key]]
Distractor (text)	[[Distractor 1]]
Distractor (text)	[[Distractor 2]]
Distractor (text)	[[Distractor 3]]

+ 🖉 −

Step 3. Generate items:

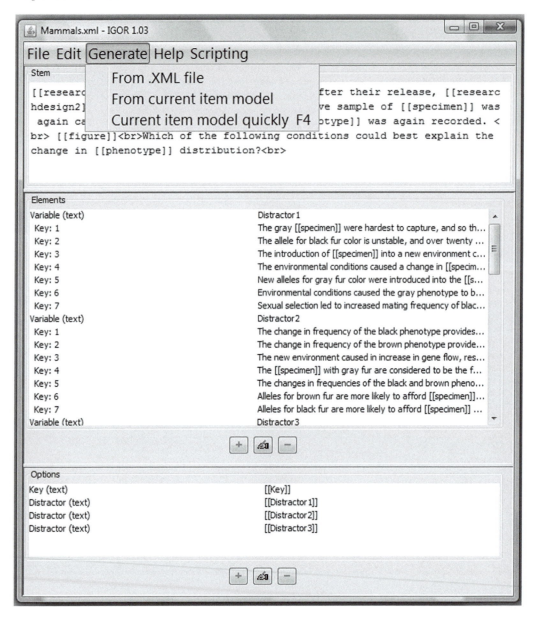

Choosing to generate **from current item template** will display a dialog for choosing where to save the .html or .doc output of the template. If one wants to create a .doc output, the **File of types** should be **All files** and an extension ".doc" should be added after the name of the file (for example, "Mammals.doc").

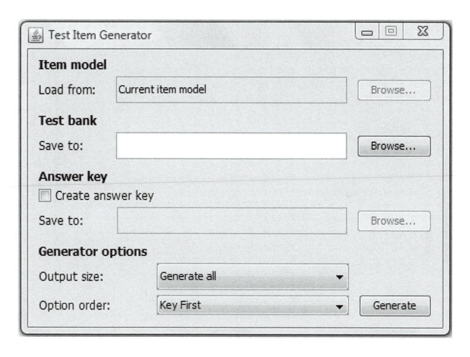

Optionally, an answer key can be created. If **Create answer key is clicked**, the resulting test bank will have the order of its options randomized. If no answer key is generated, one can choose to display the options from 5 orders:

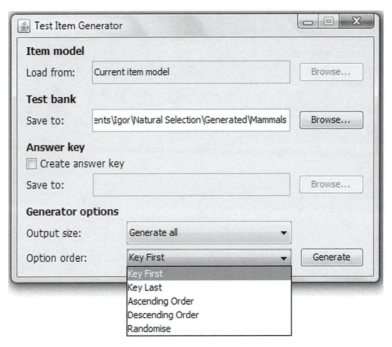

One can also choose the number of generated items. Two options are available: **Generate all** or **Limit output**. If the second option is chosen, one should specify the desired output size. In the following example, 30 items will be generated:

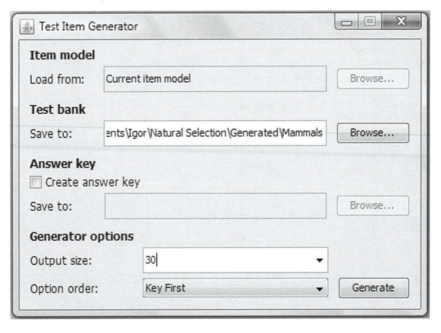

Finally, press **Generate**.

III
Psychological Foundations for Automatic Item Generation

8
Learning Sciences, Cognitive Models, and Automatic Item Generation

Jacqueline P. Leighton

Introduction

One of the goals of automatic item generation (AIG) is to standardize test-item design in the measurement of academic achievement.[1] Standardizing item design, through the use of computer technology, is expected to lead to better organization, regulation, and prediction of item characteristics than is currently the case with items designed by human writers. Although pundits have indicated that item writing is partly an art form because of its subjectivity in how item writers generate questions and options that are just right for a given purpose (e.g., Reckase, 2010; Schmeiser & Welch, 2006), item writing does have an extensive literature for the development and validation of items that possess specific psychometric properties (Drasgow, Luecht, & Bennett, 2006; Ebel, 1951; Haladyna, 1997, 2004; Schmeiser & Welch, 2006; Wesman, 1971). Despite this extensive literature for the development and validation of items, improvement is sought, namely, by minimizing the subjectivity that still characterizes traditional approaches (Bormuth, 1970). AIG is believed to standardize test-item design in *two essential ways*: (1) by making the process efficient by using computer algorithms instead of human writers to produce items and (2) by identifying the features of an item that contribute to an item's difficulty, discrimination, and construct relevance. AIG is not free from human subjectivity, as test developers must still make decisions about, for example, which features to include in item development. However, it is expected that human subjectivity will be reduced.

These two essential aspects of standardizing item design were outlined by Irvine (2002; see also Drasgow et al., 2006) in the first chapter of *Item Generation and Test Development*, one of the first volumes to describe the potential of AIG for educational measurement. In his introductory chapter, Irvine explains how Bejar's work in the mid-1980s (Bejar, 1986a,b,c), drawing from research in spatial reasoning and other areas of cognitive psychology (see, e.g., Evans, 1982; Johnson-Laird, 1983), helped to shape the thinking about these two essential aspects. For example, Bejar indicated that, to bring systematic order to item design, a computerized logical structure was needed not only to assemble items but also to tag item difficulty to figural complexity; in other words, to identify the features of items that made them cognitively demanding for examinees for construct-relevant reasons.

Other chapters in this volume focus on and discuss the first aspect of AIG—that is, the kinds of computer algorithms and logical structures that can be systematically implemented to assemble

121

and yield test items (see, for example, Lai & Gierl, this volume; Yazdchi, Mortimer, & Stroulia, this volume). For this reason, I will not elaborate on this aspect, as it has been discussed elsewhere. The purpose of this chapter is to focus on the second aspect and, specifically, to discuss the value of the learning sciences for helping to identify item features that contribute to an item's psychometric properties and construct relevance. It is in terms of this second aspect of AIG that what is called a *cognitive model of task performance* can inform test item design most directly. A cognitive model of task performance is an empirically verified representation of the knowledge and skills[2] (interchangeably used with response processes) that examinees use in order to think about and solve a set of academic achievement tasks in a specific learning domain such as reading, mathematics, or science (Leighton, 2004).

The balance of this chapter is divided into three sections. The first section elaborates on the role of the learning sciences, especially cognitive psychology, in AIG. This section explains how constructs for educational testing can be better defined, item features better identified, hypothesis tests of item features implemented, and item templates more accurately formed when learning scientific theory forms the foundation of AIG. The second section illustrates how three burgeoning lines of research, studies of examinee response processing, item difficulty modeling, and cognitive diagnostic assessment, all drawing meaningfully from learning scientific theory, can significantly inform AIG. The third section summarizes the role of the learning sciences in AIG and identifies future steps for ensuring that AIG continues to draw from a rich base of research in human learning.

Section 1: The Role of the Learning Sciences in AIG

The learning sciences can provide specific guidance to AIG programs, for example, by informing definitions of constructs and illuminating item features that are expected to elicit particular response processes in examinees. AIG programs also provide learning scientists with a unique opportunity to systematically test theories and models of cognition and academic performance. For instance, when an AIG program adopts a particular cognitive (or learning scientific) model of task performance and produces items with features that, according to the model, are expected to lead to certain levels of difficulty, the success or failure of the items in producing specific responses in examinees is essentially a test of the cognitive model. What can be learned from this test is whether the cognitive model is a useful representation of specific knowledge and skills, and also whether it is any good for item design (see Leighton & Gierl, 2011). Finding a relevant cognitive model to guide item design is difficult and may, by necessity, have to be an iterative process (Leighton & Gierl, 2011). This latter point emphasizes that there needs to be a *fit* between the AIG program and the *slice* of the learning sciences considered to inform the design of test items. Snow and Lohman (1989) emphasized this point long ago: "[T]he two most general purposes of educational measurement, the assessment of student aptitudes and achievements, would appear to *cut across the matrix of cognitive psychology in different ways ... different slices* across the field of cognitive psychology might be needed to inform test design" (p. 265, emphasis added; see also Leighton & Gierl, 2007). Factors to consider when selecting a cognitive model to inform test-item design for AIG might include not only the domain-relevance of the cognitive model, which is the most obvious, but also the grain size, and measurability of the model. For example, grain size refers to the level of specificity at which the knowledge and skills are described in the cognitive model, and measurability refers to whether the knowledge and skills can be operationalized into some type of item format (e.g., multiple-choice item; Leighton & Gierl, 2011 provide further discussion of models in reading, science, and mathematics at different grain sizes and different levels of measurability). As mentioned previously, finding an appropriate cognitive model of task performance for an AIG program can be helpful because it can guide construct definition, illuminate the item features expected to elicit specific response processes in examinees, direct hypothesis tests, and facilitate the creation of item templates. In the next section, I consider each of these in turn.

Construct Definition

According to Embretson (1983, 2007), construct definition or representation involves identifying the knowledge and skills responsible for examinees' test performance. The purpose of defining or representing constructs is to clarify the internal structure of a test, that is, what it is being measured in examinees. By clarifying what a test is measuring, test scores and inferences about examinees, based upon their test scores, are more defensible than if what the test is measuring is left unspecified. Construct definition needs to be differentiated from a related term, nomothetic *span*, which is the relationship that scores on a given test share with other tests (Embretson, 1983, 2007). This section does not focus on nomothetic span, only on construct definition.

Cognitive models of task performance can guide construct definitions for AIG programs by helping to identify the knowledge and skills required to perform on a test (e.g., Chen, Gorin, Thompson, & Tatsuoka, 2008; Embretson, & Wetzel, 1987; Gierl, Wang, & Zhou, 2008; Gorin, 2011; Gorin & Embretson, 2006; Irvine & Kyllonen, 2002; Leighton & Gierl, 2011; Leighton, Gierl & Hunka, 2004; Mislevy et al., 2010; Nichols, 1994). For example, shown in Figure 8.1 is a cognitive model for the test, the *Spanish Screener for Language Impairment in Children* (SSLIC; Gorin, 2011). Gorin (2011) describes the SSLIC as a screening measure developed to identify pre-Kindergarten to Grade 3 children who are Spanish-speaking and at risk for showing impairments in their language skills across distinct dialects, socioeconomic levels, and ethnicities. In other words, the SSLIC aims to differentiate between those Spanish-speaking children who have language impairments from those who are developing language normally.

According to the model in Figure 8.1, impairments in the Spanish language consist of two broad categories—*processing* and *linguistic*. Under the processing impairment, deficits can be related to capacity or speed. Under the linguistic impairment, deficits can be related to grammar or semantics. Classes of tasks or items which can be used to measure these deficits are listed below the categories

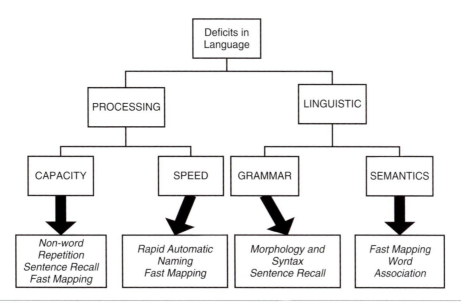

Figure 8.1 Cognitive model (theoretical framework) for SSLIC (adapted from Gorin, 2011)

of impairments. For example, items requiring examinees to engage in non-word repetition are used to measure deficits in processing capacity, and items requiring examinees to engage in rapid automatic naming measure deficits in processing speed. What is noteworthy about the model is that it explicitly identifies the constructs that the test measures (i.e., processing and linguistic) as well as sub-constructs (capacity, speed; and grammar, semantics). Further, the cognitive model shows the relationships between constructs, and the items or tasks that can be used to measure the constructs.

Identifying Item Features

Another way in which cognitive models of task performance can be useful to AIG is when they facilitate the identification of item features that can be expected to elicit particular response processes in examinees (e.g., Gorin, 2011; Irvine & Kyllonen, 2002; Leighton & Gokiert, 2008; see also Clark, 1969; Johnson-Laird, 1983; Johnson-Laird & Bara, 1984). Findings from research in deductive thinking, in particular, and problem solving on categorical, conditional, and linear syllogisms (see Newstead, Bradon, Handley, Evans, & Dennis, 2002; also Johnson-Laird & Bara, 1984) indicate that the manipulation of specific task features influences participants' task performance. Specific task features that influence performance include use of negation, marked adjectives, and content. For example, when negation is used in the text of a problem solving task such as *John is <u>not</u> as heavy as Bob* versus *John is lighter than Bob*, it increases the time required (in seconds) for individuals to process the task, and also the percentage of correct responses (Clark, 1969). Marked adjectives also influence difficulty in terms of processing time and percentage of correct responses. For example, the adjective *shorter* increases information processing time because it is *marked*, meaning that it does not embody the full dimension of height, as does the adjective *taller*, which is more often used to convey comparative information about height. Consider that when inquiring about John's height, someone is apt to ask *how tall he is* rather than *how short he is*. The content of a problem-solving task also influences its difficulty. Abstract content increases task difficulty and thematic content decreases difficulty (for a recent review of factors influencing reasoning and problem-solving tasks, see Leighton & Sternberg, in press).

Specific task features, such as use of negation or marked adjectives, make the creation of mental representations onerous, thus increasing the time and complexity of information processing for examinees (Johnson-Laird & Bara, 1984; Kyllonen & Christal, 1990). Task or item features such as use of negation can require examinees to keep track of multiple components in the mental representation of a task. For example, consider the representations below for *not tall* versus *short*:

(1) ~ Tall   (2) Short

The first representation has two components: the "~" and "tall." Now consider the second representation, which has only a single component: "short." When multiple components must be attended to in working memory, the likelihood that all components are (a) included and (b) accurately incorporated in a mental representation of the task declines, jeopardizing the fidelity of the representation created to solve the problem (Leighton & Sternberg, in press). Decades of studies have now established that tasks requiring individuals to consider multiple components in working memory are more difficult to represent than tasks requiring single components (Baddeley, 2006; Johnson-Laird, 1983; Johnson-Laird & Bara, 1984; Kyllonen & Christal, 1990; Sternberg & Pretz, 2005).

Because certain task features can either strain or lighten the load on working memory, the mental representations created, and the reasoning and problem solving that ensues from these representations, performance can be potentially undermined or enhanced (Leighton & Sternberg, in press). It is also important to note that task features, which unintentionally obscure task objectives by being ambiguous or confusing, can unnecessarily tax working memory and increase task difficulty by forcing problem solvers to create faulty mental representations. For example, Leighton and Gokiert (2008) identified problematic features in 30 items. These features were expected to pose information-processing difficulties for examinees as they responded to the items. The features included an item's *structural format* (e.g., poor graphics), *words and phrases* (e.g., unfamiliar and non-construct related words), and *background context* (e.g., poorly written background stories). Although Leighton and Gokiert were not focused on the influence of these features on an item's difficulty per se, they were interested in the influence of these features on the uncertainty and ambiguity that they might create for examinees as they answered items. Toward this end, Leighton and Gokiert created an *item ambiguity score* for each item, based on the presence of specific problematic features. They also calculated an *item misinterpretation score* for each item by asking examinees, who were unaware of the problematic items, how likely it would be for another student to have trouble understanding the items. Controlling for item difficulty, Leighton and Gokiert found that item-ambiguity scores were positively related to item-misinterpretation scores, indicating that examinees were sensitive to potentially misinterpreting items with ambiguous features. Findings from this research suggest that specific item features could negatively influence examinees' item performance.

Specific features can also directly influence the difficulty of items for examinees. For example, Gorin (2011; for a similar study in reading comprehension see Sheehan, Kostin, Futagi, & Flor, 2011) demonstrates an incidence (or Q) matrix for *sentence recall* items used in the SSLIC assessment mentioned previously. According to the SSLIC cognitive model shown in Figure 8.1, sentence-recall items are expected to measure processing capacity and knowledge of linguistics and grammar. Sentence-recall items can be designed to include increasingly more complex textual features such as intransitive, transitive, causal, relative, and conditional features. The full list of features expected to influence the difficulty of sentence recall tasks include (1) number of words, (2) number of arguments, (3) number of adjuncts, (4) phrase structure, (5) sentence complexity (i.e., complex sentence structure with subordinate or "if" clause), (6) presence of conditional verbs or adjuncts, (7) the use of temporal adjuncts, (8) causal adjuncts, and (9) presence of relative clauses. To operationalize the presence of these features in sentence-repetition items, Gorin identified features 1 through 4 as polytomous and coded these as continuous variables, and features 5 through 9 were identified as discrete and coded dichotomously.

Gorin (2011) then created 33 sentence-recall tasks to be individually administered and scored for percentage of words correct and overall correctness. Gorin evaluated the predictive value of these nine item features by conducting a variety of analyses. For example, she regressed 33 estimates of item difficulty on the nine features. The best-fitting model, showing an adjusted R^2 of 0.56, was found to have three predictors, including number of words, use of a relative clause, and complex sentence structure with a subordinate or "if" clause. Another analysis was conducted for between-group effects. That is, for each of the 33 items, the language-ability groups (i.e., language impairment versus typical development) were compared for their item performance and an eta-squared was calculated. Gorin then regressed the nine item features on the 33 effect sizes. The best-fitting model, showing an adjusted R^2 of 0.33, included four predictors: number of words, relative clauses, complex structure, and conditional clauses. Because one of the objectives of the SSLIC is to differentiate between language-impaired and typically developing students, the association between the item features and effect sizes was especially instructive in terms of illuminating which features could be used to distinguish language-impaired versus typically developing students.

Although Gorin (2011) warns that the results from this study must be interpreted with caution, as the sample size comprised only 151 students and, as such, item statistics may be unstable, the overall implementation of her study and its results suggest a promising line of research for AIG (this is further elaborated in section two of this chapter). First, Gorin demonstrates that items can be purposefully designed based on a cognitive model, thus reflecting cognitively based item features. Second, Gorin illustrates how these cognitively based item features are associated with particular psychometric properties such as producing specific values of item difficulty. The challenge then is to "scaleup" this type of item-difficulty modeling research by creating item templates or prototypes with slots that can be filled with exemplars of features that are known to elicit particular knowledge and skills in examinees. Such item templates would be expected to allow the "on-the-fly" generation (i.e., very quick production of items because of the routinized nature of the process) of many, diverse items with predictable item properties. I discuss the value of item difficulty modeling more generally in the second section of this chapter.

To scale up research on cognitively based item-difficulty modeling and leverage these findings to build AIG programs that are grounded in the learning sciences, items must be understood as consisting of component parts. The decomposition must identify those cognitive features that are expected to elicit predictable knowledge and skills in examinees (e.g., varying degrees of quantitative knowledge, sophistication in simplifying an equation, etc.) from those parts that are not. Another way of describing this is to say that the *radical* parts of the item must be distinguished from the *incidental* parts. As articulated by Irvine (2002), radicals are:

> [D]efined as those theoretically consonant structural elements of items, which, as quasi independent variables, will cause statistically significant changes in item difficulties measured by error rate and/or time to completion. These can be distinguished from *incidentals*, those surface characteristics of items that preserve serial independence but, when allowed to vary randomly within item strata, exert no significant influence on item difficulty. (p. 12)

The one limitation with this definition is that it does not emphasize why radicals exert statistically significant changes in item difficulties and why incidentals do not. Without being able to trace the effect of radicals to expected changes in elicited knowledge and skills, by way of a cognitive model of task performance, the identification of radicals is not linked substantively to a theoretical source that can continually inform the identification of new radicals. Instead, it is largely ad hoc. Irvine (2002) lists a series of learning scientific studies that have shown how item-difficulty values (i.e., classical p-values) can be predicted from variations in radicals. One of the more prominent examples is the work of Dennis, Collis, and Dann (1995) in which the p-values of verbal comprehension tasks were predicted with a linear model using sentence type, degree of grammatical transformation, and word length. In most of these examples, what makes these studies compelling is that the predictions of task difficulty are tied to theories (e.g., theories of verbal comprehension or spatial reasoning [Shepard & Metzler, 1971]), and the theoretically grounded variables that are expected to increase the complexity of, for instance, mentally rotating spatial objects.

Another concern is that the theories that have so far been used to inform the identification of radical components have tended to focus more on what we traditionally view as *abilities*, such as processing capacity and speed, and less so on knowledge and skills (see note 2; for a review see Irvine, 2002). For example, the task features (e.g., negation, marked adjectives) that are often "branded" as radical components in spatial rotation tasks, figural tasks, and categorical syllogisms (Irvine, 2002) are features that mainly influence working memory (Kyllonen & Christal, 1990), rather than knowledge of specific subject matter. Although processing capacity may be important to consider in measuring academic achievement (Sternberg & Pretz, 2005), specific subject-matter knowledge and skill mastery will also be needed, as this usually makes up the outcome information that school officials are interested in knowing for accountability purposes. For this reason, AIG initiatives might need to consider cognitive models of task performance that include not just radical components that influence processing capacity (e.g., working memory load) but also the role of knowledge and skill mastery required in academic domains—such as in reading comprehension, scientific reasoning, and mathematical reasoning for the purpose of test design (see Leighton & Gierl, 2011).

Hypothesis Tests and Item Templates

Once radicals and incidentals are distinguished, experimental tests can be conducted to evaluate hypotheses about whether the radical components identified do, in fact, lead to increased or reduced performances in examinees, in comparison to incidental components. In writing about item-difficulty modeling (IDM), Gorin (2011, pp. 18–19) recognizes the value of cognitive models for guiding this type of systematic hypothesis testing of items features:

> IDM is nothing more than good experimental design. As with IDM approaches to item and test development, one designs experimental stimuli by carefully controlling all possible variables in theoretically prescribed ways. Differences in response patterns and probabilities can then be interpreted in terms of the stimulus design. In earnest, the difference between IDM studies and traditional cognitive psychology experiments is a reflection of the disciplinary differences in theoretical and practical focus.

As Gorin points out, experimental research sophistication is required for investigating the types of item features (i.e., radical components) that elicit particular knowledge and skills in examinees and provide evidence about what makes items difficult or easy. For example, examinee performance on item Y with a negation in a sentence must be compared to examinee performance on the exact item Y (controlling all other variables) without the negation in the sentence. Examinees must be randomly assigned to each level of item Y. If item Y with the negation leads to greater processing times for examinees and a lower percentage of correct responses relative to item Y without the negation, the resulting inference of what made the item difficult is stronger—the presence of the negation is causally responsible for the increase in difficulty. It is this level of experimental rigor that needs to accompany item-difficulty modeling and other research that aims to provide evidence about item features—radicals and incidentals—to confidently fill slots in AIG templates.

According to Gierl and Lai (2011, p. 6; see also Mislevy & Riconscente, 2006) *item templates* serve "as an explicit representation of the variables in an assessment task, which includes the stem, the options [i.e., only in multiple-choice items], and often times auxiliary information [e.g., images or digital media] (Gierl, Zhou, & Alves, 2008)." Further, Gierl and Lai indicate that the stem and options included in the item template are made up of elements—that is, radical and incidental components, formalized as strings of numeric (i.e., integers) and non-numeric values (i.e., variables). These elements or components can then be systematically manipulated to generate *item exemplars*. Item exemplars are specific forms of the item that have been derived from an item template. Manipulating incidental and radical components can generate multiple item exemplars.

A variety of names have been used to refer to item templates, including item models (Gierl & Lai, 2011), templates (Mislevy & Riconscente), and schemas (Singley & Bennett, 2002). Another term that could be used to describe an item template is an item *frame* (Minsky, 1974). Similar to a script or schema, a frame is a type of representation that organizes knowledge and assigns values to *slots* within the frame (Minsky, 1974). For example, the script for dining out at a restaurant may be viewed as a frame with various slots or placeholders in which to include specific information about what to expect from the experience, such as the type of restaurant, the reasons for celebration, the cost of the meal, and the dress code. Describing general item structures as *templates* or frames signals that these are general representations that contain placeholders, which are designed to hold distinct values of item information considered critical in order to elicit response processes in examinees. Item features that would be expected to be inserted into the slots or placeholders are, for example, those radical components that have been identified from cognitive models as influencing item performance.

Item templates will not be described further in this chapter, as this concept is more technically elaborated in other chapters in this volume. However, I highlight item templates here to point out that this general structure requires the *filling in of slots* with precise information about radical and incidental components. However, without defensible data on radical or incidental components, it is unlikely that these item templates will generate good item exemplars. Consequently, AIG requires not only information about which item features might be reasonably labeled radical and incidental components, but also evidence that this labeling has been obtained from cognitive models of task performance and acquired via controlled experimentation to warrant causal inferences about which features lead to particular response processes in examinees, along with concomitant item difficulty estimates. In addition, further thought is needed on whether the differences between knowledge, skills, abilities, and a variety of other terms used to describe cognitive competencies are sufficiently well understood by educational researchers and test developers to communicate what is being measured by the particular filling of slots in item templates. Much of the early research on radical components has been focused on measuring cognitive ability, such as working memory (see Irvine, 2002). Working memory is a necessary raw material for learning, using, and coordinating academic knowledge and skills (for a review see Sternberg & Pretz, 2005). However, in order to meet specific educational accountability demands and objectives, measurement of subject-matter knowledge and skills will also be required.

Section 2: Three Lines of Research to Inform AIG

In light of the preceding discussion, this section outlines three lines of research that can be expected to inform AIG. These are not the only lines of research but they do stand out as the most promising at this point in time. The first line of research is the study of examinees' response processes, especially those studies involving think-aloud protocols, including eye-tracking data. The second line of research is item-difficulty modeling. The third line of research is cognitive diagnostic assessment (CDA). These three lines of research are not mutually exclusive, but will be treated as separate in the following sections for ease of presentation.

Think-Aloud Studies

When properly executed, the collection of verbal reports can be useful in helping to reveal the knowledge and skills that examinees use to solve educational items. In addition to providing information about the knowledge and skills examinees use to problem solve, verbal reports can also provide evidence of the features in a test item that have led to specific response processing in examinees. Because an examinee must verbalize all his or her thoughts when solving the item, often the examinee will reveal, either intentionally or not, parts of the item that are considered to be challenging in solving the task. Researchers can use this information to make a decision about whether the source of the difficulty was intended—that is, the source of difficulty is construct relevant—or is irrelevant. If the source of the difficulty is construct relevant and appears to be functioning properly, in so far as it is discriminating students who have acquired specific forms of knowledge and skills from those who have not, this information can be considered and modeled as a radical component in an item template. For example, examinees requested to think aloud while solving categorical syllogisms reported that the consideration of multiple mental models to solve categorical syllogisms made those syllogisms more difficult to solve than others requiring the consideration of a single mental model (Leighton & Gokiert, 2005; Leighton & Gierl, 2007 for a more recent discussion of this finding; see also Johnson-Laird & Bara, 1984). In particular, categorical syllogisms requiring multiple mental models in order to solve them were those that contained specific quantifiers, such as "Some ... not," in their premises. That examinees found certain quantifiers to be more cognitively demanding than other quantifiers provides evidence about the status of quantifiers as radical components that could be incorporated into item templates of categorical syllogisms (see Irvine & Kyllonen, 2002). Other studies have found that test items containing construct-irrelevant words and terms are confusing for examinees and lead to unintentional sources of difficulty (e.g., Gierl, 1997; see also Leighton & Gokiert, 2008). In cases where test item features elicit knowledge and skills in students that are different from those expected by test developers, efforts should be made to remove construct-irrelevant radical components from the items.

One limitation with think-aloud studies is that it is often not possible to isolate the specific item feature causing a specific form of response processing in examinees. In think-aloud studies, in particular those non-experimental studies conducted in education, examinees are often requested to verbally describe their thinking as they are solving items composed of many distinct features (e.g., words, graphics, and format). Many of these features are left uncontrolled and examinees may identify a variable as problematic, but, in fact, this variable may not be responsible for the increased item difficulty. As such, evidence gathered from non-experimental think-aloud studies needs to be viewed as exploratory and requiring further evaluation to ensure that the cause-effect relationships noted between item features and performance are real. For this reason, studies of item-difficulty modeling can be helpful in elucidating the cause–effect relationships between test-item variables and subsequent item difficulty. Studies of item-difficulty modeling are discussed in the next section.

Item-Difficulty Modeling

Identifying construct-relevant item features that lead to changes in item difficulty is another area of research that is useful for AIG (e.g., Gorin & Embretson, 2006). Embretson (1984; see, for example, the general multicomponent latent trait model [GMLTM]) was one of the first investigators to propose a systematic procedure for describing the relationship between item features and changes in item difficulty by incorporating information about examinee response processing. More recently, Gorin and Embretson (2006) identified features of paragraph comprehension items found in the Graduate Record Exam (GRE) that were responsible for changes in item difficulty. Through a process of cognitive decomposition made possible by developments in artificial intelligence for quantifying textual material believed to influence the response processing required of examinees, combinations of item features were identified and then tested as contributing to the difficulty of paragraph-comprehension items in the GRE. Using regression to model the relationship between an item's cognitive demands, format (i.e., decision processes required of examinees to respond to a multiple-choice item), and item difficulty, Gorin and Embretson found that decision processes contributed more to item difficulty than did examinees' text-comprehension skills. The importance of this research is twofold: First, the results suggest that item content is only one aspect of what is important to consider when modeling item difficulty, with item format being a non-trivial aspect well; and second, that systematic item-difficulty modeling can and, perhaps, must be guided by cognitive theory of what influences examinee response processing in order to ensure that combinations of item features are properly identified (see also Daniel & Embretson, 2010).

In another example of the beneficial role that the learning sciences and cognitive theory play in item-difficulty modeling, Gorin (2011) demonstrates systematic methods for linking or associating item features, based on a cognitive model, to changes in item difficulty. These methods were described in the first section of this chapter (Identifying Item Features and Hypothesis Tests and Item Templates), and so will not be repeated here. Similar investigations are being conducted in other academic domains for the purpose of designing cognitive complexity in mathematics items (Daniel & Embretson, 2010) and explaining the difficulty of computer-generated Figural Matrix Items (Freund, Hofer, & Holling, 2008). In particular, the results of Freund et al. (2008) are especially promising to AIG, as they indicate that matrix items with known psychometric properties can be generated in a relatively straightforward fashion when well-defined computerized algorithms are employed.

Although item-difficulty modeling offers an avenue for identifying reliable associations between item features and changes in item difficulty, the value of this work for AIG rests on attention to substantive details. Gorin (2011) makes four recommendations, which underscore this latter point and bear repeating here. First, the existing theory for the construct that is being assessed by the test must be considered (see also Daniel & Embretson, 2010). Constructs that have not caught the interest of learning scientists may not be associated with cognitive models or theory. Therefore, item-difficulty modeling may be most directly beneficial to AIG in domains where there are identifiable cognitive models. Second, test developers must be precise about the uses of test scores and the substance of the inferences to be made about examinees based upon test scores. Third, items developed must be viewed as tests of the theory from which the test has been developed. Fourth, the characteristics of the examinees must be considered in light of the theory from which the test is developed. To the extent that each of these four recommendations is heeded in item-difficulty modeling research, the results will be most useful to AIG programs interested in generating item exemplars (from item templates) based on cognitively rich evidence of radical components and examinee response processing.

Cognitive Diagnostic Assessment

Another area of research that may prove useful to AIG is cognitive diagnostic assessment (CDA; see Nichols, Chipman, & Brennan, 1995; see also Leighton & Gierl, 2007). CDA involves developing test items from cognitive models of task performance to support strong test-based inferences about examinees' knowledge and skills in academic domains. However, what is more often done is to apply or *retrofit* a cognitive model to an existing set of test items that has not been developed from the cognitive model directly but has been developed from a traditional set of test specifications. Much more research has been generated about retrofitting cognitive models to exiting test items than about how test items can be developed anew from a cognitive model (for review, see Leighton & Gierl, 2007, 2011). There are a number of research areas devoted to exploring CDA, including work on statistical models for diagnostic-skill classification (e.g., Roussos, DiBello, Stout, Hartz, Henson, & Templin, 2007; Rupp & Templin, 2008; Rupp, Templin, & Henson, 2010) and identifying cognitive models of task performance across academic domains (Leighton & Gierl, 2011).

Although work on CDA is being done on both statistical and learning scientific fronts, the work that is focused on the learning scientific front may uniquely contribute to AIG. This is because research devoted to identifying cognitive models of task performance, which outline the sequence of knowledge and skills (i.e., response processes) examinees use to respond to a set of test items of increasing difficulty within a task domain, may contribute to a better understanding of the *classes of features* expected to influence performance. The main difference between how CDA can inform AIG and how research on item-difficulty modeling can inform AIG is that CDA aims to identify more than independent item features and their effects on item difficulty. CDA also aims to understand the interplay of students' knowledge and skills and test-item responses. In other words, it is not sufficient for CDA to simply establish an empirical association between an item feature—for example, the use of negation in sentences—and item difficulty. It is also necessary in CDA to have a model of examinees' knowledge and skills, and to relate this model to test-item development and performance in order to provide a fuller account of what knowledge and skills are being measured in students.

To illustrate how CDA can inform AIG in terms of identifying the knowledge and skills students use to respond to items, an example taken from Leighton, Cui, and Cor (2009) is shown presently. Leighton et al. (2009) compared the adequacy of two distinct cognitive models for predicting examinee performance on a *sample* of algebra I and II items from the March 2005 administration of the SAT. The two models are shown in Figures 8.2 and 8.3.

The first cognitive model was generated from the verbal reports of 21 moderately high-ability examinees as they solved the SAT algebra items from the 2005 administration. These 21 examinees

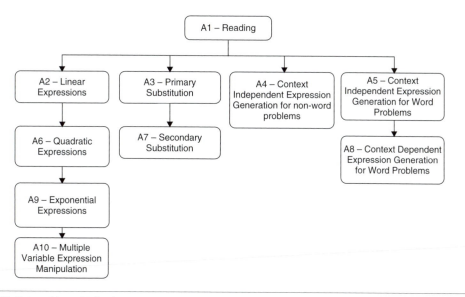

Figure 8.2 First cognitive model of performance on algebra items based on students' verbal reports

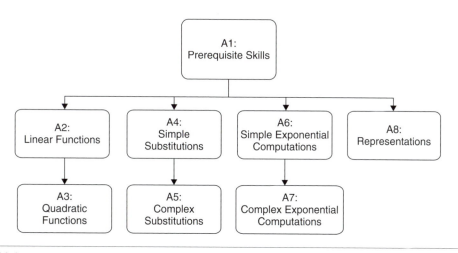

Figure 8.3 Second cognitive model of performance on algebra items based on expert's content knowledge

had taken the PSAT and were recruited using the College Board's student search service. These examinees were also en route to take the SAT. The second cognitive model was generated from the content knowledge of a mathematics and statistics expert. A cognitive IRT procedure called the *attribute hierarchy method* (AHM; Leighton et al., 2004) and its companion person-fit index, the *hierarchy consistency index* (HCI; Cui & Leighton, 2009; Cui, Leighton, Gierl, & Hunka, 2006) were then used to evaluate the adequacy of the two cognitive models for predicting the sequence of item responses of three groups or samples of examinees. The samples included (1) 5,000 randomly selected examinees who had completed the algebra items from the March 2005 administration of the SAT, (2) the 21 examinees of moderately high ability, who provided the verbal reports from which the first cognitive model was developed, and (3) 100 examinees of moderately high ability who were sampled from the group of 5,000 randomly selected examinees.

Leighton et al. (2009) found that the first cognitive model, developed from the verbal reports of 21 moderately high-ability examinees, adequately predicted the item responses of the 21 and 100 moderately high-ability examinees. However, this first cognitive model did not predict, as well, the responses of the group of 5,000 examinees. In contrast, the second cognitive model, developed from the content knowledge of the expert in mathematics and statistics, adequately predicted the responses of the 5,000 examinees, but less so the responses of the 21 and 100 moderately high-ability examinees. When Leighton et al. (2009) considered the potential reasons for the discrepancy between how the two cognitive models fit the student responses, they noted the differences between the samples (i.e., the sample of 5,000 versus the samples of 21 and 100 examinees) and how the "student reference" group considered in the development of the two models could have influenced the knowledge and skills included in the models. For example, the sample of 5,000 examinees, which was randomly selected from the larger group of students who completed the March 2005 administration of the SAT, was normally distributed around a lower level of achievement. Given this distribution, the average ability level of the students in this sample was lower than the average ability level of the students in the sample of 21 or in the sample of 100—who were specifically selected to reflect higher levels of achievement. Moreover, Leighton et al. (2009) noted that the first cognitive model had been created from the reports of these moderately high-ability examinees, so it was not surprising that this model would reflect the knowledge and skills (i.e., response processes) of higher-ability examinees. In contrast, the second cognitive model had been created by an expert in mathematics and statistics who was only provided with the general instructions to consider the knowledge and skills that a student would need to have to solve the items. As such, it is likely that the expert thought of a prototypical "average" student when developing the cognitive model—the examinees most frequently represented in the group of 5,000. In short, the differential fit of the cognitive models likely reflected the characteristics of the "student reference" group considered when the models were developed.

What Leighton et al. (2009) found in their results, then, is that a single cognitive model may not accurately reveal the knowledge and skills of groups of examinees with different ability levels. The reason for highlighting these results in light of AIG initiatives is to show that similar items may probe different response processes in examinees of differing ability. Developing algorithms to generate items with known psychometric properties may need to consider not only how specific item features influence response difficulty, but also how specific item features interact with students of particular ability levels to influence performance. Depending on the ability level of the students being considered, different response processes may underlie patterns of item responses. One limitation with this research is that specific item features are not isolated but considered simultaneously when comparing the fit between students' item responses and cognitive models.

Section 3: Discussion and Conclusion

The chapter was divided into two main sections. The first section elaborated on the role of the learning sciences, especially cognitive psychology, in AIG. The second section illustrated how three lines of research—studies of examinee response processing, item-difficulty modeling, and cognitive diagnostic assessment—all drawing meaningfully from findings in the learning sciences, can potentially inform AIG. This final section summarizes the role of the learning sciences in AIG and identifies future steps for ensuring that AIG continues to draw from a rich base of research in human learning.

A goal of AIG is to generate items systematically so that large quantities can be designed to have known psychometric properties. Achieving this goal offers a unique opportunity to generate increasingly better validity arguments because it forces test developers to better understand the features of items that elicit specific knowledge and skills in examinees. In efforts to predict what, specifically, will make one item more difficult than another, there is an opportunity to better under-stand the interaction between item features and examinees' response processes. The realm of exami-nees' response processes can be informed by the learning sciences. The learning sciences can guide the construct representation of tests and items, the specific item features that elicit particular response processing in students, and how these item features may be bundled together in item templates to systematically generate items of known psychometric properties. The learning sciences offers AIG a practical and theoretically sensible starting-place for designing items—what is known about human learning and performance within a particular academic domain, what features or variables make the domain more difficult or less difficult for a problem solver to navigate, and the specific environ-ments, made up of arrangements of features that elicit particular knowledge and skill paths. Instead of beginning from "best guesses" of what might influence problem solving, the learning sciences provide AIG a starting-point on how to begin to think about items so that their design can be made more scientific and less subjective

There are three lines of research that I believe can help AIG efforts, because each line involves actively exploring the interaction between students' response processes and test item features: think-aloud studies of examinees' response processes, item-difficulty modeling, and cognitive diagnostic assessment. The benefit of think-aloud studies is that they provide a source of evidence of how item features may be represented in students' minds, how students perceive items, and how they respond to them. These studies, while often exploratory, can be a source of hypotheses about why certain items behave in particular ways. The benefit of item-difficulty modeling is to isolate particular item features and empirically test whether they do or do not have expected effects on examinees' perform-ance. The benefit of cognitive diagnostic assessment is that a cognitive model is designed to illustrate the knowledge and skills that examinees will use to solve sequences of test items of increasing dif-ficulty and to support strong test-based inferences about examinees' test-item performance.

To conclude, in order to help ensure that the learning sciences can facilitate AIG, research into think-aloud studies, item-difficulty modeling, and cognitive diagnostic assessment must continue. However, this research needs to be thoughtfully synthesized with AIG initiatives and programs. That is, AIG enthusiasts, hopefully, recognize that they are not alone in trying to understand how a bet-ter test item can be generated, albeit more systematically, and that the major difference between a researcher in AIG and one conducting research in examinee response processing, item-difficulty modeling, or cognitive diagnostic assessment is the angle at which the problem of how to measure student learning is conceptualized and focused. Each angle provides a clue on how to build a better item, a better test, with greater scientific grounding, so that, ultimately, better psychometric results and stronger inferences about human learning can be produced. In other words, AIG provides another, perhaps more systematic, attempt to improve the validity of inferences about what students know and can do, based on their test results.

Notes

1 AIG can also be applied to generation of test items in domains other than academic achievement. However, in this chapter, my focus is on academic achievement.

2 The terms *knowledge* and *skills* are used in the present chapter. These terms are not used interchangeably with *cognitive ability* because they are viewed as theoretically distinct. Knowledge and skills are more commonly used terms in educational parlance to convey ideas about learned subject matter and share fewer associations with conceptions about innate mental ability and *intelligence*. As an example, in a recent article by Stanovich and West (2008), the terms cognitive ability, intelligence, and IQ were used interchangeably in the introductory sentence: "In psychology and among the lay public alike, assessments of intelligence and tests of cognitive ability are taken to be the sine qua non of good thinking. Critics of these instruments often point out that IQ tests fail to assess many domains of psychological functioning that are essential" (p. 672). Influential researchers in education (e.g., Lohman, 2005) and psychology (e.g., Sternberg, 1999) have put forward the argument that school curriculum and instruction are avenues for developing cognitive ability. Further, they suggest that what we label as cognitive ability may simply be very well-learned knowledge and skills. However, others debate the manipulability of cognitive ability (see Jensen, 1998).

References

Baddeley, A. D. (2006) Working memory: An overview. In S. Pickering, (Ed.), *Working memory and education* (pp. 1–31). New York: Academic Press

Bejar, I. I. (1986a). *The psychometrics of mental rotation (RR-86-19)*. Princeton, NJ: Educational Testing Service.

Bejar, I. I. (1986b). *Analysis and generation of Hidden Figure items: A cognitive approach to psychometric modeling (RR-86-20)*. Princeton, NJ: Educational Testing Service.

Bejar, I. I. (1986c). *Final report: Adaptive testing of spatial abilities (ONR 150 131)*. Princeton, NJ: Educational Testing Service.

Bormuth, J. R. (1970). *On the theory of achievement test items*. Chicago, IL: University of Chicago Press.

Chen, Y-H., Gorin, J. S., Thompson, M. S., & Tatsuoka, K. K. (2008). Cross-cultural validity of the TIMSS-1999 mathematics test: Verification of a cognitive model. *International Journal of Testing, 8*, 251–271.

Clark, H. H. (1969). Linguistic processes in deductive reasoning. *Psychological Review, 76*, 387–404.

Cui, Y., & Leighton, J. P. (2009). The hierarchy consistency index: Evaluating person fit for cognitive diagnostic assessment. *Journal of Educational Measurement, 46*, 429–449.

Cui, Y., Leighton, J. P., Gierl, M. J., & Hunka, S. (2006, April). *The hierarchical consistency index: A person-fit statistic for the attribute hierarchical model*. Paper presented at the annual meeting of the National Council on Measurement in Education (NCME), San Francisco, CA, USA.

Daniel, R. C., & Embretson, S. E. (2010). Designing cognitive complexity in mathematical problem-solving items. *Applied Psychological Measurement, 34*, 348–364.

Dennis, I.,Collis, J. M., & Dann, P. I. (1995, October). Extending the scope of item generation to tests of educational attainment. *Proceedings of the 37th International Military Testing Association Conference*. Toronto, Canada.

Drasgow, F., Luecht, R. M., & Bennett, R. E. (2006). Technology and testing. In R. L. Brennan (Ed.), *Educational measurement* (4th ed., pp. 471–515). Westport, CT: National Council on Measurement in Education and American Council on Education.

Ebel, R. L. (1951). Writing the test item. In E. F. Lindquist (Ed.), *Educational measurement* (1st ed., pp. 185–249). Washington, DC: American Council on Education.

Embretson, S. (1983). Construct validity: Construct representation versus nomothetic span? *Psychological Bulletin, 93*, 179–197.

Embretson, S. E. (1984). A general multicomponent latent trait model for response processes. *Psychometrika, 49*, 175–186.

Embretson, S. (2007). Construct validity: A universal validity system or just another test evaluation procedure? *Educational Researcher, 36*, 449–455.

Embretson, S. E., & Wetzel, C. D. (1987). Component latent trait models for paragraph comprehension. *Applied Psychological Measurement, 11*, 175–193.

Evans, J. St. B. T. (1982). *The psychology of deductive reasoning*. London: Routledge.

Freund, Ph. A., Hofer, S., & Holling, H. (2008). Explaining and controlling for the psychometric properties of computer-generated figural matrix items. *Applied Psychological Measurement, 32*, 195–210.

Gierl, M. J. (1997). Comparing the cognitive representations of test developers and students on a mathematics achievement test using Bloom's taxonomy. *Journal of Educational Research, 91*, 26–32.

Gierl, M. J., & Lai, H. (2011, April). *The role of item models in automatic item generation*. Paper presented at the annual meeting of the National Council on Measurement in Education (NCME). New Orleans, LA.

Gierl, M. J., Wang, C., & Zhou, J. (2008). Using the Attribute Hierarchy Method to make diagnostic inferences about examinees' cognitive skills in algebra on the SAT. *Journal of Technology, Learning, and Assessment, 6*(6). Retrieved [June 22, 2011] from http://www.jtla.org.

Gierl, M. J., Zhou, J., & Alves, C. (2008). Developing a taxonomy of item model types to promote assessment engineering. *Journal of Technology, Learning, and Assessment, 7*(2). Retrieved [June 22, 2011] from http://www.jtla.org.

Gorin, J. S. (2011, April). *Novel IDM applications: Special populations and testing uses*. Paper presented at the annual meeting of the National Council on Measurement in Education (NCME). New Orleans, LA, USA.

Gorin, J. S., & Embretson, S. E. (2006). Item difficulty modeling of paragraph comprehension items. *Applied Psychological Measurement, 30*, 394–411.

Haladyna, T. M. (1997). *Writing test items to evaluate higher-order thinking*. Boston: Allyn and Bacon.

Haladyna, T. M. (2004). *Developing and validating multiple-choice test items* (3rd ed.). Mahwah, NJ: Erlbaum.

Irvine, S. H. (2002). The foundations of item generation for mass testing. In S.H. Irvine & P.C. Kyllonen (Eds.), *Item generation for test development* (pp. 3–34). Mahwah, NJ: Lawrence Erlbaum Associates.

Irvine, S. H., & Kyllonen, P. C. (2002). *Item generation for test development*. Mahwah, NJ: Lawrence Erlbaum Associates.

Jensen, A. R. (1998). *The g factor: The science of mental ability*. Westport, CT: Praeger.

Johnson-Laird, P. N. (1983). *Mental models. Towards a cognitive science of language, inference, and consciousness*. Cambridge, MA: Harvard University Press.

Johnson-Laird, P. N., & Bara, B. G. (1984). Syllogistic inference. *Cognition, 16*, 1–61.

Kyllonen, P. C. & Christal, R. E. (1990). Reasoning ability is (little more than) working-memory capacity, *Intelligence, 14*, 389–433.

Leighton, J. P. (2004). Avoiding misconceptions, misuse, and missed opportunities: The collection of verbal reports in educational achievement testing. *Educational Measurement: Issues and Practice, Winter*, 1–10.

Leighton, J. P., Cui, Y., & Cor, M. K. (2009). Testing expert-based and student-based cognitive models: An application of the attribute hierarchy method and hierarchical consistency index. *Applied Measurement in Education, 22*, 229–254.

Leighton, J. P., & Gierl, M. J. (Eds.). (2007). *Cognitive diagnostic assessment for education. Theories and applications*. Cambridge, MA: Cambridge University Press.

Leighton, J. P. & Gierl, M. J. (2011). *The learning sciences in educational assessment.* Cambridge, MA: Cambridge University Press.

Leighton, J. P., Gierl, M. J., & Hunka, S. (2004). The attribute hierarchy method for cognitive assessment: A variation on Tatsuoka's rule-space approach. *Journal of Educational Measurement, 41,* 205–236.

Leighton, J. P., & Gokiert, R. (2005, April). *Investigating test items designed to measure higher-order reasoning using think-aloud methods.* Paper presented at the annual meeting of the American Educational Research Association (AERA), Montreal, Quebec, CANADA.

Leighton, J. P., & Gokiert, R. J. (2008). Identifying test item misalignment using verbal reports of item misinterpretation and uncertainty. *Educational Assessment, 13,* 215–242.

Leighton, J. P., & Sternberg, R. J. (in press). Reasoning and problem solving. In A. Healy & R. Proctor (Eds.), *Handbook of psychology* (2nd ed.), Vol. 4 Experimental psychology. New York, NY: Wiley.

Lohman, D. (2005). Reasoning abilities. In R. J. Sternberg & J. E. Pretz (Eds.), *Cognition and intelligence* (pp. 225–250). Cambridge, MA: Cambridge University Press.

Minsky, M. (June, 1974). A framework for representing knowledge. *MIT-AI Laboratory Memo 306.* Accessed on January 2, 2010, at http://web.media.mit.edu/~minsky/papers/Frames/frames.html.

Mislevy, R. J., Behrens, J. T., Bennett, R. E., Demark, S. F., Frezzo, D. C., Levy, R. et al. (2010). On the roles of external knowledge representations in assessment design. *Journal of Technology, Learning, and Assessment, 8*(2). http://escholarship.bc.edu/jtla/vol8/2.

Mislevy, R. J., & Riconscente, M. M. (2006). Evidence-centered assessment design. In S. M. Downing & T. Haladyna (Eds.), *Handbook of test development* (pp. 61–90). Mahwah, NJ: Erlbaum.

Newstead, S., Bradon, P., Handley, S., Evans, J., & Dennis, I. (2002). Using the psychology of reasoning to predict the difficulty of analytical reasoning problems. In S. H. Irvine & P. C. Kyllonen (Eds.), *Item generation for test development* (pp. 35–52). Mahwah, NJ: Lawrence Erlbaum Associates.

Nichols, P. (1994). A framework of developing cognitively diagnostic assessments. *Review of Educational Research, 64,* 575–603.

Nichols, P. D., Chipman, S. F., & Brennan, R. L. (Eds.). (1995). *Cognitively diagnostic assessment.* Hillsdale, NJ: Erlbaum.

Reckase, M. (2010). NCME 2009 Presidential Address: "What I think I know." *Educational Measurement: Issues and Practice, 29,* 3–7.

Roussos, L., DiBello, L. V., Stout, W., Hartz, S., Henson, R. A., & Templin, J. H. (2007). The fusion model skills diagnosis system. In J. P. Leighton, & Gierl, M. J. (Eds.), *Cognitive diagnostic assessment for education: Theory and applications* (pp. 275–318). Cambridge, UK: Cambridge University Press.

Rupp, A. A., & Templin, J. (2008). Unique characteristics of diagnostic classification models: A comprehensive review of the current state-of-the-art. *Measurement: Interdisciplinary Research and Perspectives, 6,* 219–262.

Rupp, A. A., Templin, J. L., & Henson, R. A. (2010). *Diagnostic measurement: Theory, methods, and applications.* New York: The Guilford Press.

Schmeiser, C. B. & Welch, C. J. (2006). Test development. In R. L. Brennan (Ed.), *Educational measurement* (4th ed., pp. 307–353). Westport, CT: National Council on Measurement in Education and American Council on Education.

Sheehan, K. M., Kostin, I., Futagi, Y., & Flor, M. (2011, April). *An automated approach for modeling the passage complexity component of reading item difficulty.* Paper presented at the annual meeting of the National Council on Measurement in Education (NCME), New Orleans, LA, USA.

Shepard, R.N., & Metzler, J. (1971). Mental rotation of three-dimensional objects. *Science, 171,* 701–703.

Singley, M. K., & Bennett, R. E. (2002). Item generation and beyond: Applications of schema theory to mathematics assessment. In S. H. Irvine & P. C. Kyllonen (Eds.), *Item generation for test development* (pp. 361–384). Mahwah, NJ: Erlbaum.

Snow, R. E., & Lohman, D. F. (1989). Implications of cognitive psychology for educational measurement. In R. L. Linn (Ed.), *Educational measurement* (3rd ed., pp. 263–331). New York: American Council on Education, Macmillan.

Stanovich, K. E. & West, R. F. (2008). On the relative independence of thinking biases and cognitive ability. *Journal of Personality and Social Psychology, 94,* 672–695.

Sternberg, R. J. (1999). Intelligence as developing expertise. *Contemporary Educational Psychology, 24,* 359–375.

Sternberg, R. J., & Pretz, J. E.(Eds.). (2005). *Cognition and intelligence: Identifying the mechanisms of the mind.* New York: Cambridge University Press.

Wesman, A. G. (1971). Writing the test item. In R. L. Thorndike (Ed.), *Educational measurement* (2nd ed., pp. 99–111). Washington, DC: American Council on Education.

9

Using Cognitive Psychology to Generate Items and Predict Item Characteristics

Joanna S. Gorin and Susan E. Embretson

In 1988, Steven Greene, a student of Yale and Northwestern, received the annual Student Award for developing a programming language to simplify the production of stimulus lists for cognitive psychology experiments. The rationale given for the research was as follows:

> Too often, an inordinate amount of an experimenter's time and mental resources is spent in the mundane task of creating stimulus lists for use in experiments. Translating the experimental design into a computer program to generate lists for individual subjects from sets of materials is not always a straightforward task, especially if the design calls for complex randomizations or counterbalancing. The process is one that is prone to error and locating the source of errors can be extremely tedious. (Greene, Ratcliff, & McKoon, 1988, p. 119)

This commentary is equally relevant in describing the view of many towards traditional, non-generative item-writing methods. Hence the motivation for automatic item generation (AIG). Like an automated stimulus generator does for experimental design, AIG can more efficiently supply high-quality items for educational and psychological testing that support inferences about individuals' cognition (Bejar, 1993; Irvine, 2002). In psychological experiments on human cognitive processes, subjects are presented with a stimulus in a particular task context and must respond to that stimulus in some way (Bower & Clapper, 1989; p. 254). The response is presumed to reflect the cognitive operations and capabilities of an individual. One designs experimental stimuli by carefully controlling all possible variables in theoretically prescribed ways. Differences in response patterns and probabilities of responses are then interpreted in terms of the stimulus design. In assessments, including AIG-based assessments, examinees are presented with items, generally composed of a stimulus situated within a given task context to which they must respond. Test items are written to evoke scorable behaviors that are interpreted as representations of the knowledge, skills, and abilities of interest. AIG offers a framework for item writing that draws it closer to the scientific approach of experimental stimulus design than does an artistic process. In point of fact, Gorin (2011) noted that AIG and related methods are merely examples of good experimental design. What distinguishes the work of the experimental psychologist from the AIG developer is the purpose of their work. For the cognitive-experimental psychologist, it is to understand the nature of intelligence and the human mind; for the test developer it is to make valid inferences about specific claims, typically in terms of current or future knowledge. We will attempt to persuade the reader that AIG endeavors are, at their core, analogous to carefully designed cognitive-experimental stimuli design.

Besides the obvious difference in development purpose for experimental stimuli and test items, a more fundamental difference exists which may explain why AIG for educational assessment has lagged until recent years. Whereas experimental stimuli are specifically designed to reflect a cognitive theory about processing, that is, to test a specific cognitive theory, educational test items are typically written in the absence of knowledge of the cognitive processes associated with solving items. The focus of item and test development for educational tests is typically on content. Test blueprints are designed to assess the content representativeness of a test relative to the domain. Little attention is paid to the cognitive processing requirements of the test items, in terms either of the impact on item difficulty or of the relationship with cognitive theory. Thus, to the extent that AIG requires knowledge of item processing, educational tests are not immediately amenable, at least not given the historic approaches to item writing.

For numerous reasons, AIG has become of increasing interest for achievement-based educational assessment. This is due primarily to the large pools of items that are required by several recent trends. Two examples are computer-based testing and through-year testing, both of which increase the frequency of testing, which in turn jeopardizes the security of test items. Large item pools are needed in order to maintain test security by minimizing item exposure while still allowing large pools of students to be tested, potentially multiple times throughout a given year (Drasgow, Luecht, & Bennett, 2006). However, some of the most promising advances in AIG have been made in aptitude testing. In comparison to educational tests designed to measure curriculum standards and behavioral objectives, aptitude tests are typically composed of cognitive tasks with well-developed cognitive theory. For example, items and tasks found on tests of abstract and spatial reasoning, like those of the Armed Services Vocational Aptitude Battery (ASVAB), are grounded on strong cognitive theory. The cognitive theory on these item types is such that the processing models include descriptions of cognitive processes for almost all examinee behavior, from the order in which examinees visually encode the stimuli to the construction of mental models representing rules relating item components to decision processes describing how examinees consider, select, and confirm their responses. We would argue that AIG systems for these items have been as successful as they have due to the theoretically derived and empirically validated cognitive models of item complexity and response processing they have undergone.

Approaches to AIG

Principled item design, whether automated or not, should begin with a clear definition of the measurement target. Gorin (2006a) suggests that item quality is directly related to the specificity of the construct definition, with definitions given at the cognitive level leading to the high-quality items. However, a strong theoretical foundation for item design is only a first step. Adherence to the construct theory in designing items will maximize the validity of score inferences (Embretson & Gorin, 2001; Mislevy, 2007). Bejar (1993) links the success of AIG projects to both the strength of the items' theoretical foundation and the extent to which the item generation process can be automated. Ideally, an a priori theoretical model of the construct should precede and direct item development. This theoretical model should not only describe the nature of the construct, but also connect characteristics of the items so as to model defined cognitive processes. Bejar (2002) calls this a top-down approach and recommends it as the most promising method for AIG. Alternatively, a bottom-up approach begins with items and item responses, from which a model of item processing can be derived statistically. As compared to the top-down approach, the bottom-up approach is more susceptible to sampling error based on the set of items and item characteristics generated for analysis (Bejar, 2002; Arendasy & Sommer, 2007).

The workflow for a bottom-up AIG approach is presented in Figure 9.1, beginning with the critical step of defining the cognitive model for the items. Early requirements for AIG implementation revolve around *cognitive-psychometric modeling* of static sets of items in order to isolate the generative components for AIG architecture. Given that no items need be generated in the first steps of the presented workflow, developing the cognitive model, identifying item structures, and modeling item difficulty may be considered a prerequisite to AIG. The current chapter will focus in large part on the first three steps in the AIG workflow, starting with the development and validation of a cognitive model.

Cognitive Models for AIG

A fully generative approach to AIG requires sufficient knowledge about the response process to predict the psychometric properties from stimulus features. Adequate knowledge of the response processes to permit accurate prediction of an item's psychometric features from its generative components must be acquired (Bejar, 1993). In fact, this requires two types of knowledge: (a) knowledge of the relevant processes guiding the item solution, and (b) knowledge of the manipulable task features corresponding to cognitive processing. Regarding the first of these, a convenient tool for representing cognitive processes is a *cognitive model.* Cognitive models refer broadly to a collection of representational types used to describe the process and structure of human knowledge and problem solving (Markman, 1999). These models serve as a useful tool for making predictions about behavior in order to test broader theories about human cognition. Specific types of cognitive models differ in terms of their representational structure, making each more appropriately suited to describe various cognitive processes. We review a few of the cognitive model types most useful for AIG purposes.

Mental Models

Irvine (2002) suggests that the use of *mental models* in item generation might be the most significant contribution of new theories of item development. A common tool for psychological explanation, a mental model is a form of knowledge representation used to explain and make predictions about behavior situations that are novel, but similar to those previously encountered (Johnson-Laird, 1989). For example, when a student encounters a test item that is similar to content learned in a classroom, he or she has an established mental model that is used to determine how to deal with a test question. The mental model is retrieved from long-term memory (LTM) and made active for use in problem solving. The mental model is selected based on a comparison of the problem to be solved and the available mental models stored in LTM (Johnson-Laird, 1980). Unlike propositional representations, the structure of a mental model is designed to represent the relevant aspects of the entity it represents. Thus, a mental model for a test item should represent the "relevant" aspects of the item that determine how an individual would solve it. Irvine's preference towards mental models for AIG

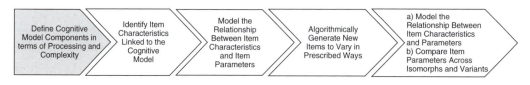

Figure 9.1 Workflow for top-down AIG development

likely stemmed from the similarity of mental models and item structures (to be discussed later). When presented with test items with similar structure, the same mental model would be retrieved and applied (i.e., the same cognitive processes would be measured). Thus, mental models for items would describe their fundamental structure in terms of physical item features, pertinent cognitive processes, and the relationship between the two.

Task Processing and Complexity Models

Despite Irvine's (2002) suggestion that mental models offer great promise for the future of test theory, the role of cognitive psychology in most test design and analysis has taken on a less "cognitive" structure. This is likely due to the emphasis on achievement versus aptitude assessment in education, as well as the role of discrete content as opposed to constructs as the measurement target. Leighton and Gierl (2007a) suggest three types of cognitive models that are appropriate to represent items on educational assessment—cognitive model of *test specifications*, cognitive model of *domain mastery*, and cognitive model of *task performance*—each of which is appropriate for distinct types of assessment. Each type of cognitive model provides information about the knowledge, skills, and abilities required by a test, though the grain size and structure of the cognitive information differs. If we consider the previously discussed mental models of psychology, then the model of task performance is most similar and thus offers the most promise for AIG development.

A cognitive model of task performance is most similar to traditional cognitive models in that it specifies the entire solution path for an examinee on an item in terms of fine-grained cognitive processes, such as activation, attention, encoding, decoding, falsification, and confirmation (Gorin, 2006a; Leighton & Gierl, 2007a). For this reason, these models are particularly well suited to tests measuring more traditional cognitive constructs than one might encounter in educational assessments. As assessments target broader content domains and less cognitively based constructs (e.g., knowledge of Western History), the model of task performance is less easily applied. With wider breadth of the content, various item types are likely to be used, each of which may require its own model of task performance.

Perhaps the closest approximation to a mental model that has been used in assessment research is the *model of cognitive complexity* (Embretson, 2009). Describing the cognitive complexity of an item or a set of test items is common for test development (e.g., test specifications). Bloom's (1956) taxonomy of cognitive behavioral objectives and Depth of Knowledge (DOK) are perhaps the most commonly used tools for labeling the complexity of assessment items. However, labeling the complexity of an item is a far cry from presenting a cognitive model of complexity. While the overall level of cognitive complexity may appropriately be described by a single term (e.g., knowledge, comprehension, analysis), such vague terms lack causal explanations of the source of the complexity. Further, the predictive power of general labels of cognitive complexity is questionable. That is, a difficult knowledge-level item can be written, even though the knowledge level of complexity is presumed to be quite low; further, a synthesis item could be relatively easy, depending on the presentation of the material and the difficulty of the information, despite the fact that synthesis is at one of the higher levels of Bloom's taxonomy. For purposes of AIG, in which the predictors of item difficulty must be fully understood (and programmed), a more detailed model of cognitive complexity is needed. Several examples of cognitive processing models describing complexity of items across a variety of domains are presented next.

Example Cognitive Models for AIG

To provide a more concrete description of cognitive models for AIG, we provide three examples of cognitive-complexity models, first for assessment of spatial reasoning, next for mathematical reasoning, and finally for measurement of abstract reasoning. For clarity, we focus our discussion at this point only on the cognitive model itself. Later, consideration of item structures derived from these models will be given. Studies of all three constructs constitute ideal conditions for top-down AIG, given the extensive cognitive literature on both the processes and tasks involved in measurement of these constructs.

Cognitive Model of Spatial Reasoning for Object-Assembly Items

The underlying processes in performing spatial tasks have interested many cognitive psychologists (Byrne & Johnson-Laird, 1989; Just & Carpenter, 1985; Mumaw & Pellegrino, 1984). A common task used to assess individuals' spatial-reasoning ability is the Object Assembly, or Assembling Objects, task (AO). The goal for AO items is to mentally assemble a set of objects presented as "separate," given several options of "assembled" objects (Figure 9.2). Support has been found for mental models theory applied to spatial tasks such as AO items (Byrne & Johnson-Laird, 1989; Glasgow & Malton, 1999), as contrasted to a rule-based or inferential approach. However, complex spatial tasks often can be solved by more than one strategy. Specific to object assembly, it has been found that instructions can determine if verbal or spatial processes are applied in item solution (Johnson, Paivio, & Clark, 1989). Consequently, Mumaw and Pellegrino (1984) developed a cognitive process theory, as opposed to a mental model representation, for object assembly tasks. In their research, shape rotation and displacement were identified as critical processes affecting items' cognitive complexity. More recent studies of cognitive complexity have added processes stemming from the multiple-choice item format, which affects response selection (Embretson, 2009; Embretson & Gorin, 2001).

Most recently, Embretson (2011) generated a large set of AO items based on an updated stage-like model of AO item complexity to represent two primary sources of cognitive complexity: spatial demand and working-memory load (Figure 9.3). The first processing stage is encoding of the stem elements. In this stage, examinees build mental representations of the shapes in the item stem for later processing. These representations could be entirely spatial, or individuals could elect to use verbal labels to facilitate encoding and subsequent processing. The second stage shown in Figure 9.3 is falsification. Falsification is a preliminary part of the response-decision process in item solution. The examinee is postulated to search for response alternatives with grossly inappropriate features as compared to the pieces in the stem. Response alternatives with the wrong number of pieces and obviously mismatched pieces can be readily rejected. It is assumed that processing of a response alternative ceases when a mismatch is detected. The final stage is the confirmation process. This process is applied only to the remaining non-falsified alternatives. This stage involves searching, rotating, and comparing shapes between the stem and the remaining response alternatives. Previous cognitive theory on spatial reasoning supports these processes as the most construct-relevant sources of cognitive complexity (Quasha & Likert, 1937).

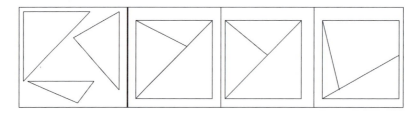

Figure 9.2 Example object assembly (AO) task

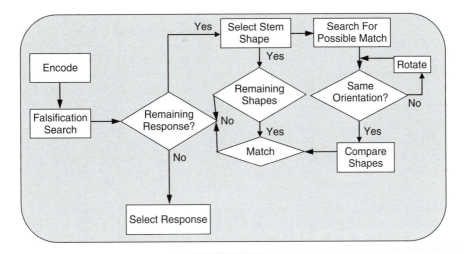

Figure 9.3 Cognitive model of object assembly items (adapted from Embretson & Gorin, 2001)

Cognitive Model of Mathematical Reasoning

Cognitive models of mathematics test items have been created to attempt to isolate the effects of a small number of key variables (e.g., Singley & Bennett, 2002; Arendasy & Sommer, 2005; Birenbaum, Tatsuoka, & Gurtvirtz, 1992). The majority of cognitive models of mathematical reasoning items are based on Mayer, Larkin, and Kadane's (1984) model. They propose two global stages of processing with two sub-stages each: problem representation, which includes problem translation and problem integration as sub-stages, and problem execution, which includes solution planning and solution execution as sub-stages (Arendasy, Sommer, Gittler, & Hergovich, 2006). In the problem-representation stage, an examinee converts the problem into equations and then, in the problem-execution stage, the equations are solved. Problem-execution processes take over once the needed equations are available in working memory. Problem execution involves (a) planning, in which a strategy for isolating the unknowns is developed and implemented, (b) solution execution, in which computations are made to obtain the unknowns and (c) decision, in which the obtained solution is compared to the response alternatives. Cognitive complexity in this stage may be reduced for items that do not require solution planning. This would be the case when equations are given in a directly useable format (see also discussion in Graf & Fife, this volume).

Embretson and Daniel (2008) extend earlier models to comprise five stages of processing: encoding, integration, solution planning, solution execution, and decision (Table 9.4). The primary distinction between previous models and Embretson and Daniel's (2008) model is modification to processing complexity based on factors associated with the presentation of the item, specifically the source of the equation in the problem. If the required equations are given directly in the item, then several stages in the solution process are bypassed and the majority of cognitive complexity stems from problem execution. However, if the necessary equations are not given directly in the item, then additional cognitive resources are needed to translate, recall, or generate equations, all of which contribute to increased cognitive complexity.

Cognitive Model of Abstract Reasoning

Among the many cognitive abilities of interest to individual differences researchers, abstract reasoning is one of the most commonly researched higher-order processes. A traditional item type used to

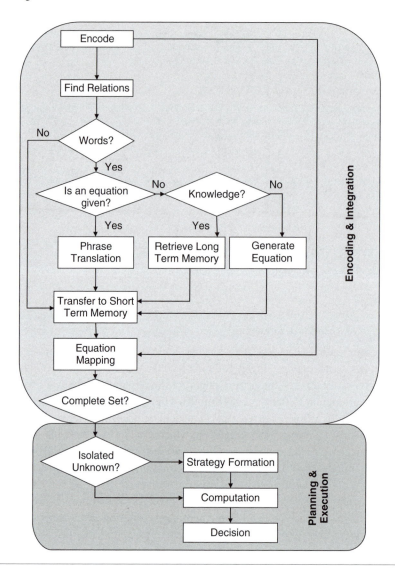

Figure 9.4 Cognitive model of mathematical reasoning item (adapted from Daniel & Embretson, 2010)

measure the ability is the progressive matrix. These items were first introduced on the classic Raven's Progressive Matrix Test (Raven, 1940) and then have been reintroduced as an online assessment called the Abstract Reasoning Test (Embretson, 1998). For these problems, students are provided with a 3 × 3 matrix of shapes, with one blank cell with a missing shape that would complete the sequence in the matrix (Figure 9.5). The examinee's task is to identify the appropriate shape for the missing cell, based on patterns (i.e., rules) governing the completed portions of the matrix. Response options for the missing cell combine different shapes, colors, and patterns, only one of which correctly completes the matrix. The shapes in each of the matrix cells are organized according to rules of association between aspects of the figures. The rules can vary in number and complexity. If the examinee is able to infer the rules of association, then the correct response option for the missing cell is selected to complete the pattern.

Figure 9.6 presents a cognitive model in terms of a sequential processing model, similar to those for spatial and mathematical reasoning. The cognitive model is driven by two general processes—

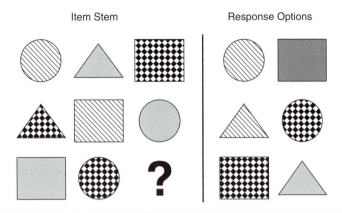

Figure 9.5 Example progressive matrix item

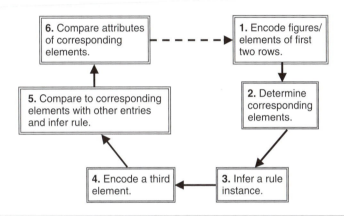

Figure 9.6 Cognitive model of progressive matrix items (adapted from Embretson, 1998)

inferring rules and applying them—which are controlled by working memory and abstraction processes (Carpenter, Just,& Shell, 1990; Embretson, 1998). Working-memory load is influenced by the number and level of relationships involved across the rows and columns of the matrix. Relationships vary in complexity, from identity relations (i.e., the same element across the row or column) as the simplest relation, to distribution of two relations (i.e., the distribution of three relations have null values where one matching element is missing). The cognitive model specifies that lower-level relationships are applied before higher-level relationships. As the lower-level relationships are applied and individuals move to application of higher-level relationships, working memory is taxed both by holding the earlier relations in mind and by the complexity of the new relations.

Building the Cognitive Model

In each of the previous examples, the existing cognitive literature is extensive. However, what happens when the targeted construct for AIG does not have an associated body of cognitive literature? The first step in the AIG process becomes infinitely more challenging; the cognitive model must be generated by subject-matter experts. In this sense, the test developer must *become* a cognitive psychologist (or employ one). To get them started, we briefly review several methods that have served cognitive scientists well in building cognitive models and have already been applied to educational test items, though in a more limited fashion.

Verbal Protocols

Verbal protocols, or think-alouds, consist of student verbalizations of response processes for an item either while solving a problem (concurrent or online verbal protocols) or once the item is completed (retrospective verbal protocols) (Ericsson & Simon, 1993). Both procedures attempt to make explicit the processes that characterize human cognition. Some educational assessment experts argue that verbal protocols can provide unique insight into individual processing, including information about student misconceptions, skill weaknesses, and uses of various problem-solving strategies (Leighton, 2004). Unlike more structured data-collection methods that presuppose the variables of interest to the researcher, verbal protocols do not restrict the information provided by the student. In terms of item difficulty modeling, this approach can be useful as an initial investigation when researchers know little about item processing, or as a confirmatory approach to verify a hypothesized processing model. Alternatively, some researchers use verbal protocols to develop objective self-report measures of processing. For example, information gained from verbal protocols of student problem solving has been used to develop strategy inventories regarding test-taking methods employed by students (Powers & Wilson, 1993; Towns & Robinson, 1993). When examined relative to item and test performance, responses to strategy inventories can provide additional support to a hypothesized processing model, or, alternatively, they may suggest processing components not previously considered in the modeling process.

Whereas just a few years ago few test-development studies employed verbal protocols (or other related methods, such as think-aloud protocols), that number is rapidly increasing (Ferrara & Chen, 2011; Gierl, Wang, & Zhou, 2008; Kaliski, Huff, & Thurber, 2011; Williamson, Bauer, Steinberg, Mislevy, Behrens, & DeMark, 2004). Recently, Leighton (2011) examined the reliability and accuracy of data generated from verbal protocols for educational assessments. Her results suggest that results from verbal protocols can be influenced by various factors, including characteristics of the interviewer as well as the difficulty level of the items used to generate the protocol. Though this does not rule out verbal protocols as a rich source of data for cognitive model development, it highlights the importance of certain factors that should be considered when designing the data-collection methods, including characteristics of the examiner and the specific tasks used for experimentation.

Cognitive Laboratories

Like verbal protocols, cognitive laboratories are designed to elicit behaviors or responses by examinees that make explicit their thought processes and knowledge representations, more so than would be available from the typical item response. Ferrara et al. (2004) developed a systematic approach to cognitive item analysis with verbal protocols called the Cognitive Laboratory Analysis (CLA) Framework. Cognitive interviews were conducted with 63 middle-school students solving problems from a state standardized science test. The interviews were then coded into four broad categories: science topics, science skills, broader cognitive processing, and examinee response strategies. The coded interviews were analyzed to compare the intended construct, specified by the state content standards, and the enacted construct, the description of the item processing coded from the CLA. Similarly, researchers examining possible item modifications for enhanced assessments to meet NCLB (No Child Left Behind) legislation used cognitive interview procedures with students with disabilities in order to gather evidence regarding possible unintended sources of item complexity that could be removed in item revisions (Parker, 2010). Researchers were able to develop a comprehensive model of task performance that improved the diagnostic capabilities of the test.

Digital Eye-Tracking

As an alternative to methods eliciting verbal responses from examinees in order to describe cognitive processes, some researchers have employed a different process-tracing method called digital eye-tracking. Eye-tracking methods record individuals' eye-movement data during stimulus processing. A relatively new methodology in psychometric research, eye-tracking data can provide many of the same benefits to cognitive model development for AIG as other process-tracing techniques, such as verbal protocols, but without some of the disadvantages (Gorin, 2006b). The assumption of the technology is that the location of an individual's eye fixation corresponds to an allocation of visual attention and, in turn, cognitive processing resources. Data on eye movement has been used across a variety of disciplines as evidence of individual differences in cognitive processing (e.g., Humphrey, Kemper, & Radel, 2004; Kemper, Crow, & Kemtes, 2004; Rayner, Warren, Juhasz, & Liversedge, 2004). Although the use of eye-trackers has been scarcer in psychometric investigations of standardized test items, some research has demonstrated its use for identifying item-solution paths or strategies (Diehl, 2004; Gorin, 2006b; Ivie, Kupzyk, & Embretson, 2004). Diehl (2004), for example, used eye-tracking data to classify problem-solving strategies for abstract-reasoning items in terms of the number and duration of looks between the problem and the response options. Further, the eye-fixation data were useful in confirming the encoding processes hypothesized by the researchers. Ivie et al. (2004) conducted similar analyses of quantitative reasoning items and also identified eye-fixation patterns associated with various problem-solving approaches.

Subject-Matter Experts

Subject-matter and domain experts provide an invaluable resource for test developers. They bring to bear useful knowledge of the skill requirements in a content domain and students' representations and misrepresentations of content domains (Gierl, et al., 2009). When presented with items in their respective domains, subject-matter experts (SMEs), through task analysis, can provide the components and the structure of a cognitive model that accurately represents how students might approach solution paths. Gierl and his team (2009) used SMEs to build learning progressions for large-scale educational tests of reading and mathematics. Experts were asked to identify and order the constituent skills required by items and then tested the model empirically with an appropriate psychometric model of item difficulty. Though the use of SMEs to review test content is not new, incorporating their feedback into cognitive model development is.

Developing AIG Item Structures from the Cognitive Model

In the second step of the AIG workflow shown in Figure 9.1, the cognitive-model components must be incorporated into an item's design. The design of an item, sometimes called the item's structure, is composed of two types of item features, *radicals* and *incidentals*. Radicals are the critical components of the item structure, or, as Bejar (1993) refers to it, the generative system, that are manipulated specifically in order to produce a predictable change in cognitive processing and, hence, item difficulty. The content of the radicals describes the sources of difficulty for sets of items. Embretson (1998) describes these components in her Cognitive Design System as *manipulables* that must be tested in order to identify their effect on item parameters such as difficulty, discrimination, and response time. Incidentals are features of items that, though they vary across items, do *not* influence item difficulty; incidentals are all non-radical features of items. Incidentals are useful when many items with identical processing components that might affect difficulty are generated, but they are perceptually different such that an examinee cannot perceive the similarity through surface processing alone. As an example of radicals and incidentals, consider a mathematics distance-word problem. The number of variables to be compared in the word problem would be a radical that would change the processing requirements of the item; the names of the characters and cities involved in the problem are incidentals. AIG development begins with a hypothesis of radicals and incidentals for items based on existing cognitive theory. However, it is critical that the item structures be tested empirically in order to determine whether incidentals unintentionally impact item difficulty. In such cases, modeling techniques can be used to include incidentals as covariates so as to control their impact on item parameters.

The cognitive model developed in the first stage of AIG should directly inform item structure. The cognitive processes that impact item processing *and* are relevant to the intended score inferences should be represented in item structures as radicals; other elements of items not tied to cognitive model components constitute incidentals. Though the verbiage is different, a similar notion of task design to reflect cognitive processes is apparent in the experimental and cognitive psychology literature. Recall the example given at the outset of stimulus design for experiments. In the early cognitive psychology research, a great deal of interest was paid to the issue of humans' ability to transfer cognitive knowledge and strategies from one problem-solving situation to another, based on similarities and differences in task structure. The typical paradigm for problem-solving research is to use tasks that appear very different on the surface, but share the same basic structure. The context and way that any specific problem is presented define its *surface structure*; the *deep structure* of a problem is independent of the particular item context. Items with common deep structures that differ only in terms of surface structure are termed *isomorphic*, a term adopted in the AIG lexicon (Bejar, 2002).

One of the most classic examples of isomorphic tasks in the cognitive psychology literature is the Tower of Hanoi (ToH) problem, used to measure individuals' ability to learn a particular solution strategy (Figure 9.7a). To solve the ToH, individuals must move a set of three wooden disks stacked on one of three wooden pegs to another of the three pegs, where allowable moves for the disks

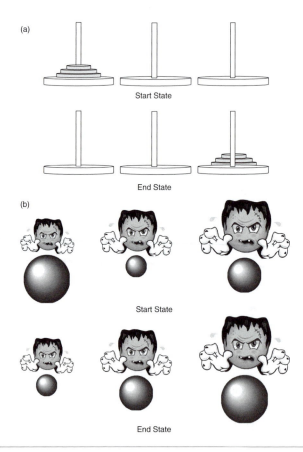

Figure 9.7 Examples of isomorphic tasks: a) Tower of Hanoi, and b) Monsters and Globes

are governed by several simple rules: (a) only one disk may be moved from peg to peg at a time, and (b) smaller disks may be placed on top of larger disks, but not the reverse. In many studies, the learning on the ToH was then followed by a transfer task, one that shares the ToH deep structure (e.g., Simon, 1975). An example of an isomorphic task is the Monsters and Globes TOH task (Kotovsky, Hayes, & Simon, 1985; Figure 7b). The goal of the Monsters and Globes task is to move the globes from one of the monster's hands to another, using only allowable rules related to the size of the globes. What makes these tasks isomorphic is that individuals use the same mental model to solve each. That is, the same fundamental cognitive processes are required to solve the problem *and* the tasks are structured to have comparable levels of complexity based on those cognitive processes. The cognitive complexity of each of the tasks can be altered by changing the number of manipulables (i.e., disks or globes) to be moved by the examinee. This suggests that the structures of the tasks are similar in terms of their relationship to the complexity of the cognitive processes. In AIG terms, one can conceive of the deep structure of an item to be defined by the item radicals; surface structure components are the item incidentals.

The structure of any two items can be compared in terms of the relationship between their radicals and incidentals (Table 9.1). Item isomorphs are identical in terms of their radicals, but vary on incidentals. Structural variants typically share a common set of item radicals, but differ in terms of the value of those radicals. Based on the structural relationship between items, certain relationships between item parameters, such as item difficulty and response time, are expected. Item isomorphs should yield item difficulty estimates as similar as two estimates of a single item administered to two separate samples of examinees. Item variants are not expected to have "equal" item difficulty parameters, though the relationship between the difficulties of item variants should be predictable based on the difference in values of the item radicals. Once AIG item structures have been defined in terms of radicals and incidentals, empirical tests to verify the expected relationships among item parameters are conducted. The results of these analyses will reflect the adequacy of the cognitive model, the validity of item structure, and the overall tenability of the generative system for AIG implementation.

Item difficulty Modeling

Theory and prior research on the constructs and item types of interest can help to generate an initial model, but empirical testing is needed in order to verify the validity of the model. Specifically, AIG implementation requires an understanding of how characteristics of individual items impact item processing and statistical properties. If the impact of item features is empirically and mathematically linked to item parameters, such as difficulty and discrimination, then item-generation algorithms can be written to create items that target specific ability levels and testing populations most efficiently.

Item difficulty modeling (IDM) has come to represent empirical examinations of the cognitive sources of item processing and items' statistical parameters (Bejar, 2002). The purpose of IDM studies is to achieve the benefits to validity arguments and efficient item development previously mentioned (IDM studies for quantitative items are also discussed in Graf & Fife, this volume). There

Table 9.1 Relationship among items with common structural radicals

		Incidentals Same values	Different values
Radicals	Same values	• Same item • Equal difficulty	• Item isomorph • Equal difficulty
	Different values	• Item variant (perceptually similar) • Different difficulty	• Item variant (perceptually distal) • Different difficulty

are two critical components to a successful IDM study—the cognitive model of item processing and the psychometric model of item-response data. The two are connected in that each model includes a description of the characteristics or features of the items. The cognitive model describes how item features are connected to each cognitive process. The psychometric model parameterizes the impact of each item feature on student response patterns. When taken together, the student responses are connected to the cognitive processes via the item features present in both models. The results of the IDM therefore allow individual item responses to be interpreted in terms of construct-relevant and irrelevant processes. Further, variations in item statistics, such as difficulty and discrimination, can be purposefully manipulated by changing the item features identified in the IDM process. Within the AIG workflow presented in Figure 9.1, IDM studies focus on the first three steps, culminating with a mathematical model of the structure of an item.

One of the most common approaches to IDM is a correlational analysis of item difficulty estimates. Item difficulty parameter estimates obtained from operational administrations of test items are typically regressed on quantified characteristics of the items, often called *item features*. Item features are attributes or properties of the items that are related to an examinee's ability to process and correctly respond to the item. For example, a feature of a mathematics test item might be the number of variables in the problem or number of operations that must be applied to correctly solve the item. Typically, the values of these features vary, resulting in generated items across a range of difficulty levels (Bejar, 2002). The key to the process of IDM is to identify the relevant features that drive item processing and to estimate their impact (Bejar, 1993; Bennett, 1999). A preliminary list of item features is often generated from theoretical literature relevant to the content area and, if available, empirical investigations of information processing. The difficulty-modeling process is often iterative, such that item features are added to or removed from the difficulty model, based on their contribution to the explanatory power of the model. The ultimate goal is to develop a model that most completely accounts for item difficulty, based on features of the test question associated with theoretical processes.

An alternative analytic tool that offers several advantages over traditional regression models is a new class of models called *cognitive psychometric models* (CPMs). CPMs can be thought of as statistical models appropriate for the analysis of student-response data that include parameters associated with cognitive sub-skills and processes. As in the regression analyses, the values of the item features (i.e., radicals and incidentals) are entered into the model as predictors of item-response behavior. However, unlike traditional regression models, the raw item-response data is modeled, as opposed to the item-level statistics. An example of a CPM that has been used frequently in IDM and AIG studies is Fischer's (1973) Linear Logistic Latent Trait Model (LLTM). The LLTM model, a member of the Rasch family of models, allows items to vary only in terms of difficulty. However, unlike in the traditional dichotomous Rasch models, item difficulty is not directly estimated from the data. Rather, LLTM structural parameters are estimated to represent item radicals and incidentals. Parameters similar to those in the regression analysis are generated including individual coefficients reflecting the contribution of individual item features to the model and estimates of overall model fit. Further, the model-predicted item difficulties can be compared to difficulty estimates directly estimated from the response data, as an alternative method for assessing model fit. Ideally, radicals would have statistically significant parameter estimates, incidentals would not, and the overall model fit would be high, including good reproducibility of Rasch-based item difficulty parameters.

IDM studies to date have shown varying success in capturing cognitive sources of item parameters, specifically item difficulty. Explained variance in item difficulty parameters from IDM studies have been as high as 90% (Sheehan & Ginther, 2001). More often, IDM models explain somewhere around 30% to 60% of the variability in item difficulty across educational test items (Embretson, 1998; Embretson & Wetzel, 1987; Enright, Morley, & Sheehan, 2002; Gorin & Embretson, 2006). The factors affecting the success of the IDM relate to the adequacy of the two IDM models—the cognitive model and the psychometric model—for capturing the features of the items and the cognitive processes. Several examples of successful IDM studies for cognitive abilities testing are presented next.

Examples of IDM Studies to inform AIG

Spatial Reasoning Tests

Early IDM studies of AO items generated and validated a set of radicals and incidentals corresponding to the cognitive model processes (Embretson, 2000; Embretson & Gorin, 2001). The radicals and incidentals derived from this model are listed in Table 9.2. During encoding of the item stem, difficulty is postulated to be influenced by the number and the complexity of the pieces in the stem. Piece complexity is affected by the number of edges and curves. In contrast, the availability of verbal labels to describe the piece reduces the impact of piece complexity. During falsification, the number of alternatives with falsifiable features will affect item difficulty, such that more falsifiable features are associated with lower difficulty. Finally, in confirmation, the radicals include item features associated only with the non-falsified alternatives. The difficulty of confirming the key is impacted by the number of displaced pieces and rotated pieces. The difficulty of confirming the key also increases with the distance of the response alternative from the stem. The difficulty of disconfirming non-falsified distractors depends on whether the pieces are mismatched by small angular disparities, as well as on the expected number of comparisons to detect a mismatched piece. For the latter variable, distractors with more mismatched pieces require fewer comparisons in order to detect a wrong piece.

In early IDM studies of AO items, hierarchical linear-regression models and LLTM analysis were employed to assess the impact of task radicals at each of the four major stages of the cognitive model. Variables from three of the four stages (encoding, falsification, and confirmation processes related to shape comparison) contributed significantly to item difficulty prediction. The full model, including an additional variable representing the position of the key in the item, accounted for approximately 66% of variance in item difficulty. IDM analysis of algorithmically generated AO items improved methodologically and theoretically upon earlier studies by assessing the impact of the two categories of cognitive processes (spatial demand and working memory) separately on two types of AO

Table 9.2 Description of cognitive model processing stages and item features (adapted from Embretson, 2009)

Processing stage	Item feature	Operational definition
Encoding	1. Number of pieces	Number of shapes in the stem.
	2. Number of edges	Number of edges on the stem pieces.
	3. Number of curved edges	Number of shapes in the stem with interior curved edges.
	4. Verbal labels	A binary variable to indicate pieces in the stem with verbal labels (e.g., circles, right triangles, hexagons, pyramids).
Falsification	1. Number of falsifiable distractors	Number of distractors falsified by gross mismatch (for Puzzle items, this variable is scored positively when the number of pieces, piece size, or the number of edges in the shapes, is mismatched between the stem and the distractor).
Confirmation	1. Displaced pieces	Number of exchanges between pieces in the item stem that must be made to locate the pieces in the same relative positions as in the key versus the item stem.
	2. Rotated pieces	Number of pieces differing in orientation between the stem and the correct response.
	3. Target distance	The distance of the correct response from the stem (same as key position, scored 1–4).
	4. Small angles	A binary variable to indicate presence of small angular disparities in the mismatch of pieces in the closest distractor to the key.
	5. Number of cycles	The expected number of comparison cycles between the stem and closest distractor to disconfirm the closest non-falsifiable distractor, which depends on the number of mismatching pieces.

items: puzzle items and marked-connection items (Embretson, 2011). In order to better represent the structure of items in terms of spatial demand and working memory, composite variables were created to represent characteristics of each item. Working-memory load and spatial demand were computed as follows for Puzzle items:

$$\text{Working memory demand} = (z_{pieces} + z_{edges} + z_{cycles} + (-1^*z_{falsify})) /4$$

$$\text{Spatial demand} = (z_{displaced} + z_{rotated} + z_{targetdist} + z_{angles} + (-1^*z_{labels})) /5,$$

where z-scores for each variable are calculated based on the mean and standard deviation of the item feature for the set of generated items.

Biserial correlations of the two composite scores with item difficulty for the AO Puzzle items were moderate, .52 and .49 respectively. Item difficulty then was regressed on the two composite scores. Overall prediction was significant statistically, with a moderately strong relationship of $R = .59$; $F(2, 233) = 61.52$, $p < .05$. The standardized regression coefficients for both spatial processing demand ($\beta = .37$, $t = 5.35$, $p < 0.05$), and working memory load ($\beta = 0.27$, $t = 6.15$, $p < 0.05$) were statistically significant, which supports their unique impact on item difficulty. The moderately strong correlations found for this model are certainly lower than results from the Embretson and Gorin (2001) study including 10 individual item features as predictors. However, the use of the composite variables has advantages. For one, with only two item features to describe item difficulty, banking items in terms of cognitive complexity or generating item specifications to support validity arguments is easier than with a larger number of item features.

Mathematical Reasoning Tests

Returning to the example of mathematical reasoning, recall the cognitive model presented in Figure 9.3. This model was used both for an IDM study of existing items as well as newly generated items (Embretson & Daniel, 2008; Daniel and Embretson, 2010). Embretson and Daniel (2008) hypothesized that item difficulty would be higher if the examinee was required to recall, generate, or translate the equations as opposed to items for which the necessary equation was provided. Additionally, item difficulty was expected to increase as the number of sub-goals for items increased. The hypothesized cognitive model and item difficulty model was tested via LLTM modeling of item responses to 112 problem-solving items from the Graduate Record Examination. As shown in Table 9.3, coefficients

Table 9.3   Rescaled LLTM parameter estimates for mathematics reasoning items (adapted from Daniel & Embretson (2010)

	Item Predictor	η	se	t	Prob.	η
	Constant	0.116	0.208	0.56	0.5769	−0.549
	Discrimination Constant	0.864	0.041	21.09	<.0001	1
Encoding and Integration	Encoding	0.015	0.003	5.51	<.0001	0.013
	Equation Needed	−0.355	0.095	−3.72	0.0002	−0.307
	Translate Equation	0.291	0.083	3.51	0.0005	0.251
	Generate New Equation	0.472	0.072	6.53	<.0001	0.408
	Visualization	0.616	0.128	4.83	<.0001	0.532
	Maximum Knowledge	−0.023	0.029	−0.78	0.4371	−0.02
	Equation Recall Count	0.015	0.047	0.03	0.7521	0.013
Planning and Execution	Subgoals Count	0.135	0.049	2.76	0.006	0.117
	Relative Definition	0.285	0.076	3.73	0.0002	0.246
	Procedural Level	0.037	0.019	1.95	0.0516	0.032
	Computation Count	−0.004	0.017	−0.23	0.8154	−0.003
	Decision Processing	1.23	0.186	6.63	<.0001	1.063

Note: Rescaling of LLTM coefficients was needed in the Embretson & Daniel (2008) study due to differing manners of model identification across analyses.

for all but three of the item features were statistically significant in their effect on item difficulty. This model accounted for 73% of the variance in item difficulty. Subsequently, Daniel and Embretson (2010) used the validated item structure to generate cognitive model families of items (i.e., original items + item variants based on that item). One-hundred thirteen item variants were generated to systematically vary in terms of (a) number of sub-goals, and (b) equation source, while varying as little as possible on all other item features, including encoding. The LLTM model was used to estimate the effects of item manipulations on item difficulty. Additionally, linear mixed-modeling procedures analogous to modeling of binary response items were used to examine the effect of radicals on response time. Results indicated that the number of sub-goals had a statistically significant effect on item difficulty (as well as item response time) in the predicted direction, whereby item difficulty and response time increased with increased numbers of sub-goals. However, the hypothesized effect of Equation Source was only partly supported by results. Item difficulty differed only between items where the equation was provided or required recall versus any other equation source. No effect of Equation Source was observed for response time.

Abstract Reasoning Tests

Finally, we return to the progressive matrix items designed to measure abstract reasoning. Recall that the cognitive complexity of these processes for any individual item comes primarily from two features/characteristics of the item: (a) the number of rules, and (b) the complexity of the rules, both determinants of overall working-memory load for an item. Table 9.4 presents a list of item features included in various IDM and AIG studies (Diehl, 2004; Embretson, 1998). Logically, as the number and complexity of rules increases across items, so should the item difficulty. For example, items written with multiple rules rather than a single rule, and those with more complex versus simpler rules, should be more difficult to solve than other items. Further, the level of abstraction needed is controlled by several other perceptual features, including overlay (i.e., one shape is placed over another), distortion (i.e., one aspect of a shape is expanded or modified to alter its appearance slightly), and fusion (i.e., two shapes are joined to form a single new shape that contains aspects of each original shape). Statistically significant effects of (a) number and complexity of rules, (b) overlay, (c) fusion, and (d) distortion on item difficulty were detected, as shown by significant weights for these variables in the LLTM model of item difficulty. In sum, the cognitive-complexity components accounted for 80% of the variance in item difficulty for algorithmically generated items. This high proportion of explained variance in item difficulty supports AIG implementation for the progressive matrix items as a measure of individual differences in abstract reasoning.

Table 9.4 Design features for progressive matrix items

Number of relationships

Type of relationship (ordered by complexity)

- identity relations, in which an element is the same across the row or column entries
- pairwise progression relations, in which an element changes systematically from entry to entry
- figure addition or subtraction relations, in which the first two entries in the row or column sum to the last entry
- distribution of three relations, in which an object or attribute appears just once in each row and column
- distribution of two relations, in which distribution of three relations have null values

Additional perceptual features

- object overlay
- object fusion
- object distortion
- frame density
- orientation

Conclusions

We focused this chapter on advancing the idea that cognitive psychological principles and AIG are inexorably intertwined. A cognitive description of the targeted construct and the assessment task are critical at the outset of the AIG development process. Regrettably, this likely means a series of empirical studies to develop cognitive models of educational constructs for which little psychological theory exists (Leighton & Gierl, 2011). Additionally, cognitive models of novel item types must be developed to account for response processes that affect item properties and score meaning. Despite the potential delay in producing an online item generator, the payoff will be in the quality of the generated items. Mislevy (2007), Embretson, (1998), Bejar (1993), Bennett (1999), Gorin (2006a), Leighton and Gierl (2007b), and numerous others are adamant that the effort placed at the outset of test development on cognitive examinations of the construct and items will yield ultimate benefits in item quality.

Admittedly, our discussion of cognitive psychology's role in AIG has been somewhat narrow in scope. Our goal was to reference specific aspects of cognitive psychology theory and methods that have shown promise thus far in IDM and AIG research. However, we would like to take this opportunity to challenge researchers to explore the cognitive literature even further. In particular, research on expert–novice differences in problem-solving strategies and stimulus processing suggests potential challenges for AIG implementations across heterogeneous populations of examinees. Experiments in the cognitive and learning science consistently reveal that experts and novices do not process items similarly (see Ericsson, Charness, Feltovich, & Hoffman, 2006 for a comprehensive review). Expert–novice differences could pose a particular challenge for AIG in terms of the equivalency of item isomorphs. Recall that isomorphs are items that share their deep structure but vary in terms of surface structure. Since it is assumed that the surface structure does not affect the problem-solving process, particularly in terms of the cognitive complexity, item isomorphs can be used interchangeably on presumably equivalent forms. However, the cognitive-psychology literature indicates that experts and novices rely on different aspects of tasks when developing a solution strategy. Experts are more likely to be sensitive to the deep structure of items, whereas novices will rely more heavily on aspects of the surface structure when solving problems (Hardiman, Dufresne, & Mestre, 1989). Thus, what may be an incidental element for an expert could be a radical element for the novice.

The relationship between expertise and perceptions of problem and problem solving has been documented in the cognitive literature across a variety of domains. Chi, Feltovich, and Glaser (1981) in their study of expertise and problem solving in physics found that experts initially abstract underlying physics principles to determine how to approach a problem, whereas novices rely on problems' literal features. Similarly, Schoenfeld and Herrmann (1982) found that, when sorting mathematics problems based on perceived similarity, novices were more likely to sort items based on surface features, such as the words or objects described in the problem statement; experts sorted items according to similarity in deep structure. Further, after a month of intensive instruction, the novices perceived problem similarity more like the experts, suggesting that their problem perception shifted as their ability increased. When studying college students' problem solving for complex arithmetic word problems, Novick (1988) found that when problems share structural features but not surface features, experts are more likely to transfer appropriate strategies than are novices, whereas when problems share surface but not structural features, novices tended to transfer incorrect strategies. In the context of engineering design, Ball, Ormerod, and Morley (2004) found that expert designers demonstrated more schema-driven, similar to principles of deep structure, than case-driven analogizing based on concrete prior design problems when solving problems. These are only a handful of examples; however the variety of contexts suggests a general principle that has yet to be addressed by the AIG approach.

Though expert–novice differences in the cognitive literature historically suggest an increased reliance on deep structure by experts on laboratory tasks, this finding may not generalize to all content domains, nor to large-scale standardized educational tests. In some disciplines, attending to surface structure in terms of contextual information is highly relevant for selecting correct problem-solving strategies. Research on medical diagnosis suggests that surface features of problems may influence expert medical professionals' behavior, and appropriately so. Unlike the previously cited research on expert–novice differences in mathematics, physics, and design problem solving, when given diagnostic case studies, medical experts both recalled and used more contextual information than did novices. As a result, the experts more frequently reached the correct diagnosis than did the novices. It is certainly possible that, based on instructional and experiential history, experts may answer complex items based on memory of previous experiences that novices lack. In such cases, the novice is more likely to engage in complex cognitive processes based on a lack of experience.

Whether experts rely more heavily on surface structure than do novices, or the reverse, the more relevant point is that individuals with different abilities may process items differently. Most AIG studies assume a common item structure for all examinees; item radicals are radicals for everyone. To the extent that different item features determine difficulty for some examinees but not others, multiple generative structures are needed. This poses a significant challenge for AIG that has been largely unaddressed. Further, expert–novice differences are potentially only one of the "wrinkles" in AIG implementation. A more comprehensive review of the cognitive psychology literature will likely suggest other complexities related to individual differences in problem solving that may pose additional challenges for operation of AIG, many of which we may not even yet be aware.

The factors affecting the success of the AIG applications relate to the adequacy of the three primary components—the cognitive model, the psychometric model, and the programming capabilities for designing items. In general, limitations associated with the psychometric model are rare. In fact, the rate of development of mathematical models for IDM analysis has surpassed advances in cognitive modeling to the point that more psychometric models exist *without* rather than with concrete applications and appropriate data (Gorin & Svetina, 2011). Limitations in programming capabilities vary, based on testing domain. As illustrated earlier, AIG programs have been successfully authored for cognitive abilities tests, including abstract reasoning, spatial reasoning, and mathematical reasoning. Notably, tests of complex verbal abilities are absent from this list. Numerous IDM studies of reading comprehension test items have informed cognitive model development and provided guidance for item structures (Buck, Tatsuoka, & Kostin, 1997; Gorin & Embretson, 2006; Sheehan, Kostin, & Persky, 2006). However, given the complexity of the design components of these items, specifically the use of passages as a basis for question content, the programming of the generative system is fraught with additional challenges. Still, with rapid advances in natural language processing, these challenges are undoubtedly surmountable. Thus, with the more "technical" components of AIG within our current capabilities, why are so few generative systems operational? The largest challenge stems from the lack of sufficient cognitive understanding of many assessment constructs needed to support AIG implementation. We conclude that two factors are likely to affect the success of AIG and related IDM studies: (a) the existing theory regarding the construct of interest; and (b) the type of task included on the test. Regarding the nature of the construct, AIG and IDM studies of tests measuring constructs with extensive cognitive literature and theory should be more successful than those for which little cognitive theory exists. In terms of task type, tests composed of tasks akin to traditional cognitive/experimental stimuli and processes should be modeled more successfully than tests with complex/innovative item types, which will increase the success of AIG implementation.

It is not our intention to discourage AIG development of non-traditional cognitive constructs. Rather, these efforts are encouraged by highlighting the challenges and heralding the accomplishments thus far. By incorporating formal item structures, introducing strong cognitive theory of our constructs, and providing psychometric tools to evaluate the quality of the items at the cognitive level, some of the subjectivity typically associated with the item-development process may be removed. As part of a larger movement towards a principled approach to educational assessment, principles of good item *design* rather than principles of item *writing* should be promoted. With each AIG and IDM study of large-scale, standards-based educational tests, we improve our understanding of constructs and the items we use to measure them.

References

Arendasy, M., & Sommer, M. (2005). Using psychometric technology in educational assessment: The case of a schema-based isomorphic approach to the automatic generation of quantitative reasoning items. *Learning and Individual Differences, 17*(4), 366–383.

Arendasy, M., Sommer, M., Gittler, G., & Hergovich, A. (2006). Automatic generation of quantitative reasoning items: A pilot study. *Journal of Individual Differences, 27*(1), 2–14.

Ball, L. J., Ormerod, T. C., & Morley, N. J. (2004). Spontaneous analogizing in engineering design: A comparative analysis of experts and novices. *Design Studies, 25*(5), 495–508.

Bejar, I. I. (1993). A generative approach to psychological and educational measurement In. N. Frederiksen, R. J. Mislevy, & I. I. Bejar (Eds.), *Test theory for a new generation of tests* (pp. 323–359). Hillsdale, NJ: Lawrence Erlbaum Associates.

Bejar, I. I. (2002). Item generation: From conception to implementation. . In S. H. Irvine and P. C. Kyllonen (Eds.), *Item generation for test development* (pp. 199–218). Mahwah, NJ: Lawrence Erlbaum Associates.

Bennett, R. E. (1999). Using new technology to improve assessment. *Educational Measurement: Issues and Practice, 18,* 5–12.

Birenbaum, M., Tatsuoka, K. K., & Gurtvirtz, Y. (1992). Effects of response format on diagnostic assessment of scholastic achievement. *Applied Psychological Measurement, 16*(4), 353–363.

Bloom, B. S. (1956). *Taxonomy of educational objectives: The classification of educational goals* (1st ed.). Harlow, Essex, England: Longman Group.

Bower, G. H., & Clapper, J. P. (1989). Experimental methods in cognitive science. In M. I. Posner (Ed.) *Foundations of Cognitive Science* (pp. 245–300). Cambridge, MA: MIT Press.

Buck, G., Tatsuoka, K. K., & Kostin, I. (1997). The skills of reading: Rule-space analysis of a multiple-choice test of second language reading comprehension. *Language Learning, 47,* 423–466.

Byrne, R. M., & Johnson-Laird, P. N. (1989). Spatial reasoning. *Journal of Memory and Lanaguage, 28*(5), 564–575.

Carpenter, P. A., Just, M. A., & Shell, P. (1990). What one intelligence test measures: A theoretical account of processing in the Raven's Progressive Matrices Test. *Psychological Review, 97,* 404–431.

Chi, M. T. H., Feltovich, P. J., & Glaser, R. (1981). Categorization and representation of physics problems by experts and novices. *Cognitive Science, 5*(2), 121–152.

Daniel, R. C., & Embretson, S. E. (2010). Designing cognitive complexity in mathematical problem-solving items. *Applied Psychological Measurement, 34*(5), 348–364.

Diehl, K. A. (2004). Algorithmic item generation and problem solving strategies in matrix completion problems. *Dissertation Abstracts International: Section B: The Sciences and Engineering, 64,* 4075.

Drasgow, F., Luecht, R. M., & Bennett, R. E. (2006). Technology and testing. In R. L. Brennan (Ed.) *Educational measurement* (4th ed.). Westport, CT: American Council on Education and Praeger Publishers.

Embretson, S. E. (1998). A cognitive design system approach to generating valid tests: Application to abstract reasoning. *Psychological Methods, 3,* 380–396.

Embretson, S. E. (2000). Generating Assembling Objects items from cognitive specifications (PR-98-1). Alexandria, VA: Human Resources Research Organization.

Embretson, S. E. (2009). A consideration of AO item specifications. Report FR-09-76, Human Resources Research Organization: Alexandria, VA.

Embretson, S. E. (2011). Impact of differences in item features and displays on the complexity of Assembling Objects items. Report FR-10-xx, Human Resources Research Organization: Alexandria, VA. (Under review).

Embretson, S. E., & Daniel, R. C. (2008). Understanding and quantifying cognitive complexity level in mathematical problem solving items. *Psychology Science Quarterly, 50*(3), 328–344.

Embretson, S. E. & Gorin, J. S. (2001). Improving construct validity with cognitive psychology principles. *Journal of Educational Measurement, 38*(4), 343–368.

Embretson, S. E., & Wetzel, C. D. (1987). Component latent trait models for paragraph comprehension. *Applied Psychological Measurement, 11*(2), 175–193.

Enright, M. K., Morley, M., & Sheehan, K. M. (2002). Items by design: The impact of systematic feature variation on item statistical characteristics. *Applied Measurement in Education, 15*(1), 49–74.

Ericsson, K. A., Charness, N., Feltovich, J., & Hoffman, R. R. (2006). *The Cambridge handbook of expertise and expert performance.* Cambridge, MA: Cambridge University Press.

Ericsson, K. A. & Simon, H. A. (1993). *Protocol analysis: Verbal reports as data.* Cambridge, MA: The MIT Press.

Ferrara, S. & Chen, J. (2011). *Evidence from think-aloud protocols about the validity of inferences from item response demands coding framework.* Paper presented at the Annual Meeting of the American Educational Research Association. New Orleans: LA.

Ferrara, S., Duncan, T. G., Freed, R., Vélez-Paschke, A., McGivern, J., Mushlin, S., et al. (2004). *Examining test score validity by examining item construct validity: Preliminary analysis of evidence of the alignment of targeted and observed content, skills, and cognitive processes in a middle school science assessment.* Paper presented at the 2004 Annual Meeting of the American Educational Research Association.

Fischer, G. H. (1973). Linear logistic test model as an instrument in educational research. *Acta Psychologica, 48*, 315–342.

Gierl, M. J., Leighton, J. P., Wang, C., Zhou, J., Goiert, R., & Tan, A. (2009). *Validating cognitive models of task performance in algebra on the SAT.* College Board Research Report No. 2009-3.

Gierl, M. J., Wang, C., & Zhou, J. (2008). Using the Attribute Hierarchy Method to make diagnostic inferences about examinees' cognitive skills in algebra on the SAT. *Journal of Technology, Learning, and Assessment, 6*(6). Retrieved [June 22, 2011] from http://www.jtla.org.

Glasgow, J. & Malton, A. (1999). A semantics for model-based spatial reasoning. In G. Rickheit, & C. Habel (Eds.), *Mental models in discourse processing and reasoning.* Amsterdam, Netherlands: North-Holland/Elsevier Science Publishers.

Gorin, J. S. (2006a). Item design with cognition in mind. *Educational Measurement: Issues and Practice, 25*(4), 21–35.

Gorin, J. S. (2006b, April). *Using alternative data sources to inform item difficulty modeling.* Paper presented at the 2006 Annual Meeting of the National Council on Measurement in Education. San Francisco, CA.

Gorin, J. S. (2011, April). *Novel IDM applications: Special populations and testing uses.* Paper presented at the 2011 Annual Meeting of the National Council on Measurement in Education, New Orleans, LA.

Gorin, J. S., & Embretson, S. E. (2006). Item difficulty modeling of paragraph comprehension items. *Applied Psychological Measurement, 30*(5), 394–411.

Gorin, J. S., & Svetina, D. (2011). Test design with higher-order cognition in mind. In G. Schraw (Ed.) *Assessment of higher order thinking skills.* Charlotte, NC: Information Age Publishing.

Greene, S., Ratcliff, R., & McKoon, G. (1988). A flexible programming language for generating stimulus lists for cognitive psychology experiments. *Behavior Research Methods, Instruments, & Computers, 20*(2), 119–128.

Hardiman, P. T., Dufresne, R., & Mestre, J. P. (1989). The relation between problem categorization and problem solving among experts and novices. *Memory & Cognition, 17*(5), 627–638.

Humphrey, H. E., Kemper, S., & Radel, J. D. (2004). The time course of metonymic language text processing by older and younger adults. *Experimental Aging Research, 30*, 75–94.

Ivie, J. L., Kupzyk, K. A. & Embretson, S. E. (2004). *Final report of Cognitive Components Study—Predicting strategies for solving multiple-choice quantitative reasoning items: An eyetracker study.* Princeton, NJ: Educational Testing Services and Lawrence, KS: University of Kansas.

Irvine, S. H. (2002). The foundations of item generation for mass testing. In S. H. Irvine and P. C. Kyllonen (Eds.), *Item generation for test development* (pp. 3–34). Mahwah, NJ: Lawrence Erlbaum Associates.

Johnson, C. J., Paivio, A., & Clark, J. M. (1989) Spatial and verbal abilities in children's crossmodal recognition: A dual coding approach. *Canadian Journal of Psychology/Revue canadienne de psychologie, 43*(3), 397–412.

Johnson-Laird, P. N. (1989). Mental models. In M. I. Posner (Ed.) *Foundations of cognitive science* (pp. 469–500). MIT Press.

Johnson-Laird, P. N. (1980). Mental models in cognitive science. *Cognitive Science, 4*, (71–115).

Just, M., & Carpenter, P. (1985). Cognitive coordinate systems: Accounts of mental rotation and individual differences in spatial ability. *Psychological Review, 92*, 137–172.

Kaliski, P. K., Huff, K. L., & Thurber, A. (2011, April). *Using think-aloud interviews in evidence-centered assessment design for the Advanced Placement World History Examination.* Paper presented at the 2011 Annual Meeting of the American Educational Research Association. New Orleans, LA.

Kemper, S., Crow, A., & Kemtes, K. (2004). Eye-fixation patterns of high- and low-span young and older adults: Follow the garden path and back again. *Psychology and Aging, 19*, 157–170.

Kotovsky, K., Hayes, J. R., & Simon, H. A. (1985). Why are some problems hard? Evidence from Tower of Hanoi. *Cognitive Psychology, 17*(2), 248–294.

Leighton, J. P. (2004). Avoiding misconception, misuse, and missed opportunities: The collection of verbal reports in educational achievement testing. *Educational Measurement: Issues and Practice, 23*(4), 6–15.

Leighton, J. P. (2011, April). *Item difficulty and interviewer knowledge effects on the accuracy and consistency of examinee response processes in verbal reports.* Paper presented at the 2011 Annual Meeting of the American Educational Research Association. New Orleans: LA.

Leighton, J. P., & Gierl, M. J. (2007a). Defining and evaluating models of cognition used in educational measurement to make inferences about examinees' thinking processes. *Educational Measurement: Issues and Practice, 26*(2), 3–16.

Leighton, J. P., & Gierl, M. J. (Eds.), (2007b). *Cognitive diagnostic assessment for education. Theories and applications.* Cambridge, MA: Cambridge University Press.

Leighton, J. P. & Gierl, M. J. (2011). *The learning sciences in educational assessment.* Cambridge, MA: Cambridge University Press.

Markman, A. B. (1999). *Knowledge representations.* Mahwah, NJ: Lawrence Erlbaum Associates.

Mayer, R. E., Larkin, J. and Kadane, J. B. (1984). A cognitive analysis of mathematical problem solving ability. In R. Sternberg (Ed.), *Advances in the psychology of human intelligence, Vol. 2* (pp. 231–273). Mahwah, NJ: Lawrence Erlbaum Associates.

Mislevy, R. (2007). Validity by design. *Educational Researcher, 36*(8), 463–469.

Mumaw, R. J. & Pellegrino, J. W. (1984). Individual differences in complex spatial processing. *Journal of Educational Psychology, 76*(5), 920–939.

Novick, L. R. (1988). Analogical transfer, problem similarity, and expertise. *Journal of Experimental Psychology: Learning, Memory, and Cognition, 14*(3), 510–520.

Parker, C. (2010). *Design features for enhanced reading comprehension assessment: Evidence from Cognitive Interviews.* Paper presented at the 2010 Annual Meeting of the National Council on Educational Measurement. Denver, CO.

Powers, D. E., & Wilson, S. T. (1993). *Passage dependence of the New SAT reading comprehension questions* (College Board Report No. 93-3). New York: College Board.

Quasha, W. H., & Likert, R. (1937). The revised Minnesota paper form board test. *Journal of Educational Psychology, 28*(3), 197–204.

Raven, J. C. (1940). Matrix tests. *Mental Health, 1,* 10–18.

Rayner, K., Warren, T., Juhasz, B. J., & Liversedge, S. P. (2004). The effect of plausibility on eye movements in reading. *Journal of Experimental Psychology: Learning, Memory, & Cognition, 30,* 1290–1301.

Schoenfeld, A. H., & Herrmann, D. J. (1982). Problem perception and knowledge structure in expert and novice mathematical problem solvers. *Journal of Experimental Psychology: Learning, Memory, and Cognition, 8*(5), 484–494.

Sheehan, K. M., & Ginther, A. (2001). *What do passage-based multiple-choice verbal reasoning items really measure? An analysis of the cognitive skills underlying performance on the current TOEFL reading section.* Paper presented at the 2000 Annual Meeting of the National Council on Measurement in Education.

Sheehan, K. M., Kostin, I., & Persky, H. (2006). *Predicting item difficulty as a function of inferential processing requirements: An examination of the reading skills underlying performance on the NAEP Grade 8 reading assessment.* Paper presented at the 2006 Annual Meeting of the National Council on Measurement in Education.

Simon, H. A. (1975). The functional equivalence of problem solving skills. *Cognitive Psychology, 7*(2), 268–288.

Singley, M. and Bennett, R. E. (2002). Item generation and beyond: Applications of schema theory to mathematics assessment. In S. H. Irvine & P. C. Kyllonen (Eds.), *Item Generation for Test Development.* (pp. 361–384). Mahwah, NJ: Lawrence Erlbaum Associates, Publishers.

Towns, M. H., & Robinson, W. R. (1993). Student use of test-wiseness strategies in solving multiple-choice chemistry examinations. *Journal of Research in Science Teaching, 30*(7), 709–722.

Williamson, D. M., Bauer, M., Steinberg, L. S., Mislevy, R. J., Behrens, J. T., & DeMark, S. F. (2004). Design rationale for a complex performance assessment. *International Journal of Testing, 4,* 303–332.

10
Difficulty Modeling and Automatic Generation of Quantitative Items
Recent Advances and Possible Next Steps

Edith Aurora Graf and James H. Fife

Introduction and Background Terminology

In this chapter, we discuss recent research and possible future directions for difficulty modeling and automatic item generation (AIG) of quantitative items. For a summary of recent research on item generation in reasoning, verbal comprehension, and mathematics, refer to Bejar (2010). First, we define some background terminology used to discuss item modeling and AIG. Next, we consider the relationship between cognitive modeling and difficulty modeling, and review research that has identified features of quantitative items that have an impact on difficulty. We argue that an iterative approach to item design, evaluation, and revision can guide the transition from weak to strong cognitive theory and that, as a technology, AIG can facilitate an iterative approach. We explore difficulty modeling of quantitative items from the perspective of transfer of learning, and review several psychometric methods that support difficulty modeling. Finally, we discuss advances in AIG that have the potential to assist difficulty modeling, instructional diagnosis, and automatic scoring.

Different researchers use different terminology when describing difficulty modeling and AIG. For the sake of clarity and brevity, we use consistent terminology whenever possible, which is not necessarily the same as that used by the authors whose work is described. As in Bejar (2002), we use the term *item model* to describe a set of items that share a common structure, and as in Enright and Sheehan (2002), we use the term *item family* to refer to related but different sets of items (or item models).

A quantitative item model can be expressed mathematically using variables and constraints. In other words, an item model may be construed as a set definition, where each element of the set corresponds to an item that could be generated by the item model. A particular item described by an item model is referred to as an instance (Bejar, 2002). Irvine (2002) distinguished between *incidental* and *radical* item elements. An incidental item model variable does not significantly affect the psychometric characteristics of the instances; by contrast, a radical item model variable influences the difficulty or discrimination of the instances. Instances that share a common mathematical structure as well as similar psychometric parameters are referred to as *isomorphs* (Bejar, 2002). In other words, item models that include only incidental variables generate isomorphs. An item model can be encoded as a computer program, or algorithm, from which instances may be automatically generated (e.g., Macready & Merwin, 1973; Meisner, Luecht, & Reckase, 1993; Singley & Bennett, 2002; Gierl, Zhou, & Alves, 2008).

Cognitive Models and Difficulty Modeling of Test Items

Before discussing the question of how item modeling and AIG can be used to enhance difficulty modeling of quantitative items, we will consider the question of why difficulty modeling is a worthwhile pursuit. One pragmatic reason is that an understanding of how item features relate to difficulty and discrimination may be used to predict the parameters of item instances in advance (e.g., Bejar, 1993, 1996; Bejar, Lawless, Morley, Wagner, Bennett, & Revuelta, 2003; Bejar & Yocom, 1991; Embretson, 1999). Depending on the predictive accuracy of a difficulty model, it may be used alone or in combination with other data sources. For example, Mislevy, Sheehan, and Wingersky (1993) found that, while information about item features alone was not sufficient to accurately predict item parameter estimates in a three-parameter logistic (3PL) model, item features could be used in combination with examinee calibration data to predict item parameters as accurately as could be predicted with a much larger calibration sample alone. In other words, difficulty modeling (through the use of item modeling or by some other means) has the potential to make the calibration process more cost-effective.

There is a more fundamental reason why item difficulty modeling is worthwhile, however: It is a potential link in the chain of inference that affords insight into what students know and can do. Greater insight into how students represent and apply knowledge and understanding contributes to one of the fundamental pillars of assessment (Leighton & Gierl, 2011; Pellegrino, Chudowsky, & Glaser, 2001). A model of item difficulty should not stand alone as a collection of associations between combinations of item features and their predicted impact on difficulty. While associations between item features and difficulty estimates are certainly necessary to support a theory, they do not provide an explanatory mechanism for why some items are more difficult than others; in other words, they do not by themselves constitute a cognitive model of performance. In the absence of a cognitive model that explains why some items are more difficult than others, we cannot claim to understand what students know and can do. The importance of cognitive models to assessment design for the purpose of providing a more complete and valid interpretative mechanism has received increasing emphasis in the past ten to fifteen years (e.g., Gierl & Leighton, 2007; Gorin, 2006; Leighton & Gierl, 2007; Mislevy, Steinberg, & Almond, 2002; Pellegrino et al., 2001).

The presence of a cognitive model has the potential to enhance the outcome aspect of validity, which refers to test interpretation and test use (Messick, 1989). Particularly where formative applications are concerned, a cognitive model is needed to guide further instruction. While a good starting-point, associations between item features and difficulty do not suggest how to support student learning. By contrast, a cognitive model explains *why* some tasks are more or less difficult with respect to the cognitive resources required, and which steps and/or sub-processes are more likely to pose hurdles, and hence suggests a more specific approach for subsequent intervention.

Gorin (2006) distinguished between two types of cognitive models that are used to support assessment design: general cognitive models that elaborate on the construct and specific cognitive models that address a particular type of item. The latter is still the more common, particularly in mathematical and scientific domains where the set of required knowledge and skills varies considerably with the content. This is not to say that these domains consist of disparate constellations of concepts and skills; for example, in mathematics, connections among areas of study are central to the discipline (e.g., National Council of Teachers of Mathematics, 2000). Recognizing the connections, however, is one of the indicators of expertise; this level of understanding is typically developed as a result of years of studying related concepts in a variety of contexts. To the novice, many of the connections are not yet apparent, and this should be considered in the development of cognitive models of student performance.

Both kinds of cognitive models (the more general and the more specific) can support a more thorough understanding of student performance. Several frameworks are available to foster the transition from cognitive theory to assessment development. Examples of these include Nichols' framework for developing a cognitively diagnostic assessment (Nichols, 1994), the cognitive design system approach (Embretson, 1999; Embretson & Gorin, 2001; Embretson & Yang, 2007), and evidence-centered design (ECD; Mislevy, Steinberg, & Almond, 2003).

The ACED Project

The ACED project (e.g., see Shute, Graf, & Hansen, 2005) illustrates the transition from cognitive theory to assessment development. ACED was an application of the ECD approach to develop a computer-based, adaptive assessment for middle school mathematics. Following the domain analysis and domain modeling phases of ECD, a student model (sometimes also referred to as a proficiency model, student proficiency model, or competency model) was developed for arithmetic and geometric sequences and other sequences, such as the Fibonacci sequence, that are commonly taught in the middle grades (Graf, 2003). Descriptions of several of the competencies from the portion of the student model that spans knowledge and skills related to geometric sequences are described below:

- Extend Geometric Sequences (find additional and/or missing terms).
    - Example: Find the next term in the following geometric sequence: 2, 6, 18, 54, 162, …
- Identify the common ratio of a geometric sequence.
    - Example: Find the common ratio for the following geometric sequence: 2, 6, 18, 54, 162, …
- Induce Rules. This skill involves specifying the rules that can generate terms in the sequence. Rules may be expressed verbally or algebraically, in either recursive or closed form, depending on the specifics of what is being assessed.
    - Example responses:
        1. "To get the next term in the sequence, I multiply the previous term by three."
        2. "To find the tenth term, I multiply two by three to the ninth."
        3. An algebraic characterization expressed in recursive form: $a_n = a_{n-1}r$.
        4. An algebraic characterization expressed in closed form: $a_n = a_1 r^{n-1}$.
- Use geometric sequences to model situations.
    - Examples: scenarios involving bacterial growth, radioactive decay, compound interest, etc.

The model specifies the constituent competencies involved in working with geometric sequences, and suggests both the nature of the evidence that will be collected and the types of tasks that may be used to collect that evidence. (Full specifications of the nature of the evidence to be collected and the types of tasks that elicit that evidence are provided in the evidence and task models, respectively.) These specifications were used to develop item models, and close to half of the items used in ACED were automatically generated from these models.

The student model above does not quite constitute a cognitive theory, since it does not describe what student thinking processes are involved in each of the constituent competencies or how these thinking processes relate to each other. In a follow-up to this work, however, Almond, Shute, Underwood, and Zapata-Rivera (2009) uncovered some interesting trends in the data that are pertinent to elaborating on the relationships among the proficiencies in the model. The student model for geometric sequences was instantiated as a Bayesian network; the posterior distribution from the network following the collection of responses was used to calculate scores. Each proficiency variable has three states: high, medium, and low. An EAP (expected *a posteriori*) score for each student on each proficiency was calculated as the difference between the probability of being in the high state and the probability of being in the low state, in other words, as $P(S_{ik} = \text{high} \mid X_i) - P(S_{ik} = \text{low} \mid X_i)$, where S_{ik} refers to the proficiency variable of the ith student on the kth proficiency, and X_i refers to the observables for student i (Almond et al., 2009). Among the displays in the paper is a matrix of scatterplots (fig. 7, p. 457). Each scatterplot shows the student EAP scores of one proficiency variable against the EAP scores of another variable; the matrix shows all such scatterplots.

Almond et al. (2009) noted that the reversed L shapes in several of the plots strongly suggest the presence of prerequisite relationships between some of the proficiency variables—in other words, many of the plots in the matrix show that a very high EAP score must be achieved on one variable before anything above a low EAP score can be achieved on the other variable. In particular, the Extend and Common Ratio proficiencies appear to be prerequisites for most of the other proficiencies. At least one plausible explanation for this is that extending a geometric sequence or identifying its common ratio requires basic pattern-recognition skills but little background knowledge, facility with procedures, or conceptual understanding. This type of pattern recognition is likely a component of other proficiencies, but they require skills well beyond pattern recognition. For example, algebraic rule induction necessarily involves pattern recognition, but it also requires symbolization in order to formulate a response. The results from Almond et al. (2009) suggest some options for formulating a cognitive model that could be examined in further research.

The Iterative Nature of Cognitive Model Development

Having argued that a cognitive model can lend validity to an assessment and is important from the perspective of understanding what students know and can do, we will qualify the argument slightly: especially in the early stages of research and development, we are not necessarily prepared to supply a cognitive model or competing cognitive models to guide its design. For mathematics assessment, the field has reached the stage where it is possible to design assessments based on existing cognitive models. But for operational testing program purposes, the usual requirement is to design a test that addresses a broad span of content and is aligned to a particular curriculum and/or standards. This is a more complicated problem: specific cognitive models do not necessarily exist for each task type in each content area, and while general models exist that may account for some, or even substantial, aspects of student performance, a large proportion of the variance will likely be left unexplained because we know the specifics are important (Leighton & Gierl, 2011). Recent progress in the development of more specific and more general cognitive models for mathematics has been made and will be discussed in a later section.

The preceding discussion illustrates two points: first, the *pilot* versions of a test are unlikely to be based on a complete cognitive model of performance. This may occur for a variety of reasons, including the goal of the models developed for the test and the availability of existing research. In the case of the student model for ACED, one of the goals was to develop a model that would be aligned to the curriculum. Second, data collection is likely to provide information that can be used to build or revise a cognitive model of performance. Item modeling and automatic generation have a potentially important role to play in the development and revision of cognitive models of performance (Bejar, 2010).

Features That Have an Impact on the Difficulty of Quantitative Items

Most difficulty modeling efforts in quantitative domains have focused on particular content areas or particular problem types. Recently, however, Embretson and Daniel (2008) and Daniel and Embretson (2010) evaluated a more general cognitive model developed to predict difficulty of the broader pool of problem-solving items from the Quantitative Reasoning measure of the GRE General Test (see also, summary in Gorin & Embretson, this volume). The former study compared different psychometric approaches for assessing the fit of the cognitive model to existing GRE quantitative items. The latter study evaluated differences in difficulty among variants generated from item models. Two components from the cognitive model were used as item model variables to examine whether systematically manipulating these difficulty predictors would produce the expected results. The cognitive model was an extension of Mayer, Larkin, and Kadane's theory of mathematical problem solving, which encompasses two main processing stages: Problem Representation and Problem Execution. Problem Representation subsumes two sub-stages: Problem Translation and Problem Integration. Problem Execution is also composed of two sub-stages: Solution Planning and Solution Execution.

Since GRE problem-solving items are a multiple-choice response type, Embretson (as cited in Embretson & Daniel, 2008) adapted the Mayer et al. model by incorporating a Decision stage, which involves processing the distractors. Embretson and Daniel (2008) found that the model explained roughly half the variance in the difficulty of quantitative problem-solving items. This is a significant advance, given the breadth of the content covered by this pool of items. It also suggests, however, that developing more specific cognitive models particular to a narrow band of content and/or a particular item type is still a necessity. The following paragraphs review some of the features that are known to have an impact on the difficulty of algebra and arithmetic items, for which item difficulty predictors are perhaps more completely understood than in other quantitative areas. Some generalizations are made, but it is still the case that features specific to the content and/or an item type have the potential to "override" any of the general difficulty predictors discussed here.

Features That Influence Item Complexity

Mathematics problems tend to become more difficult as their complexity increases, and several design characteristics pertain to item complexity. In a study of algebra word problems, Sebrechts, Enright, Bennett, & Martin (1996) identified *nest level* as a positive predictor of item difficulty (where nest level refers either to the number of equations or the number of levels of parentheses). In examining the impact of item model variables on the difficulty of generated instances, Enright and Sheehan (2002) found that introducing an additional constraint makes rate problems more difficult. Deane, Graf, Higgins, Futagi, and Lawless (2006) found that among pure algebra problems (i.e., problems with no situating context) from the Quantitative Reasoning measure of the GRE General Test that involved linear equations and simple rational equations, two-equation problems were more difficult than one-equation problems. Embretson and Daniel (2008) found that when using Fischer's Linear Logistic Test Model (LLTM), the presence of a relative definition (where one variable is defined in terms of another) significantly predicts the difficulty of GRE problem-solving items. As cited in Tabachneck, Koedinger, and Nathan (1995), Riley and Greeno found that start-unknown arithmetic word problems are more difficult than result-unknown arithmetic word problems. Although this effect tended to diminish after 3rd grade with problems involving only one operator, Koedinger and Tabachneck (1995) found the effect among high school students for word problems involving two operators.

Another consistent finding is that items that necessitate working with symbolic representations are often more difficult than items that do not. For example, from the Quantitative Reasoning measure of the GRE General Test algebra and arithmetic items Enright and Sheehan (2002) found that among problems that require fewer than three steps, those with a key that is a mathematical or logical expression are more difficult than those for which the key is a quantity. Similarly, Deane et al. (2006) found that problems with symbolic keys were more difficult than problems with numeric keys. For rate problems generated from item models, Enright and Sheehan (2002) found that instances that use variables in both the stem and the key tend to be more difficult than instances that do not use variables in either the stem or the key.

Embretson and Daniel (2008) and Daniel and Embretson (2010) found that the need to "Generate or Recall Equations" was strongly associated with item difficulty. This is not quite the same as generating or recognizing an equation in the final step, where either generating an equation or interpreting it is an absolute requirement. For many algebra problems, the traditional solution involves generating an equation, but students apply alternative, arithmetic-based solutions in many of these situations (e.g., Tabachneck et al., 1995). These strategies are often effective, but students are less likely to apply them to problems presented in symbolic format (Nathan, Koedinger, & Tabachneck, 2000), potentially resulting in lower performance. The work of Lee and Wheeler (1989) suggests that, when asked to justify a mathematical statement, students are strongly influenced by the presentation format: when presented with a symbolic statement, they tend to search for a formal algebraic rule and to avoid substituting values; when presented with a statement involving numbers, they tend to provide numeric examples rather than an algebraic justification.

It seems reasonable to expect that quantitative items that either include variables in the stem or require a variable in the response are likely to be more difficult, since they necessarily involve some symbolic thinking. (Even if an arithmetic strategy is used, it must still be related in some way to the given or required variables.) This is not to suggest that algebraic strategies are never applied to problems that do not include variables. In some situations, an algebraic approach may be much more expedient, if less intuitive, even when the key is numeric. For this reason, whether an item "requires working with symbolic representations" is not necessarily indicated by the format of the item or the key. A potential complexity in using this interpretation as a difficulty predictor is that it is strategy dependent. Assuming that there exists a predominant strategy that is used by the examinee population, it should be used to determine whether or not an item requires working with symbolic representations.

Difficulty Predictors that Depend on Solution Strategies

In general, strategy-dependent difficulty predictors (which are likely to be uncovered in the difficulty modeling of quantitative items) deserve special consideration. Some problems may afford several quite different solution strategies, and in some cases problems that encourage multiple solution methods are a recommended design principle, and with good reason—alternative strategies can provide very rich information about student cognition. Many tests use multiple-choice and/or short constructed-response item types, where the strategy is not directly observable. Verbal protocols and/or scratchwork can be collected from a small sample of students to get a sense for the types of strategies students are using, and how they are associated with other dependent measures that are observable (such as response times). If a difficulty predictor only applies to a subset of strategies that may be used to solve an item, then there is the possibility that the item may not fit the model very well. Alternative models may be considered in this situation. Irrespective of which approach is used, however, an examination of strategy use is central to the task of modeling difficulty in quantitative domains.

Symbolic Problems and Word Problems

One feature that may not have a consistent effect on difficulty is the stem format, and whether it is expressed in words or symbols. Mayer (1982) found that college students solved linear equations in one variable more quickly when working from a symbolic stem, presumably because when such equations are expressed in words, an additional translation step is involved to express the equation in symbolic form prior to solving it. As noted earlier, however, students do not necessarily apply traditional methods when solving algebra problems, especially if the problem is not expressed in symbolic format. Koedinger and Nathan (2004) found that for high school algebra students, performance on mathematically equivalent problems is higher when the stem is expressed in words than when it is expressed as a symbolic equation, given that the language is natural and familiar.

Arithmetic word problems that are solved by using operations that are inconsistent with the word order in the stem use what is referred to as *inconsistent language*, and are more difficult than problems that use *consistent language* in the stem (Lewis & Mayer, 1987). By college, this difficulty is not apparent with arithmetic problems (Martin & Bassok, 2005), but is still strongly in evidence for algebraic translation items—items for which the correct equation is consistent with a direct word-order translation are much easier than items for which the correct equation is inconsistent with a direct word-order translation (Clement, Lochhead, & Monk, 1981; Clement, Lochhead, & Soloway, 1979; Borchert, 2003; Graf, Bassok, Hunt, & Minstrell, 2004).

In modeling the difficulty of a pool of arithmetic and algebra items from the Quantitative section of the GRE, Enright and Sheehan (2002) found that abstract problems are slightly easier than word problems. When using the LLTM to model the difficulty of a pool of GRE mathematical problem-solving items, Embretson and Daniel (2008) found that the need to translate equations from words in the stem was among the statistically significant model coefficients. By contrast, in the study that examined the difficulty of instances generated from item models, the need to translate equations (which was explicitly included as a level of an item model design variable) did not significantly affect difficulty, whether using the LLTM or Embretson's 2PL-constrained model (Daniel & Embretson, 2010). In their study, Deane et al. (2006) found that symbolic stem items tended to be easier than verbal stem items. Only 12 of the items examined had verbal stems, but upon examination it was found that five of these used direct translation-consistent stems and five used direct translation-inconsistent stems. The difference between the means was not statistically significant, though it was in the expected direction. It is likely that whether verbal or symbolic stems tend to be easier is mediated by linguistic complexity. Arendasy, Sommer, Gittler, and Hergovich (2006) explicitly took this variable into account in the design of the "quality control framework" of the AGEN item generator of quantitative reasoning items by limiting the grammatical and linguistic complexity of the generated instances.

The combined results suggest that stem format alone is not a reliable predictor of item difficulty, since the processes involved are likely to vary considerably, depending on linguistic complexity and the background knowledge of the population. The cognitive requirements involved in processing a verbal stem, even one that is not contextualized, can vary considerably. Based on the available research, however, it seems reasonable to conclude that symbolic stems are likely to be more difficult than verbal stems when linguistic complexity is limited. In practice, however, it is not uncommon for mathematics test items to include language that is direct translation-inconsistent, and so both variables (stem format and linguistic complexity) should be considered together.

Number Type—Fractions and Decimals

Although often treated as an incidental variable, number type can influence item difficulty. For example, Enright and Sheehan (2002) found that procedural GRE items that involve working only with linear relationships tend to be more difficult when the stem includes fractions or decimals, but not when they involve nonlinear relationships. A possible reason for this is that the skills involved in working with nonlinear relationships may be advanced relative to the skills involved in working with arithmetic problems or linear relationships (depending on the type of nonlinear relationship), and so it might be expected that number type would have relatively little impact on the difficulty of these more advanced problems but would impact the difficulty of problems that address more fundamental skills. Number type has also been shown to affect the difficulty of high school algebra problems (Koedinger & Nathan, 2004). Some values may simplify calculation (e.g., multiples of 10). The values of particular variables can even interact with problem structure. Some numeric values may yield special cases that can be solved using a weaker strategy or through the application of a simpler formula.

Distractors

For multiple-choice items, the composition of the distractor set can be an important predictor of difficulty. For example, the types of available distractors can influence the difficulty of object assembly items (Embretson & Gorin, 2001) and analytical reasoning items (Newstead, Bradon, Handley, Evans, & Dennis, 2002). In the following section, an example of how the distractor set impacted on the difficulty of linear inequality instances is discussed (Graf, Steffen, Peterson, Saldivia, & Wang, 2004; Graf, Peterson, Steffen, & Lawless, 2005). Embretson and Daniel (2008) found that "Decision Processing" is a significant predictor of the difficulty of GRE quantitative problem-solving items, where decision processing refers to the necessity to refer to the distractors in order to correctly respond to the item. Very few of the items require decision processing, however. The evidence suggests that for multiple-choice items, the composition of the distractor set can play an important role in item difficulty, and that the requirement to extensively process distractors, although it may occur rarely, tends to make items more difficult.

Summary: Difficulty Predictors for Quantitative Items

To summarize, a number of predictors have been identified which are likely to influence the difficulty for arithmetic and algebra items. Some of the findings have come from studies intended to model the difficulty of an existing item pool, while others have come from studies in which potential difficulty predictors are systematically varied. These two approaches play complementary roles: existing items typically encompass greater structural variation than modeled instances, and so explaining the difficulty of existing item pools is a *necessary*, though not *sufficient* condition for developing a *complete* cognitive model. It is also likely, however, that potential difficulty predictors in existing items tend to co-occur, which can potentially confound interpretation. A model-based approach has the potential to disentangle the features that contribute to item difficulty by manipulating some variables while holding others constant. Some of the general features that appear to increase the difficulty of arithmetic and algebra items include increasing mathematical complexity (for example, by including additional constraints), the requirement to work with symbolic representations, the requirement to work with more advanced number types, and, for multiple-choice items, the requirement to process the distractors.

As predictors of item difficulty, these variables will almost certainly have practical limitations. What has been observed so far is that, on the whole, items with some features tend to be more difficult than others, and that varying these features while holding others constant can produce differences in difficulty. But it is still possible that features specific to an item model can have a greater influence on difficulty than any of the variables discussed here. At this point, it is not clear how these and other variables interact to influence difficulty, or whether they influence difficulty in the same way across different populations. General predictors of difficulty may also be challenging to interpret consistently, because their meaning is likely to change as the content of the item type changes. The more general a predictor, the more human judgment is involved in interpreting it in context, and this uncertainty translates to an additional source of error. For all of these reasons, difficulty modeling of quantitative items is not at the point yet where it is possible to reliably predict the difficulty of a new item written "from scratch." Still, there has been great progress in understanding how item features contribute to the difficulty of quantitative items, and the limitations are discussed only because it is advisable to keep them in mind.

Difficulty Modeling as an Iterative Process: From Weak Theory to Strong Theory

As discussed in Enright and Sheehan (2002), one approach to investigating the influence of item features on difficulty is to design item families that systematically vary the features of interest. This is the approach taken by Koedinger and colleagues in their *Difficulty Factors Assessment* (DFA) methodology (e.g., see Koedinger & Nathan, 2004 for an application of DFA), which is applied to the purpose of refining a cognitive model of the student. The approach is usually guided by hypotheses about how variation in item features has an impact on difficulty. These hypotheses may be based on a test developers' accumulated expertise, or they may be based on previously collected data. For example, prior to the systematic generation of items, Enright and Sheehan explored the relationships between item features and item difficulty as evident from data collected earlier by Sebrechts et al. (1996), and used their findings to guide the design of item families. Extending this notion, prior rounds of data collection can inform subsequent rounds of experimental design as part of an iterative process.

A number of researchers have emphasized the importance of iterative rounds of data collection and revision where explaining difficulty is concerned (e.g, Bejar, 1993; Bejar & Yocom, 1991; Embretson & Gorin, 2001; Graf et al., 2005). In their discussion of the cognitive design-system approach, Embretson and Gorin (2001, pp. 350–352) define a sequence of seven stages. The stages prior to item generation focus on characterizing relationships between a cognitive model and item design features, and the stages following item generation focus on empirical validation. However, Embretson and Gorin also point out that "Although these stages are presented in a suggested order, one should note that the entire process is iterative, and the continued improvement of items may require returning to earlier stages of the framework. For example, if the initial cognitive model is not complete or comprehensive enough to describe the item characteristics, then it may be required to return to model generation, even after having generated items" (p. 350). This is consistent with our own experience: although expert opinion and previous research findings should inform the development of difficulty models, difficulty variables are sometimes situation specific and only become apparent *following* a cognitive analysis of generated instances and their associated statistics. Typically, empirical evaluation suggests a *refinement* to the guiding hypotheses, which in turn implicates item model revision and a subsequent round of data collection. The workflow that accompanies this approach is described in more detail in Graf et al. (2005).

Bejar (2002) made a distinction between item models developed for the purpose of generating *isomorphs* and items models developed for the purpose of generating *variants*. Isomorphs vary only with respect to their incidental features; their structural characteristics are the same. Isomorphs are usually considered interchangeable, at least when it can be empirically verified that they share similar psychometric characteristics. Variants assume different values on radical variables and, unlike isomorphs, are not considered interchangeable. The psychometric characteristics of variants are expected to vary in predictable ways, however.

Designing an item model that generates isomorphs requires an awareness of features that impact on cognitive processes, but does not demand a complete cognitive theory, because the cognitive processes only need to be understood so far as to hold the psychometric parameters relatively constant. By contrast, designing an item model that generates variants requires a much more complete cognitive theory that relates the systematic manipulation of item features to differences in difficulty. Bejar (2010, p. 202) noted considerations that are fundamental to item modeling research, the first of which was "the theoretical basis, or lack thereof, for an accounting of the variability in the psychometric attributes among instances produced from item models …" Bejar went on to say:

> With respect to the first consideration, Drasgow, Luecht, and Bennett (2006) proposed the distinction between weak and strong theory as a means of distinguishing among approaches to

item generation. Operating from strong theory enables the production of items that range in their psychometric attributes in a theoretically predictable manner. By contrast, when researchers operate from weak theory, they, in effect, apply case-based reasoning; that is, if they know the psychometric attributes on one item, they should be able to hold constant the psychometric attributes of items like it. ... Although item models designed to produce isomorphs can be an instance of case-based reasoning when our theoretical knowledge is limited, such models can also be applied in pursuit of a stronger theory or can even be based on strong theory.

(Bejar, 2010, p. 203)

The last point is especially important—often in test design, information to build a complete cognitive model is not available. Expert schemas may provide a good starting-point, but experts' predictions of item difficulty are not often accurate (e.g., Bejar, 1983; Camerer & Johnson, 1991; Nathan et al., 2000; Nathan, Koedinger, & Alibali, 2001; Nathan & Petrosino, 2003). This may occur because experts perceive the domain so much differently from novices, a circumstance Nathan and Petrosino (2003) referred to as the *expert blindspot*. Alternatively, it is possible to approach test design by using a weak theory approach, with the goal of developing a stronger cognitive theory as a result of successive iterations of design, empirical evaluation, and revision. Item modeling and automatic item generation can play a role in facilitating the transition from weak to strong theory. For more on weak and strong theory approaches to AIG, see Gierl and Lai, this volume.

An Example of the Iterative Approach

As an example of this approach, Graf et al. (2005) describe work in which the original goal was to develop item models that would generate isomorphs. As found in Meisner et al. (1993), some of the item models generated instances with comparable statistics, while others did not. Following a cognitive analysis of several of the models that generated instances with more variable statistics, the models were revised as part of several experiments designed to pinpoint which variables might account for the observed differences in difficulty. The models were based on source items from the Quantitative Reasoning measure of the GRE General Test.

First Iteration

The original item model was designed to generate difficult isomorphs testing the examinee's ability to manipulate linear inequalities. As it turned out, though, the model yielded instances with relatively variable psychometric parameters. Following is one instance generated from this model:

The statement "$t - 3 \leq -1$ or $3 - t \geq 13$" is equivalent to which of the following?

A. $t \leq 2$ (Key)
B. $t \leq -10$
C. $-2 \leq t \leq 13$
D. $-9 \leq t \leq 3$
E. $-10 \leq t \leq 2$

This item model generates multiple-choice instances and, as such, generates both a key and distractors. A *key model* refers to the set of variables and constraints that characterizes the key, and a *distractor model* refers to the set of variables and constraints that characterizes a particular distractor. Ten instances were generated from the original item model; each examinee saw only one instance from the model. The average number of examinees per instance was 793. A 3PL IRT model (Birnbaum, 1968) was fitted to the response scores; classical item statistics were also produced. The differences in difficulty are easiest to see from an examination of the proportions correct; proportions correct

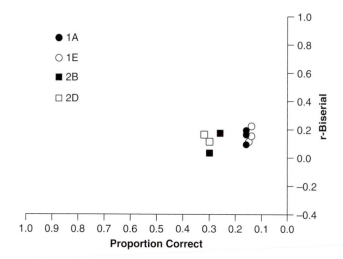

and r-biserials are shown in Figure 10.1. The figure shows two main clusters of instances; six quite difficult instances with a mean proportion correct of .15 and four somewhat easier instances with a mean proportion correct of .30. The r-biserials are low, but this item model generates quite difficult items; the IRT a-parameter estimates are between 0.40 and 1.37 for the more difficult instances and between 0.20 and 0.59 for the somewhat easier instances.

For this particular item model, the number of distractor models exceeds the number of distractors in each instance, so only a subset of distractor models is represented in each instance. The model includes additional constraints on the subsets of distractors, such that only two combinations are possible. The two clusters in Figure 10.1 correspond to two types of instances, as follows:

Type 1 instance. Lower performance, mean proportion correct: .15

The statement "$t - 3 \leq -1$ or $3 - t \geq 13$" is equivalent to which of the following?

A. $t \leq 2$ Key model ($t \leq 2$ or $t \leq -10$)
B. $t \leq -10$ Distractor Model 2 (examinee interprets *or* as *and*)
C. $-2 \leq t \leq 13$ Distractor Model 3
D. $-9 \leq t \leq 3$ Distractor Model 4
E. $-10 \leq t \leq 2$ Distractor Model 1 (reversed inequality)

Type 2 instance. Higher performance, mean proportion correct: .30

$$x - 9 < -2 \text{ or } 4 - x > 19$$

The statement above is equivalent to which of the following?

A. $-14 < x < 8$ Distractor Model 4
B. $-7 < x < 19$ Distractor Model 3
C. $x < -15$ Distractor Model 2 (examinee interprets *or* as *and*)
D. $x < 7$ Key model ($x < 7$ or $x < -15$)
E. $x < 19$ Distractor Model 5

In each of the instances above, the distractors are labeled with the corresponding distractor models that generated them. The two types have different distractor model sets: Type 2 instances replace Distractor Model 1 with Distractor Model 5. Distractor Model 1 generates potentially attractive distractors that are quite similar to an intermediate step in the solution. For example, the statement in the Type 1 instance above simplifies to $t \leq 2$ or $t \leq -10$. If an examinee interprets this as "t is less than or equal to 2 and greater than or equal to -10," then the Distractor Model 1 option is the expected response. Or, if the examinee proceeds as far as the simplification step and then searches for an option that appears similar, then the Distractor Model 1 option is again the expected response. The Distractor 5 model, however, seems far less compelling, since it just uses one of the values in the original problem statement.

The instances generated by the model also vary in other respects; for example, the stem format varies slightly, as does the order of the options. The options are presented either in the order shown above (yielding E keys and D keys, for Type 1 and Type 2 instances, respectively) or in the reverse order (yielding A keys and B keys, for Type 1 and Type 2 instances, respectively). As shown in Figure 10.1 however, it appears that these variables are incidental, at least based on this sample of 10 instances.

Figure 10.2 shows that Distractor Model 1 generates the most attractive distractors: for each instance, distractors generated by Distractor Model 1 claim 40–50% of the responses. In Figure 10.2, Distractor Models 1 and 2 produce distractors that are more popular than the key. It can also be seen that Distractor Model 5 did not produce attractive distractors, so it seems likely that replacing Distractor Model 1 with Distractor Model 5 accounts for the difference in mean proportion correct between the two types of instances.

Second Iteration

To examine this hypothesis, Graf, Steffen et al. (2004) constrained the model so that it would only generate Type 1 instances. Thirty-two instances were generated from the revised model (16 with A keys and 16 with E keys). Proportions correct and r-biserials from the revised model are shown in Figure 10.3. Constraining the model in this way was effective for generating more nearly isomorphic instances.

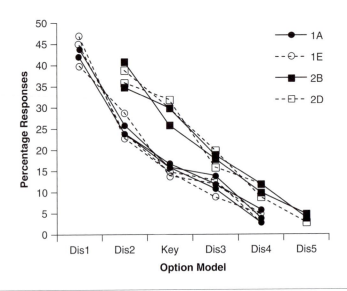

Figure 10.2 Percentage of examinees that selected options generated by different option models on instances generated by the linear inequality model (adapted from Graf et al., 2005)

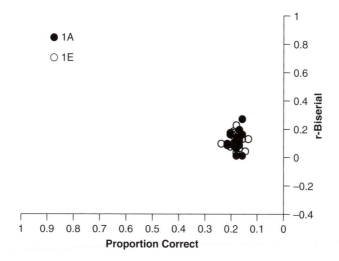

Figure 10.3 Proportions correct and r-biserial values for the revised version of the linear inequality model (adapted from Graf, Steffen et al., 2004)

Further Iterations

This particular item model was straightforward to revise because the source of the difference in difficulty between the two types was easily identified. In this case, the model was revised by eliminating a fairly obvious radical source of variation. For most of the other item models for which the instances varied in difficulty, several item model variables with radical potential were identified, and often they were confounded. In these cases, a different approach was taken: item model variables with "radical" potential became the independent variables in an experiment, and were used to create revised item models that were systematic variations on the original. Instances were generated from each of the revised versions. The results of these experiments sometimes provided more information about how combinations of item model variables interact to produce differences in difficulty. The results are not always conclusive, however; our experience has been that about half of the time the revision process raises more questions than it answers about the sources of variation that contribute to item difficulty. But when the results are interpretable, they can lead to the development of something closer to a strong theory, albeit for a specific item type. In sum, in situations where strong theory does not exist or is not a perfect fit for a planned assessment, it is possible to start from a weak theory approach and, through successive rounds of item model development, AIG, data collection, cognitive analysis, item model revision, and more data collection, approach something closer to a strong theory. Over time, it should be possible to develop many specific cognitive models, and eventually to generalize them.

Other Considerations

Sampling Issues

In the iterative approach, the sampling process to pilot instances deserves serious attention. If a sample of instances is too limited, then it may not be possible to make even a reasonable conjecture as to which variables explain most of the variance in difficulty. Of course, there is necessarily a trade-off between the number of instances and the number of examinees per instance that can be piloted; the optimal balance can be explored in simulation studies. In our experience, however, it is most important to have data from a reasonable number of instances (at least 10, and preferably more, depending on the complexity of the model). For the first iteration, the model parameter estimates need to be sufficiently precise to suggest which features are most likely responsible for producing variation. The sampling method is as important as the number of sampled instances. A simple random sample is often used, and this may be sufficient or even preferable in situations where it is expected that the item model will generate isomorphs and there is no reason to expect pockets of more or less difficult instances. As mentioned earlier, however, when instantiated with certain values, some formulas or functions may reduce to simpler, special cases that require less background knowledge, less-involved procedures, or less conceptual knowledge.

Often, item model developers may be able to anticipate the pockets and author constraints to account for them. It may also be possible to program warnings about special cases into AIG software. But unusual interactions between item model variables may still occur. In a discussion about interaction among item factors, Almond expressed this concern: "One of the assumptions coming out of this modeling work was that all these factors were more or less independent, or at least they followed an additive or generalized additive model. It was a bit worrisome to me that there might be some combination of problem story, and use of marked versus unmarked things, which would drive you up into some kind of weird corner of that distribution…" (Irvine & Kyllonen, 2002, p. 80) and "There's also some question in my mind, whether there is not some intelligent kind of sampling protocol, like the latin hypercube. That might help us get at some of these interaction effects, get some model checking for the presence of these interaction effects, into the pretesting phase…" (p. 82).

Cost Issues With Operational Programs

The iterative process is an expensive prospect and at some point yields diminishing returns where predicting difficulty is concerned. One of the potential benefits of AIG is that it may offer an economic alternative to meeting item demands (Bejar, 2002). Of course, multiple rounds of revision and data collection may defray any possible savings, and so a decision about whether or not to perform an additional iterative cycle must be considered as part of a larger picture. One aspect of this picture is whether an additional cycle has a reasonable chance to provide information that will result in a more complete model of difficulty that enhances understanding of the construct. Another aspect concerns cost: Will it be very expensive to perform an additional iteration? A final aspect concerns practical significance. Suppose an item model designed to generate isomorphs produces instances with statistically significant variation in difficulty. Are these variations sufficiently important to justify a subsequent cycle of revision and data collection? How this question is answered depends on global features of the assessment context in which the instances will be used. For example, are the consequences of the assessment high stakes or low stakes? How many items are included on the test, and what proportion of them will be generated from item models? How many students will respond to each item? Many of the practical consequences of departures from isomorphicity can be examined via a simulation study, as in Bejar et al. (2003). Other questions may need to be examined *in situ*, over a long period of time.

Interaction of Transfer and Difficulty Modeling

Modeling the difficulty of automatically generated items cannot be considered apart from questions about transfer. When using item models to generate instances for use in large-scale testing programs, the usual assumption is that multiple instances of an item model will be administered, possibly over a period of years, before the item model is retired. Since generated instances share a common structure, they may also share systematic relationships with the key. To the extent that these relationships are construct relevant, releasing instances of an item model is very similar to releasing sample items for practice. In this case, improved performance on an instance as a result of familiarity with other instances of the same model reflects learning of the subject matter, which is a positive outcome. To the extent that these relationships are construct irrelevant, however, they are problematic because they may provide a strategic advantage to test takers who have seen them, and this advantage may have nothing to do with the content area.

Morley, Bridgeman, and Lawless (2004) considered the extent to which the use of item modeling allows test takers to apply content-irrelevant strategies to solving test questions. "[I]f a variant is used in test preparation materials or [is] otherwise exposed, performance on another variant from the same family in a test situation might be better than otherwise expected, thereby compromising the validity of the item's operating characteristics" (Morley et al., 2004, p. 3). Of course, this transfer from one variant to another could be construct relevant; by working through one of the variants, the test taker's understanding of the construct may have improved.

In their study, Morley et al. (2004) administered the same posttest to all participants, but there were six forms of the pretest. Each item on each of the pretests was related to one of the items on the posttest in one of three ways:

- Some of the items on the pretest were isomorphic to the corresponding items on the posttest (i.e., they shared identical mathematical structure).
- Some of the items on the pretest were very similar in appearance to items on the posttest. These items (known as *appearance variants)* shared surface features but differed in mathematical structure and measured different aspects of the construct.
- Some of the items on the pretest were *difficulty-matched* to items on the posttest. These items were designed to assess similar skills and were similar in difficulty, but were very different in both the specifics of their solutions and in their appearance.

The six pretests had different combinations of isomorphs, appearance variants, and matched items. Additionally, some participants received feedback on items answered incorrectly on the pretest before they took the posttest; the remainder of the subjects received no feedback but took the posttest immediately after the pretest.

Test takers performed better on posttest items for which they had seen isomorphs on the pretest, which is indicative of positive transfer. Providing feedback did not have a significant effect on the posttest performance, however (Morley et al., 2004, p. 15). Also, while seeing an isomorph on the pretest seemed to enhance performance, the inclusion of appearance variants on the same test form interfered with this effect (Morley et al., 2004, p. 18). Morley et al. suggested that item models could be written in pairs, so that the models produce appearance variants of each other. Using these paired appearance variants in tests could mitigate the effects of the non-construct-related transfer (Morley et al., 2004, p. 19).

The work by Morley et al. (2004) suggests that construct-irrelevant similarities between instances can result in either positive or negative transfer, depending on the design of the item models used to generate them. Whether transfer is positive or negative, it is important for any model of difficulty to account for these kinds of effects.

Psychometric Methods to Support Difficulty Modeling and AIG

A variety of psychometric methods have been applied to the problem of accounting for differences in difficulty among related sets of quantitative items; a few more recent developments will be discussed here. Of course, classical regression models are often applied to this purpose; this was the approach taken in Sebrechts et al. (1996) and Deane et al. (2006). Enright and Sheehan (2002) used tree-based regression techniques to analyze their data. Embretson and Daniel (2008) compared the use of hierarchical regression modeling to Fischer's LLTM for explaining the difficulty of GRE quantitative problem-solving items; as expected, lower standard errors were associated with the model coefficients in the LLTM, and the LLTM approach identified more of the variables as significant. Daniel and Embretson (2010) compared the use of the LLTM to Embretson's 2PL-constrained model to examine the impact of item difficulty features on generated variants; the 2PL-constrained model was the better fit to the data, but both models were highly predictive relative to a null model. Based on the Rasch model, Fischer's model accounts for difficulty by partitioning the difficulty parameter into constituent parameters that pertain to features of an item or generated instance. Embretson's 2PL-constrained model is an extension of this idea; based on the 2PL model, it decomposes both the item difficulty and discrimination parameters into constituent feature parameters.

Michel (2007) used cluster analyses to assist the interpretation of quantitative item models. The quantitative item models were based on source items from the Quantitative Reasoning measure of the GRE General Test and the generated instances had been calibrated using a 3PL IRT model. The item models were designed to generate isomorphic instances, but a number of them generated instances with quite variable item parameter estimates. For each pair of instances, Michel used the area between the item characteristic curves as the measure of dissimilarity. The dendograms produced in her analysis can be used to identify related clusters of instances which might not be easily identified by simple inspection of the item parameter estimates. Both regression trees and dendograms are useful visuals to show clusters of related items.

Like Tatsuoka's rule-space approach, the attribute hierarchy method (AHM; Leighton, Gierl, & Hunka, 2004) interprets student response patterns with respect to a cognitive model of task performance. AHM allows for the specification of prerequisite relationships in the cognitive model, and as such might be well suited to characterizing some of the skills discussed earlier pertaining to working with geometric sequences (e.g., it is likely that a student needs to be able to extend a sequence before he or she can provide an abstract representation of the nth term). In general, the AHM approach may lend itself to modeling performance in quantitative domains, where learning is cumulative within topics.

As discussed in Enright and Sheehan (2002), difficulty modeling supports construct validation, but it also has the potential to support automatic generation of instances with known difficulty. If the difficulty of an instance can be accurately predicted in advance, it may not be necessary to calibrate each instance individually (e.g., Bejar, 1993, 1996; Bejar et al., 2003; Bejar & Yocom, 1991; Embretson, 1999). Thus, item modeling is a potentially economical solution. The question is *how* to calibrate an item model for operational use. For operational use, it is assumed that the unit of development is the *isomorphic* item model, in other words, the requirement is to hold the difficulty of the generated instances relatively constant. Hombo and Dresher (2001) suggested calibrating at the item model level by pooling the data across instances. As pointed out by Sinharay, Johnson, and Williamson (2003) and Sinharay and Johnson (2008), this approach is straightforward but ignores variation among the instances. At the other extreme, calibrating instances individually ignores their relatedness and offers no cost-savings. An alternative is to fit a hierarchical model, as in Glas and van der Linden (2003), Sinharay et al. (2003), and Sinharay and Johnson (2008). A hierarchical model can account for item model structure without ignoring variation among instances (see also Sinharay & Johnson, this volume).

Both Glas and van der Linden (2003) and Sinharay and Johnson (2008) found that the hierarchical model is a better fit to the data. However, the practical consequence of model selection is a separate issue. For the data set Sinharay and Johnson examined, which consisted of responses to instances based on items from the Quantitative Reasoning measure of the GRE General Test, there was little benefit to using the more complicated hierarchical model, at least where scoring was concerned. They suggested that, for the level of variation observed among instances in their data set, the simpler model proposed by Hombo and Dresher (2001) may suffice. But they also noted that further research is needed to determine when a particular model is preferred. When item models successfully generate psychometrically similar isomorphs, treating them as interchangeable may have little consequence. For example, in an examination of the feasibility of using AIG for NAEP mathematics, it was found that the variability in parameter estimates for generated isomorphs did not affect the population estimates (Sandene et al., 2005).

Broadening the Scope of Automatic Generation

Model Creation

One of the themes addressed in Enright and Sheehan (2002) is the inherent challenge in designing sets of items that sufficiently represent the breadth of the construct while informing cognitively based models of difficulty. Even seemingly small changes to an item can alter the cognitive processes used to solve it. Because of this, sets of items that are used to explore difficulty factors usually target only a small portion of a domain. Ensuring breadth of the construct requires the development of many item families.

Another limitation on the scope of automatically generated instances concerns the technology. Although it goes by many different names, AIG is now becoming commonplace in the assessment and textbook industries. Most often, though, AIG tools make use of *replacement-set procedures* (Millman & Westman, 1989), where slots in an item shell are replaced with alternative strings or numeric values. Deane and Sheehan (2003) and Higgins, Futagi, and Deane (2005) refer to this as a *template-based approach* and discuss its limitations, especially with respect to generating items that vary in grammatical structure, which is required for multilingual item generation. In response to these limitations, the Model Creator prototype system was developed (Deane & Sheehan, 2003; Higgins et al., 2005). In contrast to a template-based system, Model Creator uses natural language generation to support the development of more abstractly defined item models, which allow for variation in the linguistic structure of the generated instances. The Model Creator can be conceptualized as a meta-level system that automates the generation of item models rather than instances.

Template-based systems impose similar limitations on the automatic generation of quantitative items. Consider the following example: "If $2x + 1 = 16 - 3x$, solve for x." In a template-based system it is straightforward to model each of the variables and coefficients in order to generate similar instances such as "If $4y - 1 = -3 + 2y$, solve for y." It is not necessarily straightforward, however, to generate seemingly similar instances in which the terms have been rearranged. For example, the capacity to generate the instance, "If $16 + (-2)x = 3x + 1$, solve for x," would likely require the construction of a new template, even though it is mathematically equivalent to the first example. Term rearrangements constitute one type of variation that is not easily accomplished using a template-based system, but there are other similar examples in quantitative item generation. Deane et al. (2006) discuss how the Model Creator prototype was adapted to partially automate the creation of item models that vary with respect to these variables.

Diagnostic Item Models

As discussed earlier, item modeling and AIG are often used to generate large numbers of instances for large-scale testing programs. The approach has other potential applications, however, including diagnostic assessment. Different item types are better suited for different aspects of diagnosis. Multiple-choice items are useful in situations where the goal is to ascertain whether a student can *recognize* the correct response while rejecting distractors that correspond to common errors. A number of projects have discussed the development, use, and interpretation of diagnostic multiple-choice items in mathematics and science (e.g., Bart, Post, Behr, & Lesh, 1994; Briggs, Alonzo, Schwab, & Wilson, 2006; Ciofalo & Wylie, 2006; Hunt & Minstrell, 1994; Wylie & Wiliam, 2006). Constructed-response items are useful when the goal is to assess whether a student can produce a correct and well-reasoned solution or explanation, or in any circumstance where it is not advisable to restrict a response to a limited set of options. For example, consider a situation in which a response can assume many different correct forms. If the purpose of an item is to determine whether a student can *produce* any of a number of correct forms rather than whether he or she can *recognize* a particular form, then the constructed-response format is the preferred type. A diagnostic item model can be designed to generate either multiple-choice items or constructed-response items (or perhaps both, depending on the capabilities of the generation software). It is often possible to identify the reasoning behind students' incorrect responses to quantitative items (e.g., see Fife, Graf, Ohls, & Marquez, 2008). A common incorrect response for which the rationale has been identified can be represented as an *error model*. Error models might be used to generate distractors for a multiple-choice instance. Alternatively, they might be used to generate possible incorrect responses to a constructed-response instance. These incorrect responses can then be used as a basis for targeted feedback or for the development of scoring rubrics (see the following sections). Approaches to developing diagnostic item models, as well as several examples, are discussed in Graf (2008).

Extensions to Instruction

Just as error models can be used to generate possible incorrect responses (or distractors) in a diagnostic item model, *feedback models* can be used to generate targeted advice and/or solutions to the student. For example, consider an item model in which a student is asked to add two fractions. There might also be constraints on these fractions—perhaps they are expressed in lowest terms and have unlike denominators. The key would be modeled as the sum of the two fractions. One common error model might be the sum of the numerators divided by the sum of the denominators. Similarly, one could design a feedback model linked to the error model that provided specific advice about the nature of the error and the correct solution, suggestions for additional exercises to practice, and so forth. For each item model, several error models and corresponding feedback models may be constructed. As each instance is generated, so too are possible incorrect responses and linked feedback to address those responses. This was the approach taken by Morley et al. (2004) in the modeling of answer choice rationales.

Automatic Generation of Scoring Keys

As discussed, when item generation software generates an instance, it can also generate possible responses (both correct and incorrect). For items in multiple-choice format, these possible responses constitute the options. Typically, only one correct response is included among the options, and this option, however it has been modeled, corresponds to the key. Thus, modeling the key is a straightforward process when generating multiple-choice items.

For items in constructed-response format, however, the scoring key is more complicated than the simple identification of a single correct option. A constructed response may take many equivalent forms. This is true, for example, if the response provided is a mathematical expression. There are technologies that automatically score such response types quite accurately. Bennett, Steffen, Singley, Morley, and Jacquemin (1997) found an accuracy rate of 99.62% with real response data when scoring the mathematical expression type. How complicated a scoring key is also depends on how the item will be scored—dichotomously or polytomously, by humans or by automated technology, for a summative assessment or for a formative assessment. The scoring key could actually be a set of scoring rubrics that specify what features of a response warrant partial credit, or it could be a table of short feedback passages keyed to common incorrect responses. If the item is to be scored with automated technology, then the scoring key is a piece of software code that instructs the scoring engine.

Such complicated scoring keys are usually crafted individually for each item. But if users are to gain maximum efficiency from the item-generation software when generating constructed-response items, the software will need to generate the scoring keys as well as the item text. For human-scored partial-credit items, this involves generating scoring rubrics based on the common incorrect responses produced by the error models referred to earlier. For items for which the scoring is automated, the necessary software code will need to be generated.

Modeling the Key and Keying the Model

As described in Fife (2011), there are two approaches one can take to the problem of automatically generating the key to a constructed-response item. We have called these two approaches *modeling the key* and *keying the model*. The first approach involves the following steps:

- Write the item model.
- Generate an instance of the item model.
- Write a scoring model for the instance.
- Variabilize the various features of the scoring model that correspond to the variabilized features in the item model.
- Attach the variabilized scoring model to the item model.
- When instances of the item model are generated, the scoring model for that instance will also be generated.

Of course, this approach has some technical hurdles. The scoring-model-building interface must be modified to allow the variabilization of the relevant features of the scoring model and the item-generating tool must be modified to allow the addition of the "scoring-model model" to the item model. A more difficult hurdle may be the association of the proper scoring model with each instance when the items are administered, especially if item generation on the fly is employed (Bejar et al., 2003). On-the-fly item generation means that items are generated when the test is administered to examinees; each examinee is administered a different instance of the item model. Since one does not know in advance the item instance that an examinee will be administered, one cannot preload the automated scoring engine with the appropriate scoring model. This makes real-time scoring impossible. Since real-time scoring is necessary for adaptive testing, and perhaps desirable for other situations as well, generating the scoring models using a modeling-the-key approach presents some difficulties.

The other approach is to write a key that scores the item model. The key expresses the correct response in terms of the item-model parameters. For a particular response to a particular instance, the scoring model takes as input the examinee's response along with the values of the item-model parameters for that instance. The model then checks that the examinee's response is correct in terms of the values of the parameters.

This key can be preloaded into the automated scoring engine prior to the test administration. Then, when an item is generated from the item model and is administered to an examinee, the values of these parameters for this item instance are carried through to the examinee's response. This response can be viewed as a multi-part response, where only the last part is actually the examinee's response and the previous parts are the values of the various item-model parameters. If the scoring engine has the capability of scoring part of a multi-part response based on the examinee's answers to previous parts of the response, then this same capability will allow the scoring of the response to an instance based on the values of the item-model parameters. Since a single scoring model scores responses to all item model instances, it can be preloaded in the automated scoring engine, thus allowing items to be generated, administered, and scored on the fly.

The technical hurdles associated with this keying-the-model approach involve authoring the item in the test delivery software so that the instance that is generated by the item-generation tool is displayed on the screen for the examinee. In addition, the values of the parameters that determine the particular instance need to be carried through to the appropriate fields in the response.

Conclusion

This chapter reviewed research in difficulty modeling and automatic item generation of quantitative items. Although there has been new work in approaches to difficulty modeling, psychometric methods, and AIG technology, the tension between modeling difficulty and representing the breadth of the construct still exists. Although there has been substantial progress in modeling the difficulty of mathematics items in some areas (arithmetic and algebra in particular), there are many other areas that still need to be explored in depth. Also, as pointed out by Sinharay and Johnson (2008), more research is needed to determine which psychometric methods are best suited to calibrate item models. The answer to this question will certainly depend both on how the item models have been designed (i.e., whether they generate isomorphs or more variable instances) and the assessment context. AIG technologies should evolve beyond template-based systems; work has already been done in this direction as indicated by the research in many of the chapters in this volume.

Although item modeling and AIG are often applied in the context of large-scale testing programs, there are potential applications to diagnostic and formative assessment as well. In order to take full advantage of AIG efficiency, it will be necessary to generate scoring keys together with instances. This is especially true for constructed-response types, where a large portion of the development effort is invested in defining the rubrics. Future assessments will likely pose additional challenges to difficulty modeling, because they will require the integrated application of skills and make use of complex tasks that require extended responses from students. For example, as part of the Cognitively Based Assessment *of, for,* and *as* Learning (CBAL) project (Bennett, 2010; Bennett & Gitomer, 2009), competency models and complex tasks are being developed to assess competency in reading, writing, and mathematics. In mathematics, characterizing a broad model of competency that also captures the connections has been especially challenging (Graf, 2009; Graf, Harris, Marquez, Fife, & Redman, 2010). Advances in approaches to difficulty modeling are likely to support the development of new assessments that will require the application and integration of constellations of knowledge and skills.

Acknowledgment

Thanks to Issac Bejar for helpful comments on an earlier version of this chapter.

References

Almond, R. G., Shute, V. J., Underwood, J. S., & Zapata-Rivera, D. (2009). Bayesian networks: A teacher's view. *International Journal of Approximate Reasoning, 50,* 450–460.

Arendasy, M., Sommer, M., Gittler, G., & Hergovich, A. (2006). Automatic generation of quantitative reasoning items: A pilot study. *Journal of Individual Differences, 27*(1), 2–14.

Bart, W. M., Post, T., Behr, M. J., & Lesh, R. (1994). A diagnostic analysis of a proportional reasoning test item: An introduction to the properties of a semi-dense item. *Focus on Learning Problems in Mathematics, 16*(3), 1–11.

Bejar, I. I. (1983). Subject matter experts' assessment of item statistics. *Applied Psychological Measurement, 7*(3), 303–310.

Bejar, I. I. (1993). A generative approach to psychological and educational measurement. In N. Frederiksen (Ed.), *Test theory for a new generation of tests* (pp. 323–357). Hillsdale, NJ: Lawrence Erlbaum Associates.

Bejar, I. I. (1996). *Generative response modeling: Leveraging the computer as a test delivery medium* (ETS Research Report No. RR-96-13). Princeton, NJ: Educational Testing Service.

Bejar, I. I. (2002). Generative testing: From conception to implementation. In S. H. Irvine & P. C. Kyllonen (Eds.), *Item generation for test development* (pp. 199–218). Mahwah, NJ: Lawrence Erlbaum Associates.

Bejar, I. I. (2010). Recent development and prospects in item generation. In S. E. Embretson (Ed.), *Measuring psychological constructs: Advances in model-based approaches.* (pp. 201–226). Washington, DC: American Psychological Association.

Bejar, I. I., Lawless, R. R., Morley, M. E., Wagner, M. E., Bennett, R. E., & Revuelta, J. (2003). A feasibility study of on-the-fly item generation in adaptive testing. *Journal of Technology, Learning, and Assessment, 2*(3). Available from http://www.jtla.org.

Bejar, I. I., & Yocom, P. (1991). A generative approach to the modeling of isomorphic hidden-figure items. *Applied Psychological Measurement, 15*(2), 129–137.

Bennett, R. E. (2010). Cognitively based assessment of, for, and as learning: A preliminary theory of action for summative and formative assessment. *Measurement: Interdisciplinary Research and Perspectives, 8*, 70–91.

Bennett, R. E., & Gitomer, D. H. (2009). Transforming K-12 assessment: Integrating accountability testing, formative assessment, and professional support. In C. Wyatt-Smith & J. Cumming (Eds.), *Educational assessment in the 21st century* (pp. 43–61). New York, NY: Springer.

Bennett, R. E., Steffen, M., Singley, M. K., Morley, M. & Jacquemin, D. (1997). Evaluating an automatically scorable, open-ended response type for measuring mathematical reasoning. *Journal of Educational Measurement, 34*(2), 162–176.

Birnbaum, A. (1968). Some latent trait models. In F. M. Lord & M. R. Novick (Eds.), *Statistical theories of mental test scores* (pp. 397–424). Reading, MA: Addison-Wesley.

Borchert, K. (2003). *Dissociation between arithmetic and algebraic knowledge in mathematical modeling.* Unpublished doctoral dissertation, University of Washington, Seattle, WA.

Briggs, D. C., Alonzo, A. C., Schwab, C., & Wilson, M. (2006). Diagnostic assessment with ordered multiple-choice items. *Educational Assessment, 11*(1), 33–63.

Camerer, C. F., & Johnson, E. J. (1991). The process-performance paradox in expert judgment: How can experts know so much and predict so badly? In J. Smith & K. A. Ericsson (Eds.), *Toward a general theory of expertise: Prospects and limits* (pp. 195–217). New York, NY: Cambridge University Press.

Ciofalo, J. F., & Wylie, E. C. (2006, January 10). *Using diagnostic classroom assessment: One question at a time.* Retrieved December 10, 2009 from http://www.tcrecord.org/content.asp?contentid=12285.

Clement, J., Lochhead, J., & Monk, G. S. (1981). Translation difficulties in learning mathematics. *American Mathematical Monthly, 88*(4), 286–290.

Clement, J., Lochhead, J., & Soloway, E. (1979). *Translating between symbol systems: Isolating a common difficulty in solving algebra word problems.* Amherst: University of Massachusetts.

Daniel, R. C., & Embretson, S. E. (2010). Designing cognitive complexity in mathematical problem solving items. *Applied Psychological Measurement, 34*(5), 348–364.

Deane, P., Graf, E. A., Higgins, D., Futagi, Y., & Lawless, R. (2006). *Model analysis and model creation: Capturing the task-model structure of quantitative item domains* (ETS Research Report No. RR-06-11). Princeton, NJ: Educational Testing Service.

Deane, P., & Sheehan, K. (2003, April). *Automatic item generation via frame semantics: Natural language generation of math word problems.* Paper presented at the annual meeting of the National Council on Measurement in Education, Chicago.

Embretson, S. E. (1999). Generating items during testing: Psychometric issues and models. *Psychometrika, 64*(4), 407–433.

Embretson, S. E. & Daniel, R. C. (2008). Understanding and quantifying cognitive complexity level in mathematical problem solving items. *Psychological Science Quarterly, 50*, 328–344.

Embretson, S. E. & Gorin, J. (2001). Improving construct validity with cognitive psychology principles. *Journal of Educational Measurement, 38*(4), 343–368.

Embretson, S. E., & Yang, X. (2007). Automatic item generation and cognitive psychology. In C. R. Rao & S. Sinharary (Eds.), *Handbook of statistics 26: Psychometrics* (pp. 747–768). Amsterdam: Elsevier.

Enright, M., & Sheehan, K. (2002). Modeling the difficulty of quantitative reasoning items: Implications for item generation. In S. H. Irvine & P. Kyllonen (Eds.), *Item generation for test development* (pp. 129–158). Mahwah, NJ: Lawrence Erlbaum Associates.

Fife, J. H. (2011, April). Integrating item generation and automated scoring. In I. I. Bejar (Chair), *Item modeling and item generation for the measurement of quantitative skills: Recent advances and prospects.* Symposium conducted at the annual meeting of the National Council on Measurement in Education, New Orleans, LA.

Fife, J. H., Graf, E. A., Ohls, S., & Marquez, E. (2008). *Identifying common misconceptions: An analysis of the Mathematics Intervention Module (MIM) data* (ETS Research Memorandum RM-08-16). Princeton, NJ: ETS.

Gierl, M. J., & Leighton, J. P. (2007). Linking cognitively-based models and psychometric methods. In C. R. Rao & S. Sinharary (Eds.), *Handbook of statistics 26: Psychometrics* (pp. 747–768). Amsterdam: Elsevier.

Gierl, M. J., Zhou, J., & Alves, C. (2008). Developing a taxonomy of item model types to promote assessment engineering. *The Journal of Technology, Learning, & Assessment, 7*(2). Retrieved from http://www.jtla.org.

Glas, C. A. W., & van der Linden, W. J. (2003). Computerized adaptive testing with item cloning. *Applied Psychological Measurement, 27*, 247–261.

Gorin, J. S. (2006). Test design with cognition in mind. *Educational Measurement: Issues and Practice, 25*(4), 21–35.

Graf, E. A. (2003, September 25). *Designing a proficiency model and associated item models for an 8th grade mathematics unit on sequences.* Presentation given at the ETS Cross Division Math Forum, Princeton, NJ.

Graf, E. A. (2008). *Approaches to the design of diagnostic item models* (ETS Research Report No. RR-08-07). Princeton, NJ: Educational Testing Service.

Graf, E. A. (2009). *Defining mathematics competency in the service of cognitively based assessment for grades 6 through 8* (ETS Research Report. No. RR-09-42). Princeton, NJ: Educational Testing Service.

Graf, E. A., Bassok, M., Hunt, E., & Minstrell, J. (2004). A computer-based tutorial for algebraic representation: The effects of scaffolding on performance during the tutorial and on a transfer task. *Technology, Instruction, Cognition, and Learning, 2*(1–2), 135–170.

Graf, E. A., Harris, K., Marquez, E., Fife, J., & Redman, M. (2010). Highlights from the cognitively based assessment of, for, and as learning (CBAL) project in mathematics. *ETS Research Spotlight, 3*, pp. 19–30.

Graf, E. A., Steffen, M., Peterson, S., Saldivia, L., & Wang, S. (2004, October 23). *Designing and revising quantitative item models*. Presentation given at the 4th Spearman Conference, Princeton, NJ.

Graf, E. A., Peterson, S., Steffen, M., & Lawless, R. (2005). *Psychometric and cognitive analysis as a basis for the design and revision of quantitative item models* (ETS Research Report No. RR-05-25). Princeton, NJ: Educational Testing Service.

Higgins, D., Futagi, Y., & Deane, P. (2005). *Multilingual generalization of the Model Creator software for Math TCA* (ETS Research Report No. RR-05-02). Princeton, NJ: Educational Testing Service.

Hombo, C., & Dresher, A. (2001). *A simulation study of the impact of automatic item generation under NAEP-like data conditions*. Paper presented at the annual meeting of the National Council on Measurement in Education, Seattle, WA.

Hunt, E. & Minstrell, J. (1994). A cognitive approach to the teaching of physics. In K. McGilly (Ed.), *Classroom lessons: Integrating cognitive theory and classroom practice* (pp. 51–74). Cambridge, MA: The MIT Press.

Irvine S. H. (2002). The foundations of item generation for mass testing. In S. H. Irvine & P. C. Kyllonen (Eds.), *Item generation for test development* (pp. 3–34). Mahwah, NJ: Lawrence Erlbaum Associates.

Irvine, S. H., & Kyllonen, P. C. (2002). *Item generation for test development*. Hillsdale, NJ: Erlbaum.

Koedinger, K. R., & Nathan, M. J. (2004). The real story behind story problems: Effects of representations on quantitative reasoning. *Journal of the Learning Sciences, 13*(2), 129–164.

Koedinger, K. R., & Tabachneck, H. J. M. (1995). *Verbal reasoning as a critical component in early algebra*. Paper presented at the annual meeting of the American Educational Research Association, San Francisco, CA.

Lee, L., & Wheeler, D. (1989). The arithmetic connection. *Educational Studies in Mathematics, 20*, 41–54.

Leighton, J. P., & Gierl, M. J. (2007). Why cognitive diagnostic assessment? In J. P. Leighton & M. J. Gierl (Eds.), *Cognitive diagnostic assessment for education: Theory and applications* (pp. 3–18). New York, NY: Cambridge University Press.

Leighton, J. P. & Gierl, M. J. (2011). *The learning sciences in educational assessment*. Cambridge, MA: Cambridge University Press.

Leighton, J. P., Gierl, M. J., & Hunka, S. (2004). The attribute hierarchy model: An approach for integrating cognitive theory with assessment practice. *Journal of Educational Measurement, 41*, 205–236.

Lewis, A. B., & Mayer, R. E. (1987). Students' miscomprehension of relational statements in arithmetic word problems. *Journal of Educational Psychology, 79*(4), 363–371.

Macready, G. B., & Merwin, J. C. (1973). Homogeneity within item forms in domain referenced testing. *Educational and Psychological Measurement, 33*, 351–360.

Martin, S. A., & Bassok, M. (2005). Effects of semantic cues on mathematical modeling: Evidence from word-problem solving and equation construction tasks. *Memory and Cognition, 33*(3), 471–478.

Mayer, R. E. (1982). Different problem-solving strategies for algebra word and equation problems. *Journal of Experimental Psychology: Learning, Memory, and Cognition, 8*(5), 448–462.

Meisner, R., Luecht, R., & Reckase, M. D. (1993). *The comparability of the statistical characteristics of test items generated by computer algorithms* (No. 93–9). Iowa City, IA: American College Testing.

Messick, S. (1989). Validity. In R. L. Linn (Ed.), *Educational measurement* (3rd ed., pp. 13–103). New York, NY: Macmillan.

Michel, R. (2007, November). *Cluster analysis as a guide to the interpretation of quantitative item models*. Paper presented at the 52nd Annual Meeting of the Florida Educational Research Association in Tampa, Florida.

Millman, J., & Westman, R. S. (1989). Computer-assisted writing of achievement test items: Toward a future technology. *Journal of Educational Measurement, 26*(2), 177–190.

Mislevy, R. J., Sheehan, K. M., & Wingersky, M. (1993). How to equate tests with little or no data. *Journal of Educational Measurement, 30*(1), 55–78.

Mislevy, R. J., Steinberg, L. S., & Almond, R. G. (2002). On the roles of task model variables in assessment design. In S. H. Irvine & P. C. Kyllonen (Eds.), *Item generation for test development* (pp. 97–128). Mahwah, NJ: Lawrence Erlbaum Associates.

Mislevy, R. J., Steinberg, L. S., & Almond, R. G. (2003). On the structure of educational assessments. *Measurement: Interdisciplinary Research and Perspectives, 1*, 3–67.

Morley, M., Bridgeman, B., & Lawless, R. (2004). *Transfer between variants of quantitative items* (GRE Board Report No. 00-06R). Princeton, NJ: ETS.

Nathan, M. J., Koedinger, K. R., & Alibali, M. W. (2001). Expert blind spot: When content knowledge eclipses pedagogical content knowledge. In L. Chen et al. (Eds.), *Proceeding of the Third International Conference on Cognitive Science* (pp. 644–648). Beijing, China: USTC Press.

Nathan, M. J., Koedinger, K. R., & Tabachneck, H. J. M. (2000). Teachers' and researchers' beliefs about the development of algebraic reasoning. *Journal for Research in Mathematics Education, 31*(2), 168–190.

Nathan, M. J., & Petrosino, A. (2003). Expert blind spot among preservice teachers. *American Educational Research Journal, 40*(4), 905–928.

National Council of Teachers of Mathematics. (2000). *Principles and standards for school mathematics*. Reston, VA: Author.

Newstead, S., Bradon, P., Handley, S., Evans, J., & Dennis, I. (2002). Using the psychology of reasoning to predict the difficulty of analytical reasoning problems. In S. H. Irvine & P. C. Kyllonen (Eds.), *Item generation for test development* (pp. 35–51). Mahwah, NJ: Lawrence Erlbaum Associates.

Nichols, P. D. (1994). A framework for developing cognitively diagnostic assessments. *Review of Educational Research, 64*(4), 575–603.

Pellegrino, J. W., Chudowsky, N., & Glaser, R. (Eds.). (2001). *Knowing what students know: The science and design of educational assessment*. Washington, DC: National Academy Press.

Sandene, B., Horkay, N., Bennett, R. E., Allen, N., Braswell, J., Kaplan, B., et al. *Online assessment in mathematics and writing: Reports from the NAEP technology-based assessment project, research and development series* (NCES 2005–457). U.S. Department of Education, National Center for Education Statistics. Washington, DC: U.S. Government Printing Office.

Sebrechts, M. M., Enright, M., Bennett, R. E., & Martin, K. (1996). Using algebra word problems to assess quantitative ability: Attributes, strategies, and errors. *Cognition and Instruction, 14*(3), 285–343.

Shute, V. J., Graf, E. A., & Hansen, E. G. (2005). Designing adaptive, diagnostic math assessments for individuals with and without visual disabilities. In L. M. Pytlikzillig, R. H. Bruning, & M. Bodvarsson (Eds.), *Technology-based education: Bringing researchers and practitioners together* (pp. 169–202). Greenwich, CT: Information Age Publishing.

Singley, M. K., & Bennett, R. E. (2002). Item generation and beyond: Applications of schema theory to mathematics assessment. In S. H. Irvine & P. C. Kyllonen (Eds.), *Item generation for test development* (pp. 361–384). Mahwah, NJ: Lawrence Erlbaum Associates.

Sinharay, S., & Johnson, M. S. (2008). Use of item models in a large-scale admissions test: A case study. *International Journal of Testing, 8,* 209–236.

Sinharay, S., Johnson, M., & Williamson, D. (2003). Calibrating item families and summarizing the results using family expected response functions. *Journal of Educational and Behavioral Statistics, 28*(4), 295–313.

Tabachneck, H. J. M., Koedinger, K. R., & Nathan, M. J. (1995). A cognitive analysis of the task demands of early algebra. In *Proceedings of the seventeenth annual meeting of the Cognitive Science Society*. Hillsdale, NJ: Erlbaum.

Wylie, E. C., & Wiliam, D. (2006, April). *Diagnostic questions: Is there value in just one?* Paper presented at the annual meeting of the National Council on Measurement in Education, San Francisco, CA.

IV
Technical Developments in Automatic Item Generation

11
Statistical Modeling of Automatically Generated Items

Sandip Sinharay and Matthew S. Johnson

Introduction

A large pool of high-quality items is important for the efficient operation of any large-scale testing program, especially those with flexible administration times, to address concerns regarding item exposure and potential disclosure. In an attempt to produce high-quality items at reduced expense, there is an increasing interest in generating items automatically.

One way to generate items is based on a cognitive analysis of the item domain. The results from the analysis are then used to create rules for the generation of new items (Embretson, 1999). These rules were referred to as *radicals* by Irvine (2002).

Another way to generate items automatically is based on *item models* (e.g., LaDuca, Staples, Templeton, & Holzman, 1986), classes from which it is possible to generate or produce items that are equivalent or isomorphic to other items from the same model (e.g., Bejar, 2002). As an example (reproduced from Peterson, 2004), an item model on assessing mathematical aspects of graduated rates, calculations with percents, and algebraic manipulation may look like the following:

> In a certain state, for taxable incomes over y, income taxes are calculated as r percent of the first y of taxable income plus t percent of the amount greater than y. If the taxes calculated for a certain taxable income were w, what was the taxable income?

Several instances/items can be automatically generated from this model by replacing the variables y, r, t, and w with appropriate numbers and choosing appropriate distractors (if this is a multiple-choice item). An example of a radical for such an item would be whether or not the item involves calculations with percents. The surface features of an item, such as y, r, t, and w for the items generated from this item model, are referred to as the *incidentals* (Irvine, 2002). All the items generated from an item model usually share the same radicals, but have slightly different incidentals, and have item parameters, such as difficulty level, that are similar to one other.

Radicals are believed to describe the features that drive item difficulty for theoretically relevant reasons, and incidentals to describe those that do not (Mislevy, Steinberg, & Almond, 2002).

183

Items that are produced by automatic item generation (AIG) systems (Irvine & Kyllonen, 2002) and have the same radicals in common are related to one another and therefore constitute a *family* of related items. For example, items generated from an item model constitute an item family. The items in the same family are called *siblings*. They assess the same subject-matter content and have similar conceptual, psychometric and statistical properties.

There is no unanimous nomenclature in AIG literature. What we refer to as an *item model* is also referred to as an *item form* (Hively, Patterson, & Page, 1968), an *item template* (e.g., Deane & Sheehan, 2003), a *schema* (Singley & Bennett, 2002) and an *item shell* (Glas & van der Linden, 2003) by other researchers. Similarly, what we refer to as a *sibling* has been referred to as a *clone* (Glas & van der Linden, 2001, 2003), an *instance*, an *isomorph*, and a *variant* elsewhere. We refer to all the siblings generated from an item model as an *item family* (a term also used in Glas & van der Linden, 2001, 2003), for the simple reason that the siblings are related to each other; the term item family is not meant to imply that there is a *parent* item within each family, although there can be a parent item or item model for a family.

In the next section, we describe the statistical models that have been suggested for use with data involving automatically generated items. The Statistical Inference section presented later in this chapter includes discussion of estimation of the parameters of the models; model selection and model checking is also described in this section. The Example section includes an application of one such model to data from the Graduate Record Examination (GRE). The last section includes conclusions and recommendations.

Statistical Models for Automatically Generated Items

Quite possibly, the simplest approach to analyzing responses to items that have been automatically generated is to treat each item generated as a completely unique item. A major limitation of this approach for automatically generated items is that it requires hundreds or thousands of student responses to each automatically generated item in order to accurately estimate the model parameters. Therefore, the approach would not be appropriate to situations where each student is presented a unique item, or where items are generated on the fly during an adaptive test. These limitations necessitated the development of alternative models for automatically generated items. This section reviews some of these models.

The statistical/psychometric models that have been suggested for items that are automatically generated can be divided into three categories. The first category of models attempt to predict the parameters, especially the difficulty parameters, of automatically generated items from the item characteristics. One goal of these models is to determine the factors that influence the item parameters. This information may help the future item development process. The second category of models attempt to account for the dependence among the item parameters belonging to the same item family. The third category of models combine the first two categories of models.

Models That Predict the Item Parameters of Automatically Generated Items

Radicals are believed to be important determinants of item difficulty (e.g., Mislevy et al., 2002; Geerlings, van der Linden, & Glas, 2011). The linear logistic test model (LLTM; Fischer, 1973) is a psychometric model that permits one to explain item difficulty from item characteristics. Researchers such as Embretson (1999), Freund, Hofer, and Holling (2008) and Holling, Bertling, and Zeuch (2009) applied the LLTM to predict the item difficulties from the radicals.

To define the LLTM, let us first begin by presenting the Rasch model (Rasch, 1960), of which the LLTM is a generalization. The Rasch model assumes that the probability that an individual with ability θ correctly answers the dichotomously scored item j has the following functional form:

$$\Pr(Y_j = 1 | \theta, b_j) = \frac{e^{a(\theta - b_j)}}{1 + e^{a(\theta - b_j)}} \tag{1}$$

where Y_j is the score achieved on item j (0 or 1), b_j is the difficulty parameter of item c_j and a is the common discrimination parameter of the items. The LLTM (Fischer, 1973) generalizes the Rasch model by assuming that the difficulty parameter can be modeled as a linear combination of item covariates $q_{j1}, \dots q_{jk}$,

$$b_j = \eta_1 q_{j1} + \eta_2 q_{j2} + \dots + \eta_K q_{jK} = \sum_{b=1}^{K} \eta_k q_{jk} \tag{2}$$

where η_k represents the effect of item characteristic k on b_j.

In the context of automatically generated items the process would begin by using a number of items and item responses to estimate the effects (η) of the various item covariates, and then using those estimates to predict the difficulty of future generated items. For example, Embretson (1999) and Freund, Hofer, and Holling (2008) applied the LLTM to data on matrix-completion items that were automatically generated. Freund, Hofer, and Holling (2008) found that the LLTM explained approximately 50% of total variation in item difficulty; the correlation between the estimated difficulty parameters from the Rasch model and the LLTM was 0.714. Furthermore, Freund et al. (2008) reported very little difference between the estimated person ability parameters when the LLTM was used instead of the Rasch model.

In another study, Holling, Bertling, and Zeuch (2009) applied the LLTM to data on mathematical word problems that were automatically generated. Holling et al. (2009) also applied the random-effects LLTM model (e.g., Janssen, Schepers, & Peres, 2004) to their data—they concluded that the estimated difficulty parameters from this model were very close to those from the Rasch model.

Another model useful for predicting the model parameters of items that are automatically generated was suggested by Embretson (1999). The model generalizes the LLTM in two ways. First, unlike the LLTM, the model assumes that the item discrimination varies across items. Secondly, the model assumes that item discriminations are a linear combination of item covariates. As such, the model has been described as the constrained two-parameter logistic (C2PL) model. Formally, let us begin with the definition of the two-parameter logistic (2PL) model (Lord & Novick, 1968), which models the item response function as follows:

$$\Pr(Y_j = 1 | \theta, a_j, b_j) = \frac{e^{a_j(\theta - b_j)}}{1 + e^{a_j(\theta - b_j)}} \tag{3}$$

where a_j is the item discrimination or slope parameter of Item j. In addition to assuming that the difficulty is a linear combination of the item covariates,

$$b_j = \sum_k \eta_k q_{jk} \tag{4}$$

the C2PL model assumes that the item-discrimination parameter is also a linear combination of the item covariates, e.g.,

$$a_j = \sum_k \tau_k q_{jk} \tag{5}$$

in which τ_k represents the effect of characteristic k on the discrimination. Embretson (1999) applied the C2PL model to data on matrix completion items that were automatically generated. The C2PL model fitted the data significantly better than the LLTM.

Models That Account for the Dependence Among the Item Parameters of the Same Item Family

These models are employed when the automatically generated items can be divided into several item families and the primary goal is to estimate the family-level model parameters by accounting for the dependence among the items within the item families. Once the family-level parameters have been estimated from a few siblings generated from an item family, these statistical models aim to obviate the need to estimate the parameters of items generated from the same family at a later point in time. The family-level parameters estimated from a few siblings randomly sampled from the item family are used instead of these item parameters.

One way to estimate item parameters for data involving item families is to apply the identical siblings model (ISM) suggested by Hombo and Dresher (2001), which assumes a single response function (for example, the 2PL response function for multiple-choice items) for all items in a family. Effectively, fitting an ISM is equivalent to treating all the items within an item family to be the same item. This model, though easy to fit, is restrictive, as it does not account for the variation within an item family. Glas and van der Linden (2003) argued that the use of the ISM to estimate item parameters leads to the loss of accuracy in ability estimation.

The related siblings model (RSM) attempts to address the limitation of the ISM by incorporating an association structure among the items within an item family. The RSM is a hierarchical model (Glas & van der Linden, 2001, 2003) whose first component is a simple IRT model, such as the 3PL model:

$$\Pr(Y_j = 1 | \theta, a_j, b_j, c_j) = c_j + (1 - c_j)\mathrm{logit}^{-1}(a_j(\theta - b_j)), \tag{6}$$

where c_j is the guessing parameter of Item j. The transformation $\alpha_j \equiv a_j$, $\beta_j \equiv b_j$, and $\gamma_j \equiv \mathrm{logit}(c_j)$ is made.[1] Then, a normal distribution is used to relate the item parameters of the items within the same item family as

$$(\alpha_j, \beta_j, \gamma_j)' | \mu_{J(j)}, \Sigma_{J(j)} \sim N_3(\mu_{J(j)}, \Sigma_{J(j)}), \tag{7}$$

where $J(j)$ is the item family to which Item j belongs. The population distribution for the latent abilities is usually assumed to be $N(0,1)$. The family mean vector $\mu_{J(j)}$ can be partitioned as $\mu_{J(j)} = (\mu_{\alpha J(j)}, \mu_{\beta J(j)}, \mu_{\gamma J(j)})'$ and the diagonal elements of the family variance $\Sigma_{J(j)}$ will be referred to as $\sigma^2_{\alpha_{J(j)}}, \sigma^2_{\beta_{J(j)}}$, and $\sigma^2_{\gamma_{J(j)}}$ respectively.

Johnson and Sinharay (2005) extended the RSM to incorporate polytomous items so that for polytomous items, Equation 6 was replaced by the corresponding expressions from a generalized partial credit model (GPCM; Muraki, 1992) and Equation 7 is adjusted accordingly.

To summarize an item family in the RSM, Sinharay et al. (2003) suggested the family expected response function (FERF), which describes the probability that an examinee with ability θ correctly responds to a randomly selected item from the item family. The FERF for item family k is defined as

$$P(\theta | k) \equiv \int_{\mu k, \Sigma_k} \int_\eta P(\theta | \alpha, \beta, \gamma) \phi_3(\eta | \mu_k, \Sigma_k) d\eta \, p(\mu_k | \Sigma_k, | X) d\mu_k d\Sigma_k, \tag{8}$$

where $P(\theta | \alpha, \beta, \gamma) \equiv \mathrm{logit}^{-1}\gamma + (1 - \mathrm{logit}^{-1}\gamma)\mathrm{logit}^{-1}(e^\alpha(\theta - \beta))$, $\eta = (\alpha, \beta, \gamma)'$, $\phi_3(\eta | \mu_k, \Sigma_k)$ is the density function of the multivariate normal prior distribution on η and $p(\mu_k, \Sigma_k | X)$ is the joint posterior distribution of μ_k and Σ_k, given the response matrix X.

Sinharay et al. (2003) and Johnson and Sinharay (2005) demonstrated that a plot showing the estimated FERF of the family along with the estimates of the item response functions of the items provided useful information that included some idea of isomorphicity of the items within each family.

The RSM is similar to the multilevel version of the two-parameter normal-ogive model suggested by Janssen, Tuerlinckx, Meulders, and De Boeck (2000) in which no item family was involved but the second level was introduced to describe dependencies within fixed sets of items used in a standard setting procedure. The RSM also has some similarities to the testlet model (Bradlow, Wainer, & Wang, 1999). Both models describe an extra level of dependence in the observed item responses. However, the testlet model describes the extra "local" dependence between a single examinee's item responses within a testlet, whereas the RSM explains the dependence between all examinees' responses to the same single member from an item family.

Glas and van der Linden (2003) discussed how to select items from item families using a Bayesian item-selection algorithm in a computer-adaptive test. They used a criterion that required the item family selected at any point to have the minimum expected posterior variance. They commented that the smaller the variation within an item family, the better the test adapted to the examinee's ability.

A Model That Combines the RSM and the LLTM

Geerlings et al. (2011) combined the LLTM and the RSM into a model referred to as the linear item cloning model (LICM). The LICM accounts for the association among responses to a common sibling using a RSM for the first two levels of the model, and adds an LLTM-like structure for the expected value of the item difficulty parameter of each family. The structure decomposes the mean family difficulty into separate effects for each of its radicals. The LICM (Geerlings et al., 2011) utilizes the three-parameter normal-ogive (3PNO) model to specify the probability of a correct response to Item j:

$$\Pr(Y_j = 1 | \theta, a_j, b_j, c_j) = c_j + (1 - c_j)\, \Phi\, (a_j(\theta - b_j)) \tag{9}$$

The 3PNO model has the advantage of convenient sampling from the conditional posterior distributions. The transformation $\alpha_j \equiv a_j$, $\beta_j \equiv b_j$, and $\gamma_j \equiv \mathrm{logit}(c_j)$ is made. Then a normal distribution given by Equation 7 is used to relate the item parameters of the items within the same item family. If there are not too many items per item family, $\Sigma_{J(j)}$'s can be assumed to be the same, that is, $\Sigma_{J(j)} = \Sigma$. The population distribution for the latent abilities is assumed to be $N(0, 1)$. The mean difficulty of a family is postulated to be a linear combination of the effects of the radicals used to generate the items:

$$\mu_{\beta_{J(j)}} = \sum_{r=1}^{R} d_{J(j)r}\delta_r \tag{10}$$

where δ_r is the effect of Radical r on the mean difficulty of the item families and $d_{J(j)r}$ is a design variable denoting whether Radical r was used in the items of item family $J(j)$. Thus, at the item level, the difficulty of an item is assumed to follow a normal distribution with mean $\sum_{r=1}^{R} d_{J(j)r}\delta_r$, and variance $\sigma^2_{\beta_{J(j)}}$. The family covariance matrix $\Sigma_{J(j)}$ is determined by the incidentals. The idea behind the regression model given by Equation 10 is similar to that of the model suggested by Wright (2002, p. 281) that includes a regression of item difficulty and item discrimination on radicals.

Statistical Inference for Models of Automatically Generated Items

Estimation of Family and Item Parameters

Glas and van der Linden (2001, 2003), Sinharay et al. (2003), and Johnson and Sinharay (2005) described Markov chain Monte Carlo (MCMC) algorithms by fitting the RSM and estimating the family and item parameters of the model. Glas and van der Linden (2003) and Glas, van der Linden, and Geerlings (2010) suggested a Bayesian modal estimation approach for the RSM. Glas and van der Linden (2001, 2003) described how the family parameters of an RSM can be estimated using a marginal maximum likelihood method. Sinharay et al. (2003) suggested the use of Monte Carlo integration to estimate the FERF defined in Equation 8 and discussed how to attach a 95% prediction interval with the estimate.

Geerlings et al. (2011) suggested an MCMC algorithm to fit the LICM to a data set. They applied the model to data from the Analogies subtest of a non-verbal intelligence test. They found that an LICM fitted the data almost as well as an RSM.

Estimation of Examinee Abilities

Consider a test involving J items generated from item models. Suppose the observed response vector of an examinee with ability θ on such a test is $(y_1, y_2 \dots y_J)$.

Let us denote the contribution of item j to the likelihood for the examinee as

$$P(Y_j = y_j \mid \theta, \eta_j) \equiv P(Y_j = 1 \mid \theta, \eta_j)^{y_j} (1 - P(Y_j = 1 \mid \theta, \eta_j))^{1 - y_j}$$

where $\eta_j = (\alpha_j, \beta_j, \gamma_j)'$ is the transformed item parameter vector for Item j. To score individuals while using the RSM, Glas and van der Linden (2003) suggested obtaining the posterior distribution of θ as proportional to

$$p(\theta) \prod_{j=1}^{J} \int_{\eta_j} P(Y_j = y_j \mid \theta, \eta_j) N_3(\eta_j \mid \hat{\mu}_{J(j)}, \hat{\Sigma}_{J(j)}) d\eta_j \tag{11}$$

where $\hat{\mu}_{J(j)}$ and $\hat{\Sigma}_{J(j)}$ are the estimated mean and variance of the item parameters for the item family $J(j)$ that contains Item j.

However, the above approach ignores the variability of $\mu_{J(j)}$s and $\Sigma_{J(j)}$s, and fixes them at $\hat{\mu}_{J(j)}$ and $\hat{\Sigma}_{J(j)}$. Sinharay and Johnson (2008) suggested taking this variability into account and obtained the posterior distribution of θ as proportional to

$$p(\theta) \prod_{j=1}^{J} \int_{\eta_j} P(Y_j = y_j \mid \theta, \eta_j) N_3(\eta_j \mid \mu_{J(j)}, \Sigma_{J(j)}) p(\mu_{J(j)}, \Sigma_{J(j)} \mid X) d\eta_j d\mu_{J(j)} d\Sigma_{J(j)} \tag{12}$$

where $p(\mu_{J(j)}, \Sigma_{J(j)} \mid X)$ is the posterior distribution of the family parameters given the data X.

Note that if one can obtain accurate ability estimates by using Equations 11 or 12, then one would not need to estimate the parameters of all the siblings generated from the same family in future.

To approximate the integrals in Equations 11 and 12, Monte Carlo integration (e.g., Gelman, Carlin, Stern, & Rubin, 2003) is used. For Equation 11, a random sample from $N_3(\eta_j \mid \hat{\mu}_{J(j)}, \hat{\Sigma}_{J(j)})$ is generated; the average of the quantity $P(Y_j = y_j \mid \theta, \eta_j)$ computed over these sampled values provides an estimate of the integral in Equation 11. For Equation 12, for each draw of a posterior sample of $\mu_{J(j)}$ and $\Sigma_{J(j)}$, a number of η_js are generated from the prior distribution $N_3(\eta_j \mid \mu_{J(j)}, \Sigma_{J(j)})$, and finally the average of the quantity $P(Y_j = y_j \mid \theta, \eta_j)$ is computed over all the sampled values of η_j. There is a close relation between the averaging in Equation 12 and the estimation of the FERF in Equation 8.

For example, for any j, the integral in Equation 12 is $P(\theta \mid J(j))$, which is the left-hand side of Equation 8, if y_j is 1, and $1 - P(\theta \mid J(j))$ if y_j is 0. Therefore, once the RSM is fitted and the FERFs estimated, the results can be used for estimating examinee abilities without much additional computation.

The approach of integrating out the item parameters in Equations 11 and 12 is similar to the approach of computing the *expected response functions* (ERF) suggested by Lewis (1985, 2001). Note that a similar approach as described above can be used to estimate the examinee abilities under the LICM.

Model Selection and Model Checking

In an application involving item families, a researcher might be interested in comparing the different statistical models such as the ISM, RSM, LICM, and the model which ignores the relationship among the siblings, which we refer to as the unrelated siblings model (USM). Johnson and Sinharay (2005) recommended using the Bayes factor, a popular Bayesian model selection tool (e.g., Kass & Raftery, 1995) for performing such comparisons between the RSM and USM and suggested a convenient approach for estimating the Bayes factor. Sinharay and Johnson (2008) applied the posterior predictive model checking method (Gelman et al., 2003) to determine the fit of the ISM and the RSM to the observed within-family standard deviation of proportion corrects. Geerlings et al. (2011) used Bayesian residual analysis to assess the fit of the LICM. To compare the LICM and RSM, they used the deviance information criterion (e.g., Spiegelhalter, Best, Carlin, & Van Der Linde, 2002), the explained variance at the level of the item parameters, and the degree of pooling of the item parameters around their family means.

Example

Data

Items automatically generated using item models were administered in the unscored part of a recent administration of the GRE. This was among the first few known applications of automatically generated items or model-based items in a large-scale testing program. Item models were created for the GRE quantitative section after studying the features of items from previous operational item pools and choosing a number of these items as the basis of item models (Steffen, Graf, Levin, Robin, & Lu, 2011). One item model was used for each of four important content areas: remainders (RE), linear inequality (LI), quadrilateral perimeter (QP), and probability (PR). For each content area, one submodel, each corresponding to difficulty levels 1 (very easy), 2 (moderately easy), 3 (moderately hard), and 4 (very hard), was produced to cover a wide range of difficulty for each content area. Therefore, there are 16 submodels involved in all, one for each combination of content area and difficulty. We denote them as RE-1 (RE, very easy); RE-2, RE-3, and RE-4 (RE, very hard); and LI-1 etc. We treat items generated from each submodel as part of an item family. Henceforth, Item Families 1, 2, 3, and 4 refer to submodels RE-1, RE-2, RE-3, and RE-4, respectively; Families 5–8 refer to LI-1 to LI-4; Families 9–12 refer to QP-1 to QP-4; and Families 13–16 refer to PR-1 to PR-4. Ten items (siblings) from each submodel, created using the Mathematics Test Creation Assistant (TCA) software developed at the Educational Testing Service (ETS) (Singley & Bennett, 2002), were administered as part of the unscored quantitative section of the GRE. All items were multiple choice with five options. All 10 items within each family were intended to be isomorphic or equivalent.

As an example, an item generated from a LI-4 (linear inequality very hard) item model is the following (Graf, Peterson, Steffen, & Lawless, 2005):

The statement "$t - 3 \leq -1$" or "$3 - t \geq -13$" is equivalent to which of the following?

A. $t \leq 2$
B. $t \leq -10$
C. $-2 \leq t \leq 13$
D. $-9 \leq t \leq 3$
E. $-10 \leq t \leq 2$

Option A is the correct answer for the item.

The data were collected by ETS during operational computer-based testing for the GRE in January and February 2003. The computer-based GRE has four sections: analytical writing, quantitative, verbal, and an unscored variable section (quantitative or verbal and used for collecting pretest data on new items). These automatically generated items were embedded within the 28-item quantitative variable sections. Examinees did not know that these were unscored items. Hence, it can be assumed that the examinees were motivated while responding to these items. Each of the 32,921 examinees received only four model-based items, a single sibling each from four submodels, one item for each difficulty level, and one item from each content area. To avoid potential speededness and context effects, the within-section item positions of these model-based items were controlled—see Sinharay and Johnson (2008) for further details. The number of examinees receiving any of these items varied from 663 to 1,016, with the average being 821.

Figure 11.1 shows the proportion-correct scores of the items for the different item families. For each content area (RE, LI, QP, or PR—shown along the x-axis), there are four vertical lines, one each for the four difficulty levels that define the submodels, along which are plotted the proportion-correct scores for the items in that submodel. A symbol 1 corresponds to an item of Difficulty Level 1 (very easy), 2 is for Difficulty Level 2 (moderately easy), and so on.

Each item family has its own pattern. The only common pattern is that the items in Difficulty Level 1 are easier, on average, than those in Level 2, which are in turn easier than those in Level 3, and so on. The difference between the difficulty levels differs over the families. For the content area RE, there is a substantial overlap of any two successive difficulty levels. The same is mostly true for the

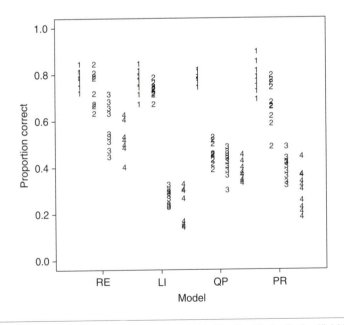

content area PR. For the content area LI, there is a big difference between the first two levels and the last two. For the content area QP, Level 1 is much easier than the other three. The proportion-correct score of each item varies within any family.

There are a few interesting outcomes in Figure 11.1. For example, the items belonging to content area LI, Difficulty Level 4, seem to be divided into two different clusters. One cluster has proportion corrects all close to 0.15 and another cluster has proportion corrects close to 0.30. This difference is due to the distracters used in the items, as will be discussed later.

Fitting of the RSM to the Data

The RSM was fitted to the data using an MCMC algorithm. We used the transformation $\alpha_j \equiv \log(a_j)$, $\beta_j \equiv b_j$, and $\gamma_j \equiv \text{logit}(c_j)$. Each examinee answers only four model-based items. Therefore, we use the posterior means and standard deviations (SDs) from the operational quantitative section (from a separate analysis performed during operational scoring of examinees) as the means and SDs, respectively, of the normal prior distributions on the proficiency parameters.

Figure 11.2 shows the estimated FERFs and corresponding 95% confidence intervals (solid lines) along with the estimated item characteristic curves (ICC; dashed lines) of the 10 items belonging to each item family. For any value of ability shown along the x-axis, the y-axis shows the value of the FERF given by Equation 8 and the value of the probability of a correct answer from the 3PL model (given by Equation 6) for the 10 items belonging to the family.[2] The figure shows that, for any family, the FERF lies roughly in the middle of the 10 ICCs. Thus, a FERF for any family is roughly a summary of all the ICCs.

Figure 11.3 summarizes the sampled values of the mean difficulty $\mu_{\beta_{J(j)}}$ (along the x-axis) and the within-family variance $\sigma^2_{\beta_{J(j)}}$ (along the y-axis) for all item families. For each item family, a point,

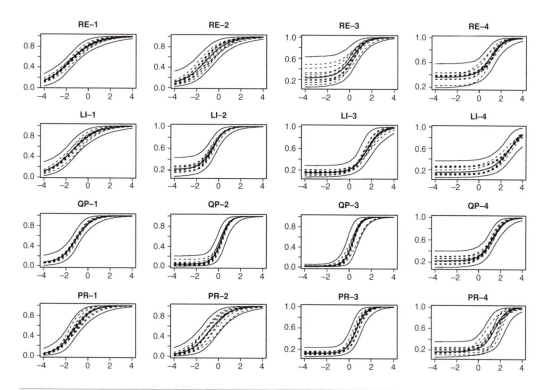

Figure 11.2 FERFs from RSM analysis.

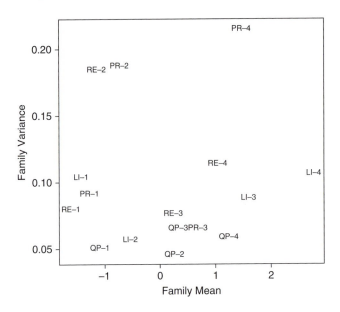

Figure 11.3 Summary of the posterior mean and variance of the difficulty parameters for all the item families. Copyright by Educational Testing Service, All rights reserved

denoted by the family name, shows the posterior median of $\mu_{\beta_{J(j)}}$ and the posterior median of $\sigma^2_{\beta_{J(j)}}$. The item families with more difficult items on an average are located towards the right of the figure. For example, item family RE-1, which includes the least-difficult items on an average (see Figure 11.1), is located to the extreme left of the figure. The item families that are less isomorphic are located towards the top of the figure.

Figure 11.3 demonstrates that the item families are well spread out, especially with respect to mean difficulty. As was found in Figure 11.1, LI-4, which is located to the extreme right of Figure 11.3, is the most difficult family by a clear margin. The content area RE seems to have the easiest families. The estimated mean difficulty for RE-1 is less than that of LI-1, QP-1, and PR-1; the same is true for the other difficulty levels. The content area QP includes item families that are, on an average, most isomorphic; the item characteristic curves for the siblings within each family for QP are close to each other in Figure 11.2. The content areas RE and PR seem to have the least-isomorphic families; the four families that have the largest estimated within-family variance (see Figure 11.3) are from these content areas. The families at Difficulty Level 1 are most isomorphic (the estimated within-family variance of item families at Difficulty Level 1 are all 0.1 or smaller), and Difficulty Level 4 are probably the least isomorphic. Figure 11.2 shows that for several families, such as RE-3, RE-4, LI-2, LI-4, QP-4, the lower asymptotes of the siblings differ substantially.

The family LI-4 shows an interesting pattern in Figures 11.1, 11.2, and 11.3—the siblings seem to belong to two different clusters. Graf et al. (2005) described this set of 10 items in detail. Six of these siblings contain a type of distractor that corresponds with a popular misconception and is an attractive distractor. Consider the example item shown earlier, which is one of these six siblings. The statement "$t − 3 ≤ −1$ or $3 − t ≥ 13$" is equivalent to $t ≤ 2$ or $t ≤ −10$ (i.e., $t ≤ 2$) so that the answer is A. However, a popular misconception is to reverse the inequality to end up with the answer $t ≤ 2$ and $t ≥ −10$ (i.e., $−10 ≤ t ≤ 2$), which corresponds with the distractor E. About 40% to 50% of examinees selected this distractor, bringing down the proportion corrects for these siblings to about 15%, even lower than the chance level of 20%. On the other hand, four other siblings use a different distractor type (not corresponding with a common mistake) instead of the attractive distractor; as a result, about 5% of examinees choose this distractor and the proportion correct for these four siblings is about 30%. As Graf et al. (2005) commented, in order to make the item families more isomorphic, one must be careful to give comparable alternative choices (distractors) across all siblings within a family. If one sibling has an attractive distractor, then all siblings should have attractive distractors. Essentially, there should be a one-to-one correspondence between the siblings' distractors.

Estimation of Examinee Abilities

Sinharay and Johnson (2008) also considered the estimation of examinee abilities under an application of RSM for these data. They simulated responses of several examinees to several items each. The parameters of each item were generated from the multivariate distribution given by Equation 7, where $J(j)$ is the item family to which the item belongs. They compared the posterior mean and posterior standard deviation of the examinee abilities obtained under RSM and ISM. They found negligible differences between ISM and RSM. This outcome is interesting because an application of the posterior predictive model checking method (e.g., Gelman et al., 2003) to these data by Sinharay and Johnson (2008) showed that the ISM does not fit the observed within-family standard deviation of proportion corrects, while the RSM does. Sinharay and Johnson (2008) also referred to some results from Glas and van der Linden (2003) to argue that the ISM performs as well as the RSM for all practical purposes, so far as the estimation of examinee abilities is concerned.

Conclusions

There has been substantial research on the statistical and psychometric modeling of automatically generated items. Models such as the RSM and LICM are the outcomes of this research. However, there are several issues that need further investigation.

Sinharay and Johnson (2008) reported that the more intuitive RSM provides little gain over the rather restrictive ISM in the estimation of examinee abilities, which can be considered as the final goal of these models. RSM does not perform much better than ISM regarding ability estimation in the simulation results of Glas and van der Linden (2003), either. These findings may indicate that the ISM is adequate (and that there is no need of the complicated RSM) for ability estimation for the level of within-family variation present in the simulations in Glas and van der Linden (2003) and in the GRE data. Thus, there is a need for more research on estimation of examinee abilities when automatically generated items are involved and on demonstrating the usefulness of the RSM or other advanced models over the simpler ISM.

The RSM provides an easy way of including collateral information. This was demonstrated by Geerlings et al. (2011), who extended the RSM to the LICM. It is possible to extend the RSM in other ways as well. For example, just like Geerlings et al. (2011) used the information on the radicals to explain the family mean, the information on the incidentals may be used to explain the family variance.

Geerlings et al. (2011) used Bayesian residual analysis (e.g., Johnson & Albert, 1999) to assess the fit of LICM. Sinharay and Johnson (2008) used the posterior predictive model checking (Gelman et al., 2003) method to assess the fit of ISM and RSM; they used, as the test statistic, the standard deviation of the proportion-correct scores within an item family. Johnson and Sinharay (2005) applied Bayes factors (Kass & Raftery, 1995) for model selection for RSMs. It is also possible to perform more rigorous model fit and model selection analysis with these models. For example, it is possible to apply the posterior predictive model checking method using a variety of test statistics to the LICM and RSM and to compute Bayes factors for comparing the LICM and RSM.

Notes

1 It is also possible to use the transformation $\alpha_j \equiv \log \Box (a_j)$.
2 Where the parameters in Equations 6 and 8 were replaced by their estimates obtained from the MCMC algorithm.

References

Bejar, I. I. (2002). Generative testing: From conception to implementation. In S. H. Irvine & P. C. Kyllonen (Eds.), *Item generation for test development* (pp. 199–217). Mahwah, NJ: Lawrence Erlbaum Associates.

Bradlow, E. T., Wainer, H., & Wang, X. (1999). A Bayesian random effects model for testlets. *Psychometrika, 64*, 153–168.

Deane, P., & Sheehan, K. (2003). *Automatic item generation via frame semantics: Natural language generation of math word problems.* Paper presented at the annual meeting of the National Council on Measurement in Education, Chicago, IL.

Embretson, S. E. (1999). Generating items during testing: Psychometric issues and models. *Psychometrika, 64*, 407–433.

Fischer, G. H. (1973). The linear logistic test model as an instrument in educational research. *Acta Psychologica, 37*, 359–374.

Freund, Ph. A., Hofer, S., & Holling, H. (2008). Explaining and controlling for the psychometric properties of computer-generated figural matrix items. *Applied Psychological Measurement, 32*, 195–210.

Gelman, A., Carlin, J. B., Stern, H. S., & Rubin, D. B. (2003). *Bayesian data analysis.* New York, NY: Chapman & Hall.

Geerlings, H., van der Linden, W. J., & Glas, C. A. W. (2011). Modeling rule-based item generation. *Psychometrika, 76*, 337–359.

Glas, C. A. W., & van der Linden, W. J. (2001). *Modeling variability in item parameters in CAT.* Paper presented at the North American Psychometric Society meeting, King of Prussia, PA.

Glas, C. A. W., & van der Linden, W. J. (2003). Computerized adaptive testing with item cloning. *Applied Psychological Measurement, 27*, 247–261.

Glas, C. A. W., van der Linden, W. J., & Geerlings, H. (2010). Estimation of the parameters in an item-cloning model for adaptive testing. In W. J. van der Linden and C. A. W. Glas (Eds.), *Elements of adaptive testing* (pp. 289–314). New York, NY: Springer.

Graf, E. A., Peterson, S., Steffen, M., & Lawless, R. (2005). *Psychometric and cognitive analysis as a basis for the design and revision of quantitative item models.* (ETS Research Report No. RR-05). Princeton, NJ: Educational Testing Service.

Hively, W., Patterson, H. L., & Page, S. H. (1968). A "universe-defined" system of arithmetic achievement tests. *Journal of Educational Measurement, 5*, 275–290.

Holling, H., Bertling, J. P., & Zeuch, N. (2009). Automatic item generation of probability word problems. *Studies in Educational Evaluation, 35*, 71–76.

Hombo, C., & Dresher, A. (2001). *A simulation study of the impact of automatic item generation under NAEP-like data conditions.* Paper presented at the annual meeting of the National Council on Measurement in Education, Seattle, WA.

Irvine, S. H. (2002). The foundations of item generation in mass testing. In S. H. Irvine & P. C. Kyllonen (Eds.), *Item generation for test development* (pp. 3–34). Mahwah, NJ: Lawrence Erlbaum Associates.

Irvine, S. H., & Kyllonen, P. C. (Eds.). (2002). *Item generation for test development.* Mahwah, NJ: Lawrence Erlbaum Associates.

Janssen, R., Schepers, J., & Peres, D. (2004). Models with item group predictors. In P. De Boeck & M. Wilson (Eds.), *Explanatory item response models: A generalized linear and nonlinear approach* (pp. 189–212). New York, NY: Springer.

Janssen, R., Tuerlinckx, F., Meulders, M., & De Boeck, P. (2000). A hierarchical IRT model for criterion-referenced measurement. *Journal of Educational and Behavioral Statistics, 25*, 285–306.

Johnson, V. E. & Albert, J. H. (1999). *Ordinal data modeling.* New York, NY: Springer.

Johnson, M. S., & Sinharay, S. (2005). Calibration of polytomous item families using Bayesian hierarchical modeling. *Applied Psychological Measurement, 29*, 369–400.

Kass, R. E., & Raftery, A. E. (1995). Bayes Factors. *Journal of the American Statistical Association, 90*, 773–795.

LaDuca, A., Staples, W. I., Templeton, B., & Holzman, G. B. (1986). Item modeling procedure for constructing content-equivalent multiple-choice questions. *Medical Education, 20*, 53–56.

Lewis, C. (1985). *Estimating individual abilities with imperfectly known item response functions.* Paper presented at the annual meeting of the Psychometric Society, Nashville, TN.

Lewis, C. (2001). Expected response functions. In A. Boomsma, M. A. J. van Duijn, & T. A. B. Snijders (Eds.), *Essays on item response theory.* New York, NY: Springer.

Lord, F. M. & Novick, M. R. (1968). *Statistical theories of mental test scores.* Reading MA: Addison-Welsley Publishing Company.

Mislevy, R. J., Steinberg, L. S., & Almond, R. G. (2002). On the roles of task model variables in assessment design. In S. H. Irvine & P. C. Kyllonen (Eds.), *Item generation for test development* (pp. 97–128). Mahwah, NJ: Lawrence Erlbaum Associates.

Muraki, E. (1992). A generalized partial credit model: Application of an E-M algorithm. *Applied Psychological Measurement, 16*, 159–176.

Peterson, S. (2004). *Test development and item modeling of mathematics questions.* Paper presented at the 30th annual conference of the International Association for Educational Assessment (IAEA), Philadelphia, PA.

Rasch, G. (1960). *Probabilistic models for some intelligence and attainment tests.* Copenhagen: Paedagogiske Institute.

Singley, M. K., & Bennett, R. E. (2002). Item generation and beyond: Applications of schema theory to mathematics assessment. In S. H. Irvine & P. C. Kyllonen (Eds.), *Item generation for test development* (pp. 361–384). Mahwah, NJ: Lawrence Erlbaum Associates.

Sinharay, S., & Johnson, M. S. (2008). Use of item models in a large-scale admissions test: A case study. *International Journal of Testing, 8,* 209–236.

Sinharay, S., Johnson, M. S., & Williamson, D. M. (2003). Calibrating item families and summarizing the results using family expected response functions. *Journal of Educational and Behavioral Statistics, 28,* 295–313.

Spiegelhalter, D. J., Best, N. G., Carlin, B. P., & Van Der Linde, A. (2002), Bayesian measures of model complexity and fit. *Journal of the Royal Statistical Society: Series B, 64,* 583–639.

Steffen, M., Graf, E. A., Levin, J. Robin, F., & Lu, T. (2011), *An investigation of the psychometric equivalence of quantitative isomorphs: Phase 1.* Unpublished manuscript.

Wright, D. (2002). Scoring tests when items have been generated. In S. H. Irvine & Kyllonen, P. C. (Eds.), *Item generation for test development* (pp. 277–286). Mahwah, NJ: Lawrence Erlbaum Associates.

12

Automatic Item Generation for Computerized Adaptive Testing

Richard M. Luecht

Introduction

Computerized adaptive testing (CAT) broadly refers to tests administered on a computer, where the items are selected so that the overall test-form difficulty is targeted to the proficiency of each examinee. This proficiency targeting results in a more efficient test where greater score or decision accuracy can be achieved using fewer items than in a typical fixed test form (i.e., a test form where every examinee sees exactly the same items). In this context, *accuracy* is referring to the magnitude of the estimation error variance. A larger error variance implies less stable score estimates. As noted further on in this chapter, another component of accuracy is bias—that is, failure of the estimate to converge to the true (but unknown) parameter of interest.

Although the efficiency benefits of CAT were anticipated by a number of researchers (Lord, 1970, 1971, 1977; Weiss, 1969, 1973, 1975, 1982, 1985; Green, Bock, Humphreys, Linn, & Reckase, 1983), it did not gain prominence until the early to mid-1990s, with implementations such as Novell's *Certified Network Engineer* program (Foster, 2011), the GRE for graduate school admissions (Eignor, Stocking, Way, & Steffen, 1993; Mills & Stocking, 1996), the NCLEX examinations for nurses, developed and administered by the National Council on State Boards of Nursing (Zara, 1994), and the *Armed Service Vocational Aptitude Battery* (Sands, Waters, & McBride, 1997). Today, CAT applications can be found for educational achievement tests, aptitude tests, certification tests, and licensure tests. Unlike conventional, standardized, paper-and-pencil tests, where all examinees receive a common test form or test battery composed of the same items, in CAT, each examinee may receive a different assortment of items, selected according to various rules, goals, or procedures.

One of the greatest challenges in CAT—actually for almost any computer-based test—is building and maintaining a pool of high-quality test items having consistent statistical parameter estimates. When testing occurs frequently or on demand, the testing organization runs the risk of examinees' collaborating to memorize and share segments of the item bank. These types of security risks are non-trivial for high-stakes examination programs used in part for professional certification or licensing, for high school graduation or college/university admissions, for job placement or employment, or even for psychological instruments used to make clinical diagnoses or decisions. A reasonable solution is to increase the size of the item bank so as to essentially dilute the exposure risk.

However, adding more items to an item bank is not without serious cost and technical complications. Professionally developed test items may each cost hundreds or even thousands of dollars when item writing, editing, pretesting, and psychometric analysis costs are factored in (Mills & Stocking, 1996; Mills & Steffen, 2000; Wainer, 2002). If ten times as many items are needed in order to reduce exposure risks, overall test development costs will likewise increase by a proportional amount. Very few testing programs can withstand order-of-magnitude increases in their test development and associated operational costs—at least, not without substantially increasing testing fees charged to the examinees or the sponsoring agency (Luecht, 2005).

A promising solution that can potentially increase the size of the item banks at substantially lower costs (per item) and also maintain the statistical integrity of the item statistics and underlying score scale is to use automatic item generation (AIG). Drasgow, Luecht and Bennett (2006) described two basic approaches to AIG: (a) a strong theory approach and (b) a weak theory approach (see, also, Gierl & Lai, this volume).

The strong theory approach to AIG employs one or more cognitive theories of item difficulty to drive the design of templates or item models so that all items developed from the same template or model perform similarly in a psychometric (statistical) sense. In addition, the cognitive theory provides a rationale that inferentially links the examinees' performance on particular tasks to an underlying proficiency of interest (Bejar, 1990, 2002; Embretson, 1999; Irvine, 2002; see also Bejar, this volume; Graf & Fife, this volume; Gorin & Embretson, this volume; Leighton, this volume).

In contrast, a weak theory of AIG primarily seeks merely to manipulate design features that affect item difficulty—so-called difficulty drivers—and other possible statistical item characteristics. A cognitive explanation is not required, provided that the item families based on item models, templates or clones of particular items perform similarly enough to essentially treat them as exchangeable within family (Meisner, Luecht, & Reckase, 1993; Glas & van der Linden, 2003; Geerlings, van der Linden, & Glas, 2010; Geerlings, Glas, & van der Linden, 2011; Glas, van der Linden, & Geerlings, 2010; Lai, Alves, & Gierl, 2009; Luecht, this volume; Sinharay & Johnson, this volume).

Ultimately, the distinctions between strong and weak theories of AIG depend on the types of inferences that test designers wish to make about the underlying construct(s). Both approaches require tying the difficulty drivers or design features of a template or item model to parameters estimated under a particular psychometric model (Embretson, 1999). A strong theory provides a plausible rationale for the design choices made and would seem to strengthen the inferential arguments made about what the test is actually measuring. However, in the end, what matters is that AIG-based item models or templates constrain design-related features of a family of items so that an examinee is indifferent[1] as to which particular item from within the family he or she sees.

This chapter first presents a basic introduction to CAT. Next, several AIG-for-CAT approaches are introduced. Finally, some results from a simulation study are presented in order to describe the basic quality-control analyses needed to monitor CAT in an adaptive context, as well as to highlight some of the benefits of good AIG implementations and pitfalls of problematic AIG implementations.

An Overview of CAT

CAT can be conceptualized as an iterative process involving the application of two types of algorithms: (1) an item-selection algorithm for constructing the test and (2) a scoring algorithm for providing provisional scores used by the item-selection algorithm. These two algorithms work together in an iterative sequence of administering and scoring items (or larger test-administration units). However, in order to understand the two algorithms, it is also necessary to understand a bit about item response theory (IRT).

Birnbaum's (1968) introduction of the IRT item information function (IIF) for the three-parameter logistic (3PL) model provided the key criterion for the item-selection algorithm used in CAT. The 3PL item information function can be expressed as

$$I_i(\theta) = \frac{\left[P_i'(\theta)\right]^2}{P_i(\theta)\left[1 - P_i(\theta)\right]} = \frac{a_i^2\left[1 - P_i(\theta)\right]\left[P_i(\theta) - c_i\right]^2}{P_i(\theta)\left[1 - c\right]^2} \tag{12.1}$$

where the 3PL response function (Lord, 1980; Hambleton & Swaminathan, 1985) is

$$P_i(\theta) = c_i + \frac{1 - c_i}{1 + \exp\left[a_i(\theta - b_i)\right]} \tag{12.2}$$

This response function, $P_i(\theta)$, mathematically describes the probability of correctly answering a dichotomously scored item—i.e., an item scored $u_i=1$ if correct or $u_i=0$ if incorrect—for an examinee having a proficiency score denoted by the Greek letter θ ("theta"). The proficiency scale is arbitrary, but is typically specified to be centered at zero, with plausible scores ranging between -4 and $+4$. In general, the probability in Equation 12.2 increases as the examinees increase in proficiency. That is, as θ increases from -4 to $+4$, so does $P_i(\theta)$.

The item parameters used in the 3PL model (Equation 12.2) are simply referred to as a_i, b_i, and c_i. These item parameters respectively denote the item slope (sometimes referred to as the item's discriminating power), the item difficulty, and a pseudo-guessing parameter that helps to fit the model to noisy data at the lower tail of the proficiency scale. At any point along the proficiency scale, an easier item usually has a higher probability of being correctly answered than a more difficult item. The slope parameter, a_i, determines the steepness of the increase in the probability function. An item having a lower a_i parameter will tend to require larger changes in θ in order to produce a comparable increase in the probability of correctly answering the item to an item with a larger a_i parameter. The 3PL model parameters are estimated by statistically fitting the mathematical model in Equation 12.2 to actual dichotomous response data.

Figure 12.1 shows the 3PL response functions for eight items. The corresponding item parameters are presented in Table 12.1. Items 1, 2, 3, and 4 have higher a-parameters, increasing the steepness

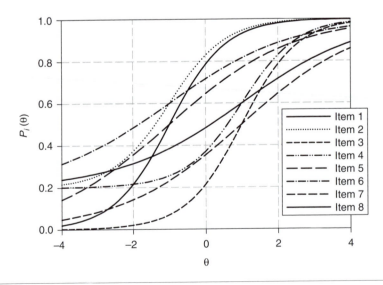

Figure 12.1 3PL probability functions for eight items (see Table 12.1)

Table 12.1 3PL item parameters for eight items

Item No.	a	b	c
1	1.3	−1.0	0.0
2	1.3	−1.0	0.2
3	1.3	1.0	0.0
4	1.3	1.0	0.2
5	0.6	−1.0	0.0
6	0.6	−1.0	0.2
7	0.6	1.0	0.0
8	0.6	1.0	0.2

of the probability functions. Items 1, 2, 5, and 6 are easier items (i.e., have b-parameters of −1.0) and the corresponding probability curves start increasing at lower values of θ than for items 3, 5, 7, and 8. Finally, the four odd-numbered items have c-parameters of zero, while the even-numbered items have c-parameters of .2. The non-zero c_i parameters raise the probability of a correct response by a constant amount to account for erratic response patterns exhibited by lower-proficiency examinees—possibly due to random guessing.

The information functions for the same eight items are shown in Figure 12.2 (also see Equation 12.1). An item information function (Birnbaum, 1968; Lord, 1980) can be interpreted as the amount of precision provided by each item at different proficiency scores. Since we *estimate* proficiency from an examinee's test responses, there will always be some amount of estimation error involved. The IIF is inversely proportional to the error (variance) of estimation. It reflects the location and amount of precision, so where the height of the curve is low, estimation error variance is high. Conversely, where information is high, the estimation error variance is relatively small. The b-parameter determines the peak of the IIF. For example, Items 1 and 3 have peak information at different points along the θ scale, corresponding to $b_1 = -1.0$ and $b_3 = +1.0$ (see Table 12.1). The amount of information (height of the IIF curve) is primarily a function of the a-parameters (see Lord, 1980 for a technical explanation). Items 1 to 4 ($a_i = 1.3$ for all four items) therefore have substantially more information near their peaks than Items 5 to 8, where $a_i = .6$. The lower-asymptote parameter, c_i, proportionally *reduces* the amount of information and moves the peak slightly to the right (see Lord, 1980). This is somewhat clear for Items 1 vs. 2 and for Items 3 vs. 4. The only differences in the item parameters are that $c_2 = c_4 = 0.2$, while $c_1 = c_3 = 0.0$.

Item information functions are highly relevant to CAT. The item-selection algorithm chooses the item that provides the most information at an examinee's provisional score—that is, his or her current estimate of θ. For example, Item 1 in Figure 12.2 ($a_1 = 1.3$, $b_1 = -1.0$, $c_1 = 0.0$) provides maximum information for examinees having θ scores from −∞ up to zero. Item 3 ($a_3 = 1.3$, $b_3 = 1.0$, $c_3 = 0.0$) is the most informative item for examinees having θ scores above zero. Item 1 is also preferred over Items 2, 5, and 6, because it has more overall information, even though all four items have difficulty parameters of exactly −1.0. Item 2 has reduced information because of the non-zero lower asymptote parameter, $c_2 = 0.2$. Items 5 and 6 have reduced information because the slope parameters are $a_5 = a_6 = 0.6$.

The scoring algorithm used in CAT requires the item parameters, a_i, b_i, and c_i, and response data ($u_i = 1$ or $u_i = 0$) to estimate θ for examinee, after each item is administered. Although there are several options for estimating θ, one of the most common algorithms for CAT uses a Bayesian procedure known as the expected a posteriori (EAP) estimator (Bock & Mislevy, 1982). The EAP can be computed as

$$\hat{\theta}^{EAP}_{u_{i_1}...u_{i_{k-1}}} = \int \theta \cdot p\left(\theta \middle| u_{i_1}...u_{i_{k-1}}\right) d\theta \tag{12.3}$$

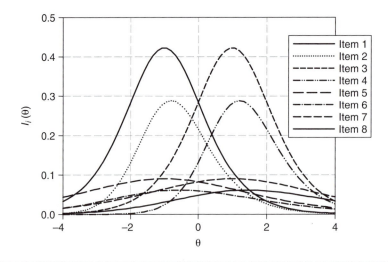

Figure 12.2 Item information functions for eight items (see Table 12.1)

where the $p()$ term is called the *posteriorlikelihood function* (PLF),

$$p\left(\theta\middle|u_{i_1}\ldots u_{i_{k-1}}\right)=\frac{g(\theta)\prod_{i=1}^{n}P_i(\theta)^{u_i}\left[1-P_i(\theta)\right]^{1-u_i}}{\int g(\theta)\prod_{i=1}^{n}P_i(\theta)^{u_i}\left[1-P_i(\theta)\right]^{1-u_i}d\theta} \tag{12.4}$$

The PLF expresses the probability of the examinee's score taking on a particular value of θ, given that examinee's pattern of responses, U_k (where k is the number of items administered to a certain point). As more items are administered, the peak of the PLF curve will (theoretically) converge to the true [but unknown] value of θ. For example, Figure 12.3 shows three posterior likelihood functions:[2] (1) the PLF after administering an 80-item test; (2) the PLF for 10 items randomly selected from the 80-item test; and (3) the PLF for 10 adaptively selected items. The PLFs are based on the 3PL model using simulated response data for an examinee whose true proficiency score is specified to be exactly $\theta=1.25$, with the a-, b- and c-parameters specified to represent a rather typical achievement test—i.e., the means and standard deviations of the a-, b- and c-parameters for the 80 items were, respectively: $a\sim(1.02, .16)$, $b\sim(.41, 1.02)$, and $c\sim(.16, .02)$. In this example, the EAP estimate of θ (applying Equation 12.3 to estimate the mean of the posterior distribution of θ) for all 80 items is $\hat{\theta}_{80}^{EAP}=1.27$, with a posterior standard deviation of $sd\left(\hat{\theta}_{80}^{EAP}\right)=0.21$. The peak of the PLF is further away from the true value and wider after only administering ten randomly selected items; that is, $\hat{\theta}_{10.random}^{EAP}=0.65$ and $sd\left(\hat{\theta}_{10.random}^{EAP}\right)=0.60$.

The larger posterior standard deviation reflects more estimation error for the shorter test. Comparatively, using a 10-item CAT moves the EAP estimate substantially closer to the true value and also reduces the uncertainty (size of the standard error) about the estimate. That is, the mean of the CAT posterior distribution is $\hat{\theta}_{10.CAT}^{EAP}=1.06$, with a posterior standard deviation of $sd\left(\hat{\theta}_{10.CAT}^{EAP}\right)=0.50$.

While the 10-item CAT is not as accurate as the full 80-item test, it presents a substantially better estimate than randomly selecting 10 items.

Van der Linden and Pashley (2010) provide a more thorough discussion than is possible here, and also offer comparisons among various IRT proficiency score estimators, including maximum likelihood estimators, EAPs and Bayesian modal estimates (also see Mislevy, 1986; Bock & Mislevy, 1982).

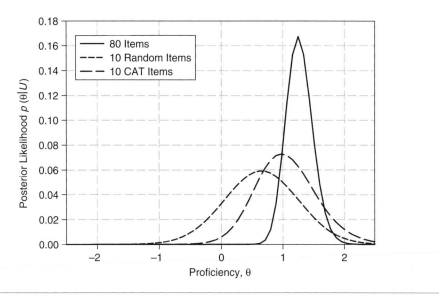

Figure 12.3 Posterior likelihood functions for 80 items, 10 randomly selected items, and a 10-item CAT (θ_{true}=1.25)

Based on each provisional estimate of θ, the CAT selects and administers another item. The examinee's responses (u_{ik}) up to that point in the test are then used to re-compute $\hat{\theta}^{EAP}$, and that new score is used to select the next item having maximum information. Formally, given the unselected items in an item database, R_k, an item is selected to satisfy the objective function:

$$i_k \equiv \max_j \left\{ I_{U_j}\left(\theta_{u_{i_1},...,u_{i_{k-1}}}\right) : j \in R_k \right\} \tag{12.5}$$

Content requirements and exposure controls can be included in the item-selection algorithm to ensure that: (a) all test forms conform to the same content blueprint and (b) the more informative items are not over-selected, placing the integrity of the test at risk if examinees conspire to memorize and share the most highly exposed items. More thorough discussions of content balancing and exposure controls are presented, for example, by van der Linden (2005) and Parshall, Spray, Kalohn and Davey (2002).

In practice, a CAT usually begins by administering a small random sample or preselected set of items to provide a reasonable starting estimate of the examinee's proficiency score, prior to activating the adaptive item-selection algorithm. Following this initial item administration period, the CAT implements the two-step process outlined above until a particular stopping criterion has been achieved. As more items are administered, the CAT software is able to incrementally improve the accuracy of the provisional score for the examinee. The CAT terminates when a stopping rule has been satisfied. Two standard stopping rules for adaptive tests are: (1) a fixed test length has been met or (2) a minimum level of score precision has been satisfied. [Note: for pass/fail mastery tests used in certification and licensure testing, a different stopping rule can be implemented related to the desired statistical confidence in the accuracy of the classification decision(s)].

Automatic Item Generation for CAT

The apparent value of AIG for computer-based testing, in general, and CAT, in particular, is three-fold.

First, being able to generate items by algorithmic or other automated or semi-automated means implies a potentially low-cost solution to the otherwise expensive option of developing items by traditional means, with incremental costs per item associated with item writing, editing, pilot testing, and analysis/calibration. For example, if items cost $300 each, doubling the size of an item bank to 2000 items implies a cost increase of $300,000. Rudner (2010) estimates that a single high-quality operational test item now costs between $1500 and $2000. Furthermore, since each item is treated as a unique commodity with a recognized, limited shelf life (due to exposure risks), retiring an item represents a lost asset. If the items can be produced on demand in whatever quantity is needed and put into operational use for a relatively low unit cost—while maintaining high quality—then the economic benefits should be obvious.

Second, by focusing on principled and efficient design, automation, and a cognitive basis for each item, AIG can improve item-writing practices by eliminating construct-irrelevant sources of variance that item writers may creatively add to a test. The result may be more valid instruments that also happen to provide more consistent scores, as well (see also Bejar, this volume).

Third, most AIG approaches depend on a hierarchy that links items to item models, families, or templates, and, possibly, templates to task models. This hierarchy can be exploited in calibrations of the items and, in some cases, used to eliminate the need for pilot testing every item—at least if the items belonging to each family meet prescribed quality-control criteria related to the allowable variation of statistical item characteristics (e.g., a maximum variance of estimated difficulties).

There are at least four variations on the theme of AIG relevant to adaptive testing contexts: (1) item modeling; (2) cloning; (3) using attribute design matrices; and (4) assessment engineering templates based on cognitive task models. I use the term *variations* to emphasize that none of these AIG methods is necessarily unique. However, there are some conceptual and operational differences that may be worth noting.

Item Modeling

Item modeling has a rich history in the measurement literature that spans many decades, including pioneering work by Hively, Patterson, and Page (1968), and Osburn (1968), all of whom suggested developing a generic parent item and then creating instances of the parent by manipulating key features to produce what Bejar and Yocom (1991) termed *isomorphs*. As Bejar (2002) notes,

> the objective is to define classes, which we later call *item models*, from which it is possible to generate or produce items that are in all respects equivalent, isomorphic, to all other items produced by a given model.
>
> (p. 201, italics in the original)

Following Irvine (2002), the features can be classified into two broad categories: (a) *incidental* parameters that alter the basic appearance of the item and (b) *radical* features that may alter the difficulty of an item if changed. (Note: Dennis, et al., 2002, similarly labeled these categories as *non-controlling* and *controlling* features, p. 56.) Under Bejar's (2002) conception, manipulating the incidental features produces isomorphs of items belonging to a common family. Manipulating radical features tends to produce variants of an item model, each of which may form an entirely new family.

Bejar et al. (2003) provided a practical proof-of-concept by developing item models from 147 Graduate Record Examination (GRE) General Test items (101 quantitative-comparison item models and 46 problem-solving item models). Educational Testing Service conducted an experimental field study involving several hundred examinees, and Bejar et al. were able to essentially replicate scores to a degree matching typical GRE test-retest correlations (see also Sinharay & Johnson, this volume). Item models have also been used in other contexts (e.g., Gierl, Zhou, & Alves, 2008; LaDuca, 1994; Singley & Bennett, 2002).

Item Cloning

Item cloning is a special case of item modeling, where an item shell (Haladyna & Shindoll, 1989) or rendered form of a class of items is generated and then used to replicate items that have the same essential look and feel, as well as content, but with enough variation to disguise each cloned item. Item cloning is essentially a weak-theory AIG method in that only the surface features are changed; an explanatory cognitive theory is not necessary. If the variation in the statistical item characteristics is sufficiently small, the cloning can be considered successful.

Each clone or item shell is usually based on a single, parent item. Variable slots or *tokens* in the shell are filled by either selecting from a list or algorithmically generating unique content or values to replace each token. The result is a family of very similar items. For example, Figure 12.4 shows a sample four-option multiple-choice item shell for a statistical item that asks the examinee to determine the probability of selecting a single item having a particular color or other attribute from a container holding three types of objects with specified quantities.

In addition to the fixed portions of the rendered form of the item, constraints are usually placed on the token values (denoted <> in Figure 12.4) so as to help to ensure that the clones are isomorphs (i.e., remain exchangeable with one another). There are many examples of successful item cloning, including Roid and Haladyna (1982), Meisner, Luecht, and Reckase (1993), Bejar (1993), Case and Swanson (2001), Devore (2002), and Haladyna (2004). There are, however, two fundamental complications associated with using item clones. One obvious complication is that the item clones from a common parent typically should not appear on the same test form. This implies that the parent-to-clone relations must be recognized within the item-management system and that the test-assembly procedures can treat the clones as mutually exclusive *enemies* (van der Linden, 2005). Glas and van der Linden (2003) also caution about a second complication where a faulty shell potentially introduces non-trivial statistical covariances among the estimated item statistics within a family of clones.

(a)

Parent Item
A canister holds 100 red objects, 150 yellow objects, and 50 blue objects. If we select one object from the canister, what is the probability that the object is red?

A. 1/300
      B. 1/100
      C. 100/250
      D. 100/300 **correct**

(b)

A *<setting.container>* holds *<object 1.count = x> <object 1.description>*
<object 2.count = y> <object 2.description>, and *<object 3.count = z>*
<object 3.description>. If you were to select *<task.action.select.object_count = k>*
<task.action.select.objectdescription> from *<setting.container>* , what is
<task.response_object> that the *<task.action.select.objectdescription>* is
<object 1.description>?

    <Option 1><task.answer.distractor 1 = $1/n$, $n = x + y + z$>
    <Option 2><task.answer.distractor 2 = $1/\{x, y,$ or $z\}$>
    <Option 3><task.answer.distractor 3 = $\{x, y,$ or $z\}$ /{$(x + y)$, $(x + z)$, $(y + z)$}>
    <Option 4><task.answer.correct = $\{x, y,$ or $z\}$ /$(x + y + z)$>

Figure 12.4 A parent item (a) and a sample item shell (b) for a statistical probability multiple-choice item

I will briefly return to this more technical point further on in the context of some CAT simulation results presented in this chapter.

Attribute Design Matrices

The use of attribute design (feature) matrices is a very general, Bayesian statistical solution to calibrating item models or clones, where *radical*[3] design features (difficulty drivers) are represented by a binary design matrix that links those design features to each item family (Glas, et al., 2010; Geerlings et al., 2011). Items are assumed to be randomly sampled from a particular family. The difficulty (and other item characteristics) associated with each family can be represented as a linear combination of the radicals. Any remaining variation in the item characteristics is assumed to be due to *incidental* features of the items and typically modeled by a family-specific covariance matrix (see Geerlings et al., 2011). A representation of radicals, families, items, and incidental features is presented in Figure 12.5.

This family-based item design approach is similar, at least at a conceptual level, to generating an item by attribute matrix for diagnostic classification models (Leighton & Gierl, 2007; Rupp, Templin, & Henson, 2010). Here, the major difference is that the attributes are the radicals (columns) and the families form the rows of the design matrix (vs. items). Item difficulty is hypothesized to result from a combination of the specified radical attributes. These hypotheses can be empirically tested and the design matrix adjusted as needed. Geerlings, et al. (2011) demonstrate some compelling empirical results of using attribute design matrices to classify items into 11 families for an analogies subtest of a non-verbal intelligence test. The results confirm that well-formed families, for the most part, allow items to be interchangeably used—that is, satisfying an examinee indifference criterion from the test-equating literature (see note 2). In addition, they provide an elaborate hierarchical IRT calibration framework based on earlier work by Glas and van der Linden (2003), and demonstrate a plausible way to estimate the model parameters using a Bayesian, data-augmented Gibbs (MCMC) sampler. Their hierarchical calibration approach appropriately incorporates uncertainty about the estimates of the item parameters and improves the efficiency and accuracy of scoring.

It also seems worth noting that self-adaptive items might be plausible in the future by essentially manipulating the radical features associated with a particular family. Luecht (2009) provides one conception of self-adapting items or performance exercises. For example, a reading comprehension task might actually rewrite the passage on the fly in order to simplify vocabulary or grammatical structures for examinees with apparently lower proficiency.

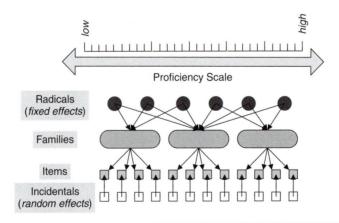

Figure 12.5 Attribute design relating radicals, families and items

Assessment-Engineering (AE) Templates

AE templates based on cognitive task models is a relatively new test design framework (see Luecht, this volume). Under AE, a task model map (TMM) is constructed to provide specific types of evidence about one or more proficiency claims along a construct (i.e., along the intended scale). The TMM is composed of independent, cognitively determined task models that represent a prescribed set of cognitive skills (procedural knowledge) being applied to a set of knowledge objects (declarative knowledge components), with additional features indicated that might alter the difficulty of a particular task (i.e., radicals). The TMM, itself, is merely a distribution of tasks models. The use of task models and a TMM accomplishes two goals. First, they provide a strong inferential validity argument that *justifies* the location of each task model as intentionally providing evidence about some level of proficiency. Second, the TMM provides a prescribed distribution of item difficulty, with the density of task models being proportional to the desired distribution of measurement information; in other words, the target test information function.

As noted above, a *task model* is a cognitive specification that details the combination of knowledge and skills (i.e., cognitive skills, declarative knowledge objects, relations among knowledge objects, and ancillary tools, settings, or conditions) that describe an entire family of test items. That is, each item in the family requires exactly the same combination of knowledge and skills and presents a highly similar challenge to the examinees. The task models can be represented in various ways. Luecht (this volume) describes using task model grammar; however, graphical or verbal descriptions of each task model are also possible. Each AE task model, in turn, is instantiated by two or more templates. A template includes a rendering model that largely controls the look and feel of the items (conceptually similar to item shells), a scoring evaluator that specifies how responses are converted to scorable information, and a data model that specifies the incidental and radical features or parameters and constraints for generating those features. Task models are further required to have multiple templates so as to ensure that the task challenges are not isolated to a particular item shell or model that only varies surface features.

An important aspect of the AE framework is that there is a direct hierarchical relationship between task models, templates, and items. Each task model has a location along the intended scale, denoting its difficulty. Each task model further has multiple templates and every template has multiple items generated from it. In other words, each task model is a family of templates and each template is a family of items. Therefore, compared to the other AIG approaches, AE expands the hierarchy by an additional level and further prescribes the relative location of each task model along the scale.

For CAT, a bank or pool of task models would be needed. A task model map for a CAT item bank with the heaviest concentration of task models near the mid-range of the proficiency scale is depicted in Figure 12.6. Each task model has a prescribed location along the scale and is represented by four templates in this representation. In practice, task models would likely have a variable number of templates. In turn, each template is capable of generating multiple items. Figure 12.6 shows a possible TMM for a pool of task models. Each task model has a prescribed location and is instantiated by multiple templates that each produce multiple items.

From a calibration perspective, it is important to preserve the direct hierarchical relations between task models, templates and items (see Glas & van der Linden, 2003; Glas et al., 2010; Geerlings, Glas, & van der Linden, 2011). Well-designed templates would allow calibrating a set of IRT hyperparameters for each template, representing the means, variances and covariances of the item parameter estimates. By extension, each task model could also have a set of (higher-order) hyperparameters (means, variances, and covariances of the IRT parameter estimates), creating a three-tiered estimation hierarchy (task models→templates→items). In practice, empirically based quality control policies would dictate whether one would calibrate and use the task model hyperparameter estimates (e.g., difficulty, discrimination) for all items in a selected family, the template-level hyperparameter

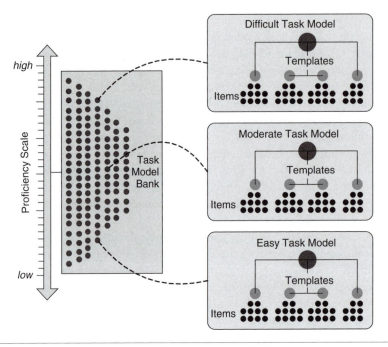

Figure 12.6 AE task models, templates and items

estimates, or calibrate individual items. For example, a minimum estimation error variance of some value would be required to migrate from using the unique item statistics to templates' hyperparameter estimates. A more stringent error variance requirement might be required in order to migrate the calibrations to the task model level. Over time, we would expect estimation error variance within families to be reduced as some of the more problematic templates are modified (e.g., sources of nuisance variance reduce by introducing tighter template specifications via the rendering model, scoring evaluator, and/or data model) and scoring could largely rely on the task model hyperparameters. The simulation study presented in the next section addresses this issue to some extent as to which set of hyperparameter estimates to use. Furthermore, new instances of the items would not need to be pilot tested, except as part of a more general quality control operation.

Using Item Family Hierarchical Structures for CAT

As noted at the beginning of this section, the four approaches to AIG (item modeling, cloning, using attribute design matrices, and AE task models and templates) have common elements. Most of the distinctions arise out of different conceptions of Irvine's (2002) notion of *radicals* (difficulty drivers or features that alter the characteristics of items in non-trivial or controlling ways) and *incidentals* (features that can be treated as random sources of variation of noise—for the most part ignorable). The attribute design matrices approach and AE add an additional level to the hierarchy, where the former regresses the family attributes on a collection of radicals and the latter regresses the items on templates and templates on task models. In a sense, AE embeds the radicals in each task model.

From an CAT perspective, we need to adapt on the radical features by either selecting families having particular combinations of radical attributes or features (Geerlings et al., 2011) or actually manipulating on the fly those features that would provide the most precision at the current, provisional estimate of an examinee's proficiency score (Luecht, 2009; also see Bejar, Lawless, Morley, Wagner, Bennett, & Revuelta, 2003). *What is apparent is that either conception of an adaptive test involves a family-based hierarchy of units and fundamentally changes both the nature of item selection as well as the nature of the scoring outlined earlier.*

The unit of selection now occurs at the *family level*—whether that is an item model, a parent item (for clones), an item family, a task model (family of templates) or an individual template (see Equation 12.5, presented earlier). Items are then randomly selected from within the family. Glas and van der Linden (2003) make the important point that, in order to treat the incidental features associated with each item as a random effect, one actually needs to randomly sample over those effects. Furthermore, scoring (i.e., Equations 12.3 and 12.4) can now include additional integrals if a multilevel model is selected to represent the statistical characteristics of the items and the family or hyperparameters in place of the individual item parameters (see Glas & van der Linden, 2003; Glas et al., 2010; Geerlings et al., 2011). Less variation of items within each family is desired, regardless of which AIG approach is adopted. That is accomplished by making credible and effective design decisions to reduce—ideally eliminate—all potential sources of nuisance variation and covariation. The simulation study summarized in the next section explores what happens when these sources of variation and covariation are managed well (or not).

A Simulation Study of CAT for Hierarchical Item Families

A number of empirical studies have demonstrated that a multilevel IRT model with hyperparameters or similar statistical modeling approaches to representing hierarchical (tree-based) families of items be used to effectively calibrate items generated using AIG (e.g., Bejar et al., 2003; Glas & van der Linden, 2003; Sinharay, Johnson, & Williamson, 2003; Shu, Burke, & Luecht, 2010; Glas et al., 2010; Geerlings et al., 2011; see also Sinharay & Johnson, this volume). One of the clear findings from most of this research is that statistically *well-behaved* item families can be used with few apparent adverse effects on scoring. That is, a majority of research studies have found that, for the most part, scores based on estimates of the item family statistics are robust with that variation at the level of the individual items, provided that the variation is random in nature (see note 10). Although there are statistical efficiency tradeoffs associated with collapsing or integrating over the incidental effects, due to unique item characteristics, hierarchical item families offer many real economic and operational benefits that offset any minor loss in inefficiency (e.g., lower-cost item production, reduction/elimination of pretesting, reduced security risks).

A simulation study was designed to help confirm some of the previous findings, and to also demonstrate the impact of encountering varying degrees of within-family variation and covariation on the accuracy of scores. The issue of residual covariance within item families has not been extensively investigated.

Simulation Study Design

An item bank was generated to match the characteristics of a large-scale mathematics test used for college admissions. The item bank was generated by isolating actual items from the mathematics test, based on their locations of maximum information,

$$\theta_{max} = b_i + \frac{1}{Da_i} ln\left(\frac{1+\sqrt{1+8c_i}}{2}\right) \qquad (12.6)$$

(see Lord, 1980, Eq. 10-4) and forming families by 10 percentage-based intervals, using inverse normal cut points for a cumulative unit normal distribution of ability. Within each interval, 3PL item parameter estimates were averaged in order to produce the true parameters used for generating items. The mean error variances of estimate for the item parameters were used to represent plausible variation of task model calibrations within family. The actual variance of the item statistics within each decile was used to provide an upper bound on the sampling variation of the item characteristics where the item modeling, cloning or engineering of the task models and templates was essentially ineffectual. Finally, the average of the mean error variances of estimate and the variances of the estimates were used to represent moderate variation of the item characteristics within families.

Nine thousand items were generated for the item pool (900 per interval) and each item had four sets of a, b, and c parameters. The item parameters for this item bank were generated by sampling from a multivariate normal distribution, $[a, b, c] \sim (\mu, \Sigma)$, where the conditional covariances within family were also varied as noted below. For the primary study, Σ was specified as an identity matrix (zero residual covariance within families). The first set of parameters included the generating parameters used to create the response data. The second set had small variation within family (i.e., variation proportional to the average error variance of estimate). The third set of parameters had moderate variation and the fourth set had large variation, essentially equal to the within-interval variation of 3PL item statistics calibrated from the real operational test. Table 12.2 summarizes the item statistics, by interval, for each of the four sets.

In addition to the increasing standard deviations (left to right), one of the interesting characteristics of this particular test is that there is a relatively strong correlation between the item difficulties and the item discriminations, where the average a-parameters at the higher deciles (more difficult items) are noticeably larger than for the lower intervals. The relationship is apparent when comparing the pairs of a- and b-parameters in Table 12.2. For subsequent simulations analyses, briefly summarized here, this covariance was incorporated into the generation of the statistics as a within-family (conditional) covariance. Perhaps not surprisingly, biased estimates of the proficiency scores resulted, carrying an important caveat to monitor the covariances of estimates as well as the variances of the errors of estimate within family. Geerlings et al. (2011) make a similar point.

Figure 12.7 shows the item-bank test information functions (TIFs) for the 9000 items in each of the four sets: generating parameters, small, moderate and large- within-family variance statistics. The TIF is the sum of the item information functions (Equation 12.1) at a particular value of θ. As indicated by Figure 12.7, the four sets of parameter estimates produced highly comparable TIFs, despite the incremental conditional variation within families for the item statistics. The implication is that, on the surface, the item banks should have performed similarly for all of the CATs. However, the magnitude of within-family variation did make a difference.

The CAT simulations were carried out by first generating dichotomous response data for all 9000 items in the bank, based on the generating parameters summarized in the third, fourth and fifth columns of Table 12.2. A random deviate sampled from a unit normal distribution was used to represent θ_j, for j=1,...,5000 simulated examinees. The item parameters and θ were used to compute the expected response function (see Equation 12.2). A random uniform number, π_{ij}, was drawn for each item and if $P_i(\theta_j) \geq \pi_{ij}$, the item response was set to $u_{ij}=1$, or zero, otherwise. This approach is a standard simulation approach for generating IRT model-based data.

This procedure created a response vector of 9000 items for each simulated examinee. Four CATs were then carried out for each simulated examinee using exactly the same data—at least for the item pool: (1) using the generating parameters (best case); (2) using the small within-family variance statistics (columns 6 to 8 of Table 12.2); (3) using the moderate within-family variance statistics (columns 9 to 11); and (4) using the large within-family variance statistics (columns 12 to 14). The CAT was able to select different items and therefore use different segments of the complete response vectors. However, the comparisons between methods reflect no additional sources of sampling variance.

A fixed-length CAT was simulated for each examinee, using the small, moderate and large within-family variation item statistics from Table 12.2, each time applied to the same response data. The

Table 12.2 Summary of item statistics by interval

Intervals	Stats.	Generating			Small			Moderate			Large		
		a	b	c	a	b	c	A	b	c	a	b	c
1	Mean	0.71	-2.44	0.16	0.71	-2.43	0.16	0.71	-2.45	0.16	0.72	-2.43	0.15
	SD	0.00	0.00	0.00	0.04	0.16	0.07	0.10	0.32	0.07	0.16	0.50	0.07
2	Mean	0.77	-1.75	0.14	0.77	-1.75	0.14	0.77	-1.75	0.14	0.78	-1.73	0.14
	SD	0.00	0.00	0.00	0.04	0.12	0.05	0.09	0.17	0.07	0.14	0.22	0.08
3	Mean	0.97	-1.26	0.11	0.97	-1.26	0.11	0.96	-1.26	0.11	0.97	-1.26	0.11
	SD	0.00	0.00	0.00	0.04	0.07	0.04	0.12	0.11	0.04	0.21	0.15	0.04
4	Mean	0.92	-1.00	0.12	0.92	-1.00	0.12	0.92	-0.99	0.12	0.91	-1.00	0.12
	SD	0.00	0.00	0.00	0.04	0.07	0.04	0.13	0.10	0.04	0.22	0.12	0.05
5	Mean	0.99	-0.68	0.17	0.99	-0.67	0.17	1.00	-0.67	0.17	0.99	-0.68	0.17
	SD	0.00	0.00	0.00	0.05	0.06	0.03	0.13	0.08	0.06	0.20	0.10	0.09
6	Mean	1.01	-0.49	0.15	1.01	-0.48	0.15	1.01	-0.48	0.15	1.01	-0.48	0.15
	SD	0.00	0.00	0.00	0.05	0.07	0.03	0.21	0.17	0.05	0.38	0.28	0.08
7	Mean	0.98	-0.18	0.15	0.98	-0.19	0.15	0.98	-0.18	0.15	1.01	-0.16	0.15
	SD	0.00	0.00	0.00	0.05	0.06	0.03	0.17	0.15	0.05	0.30	0.23	0.07
8	Mean	0.94	0.04	0.21	0.94	0.04	0.21	0.96	0.05	0.21	0.96	0.04	0.20
	SD	0.00	0.00	0.00	0.05	0.07	0.02	0.16	0.16	0.07	0.26	0.24	0.11
9	Mean	1.25	0.60	0.19	1.24	0.60	0.19	1.25	0.60	0.19	1.24	0.59	0.19
	SD	0.00	0.00	0.00	0.07	0.04	0.01	0.18	0.11	0.04	0.30	0.17	0.07
10	Mean	1.40	1.21	0.21	1.40	1.21	0.21	1.40	1.20	0.21	1.39	1.22	0.21
	SD	0.00	0.00	0.00	0.10	0.04	0.01	0.24	0.17	0.05	0.35	0.32	0.08

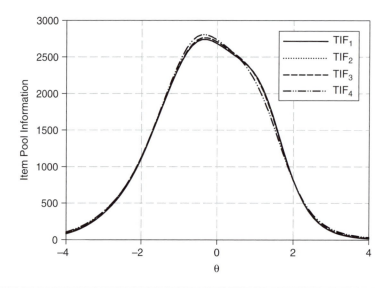

Figure 12.7 Test information functions for: (1) response-generating parameter per family; (2) small variation statistics; (3) moderate variation statistics; and (4) large-variation statistics

two-step item selection and EAP scoring algorithms[4] described earlier were applied. This simulation process was replicated for a fixed-length CAT, a sample of 5000 examinees, and repeated for seven test lengths: 10, 20, 30, 40, 50, 60, and 70 items. For each test length, four EAP estimates were obtained: EAP_1, an estimate based on the generating parameters—and expected to perform exceptionally well. EAP_2, an estimate based on the small-variance (within-family) item statistics; EAP_3, an estimate based on the moderate-variance item statistics; and EAP_4, an estimate based on the large-variance item statistics.

Simulation Results

A useful statistic for simulation research is the residual, $\hat{\varepsilon}_j = \hat{\theta}_j^{EAP} - \theta_j$, which represents the individual error of estimate for an examinee with a simulated but known proficiency score, θ_j. A non-zero expected value of the residuals implies bias in the estimates; that is,

$$BIAS^{EAP} = E_j\left(\hat{\varepsilon}_j\right) \doteq N^{-1}\sum_j^N \hat{\varepsilon}_j \tag{12.7}$$

The mean of the residuals should converge asymptotically to zero for an unbiased estimator. Taking the square root of the average of the squared residuals produces a root mean square residual (RMSE); this value is approximately the same as a standard error of estimate (SE) for relatively large samples:

$$RMSE^{EAP} = E_j\left(\hat{\varepsilon}^2\right) \doteq N^{-1}\sum_j^N \hat{\varepsilon}_j^2 \tag{12.8}$$

Table 12.3 shows a descriptive summary by test length of the *BIAS* and *RMSE* statistics, including the minimum and maximum residuals for EAP_1, EAP_2, EAP_3, and EAP_4. On average, the bias is not an overly serious concern, even for the EAP_4 results (large within-family variation). The variation of the residuals increases proportionally to the error variance within item families, but less rapidly than we might expect. For example, the EAP_3 results (moderate within-family variation) are better at each successive test length than the EAP_1 results at the preceding test length. The implication is that even fairly substantial variation in the within-family item statistics has less impact than changes in test length—at least of increments of about 10 items.

Table 12.3 BIAS and RMSE results for EAP estimates by CAT length

CAT	BIAS=Mean(Residual)				RMSE(Residual)			
Length	EAP₁	EAP₂	EAP₃	EAP₄	EAP₁	EAP₂	EAP₃	EAP₄
10	0.005	0.039	0.041	0.024	0.442	0.449	0.468	0.520
20	−0.004	0.036	0.036	0.048	0.319	0.329	0.334	0.396
30	0.001	0.039	0.038	0.052	0.257	0.265	0.273	0.339
40	0.005	0.034	0.027	0.050	0.216	0.228	0.233	0.293
50	0.002	0.034	0.028	0.046	0.198	0.203	0.212	0.260
60	0.002	0.035	0.031	0.052	0.180	0.187	0.198	0.244
70	−0.002	0.033	0.027	0.051	0.163	0.177	0.184	0.230

The residuals for the 35,000 simulated examinees (5000 examinees per each of seven CAT length conditions) were combined and organized into deciles using the true θ values. The interval-conditional mean residuals and 68% confidence bands about the mean are shown in Figure 12.8. There is a separate plot for EAP₁, EAP₂, EAP₃, and EAP₄. Although there is a tendency for positive bias in each of the plots for the lowest 20% of the sample, this may be explainable by two factors: (a) the noted lower average discrimination of the items in the lower deciles and (b) a well-known bias for EAP estimates (e.g., Bock & Mislevy, 1982; Mislevy, 1986; van der Linden & Pashley, 2010).

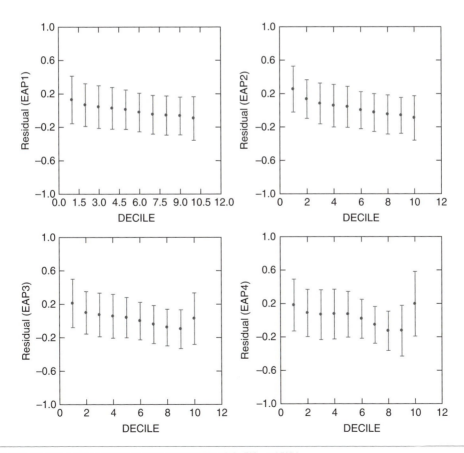

Figure 12.8 Conditional 68% confidence bands of residuals (EAP₁, EAP₂, EAP₃, and EAP₄)

Figure 12.9 shows a plot of the squared product-moment correlations between the true θ values and each of the four EAP estimates, again, by CAT length (10 to 70 items). The $R^2_{\theta,EAP}$ is reliability coefficient, where values above 0.90 are generally considered good. These results are such that the CAT length makes a substantial difference—similar to the RMSE results reported in Table 12.3. However, we also begin to see that the large within-family variation item statistics produce noticeably less accurate EAP_4 scores, except when the CAT is increased to more than 30 items.

These results suggest that any random errors of estimate associated with the item parameters (i.e., incidental variance, due to within-family item differences) is not overly serious, and may at least be partially compensated for by increasing the test length. This finding is consistent with results by Glas and van der Linden (2003) and Geerlings et al. (2011). That is *not* to imply that incidental variance is ignorable. It does contribute to score instability and potential estimation bias. However, at least for model-generated data, IRT scoring seems fairly robust with respect to random errors of observation and random sampling errors.

But what if the errors of estimate are not random? In a smaller-scale simulation study, three levels of conditional (within-family) correlations between the discrimination and difficulty parameter estimates were introduced: $r_{ab|family}=0.10$ denoting fairly minor residual covariances; $r_{ab|family}=0.25$ implying moderate residual covariances for the *a*- and *b*-parameter estimates; and $r_{ab|family}=0.50$ to mimic large residual covariances. The correlations were implemented by sampling the *a*-, *b*-, and *c*-parameter estimates from a multivariate normal distribution, with the specified correlation introduced for each family of items. The same sampling variances as before (diagonals of Σ) were used here. The actual source of the residual covariance was not specified, but would plausibly be due to population subgroup traits covarying with incidental template or item design components (e.g., resulting in differential item functioning) or virtually any plausible spurious trait or source of method variance. The CAT simulations were run at two test lengths: 10 and 40 items.

The means and standard deviations of the residuals are reported in Table 12.4 and the impact of the increasing residual covariance for item discrimination and difficulty parameter estimates is rather clear. Moving across rows (see shaded "Mean" results), the bias gets systematically worse as the error variance of estimate for the item parameters increases. That is, the residual variance induced into the item-parameter estimates used to compute the EAP_3 estimates was larger than for

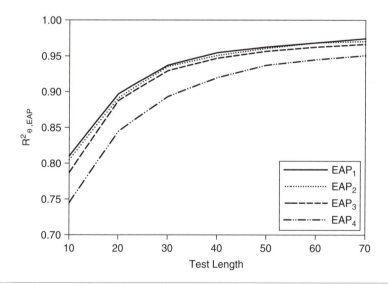

Figure 12.9 Reliability for four EAP scores as a function of CAT length

EAP_2 and larger still for EAP_4. The increases in the error variances created greater potential for the residual correlation, r_{ab}, to have an impact. Increasing the length of the CAT somewhat lowered the bias, but not entirely. When the residual correlation increased to 0.25 or 0.50, the amount of bias is rather substantial, even when the CAT length is increased.

This second simulation study makes a clear case for necessary concern over not only the error variances of estimate with hierarchical item structures, but also the residual covariance. To the extent that potential sources of any non-zero residual covariance between item discrimination and difficulty can be identified and controlled through the templates, this may not be a concern for operational CAT applications. However, the issue cannot be ignored (also see Glas et al., 2010; Geerlings et al., 2011).

Concluding Comments

This chapter provided an introduction to computerized-adaptive testing (CAT) and discussed four conceptions of AIG applicable for CAT. In addition to differences in terminology, there were differences in conceptualization of the traits, how to design traits, and how to conceptualize the item families, themselves.

Two useful concepts that helped to distinguish these approaches were Irvine's (2002) notions of *radical* (difficulty altering) and *incidental* (surface-level, ignorable) features. Item modeling and cloning were described as incorporating these two features into each item model or shell, empirically identifying and manipulating the radicals so as to change difficulty, or placing constraints on the incidental surface features in order to ensure that they did not alter the statistical properties of each family of items. Attribute design matrices were described as tying multiple radical features to each item family and providing a hierarchical IRT framework for calibrating the radicals, with the family-level statistical characteristics (e.g., difficulty) being a linear combination of the relevant radicals. This attribute design-matrices approach conceptualizes items has being incidental (random) sources of variation with each family.

The AE task model and template approach incorporates radicals by design into a cognitive specification (levels of procedural and declarative knowledge) for each task, where the task has an intended location. The primary difference with the AE approach is that there is an added level to the hierarchy where items belong to a family of templates and templates belong to a particular task-model family.

Table 12.4 Summary statistics for EAP residuals as a function of increasing covariances between item discrimination and difficulty errors of estimate

Cond. $r_{a,b}$	CAT Length			Residual for EAP_1	Residual for EAP_2	Residual for EAP_3	Residual for EAP_4
0.10	10	Mean		−0.01	0.03	0.06	0.09
		SD		0.45	0.47	0.48	0.52
	40	Mean		0.00	0.04	0.05	0.05
		SD		0.23	0.23	0.26	0.28
0.25	10	Mean		0.01	0.05	0.09	0.18
		SD		0.44	0.44	0.47	0.48
	40	Mean		0.00	0.04	0.10	0.15
		SD		0.21	0.22	0.24	0.25
0.50	10	Mean		−0.02	0.09	0.17	0.33
		SD		0.44	0.44	0.45	0.50
	40	Mean		0.01	0.09	0.16	0.29
		SD		0.23	0.24	0.24	0.26

Similar to the other three approaches, AE templates constrain the incidental features so that items within a task-model family perform in a statistically similar manner.

There must be extensive upfront verification that the item families are working as intended, as well as ongoing quality control (QC). This investment cannot be emphasized strongly enough. AIG is essentially moving from an artform to a manufacturing-engineering paradigm for item and test production. QC is an integral part of the latter paradigm. If the QC controls are properly implemented with reasonably tight tolerances and are effectively used to inform appropriate design decisions, the benefits are: (a) items that actually measure exactly what is intended by having direct linkages templates and task models, as well as being aligned to the construct map and evidence models; (b) items should perform in a psychometrically consistent manner within families; and (c) a more valid understanding of the meaning of scores, especially if the item families are constructed from evidence and task models that link the required knowledge and skills to intended, ordered proficiency claims. In short, AIG can actually increase the richness of measurement opportunities along a construct and ensure item banks that truly can provide consistent measurement where it is most needed.

Results from a CAT simulation study were also presented to highlight two important points related to the upfront verification and ongoing QC for item families. First, random variation is not overly problematic, insofar as IRT scoring is concerned, if items are, indeed, randomly sampled from within families. For CAT, this implies the need to select at the level of item families (or for task models) and then sample items (or templates and then items for AE). The variance of the errors of estimation increases under most hierarchical models, but that [minor] lost efficiency can be managed by either attempting to increase the average discrimination of the item families or increasing the test length. Also, different policies can be implemented where items within poorly estimated families (templates or task models for AE) are individually calibrated until sufficient design changes can be implemented for the templates to control the radicals as intended. Engineering policy decisions about the maximum acceptable variation over the incidental features should be implemented to guide these types of calibration decisions based on empirical results and simulations. What is considered small variation in some cases may be too large in other settings. A caveat here is that extensive variation creates the *potential* for greater bias—especially if the score estimators have known proneness to bias under certain sampling or measurement conditions.

The second point is that conditional covariances between the within-family item parameter estimates require careful attention in order to reduce or eliminate any potential sources of residual covariance—especially between the item discrimination and difficulty parameters. These types of covariances can result in biased scores in the same way that items exhibiting differential item functioning can impact on score accuracy. This may be less of a concern for Rasch-model implementations (i.e., models that do not include a discrimination parameter), but additional research seems warranted. Although the exact source of the residual covariance may be difficult to identify with any certainty, experimental studies that compare various template controls to one another or common-sense reviews of the item-family templates, constraints on variable elements, and other performance-related features may provide enough insight to implement template design changes that at least reduce the residual covariance to a nominal level. Ignoring this type of error covariance is not an option for AIG.

The potential for AIG to provide more items on demand and having consistently needed properties to generate optimal scores under CAT is enormous. The item-production cost reduction and security advantages of AIG more than offset the initial design, development and experimental pilot work needed. And that upfront work is needed. There are no shortcuts to good design. If we treat items as unique designs, they become disposable commodities with limited shelf lives and relatively high replacement costs. If we can engineer replicable and scalable production solutions though empirically proven designs based on AIG, costs will eventually go down and high-quality, consistent item production will be the result.

Notes

1 Readers may see a connection that this same rationale of indifference drives equating theories meant to link score scales (e.g., Kolen & Brennan, 2004; Holland & Dorans, 2006). The primary difference here is that the rationale is an explicit design decision, subject to empirical verification and possible design modifications.

2 A unit-normal (Gaussian) prior probability density, $g[\theta|\mu=0, \sigma^2=1]$ is assumed for this example.

3 The use of the terms *radicals* and *incidentals* follows Irvine's (2002) definitions as previously described.

4 Maximum likelihood estimates (MLE) were computed at the termination of the CAT; however, those MLE results did not substantially alter any of the findings. Therefore, only the EAP results are reported here.

References

Bejar, I. I. (1990). A generative analysis of a three-dimensional spatial task. *Applied Psychological Measurement, 14*, 237–245.

Bejar, I. I. (1993). A generative approach to psychological and educational measurement. In N. Frederikson, R. J. Mislevy, & I. I. Bejar (Eds.), *Test theory for a new generation of tests* (pp. 323–359). Mahwah, NJ: Lawrence Erlbaum Associates.

Bejar, I. I. (2002). Generative testing: From conception to implementation. In S. H. Irvine & P. C. Kyllonen (Eds.). *Item generation for test development* (pp. 199–217). Mahwah, NJ: Lawrence Erlbaum Associates.

Bejar, I. I., Lawless, R. R., Morley, M. E., Wagner, M. E., Bennett, R. E., & Revuelta, J. (2003). A feasibility study of on-the-fly item generation in adaptive testing. *The Journal of Technology, Learning, and Assessment. 2*(3). Available online: http://ejournals.bc.edu/ojs/index.php/jtla/article/view/1663/1505.

Bejar, I. I. & Yocom, P. (1991). A generative approach to the modeling of isomorphic hidden-figure items. *Applied Psychological Measurement, 15*(2), 129–137.

Birnbaum, A. (1968). Estimation of an ability. In F. M. Lord & M. R. Novick (Eds.), *Statistical theories of mental test scores* (pp. 423–479). Reading, MA: Addison-Wesley.

Bock, B. D., & Mislevy, R. J. (1982). Adaptive EAP estimation of ability in a microcomputer environment. *Applied Psychological Measurement, 6*, 431–444.

Case, S. M., & Swanson, D. B. (2001). *Constructing written test questions for the basic and clinical sciences* (3rd ed.). Philadelphia: National Board of Medical Examiners.

Dennis, I., Handley, S., Bradon, P., Evans, J., & Newstead, S. (2002). Approaches to modeling item-generative tests. In S. H. Irvine & P. C. Kyllonen (Eds.). *Item generation for test development* (pp. 53–72). Mahwah, NJ: Lawrence Erlbaum Associates.

Devore, R. (2002). *Considerations in the development of accounting simulations.* [Technical Report]. Ewing, NJ: American Institute of Certified Public Accountants.

Drasgow, F., Luecht, R. M., & Bennett, R. (2006). Technology and testing. In R. L. Brennan (Ed.), *Educational measurement* (4th ed., pp. 471–515). Washington, DC: American Council on Education/Praeger Publishers.

Eignor, D. R., Stocking, M. L., Way, W. D., & Steffen, M. (1993). *Case studies in computer adaptive test design through simulation* (RR-93–56). Princeton, NJ: Educational Testing Service.

Embretson, S. E. (1999). Generating items during testing: Psychometric issues and models. *Psychometrika, 64*, 407–433.

Foster, D. (April, 2011). Personal communication.

Geerlings, H., Glas, C. A. W., & van der Linden, W. J. (2011). Modeling rule-based item generation. *Psychometrika, 76*, 337–359.

Geerlings, H., van der Linden, W. J., & Glas, C. A. W. (2010). *Optimal design of tests with automated item generation.* Paper presented at the Annual Meeting of the National Council on Measurement in Education.

Gierl, M. J., Zhou, J., & Alves, C. (2008). Developing a taxonomy of item model types to promote assessment engineering. *Journal of Technology, Learning, and Assessment, 7*(2). Available online: from http://www.jtla.org.

Glas, C. A. W., & van der Linden, W. J. (2003). Computerized adaptive testing with item cloning. *Applied Psychological Measurement, 27*, 247–261.

Glas, C. A. W., van der Linden, W. J., & Geerlings, H. (2010). Estimation of item parameters in an item-cloning model for adaptive testing. In W. J. van der Linden & C. A. W. Glas (Eds.), *Elements of adaptive testing* (pp. 289–314). New York, NY: Springer.

Green, B. F., Bock, R. D., Humphreys, L. G., Linn, R. L., & Reckase, M. D. (1983). Technical guidelines for assessing computerized adaptive tests. *Journal of Educational Measurement, 21*, 347–360.

Haladyna, T. M. (2004). *Developing and validating multiple-choice test items* (3rd ed.). Mahwah, NJ: Lawrence Erlbaum Associates.

Haladyna, T. M., & Shindoll, R. R. (1989). Item shells: A method for writing effective multiple-choice test items. *Evaluation and the Health Professions, 12*, 97–104.

Hambleton, R. K. & Swaminathan, H. R. (1985). *Item response theory: Principles and applications.* Hingham, MA: Kluwer.

Hively, W., Patterson, H. L., & Page, S. H. (1968). A "universe-designed" system of arithmetic achievement tests. *Journal of Educational Measurement, 5*, 275–290.

Holland, P. W., & Dorans, N. J. (2006). Linking and equating. In R. L. Brennan (Ed.), *Educational measurement* (4th edition). Westport, CT: American Council on Education and Praeger Publishers.

Irvine, S. H. (2002). The foundations of item generation for mass testing. In S. H. Irvine & P. C. Kyllonen (Eds.). *Item generation for test development* (pp. 3–34). Mahwah, NJ: Lawrence Erlbaum Associates.

Kolen, M. J., & Brennan, R. L. (2004). *Test equating, scaling and linking. Methods and practices* (2nd edition). New York: Springer.

LaDuca, A. (1994). Validation of a professional licensure examination: Professions theory test design, and construct validity. *Evaluation in the Health Professions, 17*, 178–197.

Lai, H., Alves, C., & Gierl, M. J. (2009). Using automated item generation to address item demands for CAT. In D. J. Weiss (Ed.). *Proceedings of the the 2009 GMAT Conference on Computerized Adaptive Testing.* (PDF available at http://www. psych.umn.edu/psylabs/catcentral/).

Leighton, J. P., & Gierl, M. J. (2007). *Cognitive diagnostic assessment for education: Theory and applications.* Cambridge, UK: Cambridge University Press.

Lord, F. M. (1970). Some test theory for tailored testing. In W. H. Holtzman (Ed.), *Computer assisted instruction, testing and guidance* (pp. 139–183). New York, NY: Harper and Row.

Lord, F. M. (1971). The self-scoring flexilevel test. *Journal of Educational Measurement, 8*, 147–151.

Lord, F. M. (1977). A broad-range tailored test of verbal ability. *Applied Psychological Measurement, 1*, 95–100.

Lord, F. M. (1980). *Applications of item response theory to practical testing problems.* Hillsdale, NJ: Lawrence Erlbaum Associates.

Luecht, R. M. (2005). Some useful cost-benefit criteria for evaluating computer-based test delivery models and systems. *Association of Test Publishers Journal, 7*(2). (Available at http://www.testpublishers.org/journal.htm).

Luecht, R. M. (2009). Adaptive computer-based tasks under an assessment engineering paradigm. In D. J. Weiss (Ed.), *Proceedings of the 2009 GMAT Conference on Computerized Adaptive Testing.* (PDF Available at http://www.psych.umn. edu/psylabs/catcentral/).

Meisner, R. M., Luecht, R. M., & Reckase, M. D. (1993). *The comparability of the statistical characteristics of test items generated by computer algorithms* (ACT Research Report Series No. 93-9). Iowa City, IA: American College Testing Program.

Mills, C. N., & Steffen, M. (2000). The GRE computer adaptive test: Operational issues. In W. J. van der Linden & C. A. W. Glas (Eds.). *Computerized adaptive testing: Theory and practice* (pp. 75–99). Boston, MA: Kluwer.

Mills, C. N., & Stocking, M. L. (1996). Practical issues in large-scale computerized adaptive testing. *Applied Measurement in Education, 9*, 287–304.

Mislevy, R. J. (1986). Bayesian modal estimation in item response models. *Psychometrika, 86*, 177–195.

Osburn, H. G. (1968). Item sampling for achievement testing. *Educational and Psychological Measurement, 28*, 95–104.

Parshall, C. G., Spray, J. A., Kalohn, J. C., & Davey, T. (2002). *Practical considerations in computer-based testing.* New York, NY: Springer.

Roid, G. H., & Haladyna, T. M. (1982). *Toward a technology for test-item writing.* New York, NY: Academic Press.

Rudner, L. (2010). Implementing the Graduate Management Admission Test Computerized Adaptive Test. In W. van der Linden & C. Glas (Eds.), *Elements of adaptive testing* (p. 151–165), New York, NY: Springer.

Rupp, A., Templin, J., & Henson, R. (2010). *Diagnostic assessment: Methods, theory, and applications.* New York, NY: Guilford Press.

Sands, W. A., Waters, B. K., & McBride, J. R. (Eds.). (1997). *Computerized adaptive testing: From inquiry to operation.* Washington, DC: American Psychological Association.

Shu, Z., Burke, M., & Luecht, R. M. (2010, April). *Some quality control results of using a hierarchical Bayesian calibration system for assessment engineering task models, templates, and items.* Paper presented at the Annual Meeting of the National Council on Measurement in Education, Denver, CO.

Singley, M. K., & Bennett, R. E. (2002). Item generation and beyond: Applications of schema theory to mathematics assessment. In S. H. Irvine & P. C. Kyllonen (Eds.). *Item generation for test development* (pp. 361–384). Mahwah, NJ: Lawrence Erlbaum Associates.

Sinharay, S., Johnson, M. S., & Williamson, D. M. (2003). Calibrating item families and summarizing the results with expected response functions. *Journal of Educational and Behavioral Statistics, 28*, 295–313.

van der Linden, W. J. (2005). *Linear models for optimal test design.* New York, NY: Springer.

van der Linden, W. J., & Pashley, P. J. (2010). Item selection and ability estimation in adaptive testing. In W. J. van der Linden & C. A. W. Glas (Eds.), *Elements of adaptive testing* (pp. 3–30). New York, NY: Springer.

Wainer, H. (2002). On the automated generation of test items: Some whens, whys and hows. In S. H. Irvine & P. C. Kyllonen (Eds.), *Item generation for test development* (pp. 287–305). Mahwah, NJ: Lawrence Erlbaum Associates.

Weiss, D. J. (1969). *Individualized assessment of differential abilities.* Paper presented at the 77th annual meeting of the American Psychological Association.

Weiss, D. J. (1973). *The stratified adaptive computerized ability test* (Research Report 73-3). Minneapolis, MN: University of Minnesota, Department of Psychology, Psychometric Methods Program.

Weiss, D. J. (1975). Computerized adaptive ability measurement. *Naval Research Reviews, 28*, 1–18.

Weiss, D. J. (1982). Improving measurement quality and efficiency with adaptive testing. *Applied Psychological Measurement, 6*, 473–492.

Weiss, D. J. (1985). Introduction. In D. J. Weiss (Ed.), *New horizons in testing: Latent trait test theory and computerized adaptive testing* (pp. 1–8). New York, NY: Academic Press.

Zara, A. R. (1994, March). *An overview of the NCLEX/CAT beta test.* Paper presented at the meeting of the American Educational Research Association, New Orleans.

13
IGOR
A Web-Based Automatic Item Generation Tool

Todd Mortimer, Eleni Stroulia, and Meisam Vosoughpour Yazdchi

1 Introduction

The problem of automatic item generation (AIG), namely the use of algorithmic methods for automatically and systematically generating a multitude of test items, is attracting increasing interest in the educational-assessment community. After computer-supported online lesson delivery, the AIG research agenda represents the second most important use of computers in supporting education objectives.

This agenda is driven by the promise of technology to increase cost-effectiveness and to enable systematic adaptive testing. Generating individual test items is a knowledge-intensive task and test items are not reusable, or rather, they can be reused only under very carefully controlled contexts.

For purely practical reasons, automatic generation of test items is of particular interest in decentralized educational institutions, such as distance education centers, that conduct much of their testing online. For example, Athabasca University in Canada has recently started such a service for its staff and students [2], initially focusing on mathematics. Its primary objective is simply to generate a repository of different items in order to reduce staff burden and share individual items among its faculty. From an education-research perspective, educators need to be able not only to generate test items, but also to correlate test items with different knowledge and skills, in order to be able to assess the performance of students, and their progress from one level to the next, over time. This association of test items to knowledge and skill types and levels is an equally knowledge-intensive process, and fundamentally empirical in nature. Furthermore, the advancement of a student between levels is a highly individual process, which implies the need for the item-generation process to be personalized and adaptive. The ability to explicitly model test-item difficulty, and systematically generate (collections of) test items of the appropriate difficulty for an individual student and his/her current knowledge and skill level, is therefore the second educational requirement motivating this research agenda.

The general AIG problem involves several different computational challenges. First, one has to design a model for test items. The model must be expressive, i.e., it must support the specification of psychometrically valid test items in multiple fields, and at multiple knowledge and skill levels. It must also be generative, i.e., it must support the generation of multiple test-item instances. The second challenge involves the development of a systematic/algorithmic process for generating a multitude of test items, based on the specified item models. Next, one must design a process for generating tests, i.e., collections of test items, of the complexity required for a particular student. This requirement implies the need for supporting educators in assessing the knowledge and skill level of a given student, based on his/her performance on past tests. Our work in this paper builds on a particular line of research in this field [6] [8] [1], and puts forward a novel, web-based software architecture for developing AIG software systems. The fundamental contribution of our work does not involve any pedagogical innovation; instead, by migrating an existing state-of-the-art AIG system from its original single-user desktop architecture to a web-based architecture, we demonstrate how the research around AIG might find broader use and have more impact on practice.

The software architecture of AIG systems has not yet received much attention. Most publications in the area either fail to report on the software implementations of their algorithm, presumably placing little importance on it, or describe systems developed as desktop applications, whether standalone or with a server back end, hosting the repository of the test-item models. Such designs suffer shortcomings that can hinder the adoption and impact of AIG methods. First, they are designed and developed to be used primarily by individual researchers developing AIG methods, thus ignoring a range of other potential users, including teachers developing tests and students practicing their knowledge of a subject. Furthermore, such an individual-centered design essentially precludes collaboration among users, whether they may be researchers who want to share their models or teachers who want to share their in-class experience using the researchers' models. Most importantly such designs, meant to be used by individuals, are usually implemented in ways that make their extension difficult. One can conceive of many extensions for education research and applications, including (a) management of items, i.e., when they are used, by whom, and whether they can be reused or not; (b) student tracking for personal use by students and for teacher use; and (c) comparisons of alternative test-item models and generation methods.

In this chapter, we report our work on extending the Item GeneratOR (IGOR) system[6] and migrating it from its original desktop-based application architecture to a web-accessible platform (see Huff, Alves, Pellegrino, & Kaliski, this volume; Lai & Gierl, this volume). In the original IGOR system, an item model is assumed to be a multiple-choice type of item and is represented as a template, associated with a subject and a difficulty level (e.g., Grade 9 Mathematics). The template representation specifies the model stem, several options, possibly some auxiliary information, and several variables. The stem slot specifies the structure of the item (e.g., "X + Y = ?"). The variables slots constitute the item's modifiable parts (e.g., "X" and "Y"). The auxiliary-information slot specifies additional materials (e.g., pictures and diagrams) required to formulate the test items. Finally, the option slots collectively define the keys and distractors, which are possible correct and incorrect answer choices for the test items. IGOR was originally implemented as a monolithic application in Java, envisioned to be used by a single user—likely a researcher—specifying test-item models, saving them on his local hard disk as XML documents, and generating all possible test items from a particular test-item model.

In this chapter, we describe the redesign of IGOR from a single-user Java application into a web-based application designed to be used by a community. There are three important changes between the $IGOR_{v1}$ (before the redesign), and $IGOR_{v2}$ (after the redesign) (see Gierl, et al. [6], for a description of $IGOR_{v1}$). First, $IGOR_{v2}$ stores both test-item models and test items, where $IGOR_{v1}$ only stored test-item models and (re)generated the complete set of test items upon demand. By generating test items once and managing them, it becomes possible to explicitly track their lifecycle and collect information on when they are used, by whom, and with what results, thus possibly enabling their reuse by different communities, and their study. Second, $IGOR_{v2}$ uses a database as the repository, where $IGOR_{v1}$ simply stored test-item models as XML documents on the user's local hard disk. The use of a database enables the management of these models over time, including developing support for social features such as rating based on different experiences using these models and tagging for different purposes. Finally, the IGOR user interface has been re-implemented into a browser-accessible client, using Ajax (http://www.oracle.com/technetwork/articles/javaee/ajax-135201.html). This change maintains the responsiveness of the user interface, since simple user interactions generate immediate responses without necessitating the complete page to be refreshed on the browser. At the same time, the user interface becomes accessible through a variety of devices, including mobiles, thus substantially extending the opportunities for the system to be adopted and used.

This chapter is organized as follows. In Section 2 we discuss some related work in this field. Section 3 describes both the original IGOR application architecture and the architecture of the web service created in this project. We then briefly discuss the web-based user interface of the re-architected IGOR to demonstrate the currently supported usage scenarios in Section 4, including a discussion in Section 4.4 of how an envisioned sample test-taking application would be supported on this new version. Finally, in Section 5 we briefly discuss some worthwhile directions for future work and conclude with a summary of our work to date.

2 Related Research

Test-item modeling and AIG using IGOR have been the focus of research by Gierl et al. [6] [8] [1] at the Centre for Research in Applied Measurement and Evaluation at the University of Alberta. Gierl et al. have identified a taxonomy of item-model types for the purposes of performing standardized assessments. IGOR can represent each of the taxonomy of item-model types, and is designed to generate isomorphic, or equivalent, test items from a single model in the taxonomic spectrum.

In principle, most rule-based AIG methods follow the same process. First, they define a syntactic construct appropriate for capturing the semantics of the items to be generated. In general, this construct involves three types of elements: (a) background information necessary for formulating meaningful questions; (b) a set of logically related parameters that represent some aspect of the subject matter to be tested; and possibly (c) a means of generating wrong alternatives for one of the above parameters, in order to distract from the correct answer.[1] Given such a general construct, each AIG method formulates a sequence of steps for generating instances of this structure, involving a combination of (a) generating possible values for some of the construct parameters, (b) inferring values for other "dependent" parameters, and possibly (c) post-processing the generated construct instances to eliminate unwanted ones.

This computational point of view is that which we adopt in this chapter, as we are concerned with the design of a general framework that would be able to systematize many activities in this line of research. To that end, we studied an eclectic list of publications in this area, aiming at clarifying and elaborating the above computational model. IGOR is discussed in some detail in subsequent sections.

Papasalouros et al. [11] conceive test items as relatively simple conceptual paths on an ontology specified in the Ontology Web Language (OWL) (http://www.w3.org/TR/owl-ref/). In their case, the test items do not require any background information and they simply involve a statement about a relation (inheritance, instance-of or any other domain-specific relation) between two elements in the ontology. The distractors are generated through a similar path.

Goto et al. [7] describe a system for testing students on English, with emphasis on genre awareness. Their system relies on "sentences" as the general item construct and generates items by (1) extracting appropriate sentences from actual texts, (2) deciding on a blank sentence fragment (to be filled by the student), and (3) generating distractors based on statistical patterns of plausible but not as good alternatives for this fragment. Deane and Sheehan [3] also proposed a natural-language sentence structure, but for mathematics rather than English. Similarly, Fairon and Williamson [4] proposed a method for formulating natural-language items for analytical Graduate Record Exam items.

In [9], van der Linden and Diao investigate a subsequent step, namely that of presentation of the generated items, which is not addressed in this paper.

The projects discussed above, as is the case with the majority of the work in this field, are not concerned with the broader usage workflows around the AIG process, i.e., how test developers, teachers, students, and educational organizations might use these systems. This is the question at the heart of the work discussed in this chapter. The issue of the software architecture of such a system is discussed by Liu in [10], who proposes a service-oriented architecture, similar in principle to the architecture of $IGOR_{v2}$ that we discuss here. The fundamental difference between Liu's work and ours in $IGOR_{v2}$ is that our proposal is grounded to an actual AIG tool, $IGOR_{v1}$.

3 Software Architecture and Usage Scenarios

$IGOR_{v1}$, as a desktop application, provides the user with a Java-based client interface for creating and editing item models (see [6]). Models can be built using this interface and saved to an XML file for subsequent use. Given a model, IGOR can generate a collection of test items by permuting the variables within their specified ranges. Such a test-item collection is rendered as an HTML document, envisioned to be used directly by an instructor, and is associated with a corresponding answer-key HTML document. The objective of our software re-architecting activity was therefore to migrate the original IGOR java application to a web-based platform, in order to extend its functionalities as shown in Figure 13.1.

3.1 The Java-Application Architecture of $IGOR_{v1}$

The original IGOR ($IGOR_{v1}$) was organized into several modules (Java packages), as shown in Figure 13.2. At the core of the implementation, is the Template module, which specifies the representation of item models and implements the functionality for creating and modifying an item model. As we

	IGOR as a Java application	IGOR as an SOA web application
Model creation	Model creation through (de)serialization of an XML model document	√
Model editing	Model editing through a user interface	√
Model storage	Storage of complete models as XML documents	Storage of models and their constituent elements in the database
	Accessible only to the model creator (application user)	Accessible to anyone over the web
		Information about the models' constituent elements can also be accessed
		Model search based on content of the template slots, i.e., auxiliary-option images
		Model search based on metadata, i.e., grade, difficulty
Test generation	Test-item collection generation, given a model	√
		Storage of test items in the database
	HTML quiz representation, de-signed for test taking by students	XML representation of test-item collections, formatted by CSS for any desired purpose

Figure 13.1 Functionality comparison between $IGOR_{v1}$ and $IGOR_{v2}$

have briefly discussed in Section 1, templates contain options and variables. Variables can be either numeric, taking values from a range of possible values, or strings. Options represent the possible answers to the item posed by the instance of the item model, and are classified as either correct answers (keys) or incorrect answers (distractors). Constraints may be specified in order to limit the possible ways in which options and variables can be combined. This module is also responsible for (de)serializing models (from)to XML documents.

Another module, the Generator, implements the functionality of generating test items from a given model. To produce a single test item, the generation algorithm assigns to the various variables values from their ranges, subject to any applicable constraints, and evaluates at least one key option and several distractor options. By exhausting all possible valid combinations of values for its variables, a large number of items are generated and two HTML documents are produced: the item-bank document containing the complete item collection, and the answer-key document containing the correct answer for each item.

The Editor module is responsible for implementing the user interface for the application and supporting the interaction with the user for creating new models and editing existing ones.

The logical design of IGOR$_{v1}$ is intuitive and its modules directly support its model-editing and item-generation functionalities. However, it suffers from three major shortcomings. First, it lacks support for persisting items: the generator module only produces the item-bank and answer-key HTML documents and does not store the items in any intermediate, computer-accessible format. Furthermore, although models can be saved as XML documents, this representation is inefficient. On the one hand, since it is only designed as a means of producing the work of a single user, it makes assumptions about the user's environment and, therefore, sharing of XML item models across users is not possible. On the other hand, it does not support direct access to the constituent elements of the models, and if one were to produce a new model by evolving an existing one, this evolutionary relation between them would be lost. Finally, IGOR$_{v1}$ models do not have any associated metadata; the user has to maintain any such metadata separately, such as in a spreadsheet. Since neither model metadata not distinct model contents are stored, IGOR$_{v1}$ lacks any support for search.

3.2 The Service-Oriented Architecture of IGOR$_{v2}$

IGOR$_{v2}$ is architected as a RESTful [5] service-oriented application. Service orientation is a new, increasingly adopted, software-engineering paradigm, which advocates the design and development of complex software systems through the composition of independent components, i.e., services. These components, although implemented in a variety of platforms and programming languages,

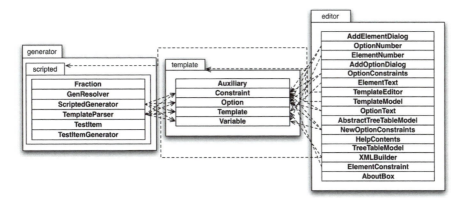

Figure 13.2 IGOR Original Package Architecture

are interoperable through open, XML-based specifications of their programmatic interfaces. Today, the term service-oriented architecture is used to refer to two distinct architecture styles: (a) hierarchical compositions of modules, specified in terms of operation-based APIs using the web-services (WS*) stack of standards (http://www.w3.org/2002/ws/), and (b) RESTful [5] applications, designed to integrate information resources, whose logical structure is specified through XML Schemas.

The critical difference between WS*- and REST-style web services is that while WS*-style objects can perform arbitrary functionality, REST-style resources are simply data structures that are fetched and stored. RESTful web services are therefore inherently data-centric, and provide a simple means for users to retrieve and update information over the web. Each resource is specified with a unique URL, and the user can perform only four operations, GET, PUT, POST, and DELETE, which retrieve, add, update, or delete the resource identified by its URL. Resources can be represented in one of many supported formats (e.g., XML, JSON, HTML, Plain Text, etc.), and the complexity of manipulating the resource data or creating complex workflows using multiple resources is put on the user, rather than embodied in the web service itself. While this style may sound limited, when we consider that modern web applications (Facebook, Twitter, Amazon, etc.) are, at their core, simply performing these same functions on a database, it becomes obvious that a rich variety of functionality can be built upon RESTful web services.

In our redesign of $IGOR_{v1}$ into a service-oriented architecture, we reused much of the original implementation of $IGOR_{v1}$ and added to it a persistent data store and a web-services layer that drives a browser-based client. As shown in Figure 13.3, $IGOR_{v2}$ contains a layer in which the complete $IGOR_{v1}$ is wrapped. This layer defines the structure of the shared resources, namely models and test items, which are stored persistently in a storage layer on the server. This storage layer is substantially redesigned, since it now includes a database. Each of these resources is then accessed via a newly developed RESTful web-service layer, upon which we created a new browser-based user interface that allows users to create, view, and manipulate item models and test items. Each of these layers has distinct responsibilities and functions.

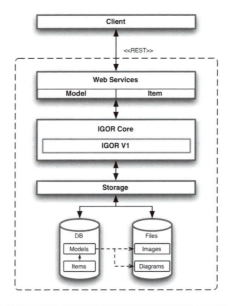

Figure 13.3 The layered service-oriented architecture of $IGOR_{v2}$. The original code from $IGOR_{v1}$ is shown in light grey, with the $IGOR_{v2}$ service layers shown in dark grey

- **The Web Client.** The client implements the new browser-based user interface through which IGOR$_{v2}$ users access the RESTful web services to add, edit, retrieve, and delete test-item models and test items.
- **The REST Web Services.** The web-services layer exposes to the client a simple set of actions (add, edit, retrieve, and delete) on two types of resources (test-item models and test items). The REST style of service-oriented software prescribes that the above actions should be implemented with PUT, POST, GET, and DELETE requests respectively, parameterized with unique IDs corresponding to the particular model or item being manipulated.
- **The Core.** The core-logic layer wraps the original IGOR$_{v1}$ functionality, and is responsible for manipulating the model and item structures, according to the specifications of the IGOR AIG theory. It is the intermediary between the storage layer and the web-services layer. All requests for models or test items are passed through this layer, which interacts with the storage layer and the original IGOR$_{v1}$ code-base as required in order to service them.
- **The Persistent Store.** The storage layer, newly implemented in IGOR$_{v2}$, handles the details of managing models and test items in the database. This layer also handles the automatic generation of test-item collections from saved or updated models, as they are committed.

Each of these layers is described in detail below.

3.3 The Persistent Store

The storage layer extends the original IGOR$_{v1}$ data-storage model from a simplistic XML file load/store system to a persistent repository of models and their associated items. This is accomplished by storing model and item information in a database, which references the original model XML files and associated auxiliary files that are now collected together on the file system and organized with unique identifiers. Sets of items are automatically generated from models and are stored in the database rather than in a monolithic HTML document, which facilitates the retrieval and tracking of individual items. In addition to managing model and item information in a database, the storage layer also maintains metadata about each model, such as the name, creation date, type, knowledge and skill level, subject, complexity, etc. This metadata allows for the classification and organization of models, and was previously maintained separately in a spreadsheet. In IGOR$_{v2}$ the user enters this metadata directly alongside the model specification.

3.4 The Core

The IGOR core layer mediates between the web-service layer and the storage layer and implements the logic required to translate a web-service request into a response. This layer also encapsulates the original IGOR$_{v1}$ application, which is leveraged to serialize and deserialize models as they are sent to or retrieved from the storage layer, and to generate banks of items for each model.

The IGOR$_{v2}$ core is where the web-service application logic is implemented. When a client sends a request to the web service, the web service parses the request into an action (PUT, POST, GET, or DELETE) and a resource (a model or item) and then calls into the core layer to execute the request. The core then performs the requested action and returns any requested data to the web service. For example, if the request is a GET request for a particular model, the web service will ask the core to fetch and return the model data. The core then finds the model information in the database, resolves any links to auxiliary files, and uses the IGOR$_{v1}$ code base to deserialize the model data into a model object representation, which is then passed back to the web service for delivery to the client. Similarly, if the request is a PUT or POST, then the core will take the new or updated data from the web service, use IGOR$_{v1}$ to serialize it, and then send it to the storage layer. Once a model is stored or updated, the core will generate any items from the model using the IGOR$_{v1}$ functionality. DELETE requests simply remove the identified model from the database, along with any associated items and auxiliary data.

In this architecture, the web-service layer serves as an interface between the user's requests and the core, and the storage layer serves as an interface between the core and the disk. Thus, the core is where the real work is done in IGOR$_{v2}$.

3.5 The REST Services

The web-services layer implements the RESTful web interface through which users can fetch and store models and items. As mentioned earlier, resources in a RESTful web service are identified by unique URLs, and clients interact with the web service by acting on these URLs, along with one of the four REST verbs: GET, PUT, POST, DELETE. The two major types of resources in our web service are those which act on models and items, and are shown in Figure 13.4, along with representative URLs.

In this figure, we see that clients can identify a model through its unique URL, */template/{modelid}*, and individual items through the unique URL */item/{modelid}/{itemid}*, where *{modelid}* and *{itemid}* indicate the unique identifier for the model or item being requested. Models and items can also be fetched in aggregate by using the plural URLs */templates* and */items*. For example, Figure 13.4 shows how a client could search for models using the */templates/search/{keywords}* URL, which could be used, for example, to fetch any mathematics-related models in the system by requesting /templates/search/mathematics. Similarly, randomly selected items for a given set of models can be returned to the user by sending a GET request to */items/formodels/{modelids}*, such as */items/formodels/4–7*, which would return a randomly selected item for each of model numbers 4 and 7. We will see later in Section 4.4 how these URLs can be combined to construct randomized tests for students in a given subject.

Because it takes input from the user and returns requested data, the web-services layer is the front end to the IGOR$_{v2}$ system. A request from the client is mapped to one of the resource objects in the system through its unique URL, which is sent to the core layer for servicing. The core returns any data for the request, which is then passed back through the web-services layer to the client.

4 Usage Scenarios in IGOR$_{v2}$

Let us now review the functionalities IGOR$_{v2}$, mentioned in Figure 13.1, through a discussion of the usage scenarios as a user of IGOR$_{v2}$ would experience them through the newly developed web-based client.

4.1 Listing and Searching through Current Models

The IGOR$_{v2}$ web-service layer supports searching for models using simple keyword matching. Thus, a user searching for models related to a particular content area or a particular knowledge or skill can search the repository for matching models, and then view or edit the returned results. We envision this functionality as primarily serving the needs of model developers, who would search through the

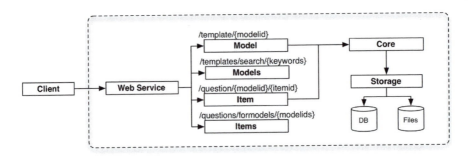

Figure 13.4 IGOR web service program flow

repository for models of a particular type or a particular model they used in the past. Alternatively, the search functionality could be used by students or instructors to find items related to a particular area or theme, which would subsequently be used for practice exercises or tests. The user interface for listing and searching through IGOR$_{v2}$'s models is shown in Figure 13.5.

As soon as the user logs in to IGOR$_{v2}$, they are presented with the list of all models currently in the repository (see Figure 13.5(a)). Each row of the table corresponds to an individual model, and the columns list model metadata. If the user is interested in a particular (set of) model(s), they can query the repository through the "Search Box" in the top right corner of the screen. After some keywords are entered in the text field, the table will refresh to only list the models whose metadata contain at least one of them. Figure 13.5(b) shows the result of a search for "*easy,*" where the resulting list contains nine models, all of which are characterized as "easy." By clicking on the "Cancel search" button, the user can return to the complete list of models.

It is worth noting that, since the user interface uses Ajax (http://www.oracle.com/technetwork/articles/javaee/ajax-135201.html) to communicate with the web service, all updates in the page are made dynamically in response to user actions, without requiring a refresh of the entire page. In this manner, the user experience with IGOR$_{v2}$ is similar to that of the original desktop-based IGOR$_{v1}$: no usability is sacrificed in allowing the shared access to the model repository over the web.

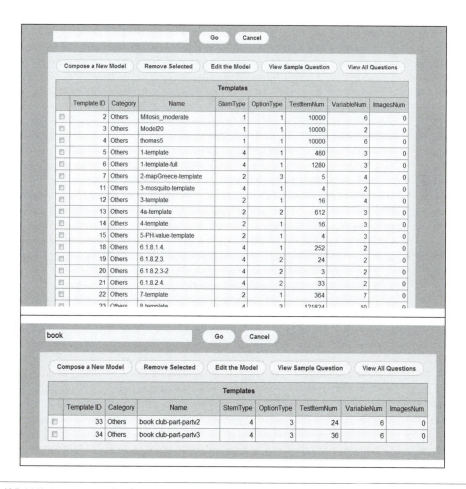

Figure 13.5 (a) Listing and (b) searching for models in IGOR$_{v2}$

4.2 Managing Models Online

When interacting with IGOR$_{v2}$, a community of users can create, edit, and share item models online. In this implementation, users are presented with a basic web interface in which they can edit model stems, variables, constraints, and options. Alternatively, a model can be imported by uploading an existing item-model XML file. Once created, several metadata fields for each model are available with which a user can identify a model, including but not limited to: (a) a content area, such as "mathematics" or "biology"; (b) a grade level, such as "Grade 6"; (c) a content theme, such as "shapes" or "words in sentences"; and (d) a knowledge or skill keyword such as "ratios," "reading comprehension," or "addition."

A user can create a new model by clicking the "Compose a New Model" button, which brings up a mode-editing form that the user can fill in with their model parameters (Figure 13.6). At the top of the form, there is a list of text boxes, where the user can define the high-level attributes of the new model, such as its name, stem, etc., and below there are four links respectively named "+ Number Variable," "+ Text Variable," "+ Number Option," and "+ Text Option". By clicking on any of these four links, a new entity of the corresponding type of variable or option appears, and can be filled in by the user. In this manner, the user may define as many variables and/or options of different types as they wish for the new model. Once the user is done composing the model, it can be saved by clicking on the "Create" button. After the model is uploaded to the server and saved in the repository, the user interface returns to the table listing the models.

To edit an existing model, the user first selects it from the list and then clicks the "Edit Model" button. This brings up a model-editing form with which the user can edit the model properties (Figure 13.7). The user can add, delete, or modify any of the model's sections and when they are done they can update the model in the repository by clicking on the "Update" button.

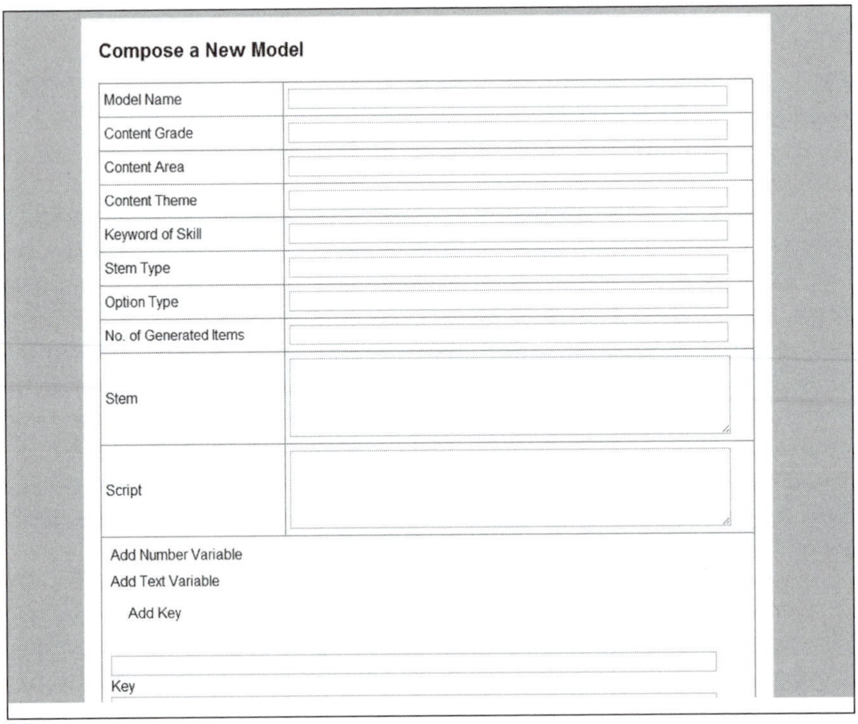

Figure 13.6 Composing a new model in IGOR$_{v2}$

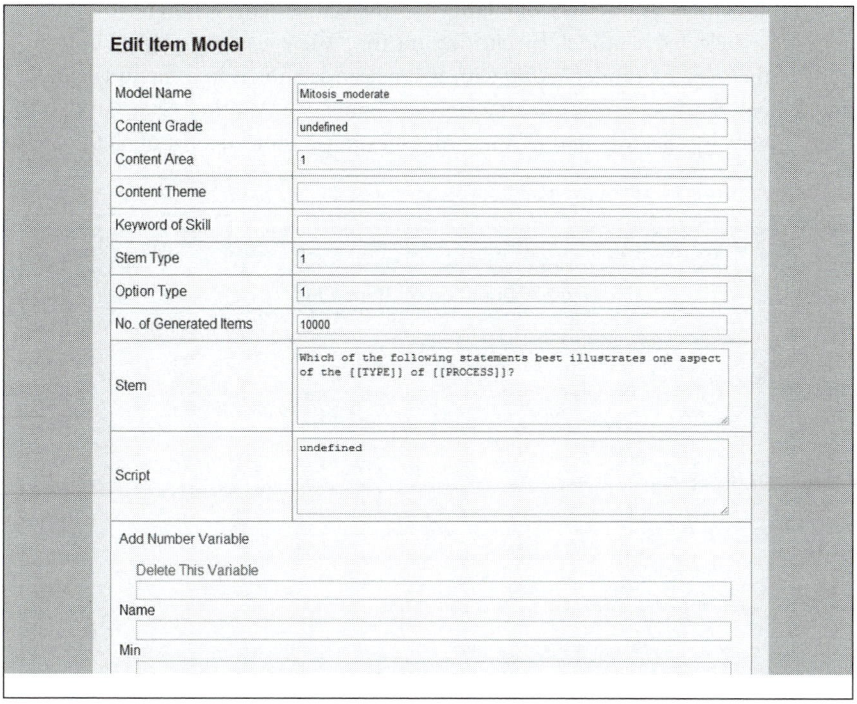

Edit Item Model

Model Name	Mitosis_moderate
Content Grade	undefined
Content Area	1
Content Theme	
Keyword of Skill	
Stem Type	1
Option Type	1
No. of Generated Items	10000
Stem	Which of the following statements best illustrates one aspect of the [[TYPE]] of [[PROCESS]]?
Script	undefined

Add Number Variable

Delete This Variable

Name

Min

Figure 13.7 Editing a model

Some models require images or other auxiliary files, such as diagrams or pictures, which can be uploaded using the "Upload Box" after selecting a model from the list. When selected, thumbnails of a given model's associated images are shown just below the "Upload Box", with names indicating which images are missing.

Having created or modified a model, a user can share it with collaborators by sending them the relevant unique URL. Alternatively, users of different IGOR$_{v2}$ instances can exchange the XML representation of their models, so that a model developed in one installation can be used by users of another. Groups of users with similar fields or interests can create and share sets of models related to a particular area, knowledge, or skill, and thus establish a repository of readily available item models from which to build new models or simply draw individual items.

4.3 Retrieving Test Items

While the primary function of IGOR$_{v2}$ is to create and manage item models, it also serves as a repository of all the individual items generated from these models. This is, in fact, a major change from the original IGOR$_{v1}$ tool, which only generated test items and rendered the complete list as HTML for a single use. Because the items generated from a single model are equivalent to each other in content and characteristics, it becomes possible for a testing agency to use multiple items from the same model over multiple tests to generate literally different tests consisting of equivalent items. IGOR$_{v2}$ facilitates this by providing easy access to specific or random items derived from a given model, and because it is easy to construct queries to the web service which retrieve items from several models concurrently, individual tests can be constructed quickly. This easy construction of individualized tests would make it easy for a testing agency to generate different "versions" of the same test, each with the same set of models but varying items.

Figure 13.8 shows the user interface of IGOR$_{v2}$ for inspecting items generated by a selected model. Once the user has selected a model, by clicking on the "View a Sample Item" button, a random sample item of the selected model, along with its answer, is shown in a menu (Figure 13.8(a)). A new, random item can be seen by clicking on the "Show Me Another Question!" button in the menu. Alternatively, by clicking on the "View All Questions" button, a list of all the model items is

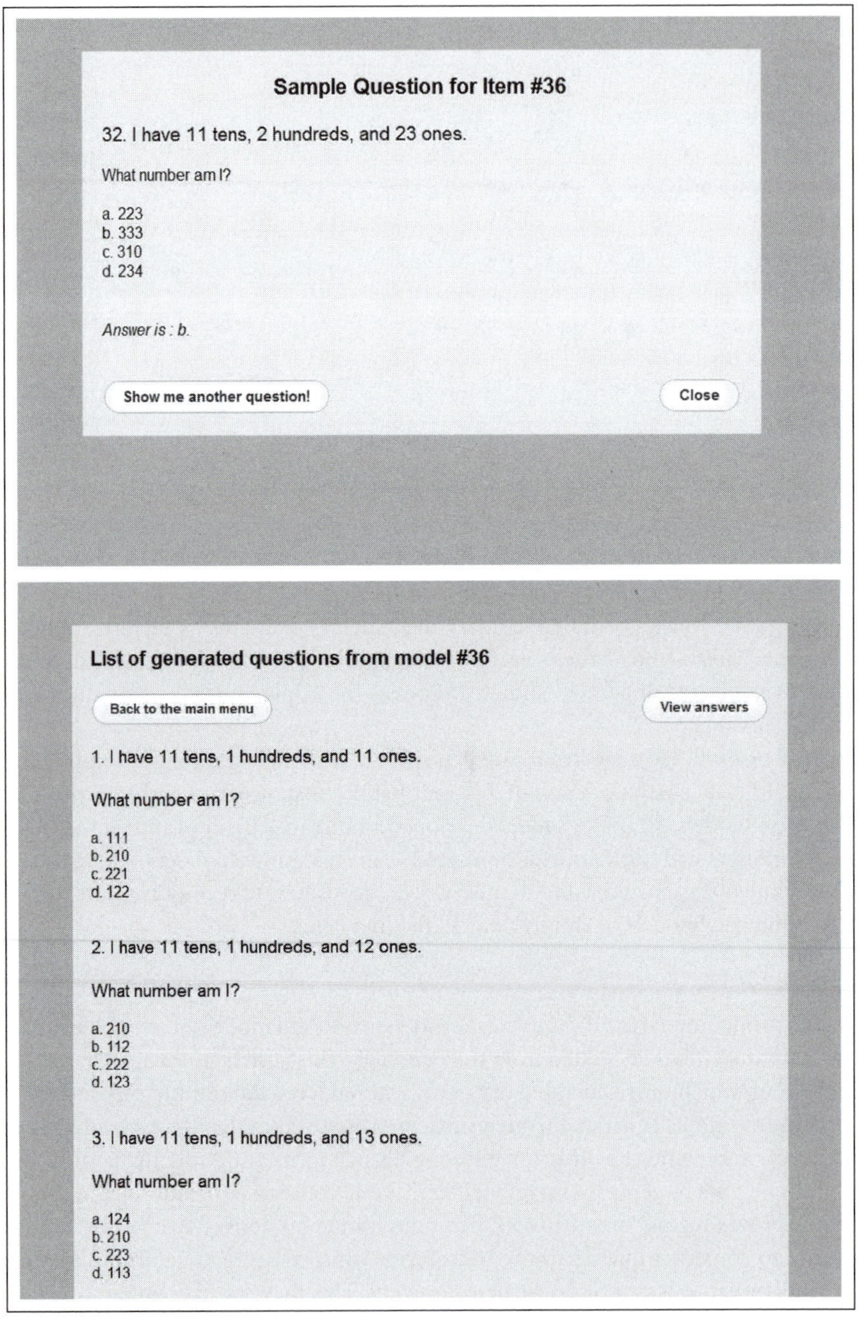

Sample Question for Item #36

32. I have 11 tens, 2 hundreds, and 23 ones.

What number am I?

a. 223
b. 333
c. 310
d. 234

Answer is : b.

Show me another question!   Close

List of generated questions from model #36

Back to the main menu   View answers

1. I have 11 tens, 1 hundreds, and 11 ones.

What number am I?

a. 111
b. 210
c. 221
d. 122

2. I have 11 tens, 1 hundreds, and 12 ones.

What number am I?

a. 210
b. 112
c. 222
d. 123

3. I have 11 tens, 1 hundreds, and 13 ones.

What number am I?

a. 124
b. 210
c. 223
d. 113

Figure 13.8 Retrieving a single item (a) or all items (b) of a selected model

shown (Figure13.8(b)). By clicking on the "View the Answers" button in the opened menu, the list of answers (keys) is presented to the user.

4.4 A Test-Administration Application with IGOR

In this section, we describe how IGOR$_{v2}$ could be used to construct a test-administration application. Note that this application is not currently implemented; however, through the redesign of the system and the development of the REST layer on top of the original IGOR$_{v1}$, all elementary functionalities are available. In this scenario, the idea is to provide a mechanism for individual students to log onto a website and take tests in a particular subject at a particular grade level. We assume that the application provider maintains its own records for students and manages any administrative information in that regard, and uses IGOR$_{v2}$ purely as an item repository that administers tests to students. There are therefore two applications involved in this scenario, the one that the student logs on to, which we will call the "Test site", and IGOR$_{v2}$, which supplies this first web server with items via its APIs.

There are three stages to the test-administration application: (a) searching the models for particular metadata, (b) getting individual items for the appropriate models, and (c) marking "used" items. Each of these steps is detailed below, and the relevant APIs are the same as those illustrated in Figure13.4.

Suppose that the student has logged into the Test site and is going to take a "Grade 9 Mathematics" test. The Test site would query IGOR$_{v2}$ for item models of this kind by accessing the web service via the following GET query:

GET /templates/search/Grade 9 Mathematics

This query would return a list of models to the Test site, which would iterate through the returned models and filter on some of the metadata, such as a theme or skill keyword, and eventually decide which models it wanted to test on. Once decided, the Test server would note the itemId from these models.

Given the list of model itemIds, the Test site would request random items for each of the models. Supposing that one of the model itemIds was 5, the corresponding query would be:

GET /question/5/rand

This query would return an individual item object, which contains a plain-text formatted item generated from the chosen model, along with the answer key. The Test site would execute one of these GET queries for each model chosen, and concatenate each of the items together to form a test. This test could then be sent to the student.

Alternatively, the Test site could query for random items from all of the models simultaneously. Given the list of model itemIds, the Test site could query IGOR$_{v2}$ in aggregate. If we suppose that the Test server wants random items for models 3, 5, 7, and 42, then it could query:

GET /questions/formodels/3–5–7–42

The above query would return a list of items—one per model—which could then be made into a test for the student.

Now that some of the items for the model have been administered, the Test site wishes to ensure that the same item is not given out again. Each item comes with a unique identifier, and so the Test site could store the identifiers of items that have been used, and subsequently filter out items with the same identifier from future tests.

Once the student has completed the test, the submitted answers can be compared with the known correct answers from the original items. The Test site can then mark the test and produce a grade, which is returned to the student.

Variations

What is described above is a very basic application of the IGOR_{v2} system. Interesting variations on the process could include giving students items one at a time rather than all at once. As students submit responses, the system can dynamically adjust the difficulty of the items, based on the student's performance, by querying for more or less difficult models and their associated items. For example, if the student answers several "Grade 9 Mathematics" items successfully, the Test site could begin querying IGOR_{v2} for more difficult items. In this way, the Test site could dynamically discover the limits of the student's knowledge and skills, providing feedback to instructors on where students' knowledge and skills are weak or strong.

5 Conclusions and Lessons Learned

In this chapter, we described a redesign of IGOR, from a desktop Java application designed for a single user to a web-based application. This new system, IGOR_{v2}, supports a superset of the IGOR_{v1} functionality. Furthermore, as we illustrated in Section 4.4, it can easily be integrated with other web-based applications to support new uses of interest to the general community of test developers, educators, and students. We believe that with the new developments in service-oriented software engineering, there is plenty of opportunity for implementing AIG methods in broadly accessible and flexibly extensible systems that can have a wider impact in education.

Acknowledgments

The authors would like to thank Mark Gierl and Hollis Lai for many long, insightful discussions that shaped this work. This work was supported by NSERC, AITF, and IBM.

Note

1 Most AIG methods generate multiple-choice test items.

References

[1] C. Alves, M. Gierl, and H. Lai. *Using automated item generation to promote principled test design and development.* In Annual Meeting of the American Educational Research Association, 2010.
[2] Athabasca University. *Pilot system explores a new dynamic for exam delivery at AU.* https://projects.athabascau.ca/node/74.
[3] P. Deane and K. Sheehan. *Automatic item generation via frame semantics: Natural language generation of math word problems.* In Annual Meeting of the National Council on Measurement in Education, April 2003.
[4] C. Fairon and D. M. Williamson. Automatic item text generation in educational assessment abstract, 2002.
[5] R. Fielding. *Architectural styles and the design of network-based software architectures.* Citeseer, Jan. 2000.
[6] M. Gierl, J. Zhou, and C. Alves. Developing a taxonomy of item model types to promote assessment engineering. *The Journal of Technology, Learning, and Assessment,* 7(2), 4–50, 2008.
[7] T. Goto, T. Kojiri, T. Watanabe, T. Iwata, and T. Yamada. Automatic generation system of multiple-choice cloze questions and its evaluation. *International Journal on Knowledge Management and E-Learning,* 2(3), 210–224, 2010.
[8] H. Lai, C. Alves, and M. J. Gierl. *Using automatic item generation to address item demands for CAT.* In GMAC Conference on Computerized Adaptive Testing, April 2009.
[9] W. J. v. d. Linden and Q. Diao. Automated test-form generation. *Journal of Educational Measurement,* 48(2), 206–222, 2011.
[10] B. Liu. Sarac. A framework for automatic item generation. In *Advanced Learning Technologies, 2009.* ICALT 2009. Ninth IEEE International Conference on, pages 556–558, July 2009.
[11] A. Papasalouros, K. Kanaris, and K. Kotis. Automatic generation of multiple choice questions from domain ontologies. In M. B. Nunes and M. McPherson(Eds.), *e-Learning,* pp. 427–434. IADIS, 2008.

14
Obstacles for Automatic Item Generation

Thomas M. Haladyna and Mark J. Gierl

The issues presented and discussed in this final chapter are (1) the status of AIG as an emerging science, (2) the role of validity for AIG, (3) the role of the learning sciences in AIG's development, (4) the construct definition problem and other content-related issues, (5) the use of different item formats, and (6) the cost and benefits of this emerging technology.

Scientific Paradigms

A scientific paradigm is a framework of interrelated concepts, principles, and procedures existing in a scientific community focusing on an issue, problem, or concept. Generally, any paradigm is supported by scholars working on the same issue, problem, or concept at about the same time. A research agenda advances the paradigm and, at times, can challenge the paradigm's validity. If there is a consensus among these scholars, we have a body of knowledge and skills that we find useful in addressing complex tasks in that science. A technology follows that makes the paradigm useful to society.

In *The Structure of Scientific Revolutions* (1962), Thomas Kuhn describes science as existing in three phases. The first phase is *pre-paradigmatic*. No particular theory exists, and there is a lack of a consensus among those studying the problem, issue, or concept. In the second phase, which he calls *normal science*, a consensus among scholars exists, and those invested in technology use the science for many useful purposes. If problems or limitations are detected in the normal science, a third phase is *revolutionary science*. In this phase, assumptions of normal science are challenged and a new paradigm replaces the old paradigm.

The term thinking *inside the box* captures this idea of a generally accepted paradigm. Scholars who think inside the box have reached a consensus and are advancing an established science. It is mostly based on theory and research. The content in this box includes essays, books, book chapters, journal articles, conference papers, and occasional papers. Thinking *outside the box* is revolutionary science. It too has a framework of concepts, principles, and procedures. However, it is not generally accepted or endorsed by the wider community of scholars who live and work *inside the box*.

Item response theory (IRT) is a good example of a revolutionary science that has occurred in educational measurement. In the mid 20th century, scholars like Fred Lord, Georg Rasch, and Ben Wright contributed substantially to IRT's advancement. In the early 1960s, it was revolutionary science. Now it is part of mainstream psychometrics, and IRT continues to grow and become more useful in different settings.

AIG: A Revolutionary Science?

Item development has a history that can be traced back to oral examinations and performance tests in ancient civilizations. However, the introduction of the multiple-choice (MC) format in the early 1900s began a series of scholarly studies that continue to this day (Coffman, 1971; Ebel, 1951; Haladyna, 2004; Haladyna & Rodriguez, in press; Roid & Haladyna, 1980, 1982; Wesman, 1971). Early critics would say that this science has not advanced very far (Bormuth, 1970; Cronbach, 1970; Nitko, 1985; Roid and Haladyna, 1980; 1982), but clearly there has been a steady stream of theory and research that results in our current technology of test-item writing.

We know that the normal science associated with item development and validation has its shortcomings. Without a doubt, there is room for growth in the science of item development. AIG is a revolutionary science. It exists outside what we commonly refer to as the science of item development. It is the result of scholars' building this emerging science. These contributors include pioneers such as Bormuth, Guttman, Hively, Tiemann, Markle, Bejar, LaDuca, Embretson, Irvine and his colleagues, and, recently, contributors to this volume. As we assert in chapter 1, we have many current influences that change terrain for AIG and makes it more promising. As the learning sciences and technology continue to grow, AIG's path will become easier. Will it become a vital aspect of the normal science of item development, or even the normal science of item writing? This is the challenge for the current group of scholars interested in AIG and those who follow.

Validity

Since the appearance of the influential manuscript on validity by Cronbach and Meehl (1955), validity has become the *sine qua non* in testing. In *The Conduct of Inquiry*, Kaplan (1964) posited validity as more than a concern for the accuracy of test scores or a magnitude on some test score scale.

> The validity of a measurement consists in what it is able to accomplish, or more accurately, in what we are able to do with it. We must take into account as well the functions in inquiry which measurement is intended to perform. The basic question is always whether the measures have been so arrived at that they can serve effectively as means to a given end.
>
> (Kaplan, 1964, p. 198)

Validity concerns the value of using a test score for specific purposes. In high-stakes testing, the value of using a test score for pass/fail promotion is a principal concern for test developers and users. Thus, a persistent focus in test and item development is how our practices affect validity.

Operational Definition and Its Failings

The above-cited writers have supported operational definition as the objective of measurement. The concept is appealing. A group of like-thinking scientists develop a consensus that a concept can be measured by applying physical operations. Time, distance, speed, and weight lend to operational definition. These are clear-cut examples of operationalism at work for the betterment of society.

Unfortunately, educational and psychological concepts do not always lend themselves to operational definition. These concepts are far too complex. Reading, writing, speaking, listening, mathematical and scientific problem solving, and critical thinking in the social and other sciences have an elusive quality that defies operationalism.

AIG is a method for operationally defining concepts. However, as Kaplan (1964) pointed out, one set of operations may not produce what another set of operations produces. Would two groups of

AIG scientists working independently produce identical items for fifth-grade reading using the same content specifications and construct definition? This is the same dilemma faced by the pioneers in item developments, Guttman and Hively. Algorithmic methods provide only one perspective on the concept being measured, and other perspectives may compete. If there is a consensus among subject-matter experts, then proposed algorithms may suffice as operationally defined.

Construct Validity

Cronbach and Meehl (1955) argued that when operationalism fails, one has a fall-back position—construct validity. Given the experience we have had with operationalism in educational measurement, we adopted the concept of validity that involves educational and psychological constructs that are abstract in nature and are explicated via item and test development. Any test is supposed to measure a construct. In educational measurement, the scope of these tests and the constructs they represent includes elementary and secondary schools curricula, course and program outcomes, admission criteria, credentialing (certification and licensure), placement, and diagnosis, among other functions. We have had many important essays on validity, and the concept continues to evolve (e.g., Cronbach, 1971; Messick, 1984, 1989; Kane, 2006a, 2006b).

AIG needs to include research and development to ensure that item responses are validated. If a claim for validity is made for test-score validity, that claim needs to be extended to item responses, which are the quintessential element in computing a test score. In other words, whether items are developed subjectively, as with the current science or through the revolutionary science of AIG, item validation remains an important and necessary condition.

Two Challenges

First, the role that AIG plays in explicating a construct needs clarification. Should we use an operational definition or construct definition? The former is more rigid, comprehensive, and closed; the latter has more flexibility and freedom. What is the role of AIG in this future? Second, item validation is an important criterion for evaluating the success of AIG. Item validation involves more than item analysis. It involves many steps in item development that comprise the normal science of item development (Downing & Haladyna, 1997; Haladyna, 2004). AIG research should lead to a conclusion that items using this method are valid for a specific testing program's purpose.

Learning Sciences

The term *learning sciences* is used by some cognitive psychologists to designate this field. It consists of a large group of scholars developing a science of human learning that contrasts sharply with behavioral learning theory, which so much dominated education and educational testing in the second half of the last century (see, for example, Leighton, this volume). Criterion-referenced and domain-referenced testing are clear-cut manifestations of the behavioral learning theory orientation. Instructional objectives are another by-product of this approach to teaching, learning, and testing.

A chapter by Snow and Lohman (1989) in the third edition of *Educational Measurement* championed the idea that the learning sciences and psychometric theory should join forces to solve the problems of developing and validly measuring cognitive abilities. The work of Mislevy and his colleagues gives evidence of progress in this union (Mislevy, 1993, 1996a, 1996b, 2006; Mislevy & Riconscente, 2006). As the learning sciences and psychometrics continue to work together, the result promises to increase understanding about learning and its measurement.

However, learning sciences is hardly unified. One might typify it in Kuhn's language as pre-paradigmatic. A variety of scholars in diverse fields continue to work on related problems, but unification seems far away. Part of the problem is unstandardized terminology, particularly for complex learning. Gierl and Lai (this volume) point out this problem in AIG terminology. Also, as noted in chapter 2 and in other sources, complex cognitive behavior has many names, and the development and classification of complex cognitive behavior continues to puzzle learning scientists.

AIG needs to advance in the context of the unrest in this young, promising field known as the learning sciences as it develops, because behavioral learning theory persists in theory and practice in much of K-12 teaching, in defining curriculums, and in testing. One practice takes extant items and converts items into item models. This is called *reverse engineering* (e.g., Masters, 2010). This is a very practical use of AIG in the current context of educational achievement testing. In effect, AIG researchers must adapt to a behavioral learning theory environment, while at the same time supporting cognitive learning theory. AIG scholars must thrive in this uncomfortable time when behavioral learning theory is waning and cognitive learning theory is growing stronger.

Construct Definition

A clear consensus among all authors in this volume is that construct definition is crucial in the development of AIG. As early as 1990, then president of the American Educational Research Association and highly respected expert in educational measurement, Nancy Cole (1990) lamented our inability to define educational constructs adequately. She also described the dilemma of competing learning theories and how we conceptualize educational content. As noted previously, the dilemma remains today. Do we focus on domains of knowledge and skills explicated by instructional objectives, or do we concern ourselves with a domain of complex tasks requiring knowledge and skills applied in complex ways?

The issues that fall into the category of construct definition include (1) elementary and secondary school curricula, (2) certification and licensure, (3) learning from prose, and (4) ill-structured problems for any domain.

Elementary and Secondary Schools Curricula

A review of state and national content standards will reveal that mainstream educational abilities such as the language arts, mathematical and scientific problem solving, social studies, and other subject matters are described in a manner consistent with behaviorism–instructional objectives.

The Common Core State Standards Initiative is a government-sponsored project to develop and disseminate national standards in the language arts, mathematics, science, and other subject matters. Teachers, administrators, and content experts were consulted in the development of these standards. The goal was to provide a clear, consistent, and valid framework for content. National organizations have long sought and supported national content standards. These organizations include the National Council of Teachers of English, the National Council of Teachers of Mathematics, the International Reading Association, the National Science Teachers Association, and the National Council for the Social Studies. Also included in the development of these content standards was input from thousands of reviewers. States traditionally have designed their own content standards, and their input was sought.

These standards define the knowledge and skills students should have within their K-12 education careers so that they will graduate high school able to succeed in entry-level, credit-bearing academic college courses and in workforce training programs. The standards:

• Are aligned with college and work expectations;
• Are clear, understandable and consistent;
• Include rigorous content and application of knowledge through high-order skills;
• Build upon strengths and lessons of current state standards;

- Are informed by other top performing countries, so that all students are prepared to succeed in our global economy and society; and
- Are evidence-based. (Taken from http://www.corestandards.org/about-the-standards, 12/20/11)

By the very nature of their quoted material, the new common core standards would appear to represent behavioral learning theory with emphasis on knowledge and skills, but with recognition of the application of knowledge and skills to higher-order thinking. We would interpret these outcomes to mean that the use of instructional objectives continues.

Table 14.1 presents three objectives taken from the common core standards in fifth-grade reading. As shown there, these appear to be fairly routine, representative content standards found in most state achievement testing programs.

Given this recent development, the challenge of AIG is to work within the current framework of the mainstream science of test and item development, but to augment item development in such a way that it increases our ability to replace the current item-development technology with a new, more efficient item-development technology, as much as it is possible.

However, the dream of an AIG system driven by cognitive psychology and operating in a way that focuses on higher-order thinking still seems distant.

Certification and Licensing

The field of certification and licensing testing appears to have advanced rapidly in terms of the technology for defining content and capturing this content into a format that can be used to develop highly effective tests. According to Raymond and Neustel (2006), content is generally developed via a practice analysis for any profession. This survey of the profession requires respondents to rate the frequency and importance of performing certain tasks in their profession. Professional training develops a curriculum based on such surveys. The goal is to articulate training with terminal testing leading to recognition and a license to practice in a profession. Thus, this field is more likely to reflect the elements of AIG that are most suitable for cognitive psychology: a domain of tasks requiring the use of knowledge and skills. Kane (2006a, 2006b) refers to this domain as the target domain. The operational domain (which Kane refers to as the universe of generalization) consists of test items that are supposed to correspond or link to this target domain.

We have many test formats to accomplish the daunting task of measuring performance on these tasks: live-patient examinations, standardized patients, mannequin examination, objectively structured clinical examinations, simulations, portfolios, oral examinations, essay examinations, and high-fidelity selected-response items, including testlets.

AIG would seem to have the best potential to make inroads here. The significant early work of LaDuca and the continuing efforts of Bejar with the architecture licensing examination appear to be two good examples of how AIG might work in certification and licensure tests of the future (Bejar, 2002; LaDuca, 1994; LaDuca, Staples, Templeton, & Holzman, 1986).

Table 14.1 Examples of learning outcomes taken from the common core reading standards for grade 5

RL.5.4.	Determine the meaning of words and phrases as they are used in a text, including figurative language such as metaphors and similes.
RL.5.5.	Explain how a series of chapters, scenes, or stanzas fits together to provide the overall structure of a particular story, drama, or poem.
RL.5.6.	Describe how a narrator's or speaker's point of view influences how events are described.

Source: http://www.corestandards.org/the-standards/english-language-arts-standards/reading-literature/grade-5/ (Retrieved 12/21/11)

Learning from Prose

Educators in the K-12 environment will argue that much learning comes from prose and text-based reading passages. Lectures and classroom activities are also important contributors, but reading is essential in most subject matters, even physical education. Bormuth (1970) recognized this fact when he proposed his linguistic theory for item development that transformed prose into test items. Unfortunately, his method produced items that measured recall only, which is unsatisfactory. However, his method worked. To date, we have not had theoretical development and a technology of AIG for prose learning. This omission is a major shortcoming in current AIG research and development. A theory of reading comprehension needs to precede a method for turning prose into test items that measure comprehension and the ability to use information gleaned from reading passages in complex ways. A review of common core reading standards for any grade level reveals the richness and diversity of learning. How can AIG produce items that capture this variation? AIG based on prose material is lacking in current AIG research and development.

Ill-Structured Problems

A problem or task that must be solved in some way is one of the most quintessential targets of testing. It is obvious in mathematics and science, and subtle but present in nearly all subject matters and central in testing for credentialing in any profession.

Well-structured problems lend themselves nicely to AIG. They have all the qualities we like with systematic replacement sets. A well-structured problem is, as expected, often clearly defined. The most common form of a well-structured problem is found in certification and licensing testing. The typical format is a testlet that contains a patient/client situation/problem with a series of 2 to 12 items. The vignette has enough replacement sets to generate a variety of vignettes and the use of generic items provides an easy path for item writers.

A simple, single-item example is provided showing a well-structured problem from a released version of the *Certified Financial Analyst Examination* (Haladyna & Rodriguez, in press).

An analyst obtained the following information regarding a company's common stock:

Weighted average cost of capital	*15%*
Intrinsic value per share	*$20*
Market value per share	*$35*

The company's investments for the fiscal year are expected to return 4 to 7 percent. Which of the following best characterizes the company's common stock?

    A. *Growth company and growth stock*
    B. *Growth company and speculative stock*
    C. *Speculative company and growth stock*
    D. *Speculative company and speculative stock*

(Adapted from Haladyna & Rodriguez, in press)

Simon (1973) is credited with introducing the dilemma presented by the ill-structured problem. An ill-structured problem is resistant to the use of an algorithm that many AIG methods use. One issue is that the problem may not be well defined or adequately defined. Another issue is that the problem may have many right answers. Background information may be lacking. The scope of the problem may be far more diverse than simply presenting a single item or a testlet consisting of a set of items targeted at solving the problem.

An example of an ill-structured problem comes from reading comprehension in a state reading test for sixth-graders. After a passage is read, the question is:

Why are people in Missouri interested in Earl?

Four options are provided. The question calls for understanding of the passage; more specifically, for motivation. These subtleties are not easy to regulate in AIG.

Further study of state and national content standards and extant released items from state and national tests will reveal a great variety of items. If AIG is to partially or completely replace subjective-item writing that is currently practiced, then many item models will need to be written and validated. The ill-structured problem represents an aspect of content that is resistant to our current methods of item modeling (see Gierl & Lai, this volume).

One approach to addressing this current limitation is to more adequately define ill-structured problems. However, by doing so, some content may be eliminated, and that poses one of Messick's main threats to validity–construct under-representation (Messick, 1989). If rules are applied, then exceptions to the rule will not be tested via AIG—unless the rule exceptions are built in somehow. Another way to increase our understanding of both well-structured and ill-structured problems is to interview students as they solve problems. Their responses can lead to greater understanding and appreciation of the complexity of some problems and test items that measure problem-solving ability. Finally, there is a considerable amount of past and recent research on ill-structured problem solving. This area of inquiry within cognitive psychology seems to have great bearing on AIG and its future. AIG must increase its network in the learning science community and include such aspects of theory and research that influence AIG's future, and ill-structured problem solving is one of these factors.

Does AIG Have Limits in Defining a Construct?

All previous discussion in this chapter raises the above question. If a construct, such as reading or mathematics, could be operationally defined in terms of item models and families, then item generation would truly be automated, formative and summative testing would be routine and very inexpensive. However, logic, arguments, and these obstacles suggest that AIG may have reasonable limitations. That is not to say that AIG cannot succeed. AIG may prove useful for certain types of test content but not all test content. Thus, as a science AIG plays an important, supportive role in mainstream item development, but it may not replace the normal science of item development currently in use. This point, of course, remains to be proven by extensive research, development, and implementation as a technology.

Item Formats

As noted in chapter 2, current AIG centers on four- and five-option multiple-choice item formats. Despite theory, research, and experience pointing to the benefits of three-option and two-option items, there is a persistent unqualified adherence to the four- and five-option format. Guidelines for item writing uniformly state that distractors should be plausible and comprise common student errors (Haladyna & Downing, 1989a; 1989b; Haladyna, Downing, & Rodriguez, 2002). There is no universal law that the number of plausible multiple-choice distractors per item are three or four. In fact, empirical analysis followed by analysis by subject-matter experts for virtually any test will show that nearly all multiple-choice test items have only one or two plausible distractors (Haladyna & Downing, 1993; Haladyna & Rodriguez, in press).

Also, we have many selected-response and constructed-response formats that provide opportunities for measuring knowledge, skills, and abilities that have not yet been adapted for AIG. One of these formats is the testlet. Haladyna (1991) presented two examples of item models that generate large numbers of test items using generic item shells and generic options for courses in statistics and art history. Although the technology for developing testlets is evolving, it has not been extensively used in AIG. Here is an opportunity for AIG to make advances in item development for a format that is increasing in popularity, due to its ability to measure complex thinking. LaDuca (1994) provided a useful concept in this stead, but more work is needed.

Subjective and objectively scored constructed-response formats provide another challenge and opportunity for those working in AIG. The task of producing these kinds of items automatically is also daunting, but a worthy long-term goal. Good examples can be found on the worldwide web.[1]

These examples are nothing more than a repository of writing prompts. But the idea that prompts must be generated with known characteristics is very attractive to the continued growth in the area of measuring writing ability. Coupled with automated essay scoring, AIG can contribute mightily to the measurement of writing ability, but this science has a long way to go.

A goal for AIG should be the use of a greater variety of formats that open opportunities for measuring complex cognitive knowledge and skills and, especially, in non quantitative areas.

Cost of AIG

As several writers have commented in this volume, the cost of a professionally developed multiple-choice item can be anywhere from $800 to $2,000. Thus, an item bank of 300 items can have a total value of up to $600,000. In this age of item theft, lack of security, and cheating, a compromised test may involve a loss of considerable value in replacing disclosed items.

Given that a technology for AIG will develop which will increase the speed of item development as well as the number of items available, it is clear from current theory and research that cognitive psychologists and measurement specialists will play important roles in any AIG system. More important are subject-matter experts (SMEs), who must marshal their expertise to assist their team mates in cognitive psychology and measurement to create item models that are universally acceptable to the wider group of SMEs for each field. The cost of such development should be factored in to the evaluation of the economy that AIG affords. Part of the research here will have to include cost-benefit studies that show that AIG for certain types of content produces reasonable economies as well as items of very high quality. As testing companies consider AIG, there will be keen interest in the cost-benefits of AIG as a useful technology for item development.

Closing

AIG has had a history with starts and stops that are characteristic of a very young, revolutionary science. Waves of small groups of scholars have whittled away at problems and issues throughout the 20th century and have made progress, but the more significant work is yet to come. Defining educational constructs and mapping the knowledge and skills needed to perform complex tasks is a project that will entail many scholars working together in a unified way. Whether AIG becomes a paradigm for item development or part of the normal science of item development depends on many factors and overcoming the obstacles ahead. AIG can contribute importantly to item development, with a sustained and coordinated effort. The evidence put forward by the authors in this volume suggests that this effort is clearly underway.

Note

1 http://jc-schools.net/write/create.htm;
   http://www.alittleleftoflogical.com/generators/randomprompts.html;
   http://www.technorhetoric.net/4.1/coverweb/barber/prompts.html.

References

Bejar, I. I. (2002). Generative testing: From conception to implementation. In S. H. Irvine & P. C. Kyllonen (Eds.), *Item generation for test development* (pp. 199-218). Mahwah, NJ: Erlbaum.

Bormuth, J. R. (1970). *On a theory of achievement test items*. Chicago, IL: University of Chicago Press.

Coffman, W. E. (1971). Essay examinations. In R. L. Thorndike (Ed.), *Educational measurement* (2nd ed., pp. 271–302). Washington, DC: American Council on Education.

Cole, N. S. (1990). Conceptions of educational achievement. *Educational Researcher, 19*(3), 2–7.

Cronbach, L. J. (1970). [Review of *On the theory of achievement test items*]. *Psychometrika, 35,* 509–511.

Cronbach, L. J. (1971). Test validation. In R. L. Thorndike (Ed.), *Educational measurement* (2nd ed., pp. 443–507). Washington, DC: American Council on Education.

Cronbach, L. J., & Meehl, P. E. (1955). Construct validity in psychological tests. *Psychological Bulletin, 52,* 281–302.

Downing, S. M. & Haladyna, T. M. (1997). Test item development: Validity evidence from quality assurance procedures. *Applied Measurement in Education, 10,* 61–82.

Ebel, R. L. (1951). Writing the test item. In E. F. Lindquist (Ed.), *Educational measurement* (1st ed., pp. 185–249). Washington, DC: American Council on Education.

Haladyna, T. M. (1991). Generic questioning strategies for linking teaching and testing. *Educational Technology: Research and Development, 39,* 73–81.

Haladyna, T. M. (2004). *Developing and validating multiple-choice test items* (3rd ed.). Mahwah, NJ: Lawrence Erlbaum Associates.

Haladyna, T. M. & Downing, S. M. (1993). How many options is enough for a multiple-choice test item. *Educational and Psychological Measurement, 53*(4), 999–1010.

Haladyna, T. M., & Downing, S. M. (1989a). A taxonomy of multiple-choice item-writing rules. *Applied Measurement in Education, 1,* 37–50.

Haladyna, T. M., & Downing, S. M. (1989b). The validity of a taxonomy of multiple-choice item-writing rules. *Applied Measurement in Education, 1,* 51–78.

Haladyna, T. M., Downing, S. M., & Rodriguez, M. C. (2002). A review of multiple-choice item-writing guidelines for classroom assessment. *Applied Measurement in Education, 15*(3), 309–334.

Haladyna, T. M., & Rodriguez, M. C. (In press). *Developing and validating test items*. New York, NY: Routledge.

Kane, M. T. (2006a). Content-related validity evidence. In S. M. Downing & T. M. Haladyna (Eds.) *Handbook of test development*, pp. 131–154. Mahwah, NJ: Lawrence Erlbaum Associates.

Kane, M. T. (2006b). Validation. In R. L. Brennan (Ed.), *Educational measurement* (4th ed., pp 17–64). Westport, CT: American Council on Education/Praeger.

Kaplan, A. (1964). *The conduct of inquiry*. New York: Chandler.

Kuhn, T. S. (1962). *The structure of scientific revolutions* (1st ed.). Chicago, IL: University of Chicago Press.

LaDuca, A. (1994). Validation of a professional licensure examinations: Professions theory, test design, and construct validity. *Evaluation in the Health Professions, 17*(2), 178–197.

LaDuca, A., Staples, W. I., Templeton, B., & Holzman, G. B. (1986). Item modeling procedure for constructing content-equivalent multiple choice questions. *Medical Education, 20*(1), 53–56.

Masters, J. S. (2010). *A comparison of traditional test blueprinting and item development to assessment engineering in a licensing context.* A doctoral dissertation. Greensboro, NC: University of North Carolina at Greensboro.

Messick, S. (1984). The psychology of educational measurement. *Journal of Educational Measurement, 21,* 215–237.

Messick, S. (1989). Validity. In R. L. Linn (Ed.), *Educational measurement* (3rd ed., pp. 13–104). New York, NY: American Council on Education and Macmillan.

Mislevy, R. J. (1993). Foundations of a new test theory. In N. Frederiksen, R. J. Mislevy, & I. Bejar (Eds.) *Test theory for a new generation of tests* (pp. 19–39). Hillsdale, NJ: Lawrence Erlbaum Associates.

Mislevy, R. J. (1996a). *Some recent developments in assessing student learning*. Princeton, NJ: Center for Performance Assessment at the Educational Testing Service.

Mislevy, R. J. (1996b). Test theory reconceived. *Journal of Educational Measurement, 33,* 379–417.

Mislevy, R. (2006). Cognitive psychology and educational assessment. In R. L. Brennan (Ed.), *Educational measurement* (4th ed., pp 257–305). Westport, CT: American Council on Education/Praeger.

Mislevy, R. J., & Riconscente, M. M. (2006). Evidence-centered assessment design. In Downing, S. M., & Haladyna, T. M. (Eds.), *Handbook of test development* (pp. 61–90). Mahwah, NJ: Lawrence Erlbaum Associates.

Nitko, A. J. (1985). [Review of Roid and Haladyna's *A technology for test item writing*]. *Journal of Educational Measurement, 21,* 201–204.

Raymond, M., & Neustel, S. (2006). Determining the content of credentialing examinations. In S. M. Downing and T. M. Haladyna (Eds.). *Handbook of test development* (pp. 181–223). Mahwah, NJ: Lawrence Erlbaum Associates.

Roid, G. H., & Haladyna, T. M. (1980). Toward a technology of test item writing. *Review of Education Research, 50,* 293–314.

Roid, G. H., & Haladyna, T. M. (1982). *Toward a technology of test-item writing*. New York: Academic Press.

Simon, H. A. (1973). The structure of ill structured problems. *Artificial Intelligence, 4*(3–4), 181–201.

Snow, R. E., & Lohman, D. F. (1989). Implications of cognitive psychology for educational measurement. In R. L. Linn (Ed.), *Educational measurement* (3rd ed., pp. 263–332). New York, NY: American Council on Education and MacMillan.

Wesman, A. G. (1971). Writing the test item. In R. L. Thorndike (Ed.) *Educational measurement* (2nd ed., pp. 99–111). Washington, DC: American Council on Education.

Author Index

240

Subject Index